Health Care Utilization in Germany

Christian Janssen • Enno Swart
Thomas von Lengerke
Editors

Health Care Utilization in Germany

Theory, Methodology, and Results

Foreword by Ronald M. Andersen

Springer

Editors
Christian Janssen
Department of Applied Social Sciences
Munich University of Applied Sciences
Munich
Germany

Thomas von Lengerke
Center of Public Health and Health Care, Medical Psychology Unit
Hannover Medical School
Hannover
Germany

Enno Swart
Institute of Social Medicine and Health Economics
Otto von Guericke University Magdeburg
Magdeburg
Germany

ISBN 978-1-4614-9190-3 ISBN 978-1-4614-9191-0 (eBook)
DOI 10.1007/978-1-4614-9191-0
Springer New York Heidelberg Dordrecht London

Library of Congress Control Number: 2013954440

Printed on acid-free paper

Springer is part of Springer Science+Business Media (www.springer.com)

Foreword

Sixty years ago, Odin Anderson, a founder of medical sociology and health services research, initiated a series of national health care utilization surveys for the USA [1]. These studies documented large differences in people's use of health services according to their demographic, social, and economic characteristics. Similar large differences were documented among other nations despite their great variations in culture and health care delivery systems [2]. I had the good fortune to serve as study director for the third of Odin Anderson's USA health care surveys conducted in 1964 [3] and collaborate with Bjorn Smedby on a comparable national health survey in Sweden [4]. In an effort to better understand the large differences in people's use we observed in both these nations, I developed the Behavioral Model of Health Services Use (BMHSU) [5].

The present volume includes theoretical, methodological and empirical analyses of health services use in Germany. Commonalities of these analyses are that they generally (1) follow perspectives from medical sociology and (2) almost half a century after its introduction, use BMHSU as a framework. The editors state that this to their knowledge is the first edited volume from medical sociology to provide an original account of social determinants of health care utilization in Germany to an international audience. I agree with their assessment and would add that they are making a significant contribution to medical sociology, international comparisons of health services use and understanding the equity of health services distribution in Germany.

The reader of this good volume might wonder about the advisability of using such an old model as a framework. As one, admittedly biased, old reader, I, personally, am delighted that the editors chose to use BMHSU. Please let me share with you my rationale and why the editors' use of BMHUS to attain the volume's objectives might be justified:

1. Quite a few colleagues both in the USA and in other countries, including Germany, are still using BMHSU [6–8]. It must have some continuing value to them?
2. While the initial version of the BMHSU was developed some time ago, it has undergone multiple revisions and, hopefully, "upgrades" over the years. In recent conversation with a neighbor who is a retired electrical engineer about

"modeling," he said, "in an engineering project we might build several models (objects that stand in the place of another) until we get it right (the final product)." The editors and some authors of this volume are working with the sixth revision of BMHSU [9].

3. A major objective of this volume is to explore the equities and inequities of health services delivery in Germany. From the beginning, a major purpose of BMHSU has been to provide a tool for defining and measuring equity according to how predisposing, enabling, and need variables were associated with health services use.
4. The editors needed a comprehensive, systematic, and integrated framework to examine the determinates and effects of health services utilization. They needed a model not a theory, and BMHSU is a model not a theory. A theory explains a relationship and can be refuted by negative findings, whereas a model predicts a relationship and "is not exposed to refutation, but is used as long as any benefit can be derived from it. A model can continue to be useful even though it yields many conclusions which are clearly wrong, provided only that it yields some conclusions that are correct (i.e. useful)" [10]. What I like about the strategy for this volume is the effort to combine theory hopefully provided by medical sociology to explain relationships established through BMHSU.
5. The volume offers useful insights and suggestions for improving health services research and the BMHUS. In closing, I would like to comment on a few of these:
   a. The importance of clarifying the role of the contextual variables and their predisposing, enabling, and need components in determining health status use and outcomes of individuals. Creative multilevel modeling and analysis is important for clarifying this role. One criticism of BMHUS is that it does not allow for contextual models to be outcomes in the analysis. This criticism is not really correct because BMHUS has recursive arrows flowing back from individual behaviors and outcomes to contextual predisposing, enabling, and need characteristics that can then be viewed as outcomes. However, it is true that BMHUS has been developed with an emphasis on understanding determinants of individual health behaviors and outcomes. If a study stresses both contextual determinants and outcomes, it may be that the model employed should be other than BMHUS.
   b. The volume highlights the need for variables to be systematically classified as predisposing, enabling, or need. For example, is social support predisposing or enabling? I have come to the conclusion it is both. One variable—the structure of social support—is predisposing. An individual must have family and friends in order to receive social support from them. Another variable—the process of social support—is enabling; family and friends must actively encourage care seeking or take the patient to the doctor to enable health services use.
   c. The volume argues for clarity as to the meaning of arrows in the model linking three or more variables. Do they suggest "mediation" or "moderation"? I must confess that I see BMHUS as a mediating model. Those linking arrows are meant to represent mediators. We want to understand

how the relationships between predisposing variables and health services use are determined by enabling variables. Do women have more visits to clinicians than men because they are more likely to have a regular source of care? Moderating relationships are not portrayed by arrows in the BMHUS. We might suspect on the basis of theory or observation that an enabling variable (having a regular source of care) moderates the relationship between a predisposing variable (gender) and number of visits received. Special analyses would be required to determine a significant moderating effect (do women respond differently to having a regular source of care than men by having more visits?)

Happy modeling to the editors, authors, and readers of this book. Can we keep trying until we get it right?

Los Angeles, CA, USA
September 23, 2013.

Ronald M. Andersen

References

1. Andersen RM. National Health Surveys and the Behavioral Model of Health Services Use. Med Care 2008;46:647–53
2. Kohn R, White K, editors. Health Care: An International Study. Report of the World Health Organization/International Collaborating Study of Medical Care Utilization. London and New York: Oxford University Press; 1976
3. Andersen RM, Anderson OW. A Decade of Health Services: Social Survey Trends in Use and Expenditure. Chicago: University of Chicago Press; 1967
4. Andersen RM, Smedby B, Anderson OW. Medical Care Use in Sweden and the United States—A Comparative Analysis of Systems and Behavior. Chicago: Center for Health Administration Studies, University of Chicago, Research Series No. 27; 1970
5. Andersen RM. A Behavioral Model of Families' Use of Health Services. Chicago: Center for Health Administration Studies, University of Chicago, Research Series No. 25; 1968
6. Andersen RM. Revisiting the Behavioral Model and Access to Medical Care: Does it Matter? J Health Social Behavior 1995;36:1–10
7. Smedby B, Andersen RM. International Comparisons of Health Care Systems: Conceptual and Methodological Developments Over Half a Century. Socialmedicinsk tidskrift 2010;87:439–52. Available at http://www.socialmedicinsktidskrift.se/index.php/smt/article/view/749
8. Andersen RM. Access to Health Care. In Oxford Bibliographies Online: Public Health. Green L, editor. New York: Oxford University Press; February 2011. Available at http://www.oxfordbibliographies.com/view/document/obo-9780199756797/obo-9780199756797–0001.xml
9. Andersen RM, Davidson PL, Baumeister SE. Improving access to care in America. In: Kominski EF, editor. Changing the U.S. health care system: key issues in health services, policy, and management. 4th edition. San Francisco, CA: Jossey-Bass; 2013. p. 33–69
10. Rubenstein A, Haberstroh C. Some theories of organization. Homewood, Il: Dorsey Press; 1960

Acknowledgements

Writing of all chapters was carried out as part of the scientific network project "Utilization of health-related services in Germany—theoretical approaches, methods and empirical results in medical sociology" (NWIn) funded by the Deutsche Forschungsgemeinschaft (German Research Foundation, grant no.: JA 1849/1-1).

The editors would like to thank to Sebastian E. Baumeister, University of Greifswald, Institute for Community Medicine, Greifswald, Germany, for his support in keeping us up-to-date on the sixth revision of the Behavioral Model of Health Services Use.

Contents

Contributors

Birgit Babitsch Department of New Public Health, University of Osnabrück, School of Human Sciences, Osnabrück, Germany

Claudia Berger Department of New Public Health, School of Human Sciences, University of Osnabrück, Osnabrück, Germany

Bernhard Borgetto HAWK—University of Applied Sciences and Arts, Faculty of Social Work and Health, Hildesheim, Germany

Cornelia Bormann Health Sciences, FH Bielefeld—University of Applied Sciences, Bielefeld, Germany

Carmen Cristina Ciupitu-Plath Berlin School of Public Health, Charité—Universitätsmedizin Berlin, Berlin, Germany

Carolin Donath Friedrich-Alexander-Universität Erlangen-Nürnberg, Clinic of Psychiatry and Psychotherapy, Center for Health Services Research in Medicine, Erlangen, Germany

Daniela Gohl Berlin School of Public Health, Charité – Universitätsmedizin Berlin, Berlin, Germany

Hannes Grau Friedrich-Alexander-Universität Erlangen-Nürnberg, Clinic of Psychiatry and Psychotherapy, Center for Health Services Research in Medicine, Erlangen, Germany

Stephanie Griehl Department of Social and Health Sciences, University of Applied Sciences, Magdeburg-Stendal, Magdeburg, Germany

Elmar Graessel Friedrich-Alexander-Universität Erlangen-Nürnberg, Clinic of Psychiatry and Psychotherapy, Center for Health Services Research in Medicine, Erlangen, Germany

Kerstin Hofreuter-Gätgens Center for Psychosocial Medicine, Department of Medical Sociology, University Medical Center Hamburg-Eppendorf, Hamburg, Germany

Rolf Holle Helmholtz Zentrum München—German Research Center for Environmental Health (GmbH), Institute of Health Economics and Health Care Management, Neuherberg, Germany

Christian Janssen Department of Applied Social Sciences, Munich University of Applied Sciences, Munich, Germany

Jens Klein Center for Psychosocial Medicine, Department of Medical Sociology, University Medical Center Hamburg-Eppendorf, Hamburg, Germany

Christopher Kofahl Center for Psychosocial Medicine, Department of Medical Sociology, University Medical Center Hamburg-Eppendorf, Hamburg, Germany

Olaf von dem Knesebeck Center for Psychosocial Medicine, Department of Medical Sociology, University Medical Center Hamburg-Eppendorf, Hamburg, Germany

Florian Kölsch Faculty of Human Sciences and the Faculty of Medicine, Institute for Medical Sociology, Health Services Research, and Rehabilitation Science, University of Cologne, Cologne, Germany

Mirjam Körner Medical Psychology and Medical Sociology, Medical Faculty, University of Freiburg, Freiburg, Germany

Ingrid Köster PMV research group at the Department of Child and Adolescent Psychiatry, University of Cologne, Cologne, Germany

Christoph Kowalski Faculty of Human Sciences and the Faculty of Medicine, Institute for Medical Sociology, Health Services Research, and Rehabilitation Science, University of Cologne, Cologne, Germany

Simone Kunz Helmholtz Zentrum München—German Research Center for Environmental Health (GmbH), Institute of Health Economics and Health Care Management, Neuherberg, Germany

Thomas von Lengerke Center of Public Health and Health Care, Medical Psychology Unit, Hannover Medical School, Hannover, Germany

Julika Loss Division of Medical Sociology, Institute for Epidemiogy and Social Medicine, University of Regensburg, Regensburg, Germany

Daniel Lüdecke Center for Psychosocial Medicine, Department of Medical Sociology, University Medical Center Hamburg-Eppendorf, Hamburg, Germany

Birte A. Maschke Department of Applied Social Sciences, Munich University of Applied Sciences, Munich, Germany

Petra Menn Helmholtz Zentrum München—German Research Center for Environmental Health (GmbH), Institute of Health Economics and Health Care Management, Neuherberg, Germany

Andreas Mielck Helmholtz Zentrum München—German Research Center for Environmental Health (GmbH), Institute of Health Economics and Health Care Management, Neuherberg, Germany

Christa Meisinger Helmholtz Zentrum München—German Research Center for Environmental Health (GmbH), Institute of Epidemiology II, Neuherberg, Germany

Eva Mnich Center for Psychosocial Medicine, Department of Medical Sociology, University Medical Center Hamburg-Eppendorf, Hamburg, Germany

Ingrid Schubert PMV research group at the Department of Child and Adolescent Psychiatry, University of Cologne, Cologne, Germany

Larissa Schwarzkopf Helmholtz Zentrum München—German Research Center for Environmental Health (GmbH), Institute of Health Economics and Health Care Management, Neuherberg, Germany

Achim Siegel Division of General Practice, University Medical Center Freiburg, Freiburg, Germany

Ulrich Stößel Division of Medical Psychology and Medical Sociology, University of Freiburg, Freiburg, Germany

Enno Swart Medical Faculty, Institute of Social Medicine and Health Economics, Otto von Guericke University of Magdeburg, Magdeburg, Germany

Holm Thieme HAWK—University of Applied Sciences and Arts, Faculty of Social Work and Health, Hildesheim, Germany

Gudrun Ulbrecht Friedrich-Alexander-Universität Erlangen-Nürnberg, Clinic of Psychiatry and Psychotherapy, Center for Health Services Research in Medicine, Erlangen, Germany

Silke B. Wolfenstetter Helmholtz Zentrum München—German Research Center for Environmental Health (GmbH), Institute of Health Economics and Health Care Management, Neuherberg, Germany

Part I
Introduction

Chapter 1
Theorizing, Empiricizing, and Analyzing Health Care Utilization in Germany: An Introduction

Christian Janssen, Enno Swart and Thomas von Lengerke

Given decades of socio-epidemiological research, the social gradients in health-related quality of life, morbidity, and mortality that favor higher social status groups and disadvantage lower social status groups are factually a truism. This holds true for Germany and Europe in general as well as for other industrialized countries such as the USA or Canada. In Germany, for instance, differences in life expectancy between the highest and lowest income groups range up to 10 years. Against this background, a crucial scientific and political question is whether the health care system increases or decreases this gap. Initial research findings in Germany indicate that the gap might be influenced more by differences in utilization than in supply.

In 2002, the working group "Health Care Research" was founded within the German Association of Medical Sociology [*Deutsche Gesellschaft für Medizinische Soziologie* (DGMS)], consisting of about 30 scientists. In the following years, several workshops at national and international conferences were held by members of this group. In 2007, a first book resulted from this collaboration, which was published by Juventa and presented medical sociological health care research in its full scope [1]. Subsequently, the special importance of the utilization of health care triggered a proposal to the German Research Foundation [*Deutsche Forschungsgemeinschaft* (DFG)] for funding a scientific network on "Health care utilization in Germany."

C. Janssen (✉)
Department of Applied Social Sciences, Munich University of Applied Sciences, Munich, Germany
e-mail: christian.janssen@hm.edu

E. Swart
Medical Faculty, Institute of Social Medicine and Health Economics, Otto von Guericke University of Magdeburg, Magdeburg, Germany
e-mail: enno.swart@med.ovgu.de

T. von Lengerke
Center of Public Health and Health Care, Medical Psychology Unit, Hannover Medical School, Hannover, Germany
e-mail: lengerke.thomas@mh-hannover.de

C. Janssen et al. (eds.), *Health Care Utilization in Germany*,
DOI 10.1007/978-1-4614-9191-0_1,

After its approval (grant no.: JA-1849, 1-1), the network started off under the designation "NWIn Research Network" (NWIn: *"Netzwerk Inanspruchnahme"* [German for "Utilization Network"]) in January 2010 for a three-year funding period. Prior to the book publication eventually intended by NWIn (the book you are holding in your hands), a special issue of General Medical Services (GMS) Psycho-Social-Medicine (P-S-M) was published [2–8]. This publication already referred to the same theoretical approach, namely one of the leading frameworks for health care utilization research: the behavioral model (BM) of health care utilization [9–12] by the US medical sociologist and health services researcher Ronald M. Andersen. Among other things, it systematically reviews empirical studies that explicitly draw on the BM [3], scrutinizes the comparability of estimated prevalences of medical services use in large-scale population surveys in Germany [4], and presents first empirical findings [5–8].

The present book carries this endeavor forward by being, to our knowledge, the first edited volume to analyze the social determinants of health care utilization in Germany via systematic use of Andersen and colleagues' BM as its recurrent theoretical approach throughout all chapters (starting with Chap. 2 in Sect. II), including a systematic update on relevant quantitative and qualitative research methods (Sect. III) and empirical results on selected predisposing and enabling factors (Part IV), need factors (Sect. V), and sectors of care (Sect. VI). To begin with, *Thomas von Lengerke*, *Daniela Gohl*, and *Birgit Babitsch* give a description of the latest versions of the BM [11–12] with reference to its psychosocial extension [10]. Subsequently, they present a basic behavioral epidemiology model which—by drawing on James S. Coleman, Paul F. Lazarsfeld, and George L. Engel, among others—intends to systematically describe somatic, mental, and social influences of health-related behavior on both individual and collective levels. By way of contrast, they discuss implications and open questions for the further development of the BM. In order to provide a better understanding of the German health care system for readers not familiar with it, the main structures and legal regulations of its statutory health insurance system are then outlined by *Cornelia Bormann* and *Enno Swart*. Roughly 85 % of the German population are covered by this system. Especially the most important sectors, outpatient and inpatient care as well as nursing care, are described. As prescriptions are an important part of the utilization of health services in Germany, the chapter describes the requirement for physician prescriptions for these services.

Starting in Sect. III, *Enno Swart* and *Stephanie Griehl* examine the comparability of instruments used in six German large-scale representative population surveys between 1991 and 2009. They find that not only do the surveys' target groups differ, but the questions on outpatient care utilization vary as well. Specifically, this relates to reference periods examined, types of physicians contacted by survey participants, and item wording in terms of clarifications and response categories. They conclude that unlike the results of the surveys' questions on inpatient care, the results of questions on the use of outpatient services are not easily comparable. In another contribution, *Enno Swart* describes the use of claims data of the German statutory health insurance for scientific purposes. In the last 20 years, such data have been systematically made available for such use. Now, claims data analysis has become an independent part of health services research with its own scientific standards. Claims data of the statutory health insurance provide a nearly complete picture of the utilization of medical services. Based on concrete examples, he discusses potentials as well as limitations of this kind of data. Concluding this part of the book, *Birgit Babitsch*, *Claudia Berger*, *Bernhard Borgetto*, and *Carmen-Cristina Ciupitu-Plath* highlight the, to some degree, neglected role of qualitative methods in research on health care utilization.

In Sect. IV, first *Birgit Babitsch*, *Cornela Bormann*, *Daniela Gohl*, and *Carmen-Cristina Ciupitu-Plath* give an overview on gender and health care use. They suggest that while there is enough evidence that women and men differ in health care utilization, it is hardly possible to sufficiently explain these findings. Picking up one, if not *the* key explanatory factor from a medical sociology viewpoint, *Jens Klein*, *Kerstin Hofreuter-Gätgens*, and *Olaf von dem Knesebeck* systematically review the associations of socioeconomic status and health care utilization in Germany. In doing so, they define socioeconomic status by education, income, and occupational status as well as insurance status, and categorize health care into outpatient care, inpatient care, and prevention. The review includes 57 publications that indicate that the strongest inequalities exist in the area of prevention, in that the lower the social status, the less people utilize prevention or early detection programs. Regarding outpatient care, higher status groups prefer visiting specialists, while lower status groups prefer primary care physicians, and only minor social disparities pertain to inpatient care. Subsequently, *Cristina Carmen Ciupitu-Plath*, *Daniela Gohl*, *Christopher Kofahl*, and *Birgit Babitsch* give an overview on migration and health care utilization in the European context. They show that in Germany, similar to findings reported for the broader European context, immigrants face more and different health problems compared to native Germans and also experience difficulties in accessing the right health service at the right time. Next, *Daniel Lüdecke*, *Eva Mnich*, and *Christopher Kofahl* discuss that home care and support of dependent elderly people are primarily provided by relatives, friends, or close acquaintances. Therefore, one major challenge for society is to support family caregivers and to provide services aimed at assisting and relieving their burden. In their chapter, the authors analyze the utilization of support services and the impact of different socioeconomic characteristics of family caregivers as well as different care situation characteristics. Predisposing and need factors turn out to be most relevant to the explanation of family caregivers' attitudes and opinions regarding service utilization as well as service utilization itself.

Two major burdens of disease in the decades ahead will be dementia and obesity. Thus, *Carolin Donath* and colleagues, at the outset of Sect. V, present two timely studies on predictors of the use of care and support services, the use of nondrug therapies, and the use of health and care services by community-dwelling persons with dementia and their family caregivers. Overall, predisposing factors, such as patient age as well as caregiver age or education level, are not as consistently predictive as the need for a service. That is, all types of services considered are used more frequently when family caregivers subjectively believe they are in need of a service.

Regarding obesity, *Thomas von Lengerke* and colleagues provide a systematic review based on population studies on the obesity-associated utilization of outpatient primary care by adults in Germany, and they empirically examine the associations between moderate and severe obesity on the one hand and the utilization of outpatient general practitioner care on the other, using data of two population surveys in the Augsburg region in Germany. Their key findings are that obese groups report more general practitioner visits than nonobese groups. In addition, among women, all overweight groups (preobesity, moderate obesity, and severe obesity) had more visits than the normal-weight group, but among men, those with severe obesity reported more visits than all other body mass groups. While this pattern parallels obesity-associated impairments in physical health-related quality of life and raises the question of sex, or gender, as an enabling rather than predisposing factor, the authors conclude that future studies should examine the roles of other enabling and contextual factors in this context, e.g., income as an effect modifier and the impact of regional density of services. Finally, *Holm Thieme* and *Bernhard Borgetto* look at rheumatic diseases and, in this context, at the use of physiotherapists as a relevant allied health profession (*Thieme* and *Borgetto*) and the participation in self-help activities as an important part of the lay health care system (*Borgetto* and *Thieme*).

Starting off Sect. VI, *Mirjam Körner*, *Birte A. Maschke,* and *Christian Janssen* examine psychotherapy as a field gaining in importance for the health care system as the rate of mental disorders in Germany increases. Currently, very little information exists on the types of patients who have access to psychotherapy, especially in the outpatient setting. Thus, the authors review studies on social inequality and use of psychotherapy. All four studies included show that patients with a higher level of education often have better access to psychotherapy than those with a lower level, although the latter more commonly suffer from mental disorders. The combined assessment of epidemiological data and studies on psychotherapy utilization indicates that patients with lower education levels receive inadequate care within the present system. Following this, *Christoph Kowalski, Julika Loss, Florian Kölsch,* and *Christian Janssen* focus on the field of disease prevention and health promotion. After a description of the German health care system with regard to prevention and health promotion, they present a systematic review in which they were able to include 48 empirical articles. Most of these studies provide quite clear evidence of an association between higher social status, female gender, and nonmigrant status on one hand and the use of prevention or health promotion services on the other. Studies dealing with tertiary prevention were rare and less conclusive. Also, they conclude that there is a lack of published intervention studies demonstrating how to better reach the socially disadvantaged. Finally, *Achim Siegel, Ingrid Köster, Ingrid Schubert,* and *Ulrich Stössel* report results of an integrated care study that is well known in Germany, namely "Gesundes Kinzigtal Integrated Care" (Healthy Kinzigtal Integrated Care [GKIC]). It represents one of the few population-based integrated care systems in Germany. By coordinating health care utilization for a defined population in the Kinzigtal region in Southwest Germany, GKIC strives to increase the quality of the local health care system and to curb rising health care costs in the region. Furthermore, GKIC wants all groups of the population to have equal access to GKIC membership and to integrated care (including older people and those with an above-average morbidity risk). Thus, GKIC has adopted an elaborate contractual framework that incentivizes GKIC providers to enroll rather high-risk and high-morbidity insured people. The authors analyze to what degree GKIC has reached its aim to preferentially enroll people with above-average morbidity, in particular the socio-demographic and morbidity structures of insured in the Kinzigtal region. Using claims data, enrolled and non-enrolled insured will be compared regarding socio-demographic variables and adjusted morbidity. The results show that GKIC has performed according to the incentives. The extended preventive and care management potential of GKIC has indeed been offered first and foremost to insurants with a higher (age- and sex-adjusted) morbidity.

In sum, all empirical contributions in this volume are based on analyses of primary or secondary data and/or results of systematic literature reviews using equivalent literature search strategies. Although all data pertain to Germany, the book is deliberately published in English in order to stimulate communication within international research communities and possibly to provide a blueprint for health care utilization analyses in other countries. At the same time, as suggested above, the impetus for this volume is to foster theoretical advancement in the field of health services utilization research in general, and particularly in regard to the BM. Thus, in the final chapter (Sect. V), *Thomas von Lengerke, Christoph Kowalski*, *Enno Swart,* and *Christian Janssen* sum up, from their points of view, the main conclusions, implications, and desiderata based on the preceding chapters. Most importantly, they highlight the need for transdisciplinary theoretical frameworks like the BM and propose to advance the specificity of variable clusters such as predisposing, enabling, and need factors in terms of mediating vs. moderating variables. Also, they call to consequently invest into multilevel modeling of health care utilization. In this latter context, Andersen's innovation of describing both contextual and individual determinants by one and the same set of variable categories [11–12] is drawn upon, and suggestions are made for future research.

References

1. Janssen C, Borgetto B, Heller G, editors. [Medical sociology and health care research: theoretical approaches, methods, instruments and empirical results]. In German. Weinheim: Juventa; 2007.
2. Janßen C, Swart E, von Lengerke T. Health care utilization in Germany: The NWIn research network. GMS Psychosoc Med. 2012;9:Doc12.
3. Babitsch B, Gohl D, von Lengerke T. Re-revisiting Andersen's Behavioral Model of Health Services Use: a systematic review of studies from 1998–2011. GMS Psychosoc Med. 2012;9:Doc11.
4. Swart E. The prevalence and the intensity of medical services. How comparable are the results of large-scale population surveys use in Germany? GMS Psychosoc Med. 2012;9:Doc10.
5. Wolfenstetter SB, Menn P, Holle R, Mielck A, Meisinger C, von Lengerke T. Body weight changes and outpatient medical care utilisation: Results of the MONICA/KORA cohorts S3/F3 and S4/F4. GMS Psychosoc Med. 2012;9:Doc09.

6. Thieme H, Borgetto B. Utilisation of rheumatology care services in Germany: the case of physical therapy and self-help groups. GMS Psychosoc Med. 2012;9:Doc08.
7. Janßen C, Sauter S, Kowalski C. The influence of social determinants on the use of prevention and health promotion services: Results of a systematic literature review. GMS Psychosoc Med. 2012;9:Doc07.
8. Lüdecke D, Mnich E, Kofahl C. The impact of sociodemographic factors on the utilisation of support services for family caregivers of elderly dependents—results from the German sample of the EUROFAMCARE study. GMS Psychosoc Med. 2012;9:Doc06.
9. Andersen RM. Revisiting the behavioral model and access to medical care: does it matter? J Health Soc Behav. 1995;36:1–10.
10. Bradley EH, McGraw SA, Curry L, Buckser A, King KL, Kasl SV, Andersen RM. Expanding the Andersen model: the role of psychosocial factors in long-term care use. Health Serv Res. 2002; 37: 1221–42.
11. Andersen RM, Davidson PL. Improving access to care in America: individual and contextual indicators. In: Andersen RM, Rice TH, Kominski GF, editors. Changing the U.S. health care system: key issues in health services, policy, and management. 3rd edition. San Francisco, CA: Jossey-Bass; 2007. p. 3–31.
12. Andersen RM, Davidson PL, Baumeister SE. Improving access to care in America. In: Kominski GF, editor. Changing the U.S. health care system: key issues in health services, policy, and management. 4th edition. San Francisco, CA: Jossey-Bass; 2013. p. 33–69.

Part II
Theory

Chapter 2
Re-revisiting the Behavioral Model of Health Care Utilization by Andersen: A Review on Theoretical Advances and Perspectives

Thomas von Lengerke, Daniela Gohl and Birgit Babitsch

Introduction

The utilization of health care services stands at the end of a help-seeking process of varying length (help-seeking behavior) and is influenced by many factors. In general, the more urgent, alarming or obvious a symptom, health complaint, or disease is perceived, the faster people seek help in the professional system and visit a physician [1]. In addition, other individual factors as well as the awareness and availability of medical facilities play a role in utilization. Germany is characterized by a high quantitative utilization of outpatient services (e.g., high number of contacts with care providers). According to analyses of the 2010 Gesundheit in Deutschland aktuell (GEDA) study by the Robert Koch Institute, 88.5 % of respondents had visited an office-based primary care physician or specialist (not including dentists) within the preceding 12 months [2]. This percentage was higher in women at 91.9 % than in men at 84.9 %. The higher percentage in women can in part be explained by regular gynecologist visits. At the same time, 11.5 % of respondents did not have any physician contact within the preceding 12 months. As possible explanatory factors, the Robert Koch Institute lists good health as well as system-related reasons, such as financial incentives for not visiting a physician or critical attitudes.

T. von Lengerke (✉)
Center of Public Health and Health Care, Medical Psychology Unit,
Hannover Medical School, Hannover, Germany
e-mail: lengerke.thomas@mh-hannover.de

D. Gohl
Berlin School of Public Health, Charité – Universitätsmedizin Berlin, Berlin, Germany
e-mail: daniela-stefanie.gohl@charite.de

B. Babitsch
Department of New Public Health, University of Osnabrück,
School of Human Sciences, Osnabrück, Germany
e-mail: bbabitsch@uni-osnabrueck.de

C. Janssen et al. (eds.), *Health Care Utilization in Germany*,
DOI 10.1007/978-1-4614-9191-0_2, © Springer Science+Business Media New York 2014

Any utilization of health services that is *not* need-induced is associated with a risk of overuse or misuse of care. Therefore, identifying any utilization-influencing factors that neither are need factors themselves nor are related to need factors can promote the effectiveness and efficiency of care. Fundamental considerations and utilization research suggest that particularly the (initial) establishment of contact to the health care system within a defined time period (any vs. no utilization) depends to a comparatively high degree on the potential user (rather than on the providers—which is the case for referrals) [3]. Hence, it can also depend on characteristics that do not represent need factors, such as individual psychosocial factors [4] or general determinants that are part of the "wide spectrum of individuality and subjectivity" [5, p. 27; English translation by authors]. In contrast, the nature and extent of utilization (if any: how much and what?), including particularly high utilization (if any: high utilization?), are typically more strongly determined by system-related factors. However, the relevance and determinants of these utilization parameters must be examined for each care sector.

Since the 1960s, several theoretical frameworks for analyzing and predicting health care utilization have been developed [6]. Worldwide, the most widely adopted model has been the Behavioral Model of Health Services Use (hereafter denoted "behavioral model" or BM) by Ronald M. Andersen, a US medical sociologist and health services researcher [4, 7–8, 9–12]. In 1968, he developed the first version of this model in his doctoral dissertation based on the third survey of the US Center for Health Administration Studies and the National Opinion Research Center [9, 13]. Interestingly, the unit of analysis in this first version was families, not individuals [9]— thus, taking a definitely sociological approach. In the following decades, the model was further developed through extensions in terms of health care system variables (1970s) [10–11], health outcomes and environments external to the health care system (1980s) [12], feedback loops (1990s) [7], psychosocial factors beyond health beliefs concerned directly with health care (2000s) [4, 14], and genetic susceptibility as an individual factor and quality of life as an outcome factor [8]. Possibly corresponding to respective trends in the zeitgeist, the initial focus on families changed to individuals as the unit of analysis. Recently, however, this shift has been at least partially counterbalanced by elaborating the contextual determinants of health services utilization to be able to cover family attributes at least on the independent side of models of utilization (i.e., determinants of utilization). However, regarding the dependent side (utilization), (empirical) emphasis seems to have been redirected toward the individual level, which is one reason that below, a behavioral epidemiology model will be suggested to be multilevel on both sides.

In its most recent version [8] (see Fig. 2.1), the BM covers a broad spectrum of contextual and individual characteristics hypothesized to influence utilization, which are classified as need, enabling, and predisposing factors [15]. Besides utilization, personal health practices as well as the process of medical care (i.e., the behavior of providers interacting with patients in the process of delivery) are supposed to be influenced by these characteristics. On the outcomes side, Andersen, Davidson, and Baumeister distinguish four types of results. Perceived health status indicates the extent to which a person can live a functional, comfortable, and pain-

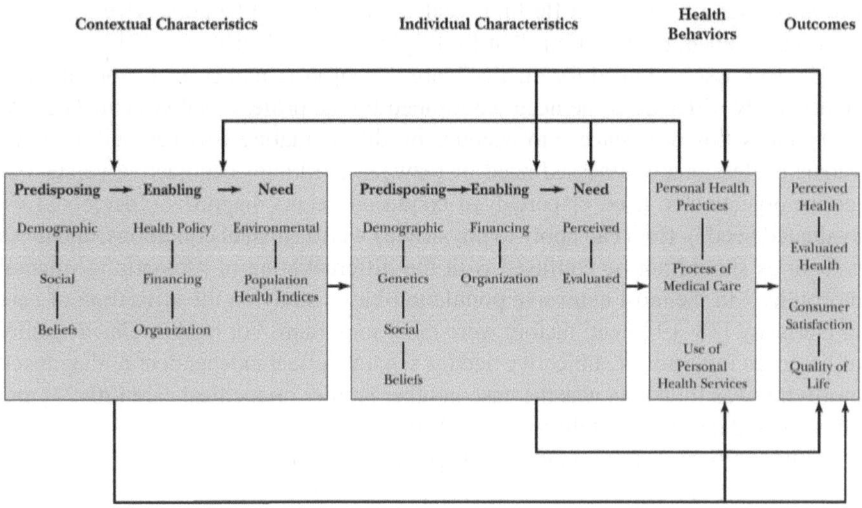

Fig. 2.1 Behavioral model of health services use, sixth revision. (Reproduced from [8])

free life. Evaluated health status is determined by professional assessment, based on established clinical standards and state-of-the-art practices. Consumer satisfaction depicts how individuals feel about the health care they receive. Finally, quality of life refers to physical and mental health, social ties, and the environments that the individual perceives as important to his or her well-being or happiness.

In the following sections, the model (2.1) and some of its previous applications (2.2)are described, and merits, potentials, and open questions are discussed (2.3). In Chap. 18, we will draw upon these considerations and all other chapters to provide suggestions to yet improve the model with, among other things, a focus on psycho-social–epidemiological factors [4, 16].

Morbidity as a Determinant: Self-Assessed and Professionally Assessed Need

People visit a physician (or other provider) when and because they are ill, feel ill, or anticipate an illness and want to prevent it. As mentioned above, this visit is often at the end of an extended process that can be defined as help-seeking behavior. This help-seeking behavior follows various decision-making phases that are generally gone through consecutively if the problem is inadequately solved or becomes more pressing, although some phases may be skipped. According to Siegrist [1], the following phases are differentiated: (1) self-treatment, (2) advice-seeking from close friends and relatives, (3) lay system, (4a) nonphysician professional system, and (4b) physician treatment. According to this model, the lay system plays a significant role in the way symptoms, health complaints, and diseases are handled. Few published studies describe help-seeking behavior in Germany. An analysis of the utilization of first aid centers in Berlin revealed that before utilizing services, patients took many self-initiated actions that fit the phases described above [17].

The self-assessed need for medical care is subject to numerous factors and can significantly differ from the need determined by the professional system. The BM [7–8] takes this difference into account by differentiating between self-assessed versus professionally assessed need or between (strikingly) subjective versus objective/objectivated need or perceived condition versus diagnosis ("perceived vs. evaluated need"). Both can apply to physical as well as mental conditions, and these categories should not be confused with the differentiation of "somatic vs. mental morbidity." In the most extensive population-based study on the utilization of care in Germany [18–19], need factors were most important. For health-related quality of life as an indicator of subjective need, a separate effect independent of diagnosed morbidity was found (as was the case in other studies on medical care [20–23] and physical and occupational therapy [24–26]).

Although such results sound unambiguous, terms such as need, diagnostic findings, and self- perceived conditions are also associated with questions about the definition of health and disease. For instance, Engel already emphasized in the biopsychosocial model: "To provide a basis for understanding the determinants of disease and arriving at rational treatments and patterns of health care, a medical model must also take into account the patient, the social context in which he lives, and the complementary system devised by society to deal with the disruptive effects of illness" [27, p. 132]. This model is now primarily interpreted as a practical orientation [28–30] rather than a general medical theory [31–32], and its discussion quickly leads to the mind–body problem and its modern solution approaches [33–34] (the discussion of which is beyond the scope of this chapter), but we should note that the question of what defines need and, therefore, appropriateness [35] is anything but trivial. In addition to the reference systems addressed by the Engel quote (medicine, patient, and society), "simple" epidemiological trends can be centrally important as well. For instance, Rose already pointed out the influence of prevalence on perceived normalcy: "What is common is all right, we presume" [36, p. 32] (in other words, statistical norms can change ideal or "should" standards).

This principle is easily illustrated on the example of obesity, a prime example of a physiological state whose pathological value is unclear [37] (contrary to the opinions expressed by many experts [38–42]). For the health care system and its users, this contributes to a situation where many questions remain unanswered about the availability and utilization of obesity-related services or services in which it plays a central role. If incidence and prevalence of obesity increase in society, this (statistical) "normalization" of markedly increased body weight can further put into question its role at least as a subjective need factor. Such an effect is suggested, for instance, by studies showing that adult women with a high body weight tend to be more satisfied with their body weight in neighborhoods with a high prevalence of overweight people [43–45]. The question whether an epidemiological increase in obesity tends to highlight it as a need factor or reduce the associated perceived need, or if both effects arise, is at least empirically valid.

Theoretically, need factors are chief determinants particularly where (potential) patients can exercise comparatively little discretion regarding utilization, such as the question to which type of specialist the primary physician refers the patient. Psychosocial factors, in contrast, can be particularly influential in cases where there is some discretion [9], for instance, in the decision whether a person first visits a primary care physician or directly sees a specialist at the start of an illness episode. Finally, some relevant factors are found on the population level rather than the individual level [8]. For instance, the prevalence or incidence of a morbidity factor can partially determine whether affected patients (and non-affected patients) utilize services.

Psychosocial and Societal Determinants: Predisposing and Enabling Factors

The BM by Andersen, Davidson, and Baumeister [8] represents an attempt to systematize utilization determinants that are not need factors by differentiating between predisposing and enabling factors. As with need factors, this is done on the individual and supraindividual (contextual) levels [8]:

Individual predisposing factors. This category includes the demographic factors—age and sex/gender ("biological imperatives" [8, p. 38]), genetic susceptibility to diseases, social factors such as education, occupation, ethnicity, and social ties (including marital status) as well as health beliefs in terms of attitudes, values, and knowledge about health and health services.

Contextual predisposing factors. This category includes the demographic and social composition of communities (including such measures as educational levels and crime rates) as well as (in terms of health beliefs) collective and organizational values, cultural norms, and prevailing political perspectives regarding health services organization, financing, and accessibility.

Individual enabling factors. This category includes financing of health services for the individual in terms of individual income and wealth available for payments. It also comprises effective prices of health care to the patient determined by personal insurance coverage and cost-sharing requirements, and characteristics of the organization of health services, such as the existence and nature of a regular source of care, means of transportation, and reported travel and waiting times required to access care.

Contextual enabling factors. Financing includes indicators such as per capita community income and wealth, i.e., measures of resources potentially available to pay for health services. Also, incentives to purchase or provide services such as rates of health insurance coverage, relative prices of medical care and other goods and services, methods of compensating providers, and per capita expenditures for health services are included here. Furthermore, organization includes the number and distribution of health services facilities and personnel. Also, structures such as ratios of physicians and hospital beds to population and facility-specific features (office hours and location of service, provider mix, utilization, quality control oversight, and outreach and education programs) are relevant. Finally, health policies in both the public and private sector are important contextual enabling factors.

We must note that the BM differentiates predisposing and enabling factors as well as need factors not only for the (basic scientific) explanation of utilization but also for the (policy-oriented) description of various dimensions of access to care [7–8]. This particularly applies to the differentiation of equitable versus inequitable access. The (political) goal of guaranteeing equitable access is achieved by ensuring that care is appropriate, while inequitable access is eliminated by reducing the influence of social and enabling factors on care [8]. However, this definition of interventions for avoiding inequitable access already suggests some inconsistencies of the BM [7–8]; these are discussed in Sect. 2.3. First, we will discuss the previous applications of the model.

Previous Applications of the Behavioral Model

In Germany, the BM has been used by the Federal Health Reporting service since 2001 [18–19, 46–47]. Recently, a systematic review has examined the use and implementation of the BM by studies that have explicitly employed it in Europe and in North America since 1998 [48]. It showed that the model has been used in several areas of the health care system and in relation to very different diseases, and that the 1995 version was used most frequently. However, the studies included in the review ($N=16$) showed substantial differences in the analyzed variables. The majority included age ($N=15$), marital status ($N=13$), gender and/or sex ($N=12$), education ($N=11$), and ethnicity ($N=10$) as predisposing factors, and income and/or financial situation ($N=10$), health insurance coverage ($N=9$), and having a usual source of care/family doctor ($N=9$) as enabling factors. As need factors, most of the studies included evaluated health status ($N=13$) and self-reported/perceived health ($N=9$) as well as a variety of diseases, most prominently diabetes and depression (both $N=5$).

Although associations of higher utilization were found with older age, female gender, higher income, and poorer health, there were inconsistencies in findings across studies. Besides differences between services as such, their context and the characteristics of the studied populations seemed to strongly impact the existence, strength, and direction of the associations. Also, the operationalizations of the model revealed that only a small common set of variables was used and that there were enormous variations in the way these variables were categorized, especially in regard to predisposing and enabling factors. This probably stems from the use of secondary data sets in most studies ($N=14$), which limited the number and variety of available variables.

The review concluded that especially primary studies are needed to improve the understanding of health care utilization and the complexity of the processes depicted in the BM. At the same time, the BM—notwithstanding its great merit as probably the classic model having guided health services utilization research for decades— is affected by a number of theoretical and conceptual inconsistencies that we will take as a starting point for further delineating its merits and potentials as well as open questions that should be answered empirically in future analyses.

Merits, Potentials, and Open Questions of the BM

As indicated above, the BM is plagued with some inconsistencies that are discussed in this section (further suggestions for improvement are outlined in Chap. 18). The first problem is that predisposing *psychological* factors (such as health beliefs) are listed as a potential source of utilization behavior ("realized access (use of services)" [8, p. 43]) but not of "inequitable access" in the form of *non*-need-induced care. This unnecessarily limits one major advantage of the BM (not only from a medical sociology perspective): the claim to explain and reduce inequity. For instance, a situation where people with pre-diabetes do not utilize adequate health services to avoid "risking" co-payments to be made with their limited personal income is not any more need-inadequate or unjust than a situation in which such insufficient care is the result of a negative body image and the associated sense of shame (quite apart from the social stratification of body image aspects, such as dissatisfaction with one's own body weight [49]).

The failure to include this aspect may also be a sign of a more structural inconsistency in the definition of predisposing and enabling factors. For instance, the former include psychological and social factors, and social relationships are sometimes considered predisposing [8], at other times enabling factors [7]. It also remains unclear why the three classic socioeconomic status indicators of education, profession, and income do not belong to the same category (although different classification, which could, in principle, be justified given the different significance for health inequalities [50–51]). Finally, the BM limited psychological factors to a few "health beliefs" for a long time; these were only elaborated in 2002 based on the development of health psychology theory [4], but have only partly found their way into the core model [8]. In sum, we see one line of further development of the BM in the integration of the mediator vs. moderator variables distinction [52-53], and the specification which predictors for which kind of utilization represent mediator and/or moderators. For example, one could hypothesize that enabling characteristics are moderators in most cases [54].

Further, the model still requires supplementation because of its focus on *individual* utilization behavior; in terms of *utilization epidemiology* and health policy, utilization by (sub) populations is more relevant than utilization by individuals. Essentially, this differentiation is based on the premise that the relationship between populations and individuals is like that of a whole that is more than the sum of its parts: Individuals and populations each have their own characteristics; therefore, causes of certain incidence or prevalence rates (of behaviors or diseases) in populations can differ from the causes of behaviors or diseases in individual members of the population (cases) [55]. The constellations in which this differentiation is particularly relevant and that were described by Schwartz and Dietz-Roux (e.g., relative ubiquitousness of individual risk factors in the population, interaction of supraindividual and individual factors in the form of context effects, or the influence of common-ness on individual manifestations of diseases or risk factors) all share assumed “social facts” that are in place and effective even outside of and independently of individuals—although not in their absence [56].

Potential Contributions from the Basic Behavioral Epidemiology Model

The expansion of the BM by *contextual* predisposing and enabling factors and corresponding need factors [8] advanced the integration of social and natural environmental factors in the prediction of utilization behavior, an integration that had already been initiated by Andersen and Newman [10]. This had the crucial advantage that multilevel models can illustrate individual and contextual influencing factors in a structurally parallel manner, meaning in corresponding categories as predisposing, enabling, or need factors. However, as mentioned above, a complete analysis of the utilization situation also requires modeling *behavioral prevalence* and *incidence* (e.g., the rate of smokers and the rate of persons who started smoking within a given time period). For such modeling of the *rates* of incidence and growth in utilization (like for other behaviors and comparable collective phenomena), the basic behavioral epidemiology model (BBEM) by von Lengerke and colleagues [16, 56] represents a basic framework to specify important basic assumptions of the BM, and will now be introduced to an Anglophone audience for the first time. Following the macro–micro model by Coleman [57] and the basic model of sociological explanation by Esser [58], it allows taking into account *collective* outcomes, meaning outcomes that do not describe individuals but groups of people. Before providing an example of such an explanation using behavioral prevalence, we will first present the BBEM in more detail (see Fig. 2.2). We intend to show that in addition to specifying important basic assumptions of the BM, it can render the BM compatible with theoretical discourses in medical sociology and render it more empirically useful by drawing on the classification of individual and supraindividual characteristics by Lazarsfeld and Menzel [59].

Like the models by Coleman and Esser, the BBEM assumes, in the spirit of methodological individualism, that supraindividual outcomes (see Fig. 2.2, top right) can only be explained by going back to the level of individual actors.[1] According to Lazarsfeld and Menzel [59], such supraindividual units (collectives) can be characterized by three types of properties:

Analytical properties can be described by a mathematical operation that is applied to characteristics of the individual members, such as the average income of a community or the prevalence of a behavior.

Structural properties can be described by a mathematical operation that is applied to the relationship of each member to other members, for instance, the cliqu-

[1] The inclusion of only one supraindividual level in Fig. 2.2 is intended to increase clarity; of course, models with more than two levels are more realistic (e.g., “patients” in “wards” in “hospitals”).

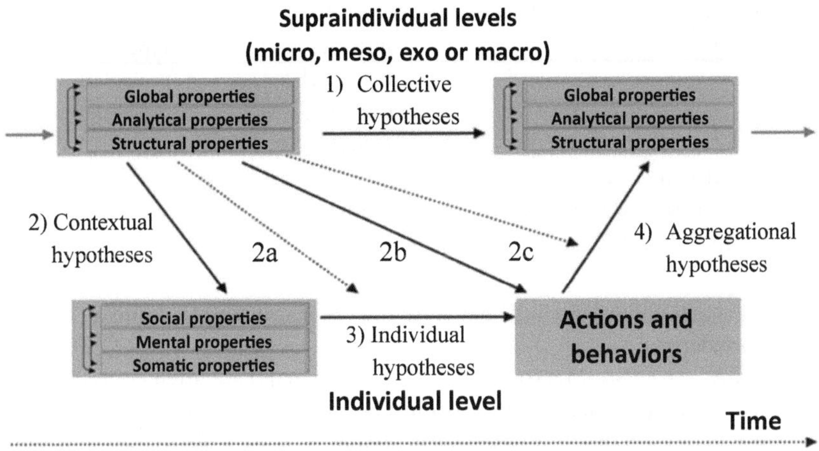

Fig. 2.2 The Basic Behavioral Epidemiology Model (BBEM) [16, 56] as a variant of the macro—micro model of sociological explanation [61]. (following Coleman [57], Esser [58], Puls [62], Engel [27] and Lazarsfeld and Menzel [59])

ishness of a school class or the proportion of ethnic enclaves in the districts of a large city (examples from [59]).

Global properties are those that are or must be defined and measured without using individual characteristics, such as the regional density of sports facilities or the ratio of national spending on education versus defense.

Relating the supraindividual and the individual levels of the BBEM to those of Andersen's BM, two main differences emerge: On the one hand, while the BM's contextual characteristics by and large would belong to the supraindividual level in the BBEM, health behaviors and outcomes are not modeled on the supraindividual level in the BM but they are in the BBEM (as analytical or structural attributes based on individual actions and behaviors or biopsychosocial morbidity parameters). On the other hand, and consequently, not all causal or otherwise influencing mechanisms within and across the levels depicted in the BBEM are found in the BM (see Fig. 2.1). Most clearly, this holds for ecological associations, i.e., mutual relationships between properties of supraindividual units (*collective hypotheses* in Fig. 2.2). This is important since ecological studies are argued to be relevant to theory and practice [60]. However, for various reasons, there are justified doubts about the sufficiency of such (macrosociological) perspectives for explaining collective circumstances [61]:

Ontological individualism: When collective phenomena are considered to be caused by individuals and their relationships, their explanations must also take into account these units since collective units themselves cannot take action.

Explanatory incompleteness: If collective hypotheses are nonlegislative but in the form of probability statements, they require assumptions about the conditions under which they apply, and these are most easily specified by going back to the individual level.

Psychosocial explanations: In cases where individuals are influenced more by their subjective perceptions than by environmental conditions, theories about so-

Table 2.1 Four types of analytical fallacies [56, 63]

Analyzed unit	Inference level	Type of fallacy
Collective	Individual	Ecological
Individual	Collective	Atomistic
Individual: No consideration of relevant collective characteristics	Individual	Psychologistic ("individualistic")
Collective: No consideration of relevant individual characteristics	Collective	Sociologistic ("collectivistic")

ciety and social conditions must generally be reconstructible in terms of this individual knowledge.

"Small N" problem: Macro-entities (like individuals) are often complex, so that the effects of many influencing factors must be assumed and investigated. However, they are also rare, so that few cases are available for testing alternative hypotheses. Analyses on the individual level can alleviate this problem (but with the risk of atomistic fallacies [63]; see Table 2.1).

Therefore, the BBEM also explains empirical collective hypotheses via the "detour" of the individual level, on which the actions and behaviors of individual actors are in turn explained by three types of individual characteristics:

Somatic properties, of which some, in certain forms, can be pathological (e.g., body mass, which can be underweight, normal, pre-obese, non-morbidly obese, or morbidly obese).

Psychological properties, of which some, in certain forms, can be pathological (e.g., depression as a morbid instantiation of depressive states).

Social properties, meaning personal characteristics related to the individual's position in terms of socioeconomic and social relational variables (especially education, income, professional status, and social relationships).[2]

Together with actions and behaviors, these properties generally form the basis of the analytical properties of supraindividual entities and are, at the same time, used on the individual level to explain actions and behaviors (*individual hypotheses* in Fig. 2.2). The model differs from the approaches by Coleman [57] and Esser [58] in that it does not prefer or even axiomatize rational choice explanations but generally allows all types of biopsychosocial explanations. In this respect, it follows Puls [62],

[2] Lazarsfeld and Menzel [59] developed a formal classification for individual properties as well:

- *Absolute properties*, which can be determined without recourse to characteristics of supraindividual units or to characteristics of relationships with other individuals.
- *Relational properties*, which are determined on the basis of information about relationships to other individuals.
- *Comparative properties*, which derive from a comparison of the value of an individual for an absolute or relational property with the distribution of this property in the considered collective.
- *Contextual properties*, which describe individuals by a (global, analytical or structural) property of the collective (and that are therefore invariable for all members of the collective).

The somatic, psychological, and social characteristics meant in the BBEM in its present form are primarily absolute properties, which means that the model is still too simplistic in this area. Since the primary goal in this context is to specify a model that can also depict *rates* of behavior, we accepted this lack of clarity here for space reasons.

who used the example of large-scale unemployment and hazardous alcohol consumption to show that theories other than expectation–times–value or comparable rational choice approaches can be integrated into the model. Accordingly, individual hypotheses can be single hypotheses or theories. This implies that somatic, psychological, and social characteristics can individually or collectively function as mediating or moderating variables in the explanation of actions or behaviors. The individual and supraindividual levels are now connected by two types of hypotheses (see Fig. 2.2):

Contextual hypotheses: They specify the influences of global, analytical, and structural properties on somatic, psychological, social, and behavioral characteristics (arrows 2 and 2b) and as moderating effects on individual and aggregation hypotheses (arrows 2a and 2c).[3]

Aggregation hypotheses: They specify the (transformation) rules according to which individual actions and behaviors (co-) determine and form the supraindividual context and its global, analytical, and structural properties.

In addition to the basic idea that it shares with the models mentioned above, the suggested form of the BBEM offers three improvements:

By following the macro–micro model of sociological explanation, the biopsychosocial analysis of causes (and effects) of health-relevant behavior becomes compatible with the theoretical discourses of (medical and health) sociology [61, 62, 67].

By (at least partially) integrating the classification of individual and supraindividual characteristics by Lazarsfeld and Menzel, who established this classification according to the relevant measurement operations [59], the model gains empirically usefulness.

By specifying somatic, psychological, and social characteristics, the model avoids at least some ([uni]disciplinary) "blind spots" [16].

A Fictitious Case Example of Causal Pathways as Suggested by the BBEM

To illustrate the BBEM, which has so far been formulated on a high level of abstraction, we will present a fictitious example of a possible causal chain. The starting point of the example is a newly established health care service: a counseling service for obese adults that is offered at the public health department. As an infrastructure, this facility represents an antecedent global property on a supraindividual (in this case community) level (see Fig. 2.2). Its ultimate goal is to reduce the prevalence of obesity, that is, to change a consequent analytical property by modifying individual behaviors. It must be noted that this newly offered service infrastructure is likely the

[3] The macro–micro model of sociological explanation typically does not contain paths 2a–c. They were included in the BBEM because they represent central health science research interests, such as moderating effects of the mean regional income on the relationship between inhabitants' individual income and their behavior (arrow 2a [64]), direct environmental effects on behavior without explicit mediation by psychological processes (arrow 2b [64]), and moderating policy effects on citizen participation in health policy decision making (arrow 2c [66]).

result of political obligations and organizational opportunities that have emerged in the context of changing political processes and framework conditions [68].

If the new health care service is considered an indicator of the quality of government administration and public service (government effectiveness), it is reasonable to expect that it may contribute to reducing the prevalence of obesity. This is particularly the case since the prevalence of obesity negatively correlates with government effectiveness in Europe as shown by Rabin et al. [69] using data of the World Health Organization (WHO) Global Noncommunicable Disease InfoBase and other international data bases (*collective hypothesis* in Fig. 2.2).[4] However, the service's contribution to reducing obesity requires that the facility be used by affected individuals (public opportunities [68]). The presence of individual obesity represents a need factor that should lead to individual utilization behavior, so that behavioral services can take effect. It is once again important to emphasize that this utilization behavior is not exclusively the result of individual decision making but is also at least influenced by the presence or absence of health policy guidelines and regulations in particular.

Awareness by members of the target group is a prerequisite for the utilization of the new counseling facility. Kersell and Milsum [73] already emphasized the importance of awareness and evaluation of health-related services as it affects their utilization and influence on health-relevant behaviors. This awareness can be promoted by social marketing (*context hypothesis* 2 in Fig. 2.2), and it then represents a psychological determinant of behavior on the individual level. Dissatisfaction with one's own body weight can be seen as another example of a psychological determinant. Awareness of services and dissatisfaction with body weight could furthermore interact in such a way that the latter, in the presence of the former, increases the likelihood of an initial visit to the facility (*individual hypothesis* in Fig. 2.2).[5] If this applies to many individuals, the summation of individual effects leads to high utilization. In addition, very early users of the service ("innovators" and "early adopters" [75]) may promote utilization by communicating ("word of mouth") with other affected individuals (*aggregation hypotheses* in Fig. 2.2).

Finally, these individual and aggregation effects can theoretically be moderated or supplemented by various other context effects (*contextual hypotheses 2a–c* in Fig. 2.2), which we will illustrate only on the example of supraindividual social factors:

---

[4] An individual's likelihood of becoming obese is also known to increase with the incidence of obesity in the individual's own social network [70] (the same is true of smoking [71] and happiness [72]). Hence, the individual somatic property "obese" is apparently influenced by the supraindividual analytical property "rate of obesity within network." However, this only applies to close social relations (friends, siblings, and partners). The relationship between the two former properties is therefore presumably moderated by the supraindividual structural property "social cohesion." However, it has not yet been determined to what extent these relationships in turn influence obesity-associated behaviors, such as utilization of care.

[5] This interaction could, in turn, be moderated by social variables, such as socioeconomic status. Rückert et al. [74], for instance, investigated the practice fee in the German health care system and found that in the chronically ill, the likelihood to avoid or delay a physician visit to avoid the practice fee was 2.45 times higher in the lowest income group than in the highest.

Social norms that favor individualized ways of dealing with individually attributable risks can prevent individuals from taking advantage of the service despite their body weight dissatisfaction (2a).

Social climates can directly correlate with individual behavior, as is the case in the societal evaluation of health policies [76] (2b).

Societal health policy support, for instance, through the allocation of financial resources [68] for quality assurance at the counseling facility, could be a constraint that influences the effectiveness of individual utilization, the changes in individual obesity status, and, in consequence, the reduction of obesity prevalence (2c).

This fictitious example of a causal chain (which naturally requires a probabilistic interpretation as is appropriate for its humanities-based subject) can, therefore, be illustrated in a multilevel structure in the BBEM. In the context of the BM, the selected example would be presented as follows: The new health care facility for obese adults is a contextual (here: organizational) factor enabling the obese adult population to utilize services to manage their obesity, and potentially to become nonobese (thus eventually reducing the prevalence of obesity). Most probably, the establishment of the new facility itself has been made possible by contextual need (high prevalences of obesity and concomitant diseases), contextual predisposing factors (such as demographic changes), and other enabling factors such as health policies and allocated financial resources.

Subsequently, the BM would predict that the utilization of the facility by individual members of the target group should at least in part be mediated or otherwise influenced by individual predisposing, enabling, and need factors (see Fig. 2.1). Factors such as those stated above (e.g., policy perception, body weight dissatisfaction) may be operative, even though their categorical labels may be different in the BBEM (biopsychosocial factors). One key difference to the BBEM, however, is that health behaviors, such as the prevalence of facility utilization by the population under scrutiny (i.e., an analytical supraindividual attribute based on individual utilization behavior in the BBEM), are not represented as contextual variables in the BM. Thus, aggregation hypotheses resulting in population behavior indices cannot be analyzed in the BM. For instance, 2c-type hypotheses as depicted in Fig. 2.2 are not represented and, thus, not testable in the BM framework.

Summary of Implications of the BBEM for the BM

In light of the above, we see the following main merits, potentials, and open questions for the BM:

Merits: To foster theoretical analysis and explanation of inequity in the utilization of health care. While it is true that the question how perceived vs. evaluated need as well as perceived health status, evaluated health status, consumer satisfaction, and quality of life are used in practice to identify inequitable access is far from trivial, and a prevailing issue within medical sociology and medicine at large, the BM is extremely useful in this regard [8].

To provide parallel structures of individual and contextual determinants, i.e., on the multilevel predictor side of the model, predisposing factors, enabling factors, and need factors are depicted in terms of corresponding categories.

Potentials: To specify factors as potential sources of (in) equitable access, further specify the role of the three classic indicators of socioeconomic status (education, income, and occupational status) in terms of predisposing vs. enabling characteristics, and more generally integrate the mediator/moderator distinction [52–53] in its theoretical and empirical calculus.

To model *behavioral prevalences* and *incidences* as outcomes beyond the focus on *individual* utilization behavior, since utilization by (sub) populations rather than individual utilization is primarily relevant for *health services epidemiology* and health policy.

Open questions: How can the categories of the model (particularly predisposing and enabling factors) be more clearly defined?

Which theories/hypotheses are valid and expedient for which types of utilization in the context of the BM^2 on individual and supraindividual levels as depicted in the BBEM?

How do contextual characteristics affect individual predictors of utilization behavior and the behavior itself as well as the relationships between the two (contextual hypotheses)?

How do individual utilization decisions influence the relevant contexts that are in turn relevant for later utilization (aggregation hypotheses)?

Can ecological relationships be used to derive health policy recommendations by applying the following research principle for testing collective hypotheses: “When predicting the behavior or status of groups, correlate means” [60, p. 363]?

Although the present volume will not be able to provide answers (leave alone empirical ones) to all of these questions, the results reported in the individual chapters should also be discussed in light of this background. This theoretical chapter is primarily intended to provide an overview of possible desiderata, which will be reexamined in Chap. 18.

References

[1] Siegrist J. Medizinische Soziologie. In German. München: Urban & Fischer; 2005.

[2] Robert Koch Institute, editor. Daten und Fakten: Ergebnisse der Studie »Gesundheit in Deutschland aktuell 2010«. In German. Berlin: Robert Koch Institute; 2012.

[3] Diehr P, Yanez D, Ash A, Hornbrook M, Lin DY. Methods for analyzing health care utilization and costs. Ann Rev Public Health. 1999; 20: 125–144.

[4] Bradley EH, McGraw SA, Curry L, Buckser A, King KL, Kasl SV, Andersen RM. Expanding the Andersen model: the role of psychosocial factors in long-term care use. Health Serv Res. 2002;37:1221–42.

[5] Andersen HH, Bormann C, Elkeles T. [Index numbers of the utilization of outpatient treatment. Methodical aspects of the value of data from surveys.] In German. Soz Praventivmed. 1993;38:26–33.
[6] Ricketts TC, Goldsmith LJ. Access in health services research: the battle of the frameworks. Nurs Outlook. 2005;53:274–80.
[7] Andersen RM. Revisiting the behavioral model and access to medical care: does it matter? J Health Soc Behav. 1995;36:1–10.
[8] Andersen RM, Davidson PL, Baumeister SE. Improving access to care in America. In: Kominski EF, editor. Changing the U.S. health care system: key issues in health services, policy, and management. 4th edition. San Francisco, CA: Jossey-Bass; 2013. p. 33–69.
[9] Andersen RM.: Families' use of health services: a behavioral model of predisposing, enabling, and need components [Dissertation]. http://docs.lib.purdue.edu/dissertations/AAI6902884 (1968). Accessed 5 June, 2013.
[10] Andersen RM, Newman JF. Societal and individual determinants of medical care utilization in the United States. Milbank Mem Fund Q Health Soc. 1973;51:95–124.
[11] Aday LA, Andersen RM. A framework for the study of access to medical care. Health Serv Res. 1974;9:208–20.
[12] Aday LA, Andersen RM, Fleming GV. Health care in the U.S.: equiable for whom? Beverly Hills, CA: Sage; 1980.
[13] Andersen RM. National health surveys and the behavioral model of health services use. Med Care. 2008;46:647–53.
[14] Andersen RM, Davidson PL. Improving access to care in America: individual and contextual indicators. In: Andersen RM, Rice TH, Kominski GF, editors. Changing the U.S. health care system: key issues in health services, policy, and management. 3rd edition. San Francisco, CA: Jossey-Bass; 2007. p. 3–31.
[15] Hulka BS, Wheat JR. Patterns of utilization. The patient perspective. Med Care. 1985;23:438–59.
[16] von Lengerke T. Sozialpsychologische Grundlagen der Medizinischen Psychologie. In German. In Brähler E, Strauß B, editors. Medizinische Psychologie [Enzyklopädie der Psychologie, Band D/VIII/1]. Göttingen: Hogrefe; 2012. p. 285–316.
[17] Babitsch B, Braun T, Borde T, David, M. Doctor's perception of doctor-patient relationships in emergency departments: What roles do gender and ethnicity play? BMC Health Serv Res. 2008;8:82.
[18] Thode N, Bergmann E, Kamtsiuris P, Kurth B-M. Einflussfaktoren auf die Inanspruchnahme des deutschen Gesundheitswesens und mögliche Steuerungsmechanismen. In German. Berlin: Robert Koch Institute; 2004 http://www.rki.de/DE/Content/Gesundheitsmonitoring/Themen/Versorgung/projektbericht.html, Accessed 5 June, 2013.
[19] Thode N, Bergmann E, Kamtsiuris P, Kurth B-M. Einflussfaktoren auf die ambulante Inanspruchnahme in Deutschland. Bundesgesundheitsbl Gesundheitsforschung Gesundheitsschutz. 2005;48:296–306,
[20] de Boer AGEM, Wijker W, de Haes HCJM. Predictors of health care utilization in the chronically ill: a review of the literature. Health Policy. 1997;42:101–15,
[21] Henton FE, Hays BJ, Walker SN, Atwood JR. Determinants of Medicare home health care service use among Medicare recipients. Nursing Res. 2002;51:355–62,
[22] McCusker J, Karp I, Cardin S, Durand P, Morin J. Determineants of emergency department visits by older adults: a systematic review. Acad Emerg Med. 2003;10:1362–70,
[23] Padgett DK, Brodsky B. Psychosocial factors influencing non-urgent use of the emergency room: a review of the literature and recommendations for research and improved service delivery. Soc Sci Med. 1992;35:1180–97,
[24] Cook C, Stickley L, Ramey K, Knotts VJ. Variables associated with occupational and physical therapy stroke rehabilitation utilization and outcomes. J Allied Health. 2005;34:3–10,
[25] Finlayson M, DalMonte J. Predicting the use of occupational therapy services among people with multiple sclerosis in Atlantic Canada. Can J Occup Ther. 2002;69:239–48,
[26] Kadushin G. Home health care utilization: a review of the research for social work. Health Soc Work. 2004;29:219–44,

[27] Engel GL. The need for a new medical model: a challenge for biomedicine. Science. 1977;196:129–36,
[28] Borrell-Carrió F, Suchman AL, Epstein RM. The biopsychosocial model 25 years later: principles, practice, and scientific inquiry. Ann Fam Med. 2004;2:576–82,
[29] Epstein RM, Borrell-Carrio F. The biopsychosocial model: Exploring six impossible things. Fam Syst Health. 2005;23:426–31,
[30] McDaniel SH, Campbell T, Hepworth J, Lorenz A. Family-oriented primary care. 2nd edition. New York: Springer; 2005.
[31] McLaren N. A critical review of the biopsychosocial model. Aust N Z J Psychiatry. 1998;32:86–92.
[32] McLaren N. The myth of the biopsychosocial model. Aust N Z J Psychiatry. 2006;40:277–8.
[33] Kendler KS. A psychiatric dialogue on the mind-body problem. Am J Psychiatry. 2001;158:989–1000.
[34] McLaren N. Interactive dualism as a partial solution to the mind-brain problem for psychiatry. Med Hypotheses. 2006;66:1165–73.
[35] Advisory Council for the Concerted Action in Health Care. Appropriateness and Efficiency (Report 2000/2001, Summary). http://www.svr-gesundheit.de/index.php?id=18. Accessed 5 June, 2013.
[36] Rose G. Sick individuals and sick populations. Int J Epidemiol. 1985;14(1):32–8.
[37] World Health Organization. Obesity and overweight [Fact sheet N°311]. Geneva: WHO; 2013. http://www.who.int/mediacentre/ factsheets/fs311/en/index.html. Accessed 5 June, 2013.
[38] Allison DB, Downey M, Atkinson RL, Billington CJ, Bray GA, Eckel RH, Finkelstein EA, Jensen MD, Tremblay A. Obesity as a disease: a white paper on evidence and arguments commissioned by the Council of the Obesity Society. Obesity. 2008;16:1161–77.
[39] Bray GA. Obesity is a chronic, relapsing neurochemical disease. Int J Obes. 2004;28:34–8.
[40] Council of the Obesity Society. Obesity as a disease: the Obesity Society Council resolution. Obesity. 2008;16:1151.
[41] Dausch J. Determining when obesity is a disease. J Am Diet Assoc. 2001;101:293.
[42] Kossmann B, Aidelsburger P, Wasem J. Adipositas – eine Krankheit? In German. Essen: Universität Duisburg-Essen; 2006. http://www.magenband-hilfe.de/attachment. php?attachmentid =120. Accessed 5 June, 2013.
[43] McLaren L, Gauvin L: Neighbourhood level versus individual level correlates of women's body dissatisfaction: Toward a multilevel understanding of the role of affluence. J Epidemiol Community Health. 2002, 56:193–199.
[44] McLaren L, Gauvin L: Does the 'average size' of women in the neighbourhood influence a woman's likelihood of body dissatisfaction? Health Place. 2003, 9:327–335.
[45] von Lengerke T, Mielck A;KORA-Studiengruppe. Unzufriedenheit mit dem eigenen Körpergewicht nach Einkommensarmut: eine Mehrebenenanalyse in der Region Augsburg. In German. In Berth H et al., editors. Psychologie und Medizin – Traumpaar oder Vernunftehe? Lengerich: Pabst; p. 69–80.
[46] Bergmann E, Kalcklösch M, Tiemann F. Inanspruchnahme des Gesundheitswesens – Erste Ergebnisse des telefonischen Gesundheitssurveys 2003. Bundesgesundheitsbl Gesundheitsforsch Gesundheitsschutz. 2005;12:1365–73.
[47] Kamtsiuris P, Bergmann E, Rattay P, Schlaud M. Inanspruchnahme medizinischer Leistungen. Ergebnisse des Kinder- und Jugendsurveys (KiGGS). Bundesgesundheitsbl Gesundheitsforsch Gesundheitsschutz. 2007;50: 836–50.
[48] Babitsch B, Gohl D, von Lengerke T. Re-revisiting Andersen's Behavioral Model of Health Services Use: a systematic review of studies from 1998–2011. GMS Psychosoc Med. 2012;9:Doc11.
[49] von Lengerke T, Mielck A; KORA Study Group. Body weight dissatisfaction by socioeconomic status among obese, preobese and normal weight women and men: results of the cross-sectional KORA Augsburg S4 population survey. BMC Public Health. 2012;12:342.

[50] Geyer S, Hemström Ö. Peter R, Vågerö D. Education, income, and occupational class cannot be use interchangeably in social epidemiology. Empircal evidence against a common practice. J Epidemiol Community Health. 2006;60:804–810
[51] Geyer S. [Single indicator or index? Comparison of measures of social differentiation]. In German. Gesundheitswesen. 2008;70:281–8.
[52] Baron RM, Kenny DA. The moderator-mediator variable distinction in social psychological research: conceptual, strategic and statistical considerations. J Pers Soc Psychol. 1986;51:1173–82.
[53] Hayes AF. Introduction to mediation, moderation and conditional process analysis: A regression-based approach. New York, NY; Guilford; 2013.
[54] Stokols D. Establishing and maintaining healthy environments: Toward a social ecology of health promotion. Am Psycholog. 1992;47:6–22.
[55] Schwartz S, Diez-Roux AV. Causes of incidence and causes of cases – a Durkheimian perspective on Rose. Int J Epidemiol. 2001;30:435–9.
[56] von Lengerke T, Abu-Omar K. Verhaltensepidemiologie: Einblicke in ein neues Wissensgebiet. In German. In: von Lengerke T, editor. Public Health-Psychologie: Individuum und Bevölkerung zwischen Verhältnissen und Verhalten. Weinheim: Juventa; 2007. p. 32–44.
[57] Coleman JS. Foundations of social theory. Cambridge, MA: Belknap Press; 1990.
[58] Esser H. Soziologie: Allgemeine Grundlagen. In German. Frankfurt: Campus; 1999.
[59] Lazarsfeld PF, Menzel H. On the relation between individual and collective properties. In Etzioni A, Lehman EW, editors. A sociological reader on complex organizations. 3rd edition. New York: Holt, Rinehart and Winston: 1980. p. 508–21.
[60] Lubinski D, Humphreys LG. Seeing the forest from the trees: When predicting the behavior or status of groups, correlate means. Psycholog Public Policy Law, 1996;2:363–76.
[61] Greve J, Schnabel A, Schützeichel R. Das Mikro-Makro-Modell der soziologischen Erklärung – zur Einleitung. In German. In: Greve J, Schnabel A, Schützeichel R, editors. Das Mikro-Makro-Modell der soziologischen Erklärung. Zur Ontologie, Methodologie und Metatheorie eines Forschungsprogramms. Wiesbaden: VS; 2008. pp. 7–17
[62] Puls W. [Mass unemployment, stress and risky alcohol consumption An attempt at a sociological explanation based on the model of effort-reward imbalance]. In German. J Public Health. 2004;12:259–70.
[63] Diez-Roux AV. Bringing context back into epidemiology: variables and fallacies in multilevel analysis. Am J Public Health. 1998;88:216–22.
[64] Twigg L, Moon G, Jones K. Predicting small-area health-related behaviour: a comparison of smoking and drinking indicators. Soc Sci Med. 2000;50:1109–20.
[65] Sallis JF, Hovell MF, Hofstetter CR, Elder JP, Hackley M, Caspersen CJ, Powell KE. Distance between homes and exercise facilities related to frequency of exercise among San Diego residents. Public Health Rep. 1990;105:179–85.
[66] Council of Europe. The development of structures for citizen and patient participation in the decision-making process affecting health care. Straßburg. Council of Europe; 2001.
[67] Cockerham WC. Medical sociology. 12th edition. Upper Saddle River, NJ: Pearson; 2012.
[68] Rütten A, Lüschen G, von Lengerke T et al. Determinants of health policy impact: comparative results of a European policymaker study. Soz Praventivmed. 2003;48: 379–91.
[69] Rabin BA, Boehmer TK, Brownson RC. Cross-national comparison of environmental and policy correlates of obesity in Europe. Eur J Public Health. 2007;17:53–61.
[70] Christakis NA, Fowler JH. The spread of obesity in a large social network over 32 years. N Engl J Med. 2007;357:370–9.
[71] Christakis NA, Fowler JH. The collective dynamics of smoking in a large social network. N Engl J Med. 2008;358:2249–58.
[72] Fowler JH, Christakis NA. Dynamic spread of happiness in a large social network: longitudinal analysis over 20 years in the Framingham Heart Study. BMJ. 2008;337:a2338.
[73] Kersell MW, Milsum JH. A systems model of health behavior change. Behav Sci. 1985;30:119–26

[74] Rückert IM, Böcken J, Mielck A: Are German patients burdened by the practice charge for physician visits ('Praxisgebuehr')? A cross sectional analysis of socio-economic and health related factors. BMC Health Serv Res. 2008;8:232.
[75] Rogers EM. Diffusion of innovations. 5th edition. New York: Free Press; 2003.
[76] von Lengerke T, Vinck J, Rütten A, Reitmeir P, Abel T, Kannas L, Lüschen G, Rodríguez Diaz JA, van der Zee J. Health policy perception and health behaviours: a multilevel analysis and implications for public health psychology. J Health Psychol. 2004;9:157–7.

Chapter 3
Utilization of Medical Services in Germany—Outline of Statutory Health Insurance System (SHI)

Cornelia Bormann and Enno Swart

Introduction

In Germany, the utilization of medical and health services is largely governed by structural and statutory provisions. These provisions are briefly described below to ensure a better understanding of relationships within utilization research and within the care sectors presented in this book, particularly for readers who are not familiar with the German system. For more detailed discussions, refer to the basic literature and relevant legal texts [1–6]. Unless otherwise indicated, the empirical data on the German health-care system were current as of the fall of 2012.

The Statutory Health Insurance System

In Germany, health insurance has been compulsory since 2009. Approximately 85% of the population (70 million people) is insured through the statutory health insurance (SHI) and 10% is covered by private health insurance (PHI). The SHI covers all employees with a gross income of up to EUR 3,825 per month or EUR 45,900 per year (=contribution assessment ceiling; as of 2012) and their nonworking family members (spouses and children). Individuals whose income is above the contribution assessment ceiling can voluntarily enroll in the SHI or switch to PHI. The PHIs also insure self-employed persons, freelancers, and civil servants (in the latter case, at least the portion

C. Bormann (✉)
Health Sciences, FH Bielefeld—University of Applied Sciences, Bielefeld, Germany
e-mail: cbormann@uni-bremen.de

E. Swart
Institute of Social Medicine and Health Economics, Medical Faculty, Otto von Guericke University of Magdeburg, Magdeburg, Germany
e-mail: enno.swart@med.ovgu.de

C. Janssen et al. (eds.), *Health Care Utilization in Germany*,
DOI 10.1007/978-1-4614-9191-0_3,

Table 3.1 Health insurance funds, health insurance types, insured persons and members in 2011 (annual average in thousands)

	Number[a]	Avg. contribution in %[b]	Insured members, total	Compulsory members		Voluntary members		Retirees		Coinsured family members	
			in 1,000	in 1,000	in %	in 1,000	in %	in 1,000	in %	in 1,000	in %
SHIs	147	15.5	69,637	29,878	42.9	4,919	7.1	16,806	24.1	18,035	25.8
Regional health insurance funds	12	15.5	24,243	10,175	42.0	977	4.0	6,905	28.5	6,186	25.5
Company health insurance funds	122	15.5	12,817	5,808	45.3	1,052	8.2	2,307	18.1	3,651	28.5
Guild health insurance funds	7	15.5	5,431	2,837	52.2	315	5.8	797	14.7	1,482	27.3
Substitute SHIs	6	15.5	24,614	10,390	42.2	2,464	10.0	5,596	22.7	6,164	25.0
Other	10	15.5	2,531	669	26.4	110	4.3	1,202	47.5	551	21.8

[a] Number of insurances in January

[b] Including additional contribution by the insured equaling 0.9%; Source: Federal Ministry of Health, National Association of Statutory Health Insurance Funds statistics (calendar month 1/13), cited according to [7]

that is not covered by the government allowance). Table 3.1 presents the number of SHIs and the distribution of insured persons among the different insurance types.

In recent years, the number of SHIs has significantly decreased as a result of closings and particularly fusions. By early 2012, 145 health insurances remained (as of March 1, 2012; National Association of Statutory Health Insurance Funds, 2012; http://www.gkv-spitzenverband.de/ITSGKrankenkassenListe.gkvnet). A further decrease is expected. SHIs are primarily funded by a uniform contribution rate of 15.5 % of their members' income. Of this contribution, 7.3 % is paid by the employer and 8.2 % by the employee. In addition, a few government grants are available, for instance for contribution-free coverage of nonworking family members.

Expenses

For almost 15 years, the expenses in the health-care system have been in the range of 10.0–10.6 % of the gross domestic product (GDP); in 2011, they equaled about EUR 250 billion. The SHIs cover more than two-third of all health-care expenditures,

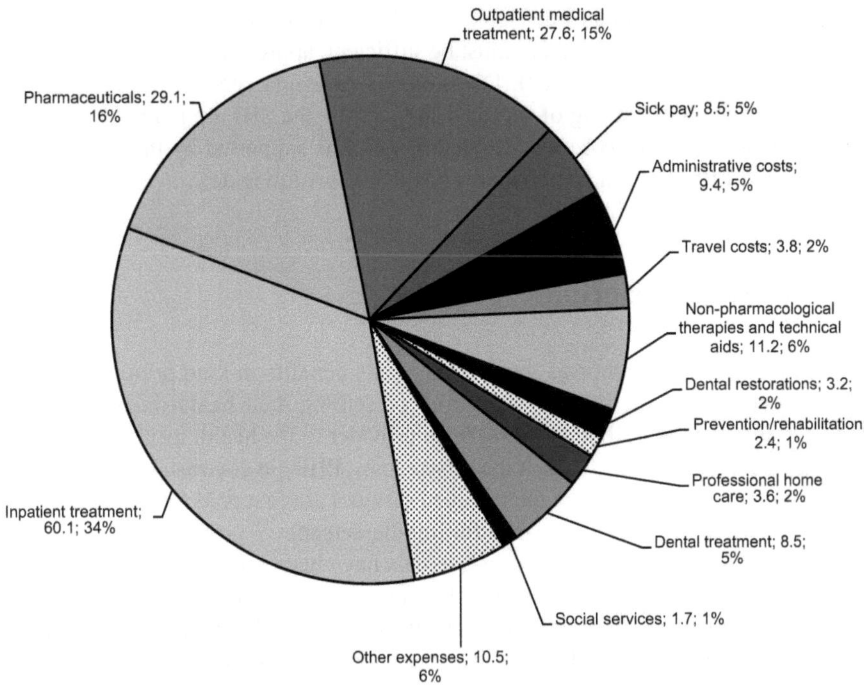

Fig. 3.1 SHI services and expenses in 2011. (Source: Federal Ministry of Health; National Association of Statutory Insurance Funds statistics: key figures and rules of thumb [8])

a good EUR 170 billion, which equals to 6–7 % of the GDP. However, the political discourse has repeatedly been critical of the development of SHI expenses in view of flat or dropping revenues. In recent years, many steps were therefore taken to reduce the SHI catalog of services, increase co-payments by the insured for certain services, and change the entire funding basis. Figure 3.1 presents the distribution of expenses in 2011.

The listed expenses refer to the standard benefits as required by law and as specified in the SHI catalog of services as well as to special services identified in the health insurances' statutes. Standard benefits include the following:

- Outpatient medical treatment
- Hospital treatment
- Disease prevention
- Early detection of diseases
- Dental treatment, including dental restorations
- Provision of pharmaceuticals, dressing materials, remedies, and technical aids (in some cases, co-payments by the insured apply)
- Home nursing care and domestic help
- Palliative care
- Services for geriatric rehabilitation and occupational therapy and
- Sick pay (80 % of net wages).

§ 12 of the German Social Code Book V (SGB V) sets out that the services provided to patients within the SHI system must be sufficient, appropriate, and economically efficient ("efficiency principle"). Decisions as to which specific services should be added to the SHI catalog of services and paid by the SHI are made by the Joint Federal Committee (G-BA; www.g-ba.de), which is supported by the Institute for Quality and Efficiency in Health Care (IQWiG; www.iqwig.de).

Remuneration Principles

Generally, the SHI reimburses services using the benefits-in-kind principle, that is, the insured receive medical services after presenting their health insurance card. The services are then billed by the service provider to the health insurance without the insured being informed about the arisen costs. PHIs, in contrast, use the cost reimbursement principle, where the received services are first paid for by the insured, who can then apply to the insurance for reimbursement.

For several years, SHI-insured individuals have been required to make co-payments for certain health services in addition to paying monthly SHI contributions; these co-payments are the sole responsibility of the insured (that is, the costs are not shared with the employer). For instance, they apply for the following:

- Practice fee: EUR 10 per quarter. In case of referral by the primary care physician, who is always seen first, the practice fee is only paid at that first office and not at the visited specialist offices. The practice fee was dropped as of January 01, 2013 since it did not have the intended effect of reducing physician visits.
- Co-payments at hospitals and rehabilitation facilities: EUR 10 per day for no more than 28 calendar days per year.
- Co-payments for pharmaceuticals and dressing materials: 10 % of costs, but at least EUR 5 and no more than EUR 10.
- Co-payments for non-pharmacological therapies: 10 % of costs and EUR 10 per prescription.
- Co-payments for professional home care: 10 % of costs and EUR 10 per prescription.

To ensure that these co-payments do not cause social hardship, the insured can apply to the health insurance for relief if the co-payments exceed 2 % of their gross annual income (or 1 % of income if they are chronically ill).

Since 2009, employee and employer contributions as well as tax subsidies for extraneous benefits, such as coverage of nonworking family members, maternity allowance, etc., have been paid into a so-called Health Fund [*Gesundheitsfond*]. To fund their benefits, the health insurances are allocated money from the Health Fund according to the number of insured individuals and their age, gender, and morbidity distribution. If the allocations do not cover the SHI's expenses, the insurance can ask its members for an additional contribution. A few insurers have done this in the past, and in some cases, it led to many members leaving the respective SHI.

The above-described services within the SHI catalog of services (standard benefits) must be prescribed by a physician, even if they are not actually provided by a physician [*Arztvorbehalt*]. This applies to occupational and physical therapy, for instance. There are very few services that the insured can receive directly and still be reimbursed by the SHI. One example is participation in disease prevention courses. The insured can participate in these courses but must initially pay the course fees. The insured can then apply to the SHI for partial reimbursement of up to two different courses per year. This rule is particularly problematic for chronically ill patients, whose continuous, long-term participation (e.g., in back pain exercises) is medically desirable. In 2011, the SHI therefore allowed participation in functional and rehabilitation exercise programs. They must be prescribed by a physician, and an application for reimbursement must be submitted to the health insurance and be approved before the program starts. The SHI may approve the reimbursement of expenses for 50 or 120 h of exercise that can be completed in 1.5–3 years.

PHIs are structured differently than SHI. The following are the most important differences:

- In the PHI, member contributions are based on their individual health risks.
- The insurance is voluntary and not regulated by law.
- A contribution is paid for each insured person, that is, there is no contribution-free family member coverage.
- The PHI uses the cost reimbursement principle.
- The PHI may provide more benefits (e.g., corrective lenses, nonprescription pharmaceuticals, and dental restorations) and in some cases fewer benefits than the SHI (e.g., technical aids).

Sectors

The medical services infrastructure in the German health-care system primarily rests on the following pillars: outpatient medical care, inpatient care, long-term nursing care, and rehabilitation. Below, we will briefly discuss the structure of the two most important and expensive pillars—outpatient and inpatient medical care—as well as long-term nursing care.

Outpatient Medical Care

According to Simon, outpatient medical care features the following structural characteristics (Simon, 2010, p. 183):

- Physicians' freedom of establishment
- Patients' free choice of physician (§ 76 SGB V)
- Transfer of central tasks to the Association of SHI Physicians (§§ 77–81 SGB V)
- Needs planning and restrictions on approval to practice (§§ 99–105 SGB V)

- Structural organization into primary care and specialist care (§ 73 SGB V)
- Group negotiations between associations of SHI physicians and health insurances
- Joint self-administration by associations of SHI physicians and health insurances

In the German outpatient sector, SHI-accredited physicians who are members of the Associations of SHI Physicians have a treatment monopoly. At the same time, the Associations of SHI Physicians must ensure the sufficient availability of outpatient care on a federal state [*Bundesland*] level. A few years ago, hospital physicians were granted permission to participate in outpatient care, for instance within the framework of medical care centers [*Medizinische Versorgungszentren*], which are cross-specialty physician-run facilities. Vice versa, SHI-accredited physicians in private practice may only participate in inpatient care to a limited extent, for instance, as affiliated doctors in smaller hospitals. To become an SHI-accredited physician, physicians must register in the medical register of their State Association of SHI Physicians and apply to become an SHI-accredited physician. The accreditation decision is made by the Admissions Committee, which is made up equally of health insurances and representatives of the Association of SHI Physicians. In addition to the applicant's qualifications, regional needs are an important criterion for admission as an SHI-accredited physician. The same procedure also applies for the medical care centers, which have been permitted since 2004.

In 2011, around 139,500 physicians provided outpatient care in Germany, of which around 120,500 were SHI-accredited [9], that is, they invoiced their services through the SHI. Among the 120,500 SHI-accredited physicians, around 43 % provided primary care, but this percentage has been slowly dropping for years [9].

The dominant structure in the outpatient sector is still the individual practice, where a single physician provides patient care with the aid of medical assistants. In a joint practice [*Praxisgemeinschaft*], the facility is used by multiple physicians, but billing and liability remain separate. Physicians in group practices [*Gemeinschaftspraxis*], in contrast, submit joint bills through the Association of SHI Physicians using a single billing code. Among the roughly 120,000 SHI-accredited physicians, about 46,300 worked in group practices in 2011 [9].

In European comparison, the German health-care system is lamented to be excessively utilized. According to the 1998 Federal Health Survey, 90 % of respondents visited a physician at least once a year [10]. Women had an average of 12.8 physician visits per year (not including dentist visits), and men had 9.1 visits [10]. The average number of visits rises with age, ranging from 8.7 visits on average for 18–19-year-olds to 14.9 in 70–79-year-olds. The 2002 Socio-Economic Panel shows a similar trend, albeit with different absolute numbers: At the time, 68.5 % of respondents had seen a physician at least once in the 3 months preceding the survey. The average number of physician visits was 3.9 in the preceding 3 months. The average number of visits rose from 3.3 in patients under age 40 to 4.5 in people aged 60 and above [11, p. 16]. [Also, compare the contribution by Swart and Griehl in this volume.]

Multiple studies have investigated the factors that influence this high utilization of medical care. Since morbidity is not greater in Germany than in other European countries, organizational and economic factors within the health-care system must be considered as potential causes of higher utilization. On the provider side, follow-up appointment scheduling and referrals by physicians are associated with system-related incentives for the expansion of services. On the demand—or patient—side, it must be noted that until a few years ago (up to 2003), visiting a physician was very easy and free of charge, so that multiple physicians could be seen simultaneously for the same disease.

Inpatient Care

According to § 107 para. 1 SGB V, hospitals are facilities that "are under permanent medical management by a physician… and serve to… diagnose, cure, and prevent deterioration of patients' diseases and ameliorate symptoms of disease, primarily through medical and nursing services." In case of a diagnosed or suspected serious illness for which permanent accommodation and medical monitoring are required, SHI members have a legal right to inpatient treatment at a licensed hospital. Inpatient treatment is only justified, however, if the treatment objective cannot be met by another form of treatment (outpatient, semi-inpatient, etc.). Hence, the other treatment forms are always preferable over inpatient treatment, which is ordered by a physician in private practice through a referral, except in emergencies. Generally, patients can freely choose their hospital but not their treating physicians at the hospital.

The federal states [*Bundesländer*] must ensure sufficient availability of inpatient care in the context of hospital planning, which is conducted by the responsible ministry, the state hospital trust, and the state associations of the SHIs. The result is the general hospital plan, which is now needs-oriented in most federal states and lists the hospitals by care levels (basic care, regular care, intermediate care, centralized or maximum care, and specialist care), departments, and number of beds. Only hospitals listed in the general hospital plan are eligible for state support of investment activities in the context of the dual system of hospital financing [5].

In general, German hospitals can be categorized by ownership into public, nonprofit, and private hospitals. Since 1991, general hospitals have further been differentiated from other hospitals. The category 'Other hospitals' includes all hospitals that offer only psychiatric and/or neurological beds. 'General hospitals' therefore include all forms and beds other than 'Other hospitals'.

Table 3.2 displays the 2010 ownership distribution of general hospitals and their development within the preceding 20 years.

The table shows that in the past 20 years since German re-unification, the number of general hospitals has distinctly dropped. This reduction applies to public and nonprofit hospitals, while the number of private hospitals has grown. Taking into account the absolute numbers of hospital beds, it becomes clear that privately

Table 3.2 Hospitals and beds by ownership status in 2010. (Source: [12])

	Hospitals with somatic departments		All hospitals (incl. Psychiatric hospitals)	
	2010	Change since 1991 in %	2010	Change since 1991 in %
General hospitals	1,758	−18.8	2,064	−14.4
Public	539	−45.9	630	−44.2
Nonprofit	644	−23.2	755	−19.9
Private	575	+74.2	679	+89.7
Beds	462,457	−22.7	502,749	−24.5
Public	223,385	−39.2	244,254	X
Nonprofit	164,337	−20.6	173,457	X
Private	74,735	+211.4	85,038	X
Beds/100,000 inhabitants			615	−26.1
Cases/100,000 inhabitants			22,057	+21.0

X no data available

owned hospitals tend to be smaller with fewer beds, while public and nonprofit hospitals tend to be larger and offer all care levels. Despite the massive reduction in the number of beds and hospitals, the majority of inpatient care is still provided by public and nonprofit hospitals. Nonetheless, there is a clear trend toward privatization.

Around 17–18 million cases are treated at German hospitals every year [12]. Compared with other European countries, these numbers are fairly high. In the past 10 years, the number of inpatient cases has increased. In 1991, 14.5 million cases were treated at hospitals, versus 18 million cases in 2010; this represents an increase of around 25 % [12]. In parallel with the growing case numbers, the average length of stay dropped, equaling 14 days in 1991 versus 7.9 days in 2010 [12]. About one-third of cases involve patients aged 65 years or older, despite the fact that this group makes up less than 20 % of the population [12]. In terms of the indications that most frequently lead to hospitalization, high rates of cardiovascular diseases and cancer stand out. They are followed by diseases of the digestive organs, injuries, and poisoning as well as diseases of the musculoskeletal system [13]. These five groups represent more than half of all inpatient cases.

To limit expenditures in the inpatient sector, Diagnosis Related Groups (diagnosis-related flat rates; www.g-drg.de) were introduced in 2004, thereby eliminating the financial incentive for hospitals to extend the length of stay. It now makes economic sense for hospitals to admit and treat patients as rapidly as possible.

Long-Term Nursing Care

Compulsory long-term care insurance was introduced in Germany in response to the growing number of patients in permanent need of care, which is the result of demographic changes. Social long-term care insurance (SLTCI), which was established

Table 3.3 Reimbursement amounts (in Euro) as of January 01, 2010, for the various Care Levels and types of care. (Source: SGB XI, §§ 36)

Type of nursing service	Level 1 Significant need of care	Level 2 Intermediate need of care	Level 3 Highest need of care
Duration of daily care	1.5 h	3 h	5 h
Monetary allowance for home care	225	430	685
Benefits-in-kind for outpatient nursing services	440	1,040	1,510
Semi-inpatient nursing care (daytime or nighttime care)	440	1,100	1,510
Combination of nursing care allowance, nursing benefits-in-kind, and semi-inpatient nursing care (maximum amount)	660	1,560	2,265
Inpatient nursing care	1,023	1,279	1,510

in 1994 based on the model of the SHI, provides the insured with services, benefits-in-kind, and payments for basic care and domestic help if the Medical Service of the Statutory Health Insurance (Medizinischer Dienst der Krankenversicherung (MDK)) has confirmed the need for long-term care. Unlike the statutory health insurance, where meeting needs takes priority over stable contribution rates and contribution rates are adjusted to ensure that they cover the medically required services, stable contribution rates have priority over meeting needs in the SLTCI [5, p. 324 f.]. The SLTCI is referred to as 'partial coverage' insurance or as a budgeting system because a fixed amount is reimbursed on the basis of the patient's Care Level, regardless of the patient's actual needs.

Patients are placed in a Care Level, from I to III, depending on the type, frequency, and duration of required assistance per day. The SLTCI offers payments and benefits-in-kind, the height of which depends on the determined Care Level. The following are the major benefit types:

- Nursing care allowance for home care provided by privately hired caregivers
- Professional home care provided by an outpatient nursing service
- Semi-inpatient nursing services
- Benefits for long-term care at nursing homes (institutional care).

The benefit amounts depend on the Care Level, and monthly reimbursements vary widely. Table 3.3 lists them by reimbursement type as of January 01, 2010.

In addition to these reimbursement options, substitute or 'respite' care can be granted for no more than four weeks per year if a substitute must be hired to cover for the primary caregiver due to illness, vacation, or other reasons; this option is available if home care is provided for more than six months. In addition, the SLTCI may reimburse the costs for necessary short-term care in an inpatient facility for four weeks per calendar year and up to an amount of EUR 1,510.

To enable patients to stay in their homes, improvements to the living environment, such as elimination of thresholds, attachment of handles and rails, and installation of wheelchair ramps, stair lifts, etc., may be reimbursed by the SLTCI up to an amount of EUR 2,557, but the patient must bear 10 % of the costs of the alteration project. The umbrella organization of SLTCIs has laid out general rules on this topic in a 2002 joint newsletter. In general, the necessity of improvements to the living environment must be confirmed by a nursing care service.

Home and partial inpatient care are preferable over inpatient nursing care. Except in patients in Care Level 3, the necessity of inpatient nursing care must be verified by the MDK. The SLTCI pays a monthly flat fee to the nursing home (see Table 3.3). The costs for food and lodging as well as investment costs are the patient's responsibility. If the income of the patient and any financially responsible relatives is insufficient, they can apply for "Help with care" to the responsible welfare agency in their respective federal state.

Since July 01, 2008, the SLTCI contributions have been the same throughout Germany, at 1.95 % of income up to the contribution assessment ceiling, with employers and employees each paying 0.975 %, except in the state of Saxony. Childless people aged 23 and above pay an additional 0.25 %, payable by the insured only. In 2009, just below 70 million people were members of the SLTCI [14]. More than 60 % of care recipients are 80 years or older (total number of care recipients: 2.34 million). More than half of beneficiaries are in Care Level 1; two-thirds (69 %) of those in need of nursing care receive care at home from family caregivers, and one-third of these are supported by nursing services. The percentage of those receiving long-term care increases continuously from almost 5 % of people aged 70–75 to almost 60 % of people aged 90+ [15].

In Germany, outpatient nursing services include welfare centers [*Sozialstationen*] and private nursing services. In total, more than 12,000 outpatient nursing services are currently in operation [15]. Simon [5] describes outpatient nursing services using the following structural characteristics:

- SLTCIs must ensure sufficient availability of nursing care for the insured.
- The government does not engage in capacity planning. Capacities are primarily managed through health service agreements between long-term care insurances and nursing facilities.
- The services are almost exclusively rendered by nonprofit and private entities; public entities play only a minor role.
- The reimbursement system is not uniform but differs by insurer [5, p. 354].

Outpatient nursing services offer a very wide range of services. In addition to home help, they can provide basic and therapeutic nursing care as well as intensive nursing care. The beneficiary may claim monetary payments or outpatient benefits-in-kind, the extent of which is determined by the Care Level.

Unlike medical care, outpatient nursing care is not subject to government capacity planning. The available services are largely governed by supply and demand. However, providers in particular are subject to government regulations, primarily regarding the quality of care. According to SGB XI, long-term care insurances must enter into health service agreements with the operators of nursing facilities, specifying the type, scope, and content of general nursing services that the facility must provide to the patient. Only those services are reimbursed. This agreement approves the facility for providing care and serves as a mandate to provide care. To fulfill the health service agreement, the nursing facility must meet legal requirements to the effect that the nursing facility is managed by a trained nurse, ensures efficient and economic nursing care, and agrees to establish and further develop an internal quality management system (SGB XI, §§ 71, 72). In addition to the health service agreement with the long-term health insurance, the nursing facility must enter into a separate agreement with each patient. This agreement specifies the type, content, and scope of the services to be rendered for each individual patient and the payments to be made. The agreement is intended to strengthen the patient's position toward the facilities.

As a further peculiarity of the long-term care sector, nursing facilities must regularly supply the long-term insurances with proof of performance and quality, which is reviewed by experts and inspection bodies. This proof of quality confirms that quality requirements according to SGB XI are met and justifies the claim for reimbursement of the provided services.

In Germany, inpatient care for patients requiring long-term care is provided by inpatient nursing facilities. According to Simon, the range of services of inpatient nursing facilities includes basic and therapeutic nursing care as well as domestic help [5, p. 380]. The following care types are differentiated:

- Inpatient nursing care (around the clock)
- Semi-inpatient care (only daytime or only nighttime)
- Short-term care (temporary inpatient care for up to 4 weeks per calendar year).

Outpatient and inpatient nursing care are similar in many respects, as both are governed by SGB XI. Simon summarizes the following central structural characteristics for inpatient nursing care:

- The long-term care insurances must ensure sufficient availability of nursing care for the insured.
- There is no capacity planning by the government or the joint self-administration. Capacities are primarily managed through health service agreements between the long-term health insurances and the nursing facilities.
- The services are almost exclusively rendered by nonprofit and private entities; public entities play only a minor role [5, p. 380].

The number of nursing homes has grown by some 30 % between 1999 and 2009; in 2009, more than 11,000 homes were available [15]. Most homes are nonprofit (n=6,373), followed by 4,637 private facilities, and only 624 public facilities [15]. Separate homes exist for older people, disabled people, the mentally ill, and the seriously ill and dying. The growing number of homes particularly results from an increase in homes for older people, where about three-fourths of residents suffer from dementia. The total number of resident places at homes has increased from 645,456 in 1999 to 845,007 in 2009, with the majority being for long-term inpatient care (some 86 %). This is also the area with the largest increases in the past 10 years.

Both outpatient and inpatient nursing care are characterized by a large percentage of part-time and female workers. Inpatient care is organized following similar principles as outpatient care according to SGB XI, §§ 71 and 72 and is based on numerous health service agreements between the long-term care insurances and the nursing facilities. In addition to this health service agreement, the home operator must enter into a nursing home agreement with the resident as specified by the Nursing Home Act [*Heimgesetz*]. The nursing home agreement governs the rights and duties of both parties as well as the applicable payments.

Summary

As regards the influence of system-related factors on utilization behavior, numerous health services are covered by health insurance, but SHI-financed services must be included in the catalog of services. Services are included in the catalog on the basis of criteria such as being evidence-based, necessary, and economical. The majority of health-care services are billed by the service provider directly to the insurance without involving the insured, who pay monthly contributions. A few services must be paid for by the insured or require co-payments. This may influence the utilization of necessary medical services, especially by patients of low socioeconomic status. In Germany, the range of available services and the frequency of actually provided services are strongly physician-dominated since many health-care services are restricted to physicians. In some cases, approval by the health insurance is required in addition to a physician prescription, a situation that may further affect utilization.

Acknowledgment We wish to thank Ms. Stephanie Griehl, B.A., for her support in researching current data on the German health-care system.

References

1. Beske F, Hallauer JF. Das Gesundheitswesen in Deutschland. Struktur—Leistungen—Weiterentwicklung. 3rd ed. Köln: Deutscher Ärzte-Verlag; 2005.
2. Busse R. Das deutsche Gesundheitssystem im Überblick. Daten, Fakten, Trends. 2nd ed. München: MMW Verlagsgesellschaft; 2013.
3. Nagel E, editor. Das Gesundheitswesen in Deutschland: Struktur—Leistungen—Weiterentwicklung. 4th ed. Köln: Deutscher Ärzte-Verlag; 2007.
4. Preusker UK. Das deutsche Gesundheitssystem verstehen: Strukturen und Funktionen im Wandel. Heidelberg: medhochzwei Verlag; 2013.
5. Simon M. Das Gesundheitssystem in Deutschland. Eine Einführung in Struktur und Funktionsweise. 3rd ed. Bern: Verlag Hans Huber; 2010.
6. Gesetze für die Soziale Arbeit. Textsammlung. Ausgabe 2011/12. Sozialgesetzbücher V, IX und XI. Baden-Baden: Nomos Verlag; 2011.
7. www.Sozialpolitik aktuell.de.
8. Bundesministerium für Gesundheit (BMG). Zahlen und Fakten zur Krankenversicherung. Berlin; 2012.

9. Kassenärztliche Bundesvereinigung. Statistische Informationen aus dem Bundesarztregister (Stand: 31.12.2011). Berlin; 2012.
10. Bergmann E, Kamtsiuris P. Inanspruchnahme medizinischer Leistungen. Das Gesundheitswesen 1999; 61: S138–144.
11. Grabka M, Schreyögg J, Busse R. Die Einführung der Praxisgebühr und ihre Wirkung auf die Zahl der Arztkontakte und die Kontaktfrequenz –Eine empirische Analyse. Berlin: DIW Discussion Papers 506; 2005.
12. Statistisches Bundesamt, editor. Grunddaten der Krankenhäuser 2010 (Fachserie 12 Reihe 6.1.1). Wiesbaden; 2012.
13. Schellhase T. Statistische Krankenhausdaten: Diagnosedaten der Krankenhauspatienten 2009. In: Klauber J, Geraedts M, Friedrich J, Wasem J, editors. Krankenhausreport 2012. Stuttgart: Schattauer Verlag; 2012. p. 377–405.
14. Bundesministerium für Gesundheit (BMG). Daten zur Pflegeversicherung. Berlin, 2010. http://www.bmg.bund.de. Accessed 12 Jul 2012.
15. Statistisches Bundesamt, editor. Pflegestatistik 2009. Pflege im Rahmen der Pflegeversicherung—Deutschlandergebnisse. Wiesbaden; 2011.

Part III
Methodology

Chapter 4
The Problem of Repeated Surveys. How Comparable are their Results Regarding the Utilization of Medical Services?

Enno Swart and Stephanie Griehl

Background

In the course of the past 20 years since German reunification, several large-scale representative population surveys have been conducted under the leadership of the Robert Koch Institute (RKI; formerly Federal Health Office). In addition to questions about health and its determinants, these surveys asked about the prevalence and frequency of utilization of outpatient, inpatient, preventative, and rehabilitative services as well as the pharmaceutical treatment of certain symptoms and diseases. The Socioeconomic Panel (SOEP) and the Bertelsmann Foundation's Healthcare Monitor survey the utilization of medical services as well. This contribution examines the extent to which these survey questionnaires use the same or at least similar questions to measure the utilization of medical services, including services for health promotion, prevention, rehabilitation, and drug treatment. In this context, this chapter also explores the comparability of the results of these surveys.

This is a relevant topic in health services epidemiology and health-care systems research in Germany because particularly the RKI surveys and to a lesser degree the results of the SOEP and Healthcare Monitor are often referenced by other studies to estimate disease prevalence or to study determinants of health and disease. When using these surveys, it is important to know the extent to which the results of these surveys may be considered valid reference data.

E. Swart (✉)
Medical Faculty, Institute für Social Medicine and Health Economics,
Otto-von-Guericke-University Magdeburg, Leipziger Straße,
39120, Magdeburg, Germany
e-mail: enno.swart@med.ovgu.de

S. Griehl
Department of Social and Health Sciences,
University of Applied Sciences, Magdeburg-Stendal,
Breitscheidstr 1, 39114 Magdeburg, Germany
e-mail: stephanie.griehl@web.de

C. Janssen et al. (eds.), *Health Care Utilization in Germany*,
DOI 10.1007/978-1-4614-9191-0_4, © Springer Science+Business Media New York 2014

With regard to these two central questions, this contribution explores the following aspects:

- What reference periods are used to ask about outpatient and inpatient utilization?
- How are the prevalence and frequency of utilization measured, e.g., by using the number of outpatient contacts, inpatient admissions, or number of nights spent in hospital?
- To what extent do questions differentiate between the outpatient utilization of specific types of specialists?
- To what extent do the surveys ask about preventative and rehabilitative services and drug treatment?
- How do the results differ on the basis of the survey design and survey questions?

We have already published the principal results of this comparative analysis of field research on health-care utilization in Germany [1]. As this book aims to provide a complete account of theories, methods, and results of health-care utilization (HCU) research in Germany, the first author and the editor have agreed to include a revised version of this chapter on the comparability and validity of primary data in the book. In the context of the two other methodological contributions on secondary data and qualitative approaches in HCU research, the book will then present all three central methodological approaches for measuring health services utilization behavior.

Underlying Data

This analysis draws on the public use files (PUFs) of four representative population surveys conducted between 1991 and 2009, data from the 16 waves of the Bertelsmann Healthcare Monitor conducted between 2001 and 2009, and data from the 26 waves of the SOEP conducted between 1984 and 2009. All surveys included questions on the utilization of outpatient, inpatient, and preventative services.

In the context of the German Cardiovascular Prevention Study (DHP; [2]), two waves of surveys with representative samples of the population of former West Germany had already been conducted in the 1980s. Participants underwent a standardized medical examination and participated in an extensive interview on health-related topics (National Health Survey). To supply comparative data for the reunified Germany for the first time, a third wave of surveys was conducted in 1990/1991 in former West Germany and in 1991/1992 in former East Germany, using largely thc samc methodology (East-West Survey, OW91). The data of these health surveys were meant to provide information about the prevalence of certain diseases or disease characteristics, risk factors, symptoms, and health-related behaviors and living conditions in the German resident population. The population of OW91 included all Germans aged 25–69 in former West Germany and all Germans aged 18–79 in former East Germany. Samples were randomly selected with equal probability using a two-stage, multi-stratified sampling procedure. The net samples of the health surveys comprised 5,255 individuals (former West Germany) and 2,211 individuals (former East Germany), with response rates of approximately 70 % [3].

The 1998 National Health Survey (BGS98) involved a health-related interview and examination of a representative sample of the resident population of Germany between the ages of 18 and 79. The primary goal of the survey is to produce data for Federal Health Reporting and intra-European comparisons. Using data from previous surveys also reveals trends in the distribution of risk factors and diseases in the population. Question sets pertained to subjective and objective health, the utilization of medical services, and numerous potential determinants of health. The sample was randomly selected using a multi-stratified procedure according to regional and spatial planning aspects. A total of 7,124 people completed the survey questionnaire and underwent a medical examination, which corresponds to a response rate of 61 % [4, 5].

In continuation of the BGS98, the RKI conducted the first nationwide representative Telephone Health Survey in 2003, with a focus on chronic diseases (Tel03). A total of 8,362 people aged 18–79 were surveyed (response rate: 52 %). The method was based on the Gabler–Häder procedure for selecting a representative sample of the population for telephone surveys (landline numbers) in the Federal Republic of Germany. The catalog of questions was based on BGS98 [6].

The 2009 German Health Update (GEDA09) is a representative survey of the adult German-speaking population living in private households in Germany with a landline telephone. A total of 21,626 interviews were completed (response rate: 51 %). The GEDA survey is regularly repeated as part of health monitoring [7] in order to continuously monitor developments in disease occurrence and in health and risk behaviors. It is meant to provide the health reporting system and health policymakers with timely information regarding health trends in the population or in specific subgroups. The survey follows the annual telephone health surveys conducted between 2003 and 2006 and uses the same methods [8].

Since 2001, the Bertelsmann Healthcare Monitor has surveyed insured individuals and physicians about outpatient care at regular intervals. The main focus of the interviews with the insured is to assess the utilization of services, patient orientation in care delivery, patient expectations of the health-care system, and patient satisfaction. The written survey of the insured is conducted semiannually, while the survey of physicians in private practice is conducted annually by telephone. The questionnaires contain a core of identical questions, for instance, about the frequency of outpatient and inpatient utilization, as well as supplementary questions on selected current health policy-related topics. TNS Healthcare (formerly NFO Infratest Gesundheitsforschung) draws the sample for the survey of the insured from a panel of households that have agreed to participate (the so-called Access Panel). This panel contains about 70,000 households with more than 160,000 household members [9, 10].

The SOEP is the largest and longest-running (since 1984) multidisciplinary longitudinal study in Germany. The SOEP is commissioned by the German Institute for Economic Research (DIW) in Berlin. For the SOEP, more than 20,000 people in about 11,000 households are surveyed every year by the survey institute TNS Infratest Sozialforschung [11]. Data collected through the SOEP provide information on topics such as income, employment status, education level, and health. Since the same people are surveyed each year, the survey lends itself to the analysis of

Table 4.1 Characteristics of included surveys

	OW91	BGS98	TEL03	GEDA09	SOEP	MONI
Year of survey	1991	1998	2003	2009	Annually since 1984	Semiannually since 2001
Number of participants	7,466	7,124	8,318	21,262	12,000–20,000	approx. 1,500
Age group	25–69 years of age	18–79 years of age	18+ years old	18+ years old	18+ years old	18 of 79 years of age
Access	Representative samples	Representative samples	Representative samples	Representative samples	Access panel	Access panel
For more information	www.rki.de	www.rki.de	www.rki.de	www.rki.de	www.diw.de	www.bertelsmann-stiftung.de

OW1991 East-West Survey 1991, *BGS 1998* German National Health Survey 1998, *TEL2003* Telephone Health Survey 2003, *GEDA2009* Telephone Health Survey 'German Health Update' 2009, *SOEP* Socioeconomic Panel, *MONI* Bertelsmann Healthcare Monitor; modified according to [1]

long-term societal trends as well as the life courses of specific groups. Although health-related questions are not the main focus of the survey, it regularly asks questions about the utilization of medical services.

The PUFs of the RKI population surveys, including extensive documentation, can be ordered from the RKI for a small usage fee (www.rki.de). The same applies to data from the SOEP, which can be ordered from the DIW (www.diw.de). The data from the Bertelsmann Healthcare Monitor, including a data set description and the employed participant questionnaires, are available for download free-of-charge on the Bertelsmann Foundation website (www.bertelsmann-stiftung.de).

Survey Instruments

Table 4.1 lists the study characteristics of the included surveys. Depending on the objectives of the surveys, distinct differences are found in the study population and design. The RKI surveys are one-time cross-sectional surveys using differentiated sampling plans [7] designed to render them representative of the population. The SOEP and Healthcare Monitor, in contrast, involve repeated panel surveys [9–11].

There are similarities in the individual sets of questions on health and hence health services utilization as well as in individual questions on their potential determinants (age, gender, sociodemographic characteristics, subjective health status, symptoms, diagnoses, individual risk factors, and health-relevant behaviors). However, the SOEP includes markedly fewer questions on subjective health, disabilities, and limitations in activities of daily living (Table 4.2).

Analyzing the surveys' question sets reveals distinct differences in the questions on outpatient utilization (Table 4.3). Only three of the six surveys ask participants

Table 4.2 Sets of questions in included surveys on health, utilization, and their determinants

	OW91	BGS98	TEL03	GEDA09	SOEP	MONI
Schooling	x	x		x	x	x
Educational attainment	x	x		x	x	x
Employment status	x	x	x	x	x	x
Income	x	x	x	x	x	
Social class (score)	x	x	x	x		x
Migration status	x	x	x	x	x	x
Insurance status	x	x	x	x	x	x
Marital status, household	x	x	x	x	x	x
Chronic diseases	x	x	x	x	x	x
Psychosomatic complaints	x	x				(x)
Subjective health	x	x	x	x	x	x
Pain	x	x	x	x		x
Need for help in activities of daily living		x	x	x		
Recent limitations	x	x	x	x		x
Disability		x	x	x	x	
Indiv. risk factors (e.g., smoking)	x	x	x			x
Occupational, environmental exposures	x	x		x	x	(x)
Satisfaction, social network	x	x		x	x	

OW91 East-West Survey 1991, *BGS98* German National Health Survey 1998, *TEL2003* Telephone Health Survey 2003, *GEDA09* Telephone Health Survey 'German Health Update' 2009, *SOEP* Socioeconomic Panel, *MONI* Bertelsmann Healthcare Monitor, (x) not in all waves; modified according to [1]

when they last contacted a physician, and only the German National Health Survey and the Bertelsmann Healthcare Monitor inquire about more details, such as the reason for this contact. With regard to questions on physician contact within a certain time period preceding the survey, the time period mentioned ranges from 4 weeks to 12 months. Marked differences were also found in the questions about contacts with

Table 4.3 Questions on the utilization of outpatient services

	OW91	BGS98	TEL03	GEDA09	SOEP	MONI
Time of most recent physician contact	x	x		x		
Reason for most recent contact		x				x
Details of most recent contact (where, who)		x				x
Outpatient contact within the preceding 4 weeks (yes/no)	x	x		x		
Outpatient contact within the preceding 3 months (yes/no)			x		x	
Number of outpatient contacts within the preceding 3 months (n)					x	
Outpatient contact within the preceding 12 months (yes/no)				x		
Number of outpatient contacts within the preceding 12 months (n)				x		
Have a regular primary care physician (yes/no)		x	x	x		x
Contacts with specific specialists						
Primary care physician/GP	§, $	%, $, &	%, $			%
Internist	§, $	%, $, &				%
Gynecologist	§, $	%, $, &				%
Surgeon/orthopedic surgeon	§, $	%, $, &				%
Ophthalmologist	§, $	%, $, &				%
ENT specialist	§, $	%, $, &				%
Neurologist	§, $	%, $, &				%
Urologist	§, $	%, $, &				%
Dentist	§, $	%, $, &				%, $

OW91 East-West Survey 1991, *BGS98* German National Health Survey 1998, *TEL2003* Telephone Health Survey 2003, *GEDA09* Telephone Health Survey 'German Health Update' 2009, *SOEP* Socioeconomic Panel, *MONI* Bertelsmann Healthcare Monitor, *§* within the preceding 4 weeks, *%* within the preceding 12 months, *$* number of contacts within this time period, *&* treatment satisfaction; modified according to [1].

specific types of specialists: These questions are completely missing from some surveys, and in others, the included specialties differ.

Greater similarities are found in the questions about the prevalence of inpatient admissions. All six surveys ask about inpatient stays within the preceding 12 months. They only differ in the way in which they inquire about the frequency of inpatient care (number of nights or number of admissions within the preceding 12 months; Table 4.4).

Finally, only a few surveys include questions about participation in screening and prevention services. Comparative analyses particularly include services from the statutory health insurance (SHI) catalog of services, namely cancer screening services (breast, bowel, prostate, skin, and cervical cancer), "health checkup" services (screening for diabetes mellitus, cardiovascular diseases, and renal disease), and prenatal examinations (Table 4.5). The questions about screening examinations are very similar or virtually identical in the various RKI surveys, but there are

Table 4.4 Questions on the utilization of inpatient services

	OW91	BGS98	TEL03	GEDA09	SOEP	MONI
Inpatient stay within the preceding 4 weeks	x					
Inpatient stay within the preceding 12 months	x	x	x	x	(x)	(x)
Number of hospital admissions within the preceding 12 months	x		x	x	(x)	(x)
Number of nights spent in hospital within the preceding 12 months	x	x			(x)	(x)

OW91 East-West Survey 1991, *BGS98* German National Health Survey 1998, *TEL2003* Telephone Health Survey 2003, *GEDA09* Telephone Health Survey 'German Health Update' 2009, *SOEP* Socioeconomic Panel, *MONI* Bertelsmann Healthcare Monitor; (x) not throughout; modified according to [1].

differences in the use of filters. In the 2003 Telephone Health Survey and GEDA 2009, the questionnaire included filters that restricted answers about screening examinations to participants who are entitled to these services [12].

All other preventative and health promotion services (e.g., physician consultations) are rarely asked about in the respective surveys. Questions regarding the utilization of other services (rehabilitation services, services from non-physician service providers such as occupational or physical therapists, or the use of prescription or over-the-counter medications) are not standard questions and will not be further discussed here [1].

Results

The East-West Survey, the German National Health Survey, and GEDA2009 ask respondents about when they last contacted a physician. The results for contacts within the preceding 4 weeks differ by approximately 10 % points, varying from almost 40 to almost 50 %. When extending the reference period to 3 months, the same differences in percentage points are observed, with utilization prevalence ranging from 63 to 72 %. Age-specific and sex-specific utilization patterns are consistent, and the various surveys' results again differ by approximately 10 percentage points. The Healthcare Monitor does not supply any data on this topic because it only asks about the number of contacts made with various physicians within the preceding 12 months (Table 4.6).

Table 4.5 Questions on the utilization of preventative services

	OW91	BGS98	TEL03	GEDA09	SOEP	MONI
Cancer screening	x		x	x		x
Health checkup	x		x	x		x
Prenatal examination	x					
Screening of blood pressure, blood sugar, and weight	x					
Dental checkup	x			x		
Vaccinations		x	x	x		
Medical consultation regarding nutrition, exercise, etc.	x	x		x		
Medical consultation regarding back exercises, relaxation, etc.		x				

OW91 East-West Survey 1991; *BGS98* German National Health Survey 1998; *TEL2003* Telephone Health Survey 2003, *GEDA09* Telephone Health Survey 'German Health Update' 2009, *SOEP* Socioeconomic Panel, *MONI* Bertelsmann Healthcare Monitor; (x) not included in all waves; modified according to [1].

OW91 reveals a 4-week prevalence of contact with primary care physicians of 29 %, and BGS98 shows a 12-month prevalence of 71 %. OW91 reports an average of 1.8 contacts with primary care physicians within the preceding 4 weeks, while BGS98 and the Healthcare Monitor each show 4.9 contacts over the preceding 12 months. The 2003 Telephone Health Survey reports 4.0 contacts for the same time period but only includes respondents who reported having a regular primary care physician. The reported number of physician contacts varies widely. GEDA 2009 and SOEP ask only about the total number of physician contacts and calculate an average of 6.1 for a 12-month period (GEDA09) and 3.6 for a 3-month period (SOEP). The Healthcare Monitor distinguishes between contacts made with four additional types of specialists, and OW91 and BGS98 measure the frequency of utilization of more than ten types of specialists. Despite the fact that primary care physicians make up only about 50 % of all physicians in private practice in Germany, the surveys do not offer a detailed differentiation between outpatient specialist contacts (Table 4.7).

The questions about hospitalizations are much more comparable than those about outpatient utilization. Even for identical questions about hospital stays within the preceding 12 months, results vary by nearly 9–15 %. These variations are only partially attributable to differences in survey populations since distinct differences persist even after stratification by age group. However, the patterns of age-specific and sex-specific utilization are the same in all surveys (Table 4.8).

The question whether the respondent has ever participated in cancer screening was answered affirmatively by 76 % of entitled respondents in OW91, by 78 % in the 2003 Telephone Health Survey, and by 72 % in GEDA2009. The 2003 Telephone

Table 4.6 Time of most recent outpatient physician contact, by age groups and gender

	OW91	BGS98	TEL03	GEDA09	SOEP	MONI
Contact within the preceding 4 weeks (%)	48.4	42.6	x	39.3	x	x
Men	43.0	37.5	x	34.5	x	x
Women	53.6	49.4	x	42.9	x	x
40–49 years of age	44.3	35.6	x	34.4	x	x
50–59 years of age	55.3	47.6	x	41.7	x	x
60–69 years of age	62.1	58.6	x	46.6	x	x
70–79 years of age	x	68.3	x	54.0	x	x
Contact within the preceding 3 months (%)	69.8	66.9	63.3	66.3	72.2	x
Men	63.1	59.0	57.8	60.6	66.9	x
Women	75.3	74.4	68.1	70.6	77.2	x
40–49 years of age	66.4	60.9	57.9	60.6	66.4	x
50–59 years of age	74.9	70.9	64.4	67.4	72.0	x
60–69 years of age	80.2	80.5	74.6	73.8	82.5	x
70–79 years of age	x	86.4	80.2	79.7	89.2	x

OW91 East-West Survey 1991, *BGS98* German National Health Survey 1998, *TEL2003* Telephone Health Survey 2003, *GEDA09* Telephone Health Survey 'German Health Update' 2009, *SOEP* Socioeconomic Panel, *MONI* Bertelsmann Healthcare Monitor (only inquires about utilization within the preceding 12 months); modified according to [1].

Health Survey and the 2009 GEDA study additionally asked about utilization within a 12-month period. The results show that 73 % of respondents participated in cancer screening within a year before the survey (Table 4.9). In the Healthcare Monitor, more than half of all respondents reported regularly participating in cancer screening, either annually or every other year. In contrast, 17 % of the respondents reported not utilizing any cancer-screening services. This result is comparable with the percentage of RKI survey respondents who report never having participated in cancer screening, revealing deviations of 5–10 %.

Analyses of participation in the Health Checkup screening program reveal greater differences than in the utilization of cancer screening. In the 1991 East-West Survey, 33 % of entitled respondents reported having participated in a Health Checkup at least once. However, this preventative service had only been added to the SHI catalog of services briefly before reunification. In the 2003 and 2009 telephone health surveys, about 20 % more respondents had participated. The question about utilization within the preceding 24 months—the planned examination interval—is

Table 4.7 Prevalence and frequency of outpatient contact with various specialists, by age groups and gender

	OW91	BGS98	TEL03	MONI
Specialist contacts within the preceding 4 weeks (%)				
Primary care physician/general practitioner	28.8	x	x	x
Internist	7.3	x	x	x
Gynecologist	14.0	x	x	x
Specialist contacts within the preceding 12 months (%)				
Primary care physician	x	70.8	86.6 (76.2)#	82.8
Internist	x	20.0	x	18.6
Gynecologist	x	67.1	x	74.3
Primary care physician contacts within the preceding 12 months	1.8§	4.9	4.0#	4.9
Mean	1.8§	4.9	4.0#	4.9
Median	1§	3	2#	3
Lower–upper quartile	1–1§	2–6	1–3#	2–6
Minimum–maximum	1–30§	1–99	1–92#	1–98
At least one primary care physician visit within the preceding 12 months (%)				
Men	25.9§	69.1	57.8	81.1
Women	31.5§	72.4	68.1	84.2
40–49 years of age	24.1§	69.2	57.9	84.2
50–59 years of age	35.4§	69.7	64.6	81.9
60–69 years of age	44.6§	73.3	74.6	81.6
70–79 years of age	x	77.1	80.2	87.5

OW91 East-West Survey 1991, *BGS98* German National Health Survey 1998, *TEL03* Telephone Health Survey 2003, *MONI* Bertelsmann Healthcare Monitor, wave 16, *GEDA09 and SOEP* No information provided # study participants with regular primary care physicians; in parentheses (total), *§* deviating: Within the preceding 4 weeks, & deviating: Within the preceding 3 months, *$* within the preceding 12 months; modified according to [1]

also only included in the two telephone health surveys. Among the respondents who reported having "ever" taken part in a Health Checkup, participation within the preceding 24 months was reported by 82 % in the 2003 Telephone Health Survey and by 89 % in GEDA09. In the Bertelsmann Healthcare Monitor, in contrast, 42 % of respondents stated that they regularly utilize the Health Checkup every 2 years (Table 4.9). On the other hand, 19 % report not participating in this type of screening at all. Comparing this value with the non-participation information from the RKI surveys reveals differences of about 25 % [12, 13].

As a result of inconsistent questions, the RKI's surveys are less suitable for depicting changes in utilization over time. The Bertelsmann Healthcare Monitor and the SOEP, on the other hand, use identical questions for a longer time period. In the Bertelsmann Healthcare Monitor, some 95 % of all respondents report at least

Table 4.8 Frequency of inpatient treatment within the preceding 12 months, by age groups and sex

	OW91	BGS98	TEL03	GEDA09	SOEP§	MONI$
Hospitalized at least once (%)	8.8	14.3	14.1	14.0	12.8	15.5
Hospitalized more than once (%)	1.7	x	x	x	x	4.0
Nights in hospital						
Mean	18.1	14.5	13.6	12.4	12.6	12.2
Median	10	9	7	6	7	9
Lower–upper quartile	6–21	5–15	4–14	3–14	5–14	4–15
Minimum–maxi-mum	0–350	1–240	1–300	1–365	1–300	1–90
Hospitalized at least once (%)						
Men	9.2	10.6	12.4	12.9	12.0	15.2
Women	10.6	13.9	15.3	14.9	13.6	15.7
40–49 years of age	9.2	9.5	11.1	10.6	8.6	14.3
50–59 years of age	10.1	12.3	13.2	13.2	11.8	16.1
60–69 years of age	12.6	16.0	18.2	17.9	16.1	18.6
70–79 years of age	x	19.0	23.6	22.6	21.6	18.9

OW91 East-West Survey 1991, *BGS98* German National Health Survey 1998, *TEL2003* Telephone Health Survey 2003, *GEDA09* Telephone Health Survey 'German Health Update' 2009, *SOEP* Socioeconomic Panel, *MONI* Bertelsmann Healthcare Monitor, *§* wave 26 (2009), *$* wave 7(2004); modified according to [1].

one contact with their primary care physician within the preceding year, and the survey finds an average of about five contacts within this time period. Within the total 8-year reporting period, there are only minor variations in this utilization level (Fig. 4.1).

For the past 25 years, SOEP results on inpatient stays within the preceding 12 months reveal a constant level of 11–12% of respondents with at least one hospitalization and a continuously dropping average number of nights in hospital (among the respondents with at least one hospitalization; Fig. 4.2).

Discussion

This study examined large-scale representative population surveys and panel surveys in Germany whose data are readily accessible to the scientific community and whose results are therefore frequently used in estimates of health-care needs and health services utilization. This comparative analysis did not primarily aim to determine the "actual" level or frequency of health services utilization or the determinants of utilization. Such investigations have been published in the literature elsewhere [14–17].

Table 4.9 Participation in preventative services

	OW91	TEL03	GEDA09	MONI$
Participation in cancer screening, ever (%)	76%	78%	72%	x
Among these, participation within the preceding 12 months (%)		73%	73%	
Regular participation every 12 months (%)				42%
Participation in a health checkup, ever (%)	33%	56%	54%	x
Among these, participation within the preceding 12 months (%)	x	82%	89%	x
Regular participation every 2 years				39%

OW91 East-West Survey 1991, *TEL03* Telephone Health Survey 2003, *GEDA09* Telephone Health Survey 'German Health Update' 2009, *MONI* Bertelsmann Healthcare Monitor; no information from BGS98 and SOEP

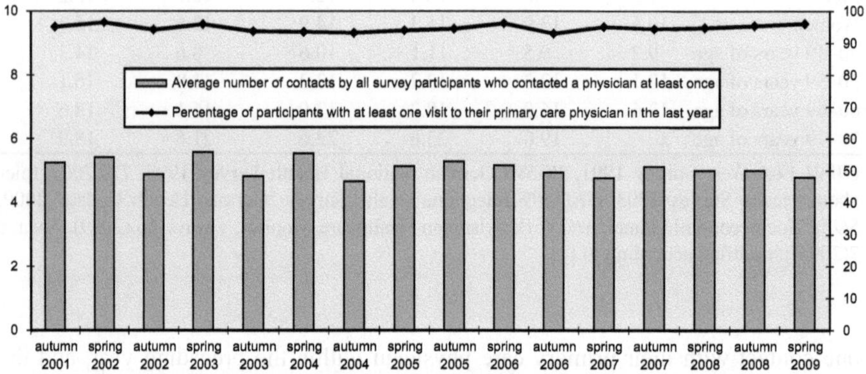

Fig 4.1 Prevalence of primary care physician visits in the last 12 months, from 2001 to 2009, Bertelsmann Health Monitor, waves from 1 to 16 (source [1])

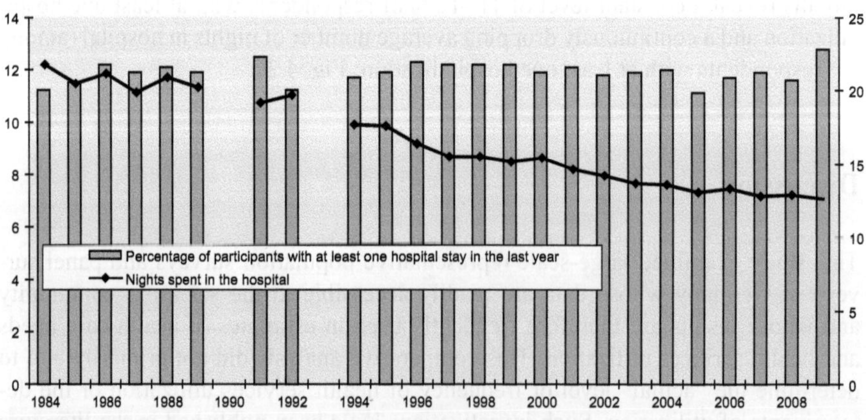

Fig. 4.2 Prevalence of inpatient admissions and number of nights spent in hospital in the last 12 months, from 1984 to 2009, SOEP, waves from 1 to 26 (source [1])

Rather, the aim of this study was to compare the employed instruments and differences in results using simple analyses of the overall population or broken down by sociodemographic characteristics. It is beyond the scope of this contribution to present utilization by population subgroups [e.g., 18–20], or specific patient groups [e.g., 21], or even multivariate modeling of utilization, for instance, on the basis of the Andersen model [22–24].

The survey results on outpatient utilization are comparable only to a limited degree. There are considerable differences in terms of individual questions even among the surveys by the RKI. The RKI surveys, SOEP, and the Bertelsmann Healthcare Monitor differ not only in target groups but also in their questions on outpatient utilization, the surveyed time interval, the differentiation by specialist groups, the wording of questions, including clarifications (for instance, on the inclusion of non-personal contacts), as well as response categories. For outpatient treatment and the utilization of preventative services, the variations in questions and hence results are much smaller.

The differences in methodological approaches, using representative samples (RKI surveys) versus panel surveys (SOEP and Healthcare Monitor), additionally affect results. The authors of the Healthcare Monitor, for instance, state that the participants of the individual waves are either representative of the total population in terms of age and gender structure as well as regional and sociodemographic characteristics or representativeness can be established through calculations or weighting factors [10]. However, the households' fundamental willingness to respond—a prerequisite for inclusion in the Access Panel—in itself introduces a systematic bias to the distributions of responses. To the authors' knowledge, no related analyses on selection bias have been conducted so far, but care should be exercised when generalizing the results, particularly as regards behaviors and attitudes.

Unlike results on hospital stays, the results for contacts with primary care physicians and specialists are not necessarily comparable. In addition, some questions are not clearly worded as to whether physician contacts should include direct contacts only or also telephone consultations and office contacts for picking up referrals or prescription renewals in patients with chronic diseases. (Example 1 from the Healthcare Monitor: "With which of the following physicians or their office staff were you in contact within the previous 12 months, and how often were you in contact?"; Example 2 from GDA09: "And how often did you visit a physician in private practice, either a primary care physician or specialist, within the past 12 months? *Note to participants*: Picking up a prescription counts as a physician visit. Dentist visits are not counted.")

The objection that secular trends over a time period of almost 20 years render comparisons generally problematic is largely countered by the fact that Figs. 4.1 and 4.2 show little change in the levels of outpatient and inpatient utilization (except regarding the average length of stay, which is not discussed in more detail in this contribution). Further, there is a fundamental question about the validity of self-reported information on the utilization of medical services, particularly in terms of the frequency of contact within a time interval of more than 3 months. Simply imagine asking a chronically ill patient with multiple morbidities who visits a physician several times per month exactly how many total contacts he or she has had within the past year with primary care physicians or various specialists.

Robra et al. [25] conducted an early comparison of results from the EVaS study and the DHP study's national survey on outpatient utilization. Regarding the frequency of personal physician–patient contacts, the survey participants' self-reported results were strikingly similar to the data from the physicians' documentation. However, the study did not validate information on an individual basis, but rather validated the results of extrapolations with regard to the number of contacts within a quarter, performing essentially an ecological "validation." The authors are not aware of recent German comparative analyses on the validity of self-reported information using an external data source on an individual basis.

According to a slightly older review by Harlow and Linet [26], which examined validation studies comparing data on the utilization of medical services obtained from questionnaires, there was a good agreement between self-reports and hospital record data on hospital stays and surgeries. However, there was less agreement about dentist contacts, specific medical services (e.g., X-rays), and medications. The study did not investigate the frequency of outpatient services utilization.

Walihan et al. [27] evaluated the accuracy of older Americans' (aged 60+) self-reported utilization of medical services (hospital admissions, utilization of emergency rooms, outpatient contacts, and house calls). One-fourth of people who were hospitalized did not report it, and the same fraction failed to report emergency room utilization. For outpatient visits, particularly the number of visits was severely under-reported, and the degree of under-reporting was correlated with age and the frequency of outpatient visits. The under-reporting of utilized medical services was found to be much higher in people with mental illnesses [28]. As the primary reasons for this under-reporting, the study lists recall bias and social desirability bias. A Korean study also estimated that survey information regarding outpatient visits (within 2 weeks preceding the survey) and inpatient admissions (within the year preceding the survey) had a sensitivity of less than 60 % as measured against the gold standard of billing data [29].

A review by Bhanderi et al. [30] examined factors affecting the degree of under-reporting. Determinants of under-reporting were found to be age, the type of, and reason for utilization, its frequency, and the extent of perceived 'stigma' associated with utilization. This is a relevant issue in mental illnesses and addiction disorders, for instance. In addition, the study design (personal interview, telephone-based interview, and questionnaire), question wording and comprehensibility, length of the period for which utilization is measured, the order of survey questions, and memory aids for the participants can influence the validity of self-reported data, as suggested by the inconsistencies in German survey instruments. In general, self-reported utilization data must bc assumcd to widely vary in validity and hence to be of limited comparability.

Given the mentioned difficulties associated with the validity of self-reported utilization of medical services, SHI routine data (claims data) on the utilization of medical services lend itself for epidemiological studies in general and specifically for validating self-reported data. In recent years, these data have systematically been made available for utilization in health services research [31, 32], and during the same time, the large health insurers have developed continuous (health data) reporting systems [e.g., 33, 34]. Another contribution in this book by *Swart* discusses the content of these data, potential applications in health services and utilization research, and methodological limitations of scientific utilization beyond their primary billing-related purpose.

Two additional challenges arise if SHI routine data are not used solely as routine data but are individually linked with primary data [35]. Numerous technical, organizational, and data privacy issues must be solved [36–38], and many study participants will not consent to having their survey data and SHI data linked. This group may well include up to 40 % of the participants [36]. Therefore, the potential of individual data linkage cannot be finally assessed at this time.

Several current German epidemiological studies are designed to include individual-based data linkage of primary data and SHI billing data and are expected to reveal insights, opportunities, and limitations of the linkage of primary and secondary data in the coming years. An important example is the German National Cohort (www.nationale-kohorte.de), which plans to include reconciliation with SHI billing data as well as with the data of other social insurances (statutory pension insurance and Federal Labor Office) for all 200,000 study participants [39]. Prerequisites and problems have already been described for a smaller cohort study with some 6,500 participants [36]. Linking primary data with not only individual-based secondary data but also context-related secondary data on an aggregated level, such as physician density, access to inpatient facilities, and regional socioeconomic variables, can potentially result in a multilevel model as an extension of the Andersen model as opposed to pure modeling on an individual level [24].

Nevertheless, these studies enable the direct cross-validation of primary and secondary data, for instance, as regards the type and extent of outpatient and inpatient service utilization. However, both primary and secondary data can be plagued by over-reporting and under-reporting. For instance, SHI billing data do not include over-the-counter medications, and not all individual contacts with a physician in private practice will be recorded in an outpatient care system that is strictly based on a flat-fee reimbursement scheme. Therefore, neither primary data nor SHI billing data can be considered the gold standard in Germany. Secondary data from the office information systems of physicians in private practice are only incrementally made available to scientific research and are not yet available on a routine basis [40, 41].

Future surveys and epidemiological studies will therefore still need to include sets of questions on health services utilization. The various potential biases then need to be considered and controlled [30]. In this context, we must also mention qualitative methods, which supply additional insights and information that are difficult or impossible to attain with primary and secondary data, for instance, [subjective] access barriers and knowledge about entitlement and the ability to influence health. The contribution by *Babitsch* et al. in Chap. 6 will discuss these aspects.

References

1. Swart E. The prevalence and intensity of medical services use. How comparable are the results of large-scale population surveys in Germany? Psycho-Social-Medicine. GMS online. 2012. DOI: 10.3205/psm000088.
2. Forschungsverbund DHP, editor. Die Deutsche Herz-Kreislauf-Präventionsstudie. Bern: Hans Huber Verlag; 1998.
3. Stolzenberg H. Gesundheitssurvey Ost-West. Befragungs- und Untersuchungssurvey in den neuen und alten Bundesländern. Dokumentation des Public Use File OW91. Berlin: Robert-Koch-Institut; 1995.
4. Potthoff P, Schroeder E, Reis U, Klamert A. Ablauf und Ergebnisse der Feldarbeit beim Bundes-Gesundheitssurvey. Das Gesundheitswesen. 1999; 61: S62–S67.
5. Thefeld W, Stolzenberg H, Bellach B-M. Bundes-Gesundheitssurvey: Response, Zusammensetzung der Teilnehmer und Non-Responder-Analyse. Das Gesundheitswesen. 1999; 61: S57–S61.
6. Kohler M, Rieck A, Borch S. Methode und Design des telefonischen Gesundheitssurveys 2003. Bundesgesundheitsblatt. 2005; 48: 1224–1230.
7. Kurth B-M. Gesundheitssurveys des Robert-Koch-Instituts-Instrument eines Monitorings der gesundheitlichen Versorgung der Bevölkerung? In: Kurth B-M (ed.) Monitoring der gesundheitlichen Versorgung in Deutschalnd. Konzepte, Anforderungen, Datenquellen. Köln: Deutscher Ärzteverlag; 2008. P. 95–110.
8. Lange C, Ziese T. Daten und Fakten: Ergebnisse der Studie Gesundheit in Deutschland aktuell 2009. Berlin: Robert-Koch-Institut, 2011.
9. Güther B, Schnee M, Potthoff P. Zur Methode des Gesundheitsmonitors. In: Böcken J, Braun B, Schnee M, editors. Gesundheitsmonitor 2002. Die ambulante Versorgung aus Sicht von Bevölkerung und Ärzteschaft. Gütersloh: Verlag Bertelsmann-Stiftung; 2002. p. 188–199.
10. Güther B. Gesundheitsmonitor: Feld- und Methodenbericht—Welle 16 Bevölkerungsbefragung/Versichertenstichprobe. München: TNS Health Care; 2009.
11. Wagner GG, Göbel J, Krause P, Pischner R, Siebel I. Das Sozio-ökonomische Panel (SOEP): Multidisziplinäres Haushaltspanel und Kohortenstudie für Deutschland—Eine Einführung (für neue Datennutzer) mit einem Ausblick (für erfahrene Anwender). Wirt Sozialstat Archiv. 2008; 2: 301–328.
12. Griehl S. Präventionsleistungen der gesetzlichen Krankenversicherung—zeitliche Entwicklung und Faktoren der Inanspruchnahme. Hochschule Magdeburg-Stendal; 2012.
13. Kahl H, Hölling H, Kamtsiuris P. Inanspruchnahme von Früherkennungsuntersuchungen und Maßnahmen zur Gesundheitsförderung. Das Gesundheitswesen. 1999; 61: S163–S168.
14. Baumeister SE, Alte D, John U. Inanspruchnahme medizinischer Leistungen. Welche Rolle spielt die soziale Unterstützung. Ergebnisse der Study of Health in Pommerania (SHIP). Das Gesundheitswesen. 2004; 66: 175–179.
15. Bergmann E, Kalcklösch M, Tiemann F. Inanspruchnahme des Gesundheitswesens. Erste Ergebnisse des telefonischen Gesundheitssurveys 2003. Bundesgesundheitsblatt. 2005; 48: 1365–1373.
16. Bergmann E, Kamtsiuris P. Inanspruchnahme medizinischer Leistungen. Das Gesundheitswesen. 1999; 61: S138–S144.
17. Winkelhake O, Mielck A, John J. Einkommen, Gesundheit und Inanspruchnahme des Gesundheitswesens in Deutschland 1992. Soz.-Präventivmed. 1997; 42: 3–10.
18. Hessel A, Gunzelmann T, Geyer M, Brähler E. Inanspruchnahme medizinischer Leistungen und Medikamenteneinnahme bei über 60jährigen in Deutschland. Z Gerontol Geriat. 2000; 33: 289–299.
19. Kamtsiuris P, Bergmann E, Rattay P, Schlaud M. Inanspruchnahme medizinischer Leistungen. Ergebnisse des Kinder- und Jugendgesundheitssurveys (KIGGS). Bundesgesundheitsblatt. 2007; 50: 836–850.

20. Röckl-Wiedmann I, Meyer N, Fischer R, Laubereau B, Weitkunat R, Überla K. Schichtspezifische Inanspruchnahme medizinischer Leistungen und Vorsorgeverhalten in Bayern. Ergebnisse einer repräsentativen Bevölkerungsbefragung. Soz.-Präventivmed. 2002; 47: 307–317.
21. Lengerke T von, Happich M, Reitmeir P, John J. Utilization of out- and inpatient health services by obese adults: a population based study in the Augsburg region, Germany. Das Gesundheitswesen. 2005; 67: S150–S157.
22. Andersen RM. Revisiting the behavioral model and access to medical care: does it matter? J Health Social Behavior 1995; 36:1–10.
23. Andersen RM, Davidson PL. Improving access to care in America: individual and contextual indicators. In: Andersen RM, Rice TH, Kominski GF, editors. Changing the U.S. health care system: key issues in health services, policy, and management. 3rd edition. San Francisco, CA: Jossey-Bass; 2007. p. 3–31.
24. Thode N, Bergmann E, Kamtsiuris P, Kurth B-M. Einflussfaktoren auf die ambulante Inanspruchnahme in Deutschland. Bundesgesundheitsblatt. 2005; 48: 296–306.
25. Robra B-P, Lü C, Kerek-Bodden H, Schach E, Schach S, Schwartz FW. Die Häufigkeit der ärztlichen Inanspruchnahme im Spiegel zweier Repräsentativerhebungen. DHP-Survey und EVaS-Studie. Das Gesundheitswesen. 1991; 53: 228–232.
26. Harlow S, Linet MS. Agreement between questionnaire data and medical records, the evidence for accuracy recall. American Journal of Epidemiology. 1989; 129: 233–248.
27. Wallihan DB, Stump TE, Callahan CM. Accuracy of self-reported health services use and patterns of care among urban older adults. Medical Care. 1999; 37: 662–670.
28. Drapeau A, Boyer R, Diallo FB. Discrepancies between survey and administrative data on the use of mental health services in the general population: findings from a study conducted in Québec. BMC Public Health. 2011; 11: 837 (doi:10.1186/1471–2458-11–837).
29. Rim H, Kim H, Lee K, Chang S, Hovell MF, Kim Y-T, Kim Y, Kang G, Tak Y, Im J. Validity of self-reported healthcare utilization data in the community health survey in Korea. J Korean Med Sci. 2011; 26: 1409–1414.
30. Bhandari A, Wagner T. Self-Reported Utilization of Health Care Services: Improving Measurement and Accuracy. Medical Care Research and Review. 2006; 63: 217–235.
31. Swart E, Heller G. Nutzung und Bedeutung von GKV-Routinedaten. In: Janßen C, Borgetto B, Heller G, editors: Medizinsoziologische Beiträge zur Versorgungsforschung: Theoretische Ansätze, Methoden und Instrumente sowie ausgewählte Ergebnisse. Weinheim: Juventa; 2007. p. 93–112.
32. Swart E, Ihle P, editors. Routinedaten im Gesundheitswesen. Handbuch Sekundärdatenanalyse: Grundlagen, Methoden und Perspektiven. Bern: Hans Huber Verlag; 2005.
33. Bitzer EM, Grobe TG, Neusser S, Mieth I, Schwartz FW. BARMER GEK Report Krankenhaus 2011. St. Augustin: Asgard-Verlag; 2011.
34. Grobe TG, Dörning H, Schwartz FW. BARMER GEK Arztreport 2011. St. Augustin: Asgard-Verlag; 2011.
35. Hoffmann W, Bobrowski C, Fendrich K. Sekundärdatenanalyse in der Versorgungsepidemiologie. Potenzial und Limitationen. Bundesgesundheitsblatt 2008; 51: 1193–1201.
36. March S, Rauch A, Thomas D, Bender S, Swart E. Datenschutzrechtliche Vorgehensweise bei der Verknüpfung von Primär- und Sekundärdaten in einer Kohortenstudie: die lidA-Studie. Das Gesundheitswesen. 2012; 74: e122–129.
37. Swart E, March S, Thomas D, Salomon T, von dem Knesebeck O. Erfahrungen mit der Datenverknüpfung von Primär- und Sekundärdaten in einer Interventionsstudie. Das Gesundheitswesen. 2011; 73: e126–e132.
38. Swart E, March S, Thomas D, Salomon T, von dem Knesebeck O. Die Eignung von Sekundärdaten zur Evaluation eines Interventionsprojekts—Erfahrungen aus der AGil-Studie. Prävention und Gesundheitsförderung. 2011; 6: 305–311.
39. Wichmann H-E, Kaaks R, Hoffmann W, Jöckel K-H, Greiser K-H, Linseisen J. Die Nationale Kohorte. Bundesgesundheitsblatt. 2012; 55: 781–789.

40. Hauswaldt J, Kersting M, Hummers-Pradier E Influenza-Impfungen durch Niedersächsische Hausärzte—eine Sekundäranalyse vertragsärztlicher Versorgungsdaten aus 1995/1996, 2002/2003 und 2005/2006. Das Gesundheitswesen. 2010; 72: 332–339.
41. Kersting M, Gierschmann A, Hauswaldt J, Hummers-Pradier E. Routinedaten aus hausärztlichen Arztinformationssystemen Export, Analyse und Aufbereitung für die Versorgungsforschung. Das Gesundheitswesen. 2010; 72: 323–331.

Chapter 5
Health Care Utilization Research using Secondary Data

Enno Swart

Preliminary Remarks

As defined by Good Practice in Secondary Data Analysis (GPS; see below), secondary data are "data which are provided for analysis over and above their original, primary purpose." Their classification as secondary data critically rests upon differences between the primary purpose for which the data are collected and their subsequent utilization. It is irrelevant for classification whether the data owners themselves or third parties undertake the further utilization of the data. Therefore, routine data of health insurances ('claims data') are considered secondary data not only if they are used for scientific purposes but also if they are used by the health insurance for health services planning, for instance. GPS further specifies: "Secondary data analysis defines the utilization of secondary data. Secondary data analysis includes the survey and preparation steps of the secondary data body that are required for the analysis. By these preparation steps the data are accessible for scientific questions" [1].

In recent years, a variety of data sets have been made available for scientific utilization in the context of secondary data analyses. Since the 1990s, the initial focus was almost exclusively on routine data[1] from the statutory health insurances (SHIs), which was promoted by initial extensive studies and an early memorandum on the analysis and utilization of health care and social data; in recent years, routine data from the German statutory pension system and Federal Employment Agency have increasingly been made available to researchers as well [2–5].

This chapter focuses on the utilization of SHI-financed medical services, so we will not further discuss the latter data sets. For additional information, refer to the websites of the research data centers of the statutory pension fund (www.fdz-rv.de) and the Institute for Employment Research (IAB; http://fdz.iab.de). The health-related data in official statistics (e.g., hospital diagnosis statistics) can be utilized as

[1] The term 'routine data' is used synonymously with secondary data in the context of the SHI.

E. Swart (✉)
Medical Faculty, Institute of Social Medicine and Health Economics, Otto von Guericke University of Magdeburg, Magdeburg, Germany
e-mail: enno.swart@med.ovgu.de

C. Janssen et al. (eds.), *Health Care Utilization in Germany*,
DOI 10.1007/978-1-4614-9191-0_5, © Springer Science+Business Media New York 2014

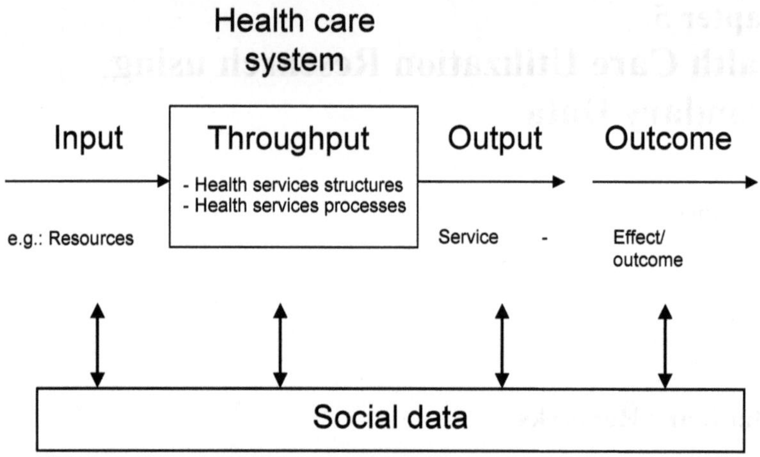

Fig. 5.1 Social data and the health-care system. (Source: [10])

well through the research data center of the German federal states' and federal government's statistical offices (www.forschungsdatenzentrum.de). Since these data are very similar in content to SHI data, these sources are not explicitly discussed here. However, the opportunities and limitations of the utilization of secondary data as discussed in this chapter generally apply to these data sets as well. Additional discussions of these data sets are found in [6, 7]. Kurth (2008) presents additional specific data sets that could be used for health-care utilization (HCU) research and health services monitoring (e.g., data from clinical registries, networks of expertise, or external quality assurance) [8].

This chapter focuses on discussing the scientific utilization of SHI routine data since these data provide an almost complete picture of the utilization of medical services, namely of all SHI-financed services. In addition, we are guided by the idea that "health services [and particularly utilization; E.S.] research requires data collected in routine care" [9]. Figure 5.1 shows that social data and particularly the discussed SHI data can provide information about the entire utilization process, particularly about the specific health services processes (throughput), the provided services (output), and the results of medical services (outcomes). This will be discussed in greater detail under 'Examples of use' [10].

Data Structure

Discussing the methodological, technical, and data protection aspects of the scientific utilization of SHI routine data first requires an overview of the data stored by the SHIs. The German *Social Code Book V* (SGB V), Chap. 10, "Transmission of health services data" [*Übermittlung von Leistungsdaten*] (§ 295 ff.) lays down provisions regarding the standardized transmission of data about rendered services

Table 5.1 Provisions in the *Social Code, Book V* on the transmission of routine data from the statutory health insurance

	Health care sector	Case-related contents (among others)[a]
§ 295	Outpatient care	Type of case (e.g., direct contact, referral, emergency), specialties of the treating physician and any referring physician, diagnoses (ICD), services (EBM, OPS)
§ 295	Incapacity to work	Diagnosis (ICD) that justifies the incapacity to work, initial versus follow-up certificate
§ 300	Pharmaceutical prescriptions	Proprietary medicinal products; central pharmaceutical number (PZN) indicates active ingredient, price, and quantity of the pharmaceutical (ATC Code); prescription date
§ 301	Inpatient care	Admitting hospital, diagnoses at admission and discharge, secondary diagnoses (ICD), procedures and diagnostics (OPS), reimbursement (DRG), reason for admission and discharge, date of admission and discharge
§ 302	Prescriptions of non-pharmaceutical therapies and technical aids	Rendered services by type, quantity, and price, as well as medical diagnosis

[a] Member-related data (age, sex, etc.) are available for every sector

and associated costs by the service providers (physicians in private practice, hospitals, rehabilitation facilities, pharmacies, and nonphysician service providers such as occupational and physical therapists) to the insurances. With the exception of dental care[2], every major health-care sector requires specific case-based documentation for every physician–patient contact (Table 5.1), and the specific content of the transmitted data is specified down to individual variables. The 2004 revision of § 295 included the outpatient sector in this documentation requirement.

The routine data are owned by the individual SHIs. The scientific utilization of these data within the context of health services research, therefore, requires contacting the insurances and discussing and contractually agreeing on the objectives of use under aspects of health services epidemiology. This aspect is discussed in greater detail below.

Methodological Aspects of Handling Routine Data

SHI routine data are primarily collected for the billing of medical services. The transmitted variables and the type of coding are specified in accordance with this primary purpose. This fact must always be borne in mind when discussing the advantages and disadvantages of utilizing routine data in the context of HCU research.

[2] Dental care is an exception since considerable portions of dental services (such as dental restorations and prosthetics) are not included in the SHI catalog of services and are therefore not reimbursable. For additional information, please refer to the publications by the Institute of German Dentists (IDZ; www.idz-koeln.de).

It also affects validation and data processing as central steps before the actual data analysis can start. Before presenting the associated methodological problems and solution approaches, we list a series of distinctive characteristics that reveal the suitability of these data for research purposes:

- *Population-based*: Epidemiological figures are typically expressed as rates, with the absolute number of target events in the numerator and a definable and quantifiable population in the denominator. Such rates are also relevant for HCU research, for instance, when expressing treatment frequencies (e.g., number of diabetics per 1,000 insured) or distinct events (e.g., number of hospital admissions with diabetes as the main diagnosis), which may be further differentiated by age, gender, and other socio-demographic characteristics. Typical epidemiological figures such as incidence (new cases or initial documentation of diagnosis) and prevalence (number of treated patients with a certain diagnosis) can be clearly determined on the basis of SHI routine data by using the number of members insured by an SHI at a specific date or during an observation period (the so-called population at risk). Since exact insurance coverage periods are available for each member, the denominator can list precise member-years. Other HCU-relevant data from physician practices, hospitals, or disease registers generally do not include this precise population-based information.
- *Individual-based*: SHI routine data are highly significant for HCU research because the health services provided to individual insured members can be tracked over an extended time period, both retrospectively and prospectively. Through pseudonymized health insurance-member numbers, all of the member's contacts in all sectors can be pooled, regardless of service provider and location of service provision [11]. This is not true for statistics that are merely case-based or sector-based (such as the German federal hospital diagnostics statistics). For instance, these statistics present transfers and readmissions as separate cases without a clear link to the insured individual. The official diagnostics statistics, therefore, do not reveal how many patients were involved in the roughly 18.5 million hospitalizations (2010; www.gbe-bund.de).
- *Residence-based and location-based*: The postal code of the insured, with the fifth digit often removed for data protection purposes, allows the detailed resolution of epidemiological figures to the district and community level, irrespective of the difficulties associated with the clear matching of postal codes to communities and districts. No other health services data currently allow such small-scale regional representation of the health services situation with clear population-based information. Local health services analyses can be performed with regard to the service providers as well, in compliance with data protection regulations [1, 12].
- *Data quality*: In the context of their primary purpose, routine data are checked for completeness and accuracy, for instance, regarding the consistency of reimbursement-relevant diagnostic and surgical data. However, variables that are not checked for quality by the data owner, such as information on specialty departments or causes of inpatient admission, must be separately validated by the secondary user. This also applies to specific content-related questions, such as

the review of the documentation of diagnoses and services in the context of disease-specific and procedure-specific examinations [13, 14].

- *Completeness*: Because they are relevant to reimbursement, most SHI data sets can be assumed to be nearly 100% complete (inpatient cases, pharmaceutical prescriptions, non-pharmaceutical therapy, and technical aid prescriptions), and they are associated with an extremely low risk of selective reporting bias, which is often a suspected problem in external quality assurance. However, only information about SHI-financed services can be assumed to be complete. Privately financed services, such as the purchase of over-the-counter (OTC) pharmaceuticals, are by definition missing from SHI routine data. Private prescriptions and so-called IGeL services (*Individuelle Gesundheitsleistungen,* individual self-paid health services) are not systematically documented. Data of incapacity to work also underrepresent short-term sick leave lasting 3 days or less because many employers only require employees to submit an incapacity certificate starting on the fourth missed working day [6].
- *Low cost*: Routine data are created through standardized pathways within the day-to-day operation of the health-care system. The only cost-relevant aspects for HCU researchers are expenses arising for data processing, supply, and transmission beyond the routine administration process. At the insurances, these expenses are comparatively low since only filtration is typically required, and the data are not assessed further for content. The data are typically available in a form that facilitates subsequent information technology (IT) processing. Nevertheless, the expenses and time required for supplying the SHI data can represent obstacles to scientific utilization in light of the routine tasks of the data owners.

For many years, the scientific utilization of routine data was deemed 'second-class research' because it used supposedly inferior (secondary) data and did not employ specific instruments. Its problems, methods, and results did, therefore, not receive appropriate recognition. This negative perception changed with the growing availability and scientific utilization of SHI routine data and the initial publication of a scientific standard for the proper use of these data (GPS), which drew on Good Epidemiological Practice (GEP) [17, 18]. GPS was the first established standard for conducting secondary data analyses, and it represented a basis for contracts be tween data owners and external secondary users as well. GPS has now been revised twice, most recently in 2012 (download available at www.dgepi.de, also in English translation).

The first revision structurally aligned GPS with GEP. GPS now also features 11 guidelines, each with explanations and recommendations. The guidelines primarily reflect the entire secondary data analysis process from data generation and verification to analysis and interpretation. Specifically, GPS provides recommendations on study design, data processing, data analysis, quality assurance, data privacy, and contractual frameworks as well as the scientific independence of secondary users. GPS particularly emphasizes the documentation and transparency of data processing. Herein lies the biggest difference to research with primary data since the subsequent secondary users cannot influence the generation and collection of routine data. GPS additionally stresses the need for contractually regulating the secondary utilization by defining the rights and duties of data owners and health services researchers. Finally, the utilization of SHI data within the context of health services research requires full compliance with the applicable data privacy provisions and the SGB [19–21].

The GPS' target group is data owners, secondary users involved in social medicine and health services epidemiology, and those who use their research results. This includes not only members of universities but also all those who apply scientific methods to secondary data and their analyses from a scientific perspective. GPS is now an established standard. The improved reputation of secondary data analysis and recognition of its importance in health services research and hence HCU research are highlighted by the methodology memos issued by the German Network for Health Services Research, which explicitly discuss the utilization of secondary data [22, 23].

The next section covers the specific uses of SHI routine data and the associated methodological problems and solution approaches.

Examples of Use

SHI routine data supply information about all phases of the health services process that were outlined above (see Fig. 5.1), although to a varying extent. Input-oriented health services research includes needs research and the investigation of health services utilization. The analysis of routine data primarily aims to reveal utilization; on the basis of retrospective contact analyses, they can also provide approximate information about objective needs but not subjective needs. Throughput-oriented health services research deals with structures and institutions; here, routine data can supply suitable process and outcome parameters for comparisons between service providers. Routine data directly indicate the output of the health-care system through billed services. Increasingly, SHI routine data are also used to identify the outcomes of medical services. Table 5.2 presents the fields in which SHI routine data can be scientifically utilized [24].

A 2009 review found 70 studies on the use of pharmaceutical prescription data alone [25]. Newer studies and studies with a different focus add to this number. At this point, a complete overview of the use of SHI routine data in Germany can, therefore, not be provided. Instead, a few brief examples of current questions that are investigated using SHI routine data will be presented below. These examples are intended to demonstrate the wide range of potential uses and to encourage more intensive utilization. Some of the examples come from analyses of the Sample Survey of Persons Insured in SHI Institutions in Hessen [*Versichertenstichprobe AOK Hessen/KV Hessen*] since the author considers this database the most extensive and longest used data source for secondary data analysis in Germany [26]. Numerous additional examples are found, for instance, in Swart and Heller (2007), Schubert et al. (2008), Swart and Ihle (2005), Grobe (2008), and the Health Care Report of the AOK Research Institute (WIdO), which has been published annually since 2011 [7, 24, 27–29].

Table 5.2 Selected applications for SHI data. (Source: [24], shortened)

Topics	Contents	Variables, methodological approach
Morbidity estimates	Incidence and prevalence estimates	Outpatient and inpatient main and secondary diagnoses, incapacity to work diagnoses
Utilization of services	Type and frequency of service	Physician visits, hospital admissions, prescriptions of pharmaceuticals, non-pharmacological therapies, and technical aids
Patterns of care	Patient-specific courses of utilization over time	Longitudinal data on outpatient and inpatient services and prescriptions; utilization of various service providers
Resource utilization	Studies of costs of illness	Costs of outpatient and inpatient utilization, of pharmaceuticals, non-pharmacological therapies, and technical aids
Quality of care (process)	Indicator-supported assessment of care	Comparison of documented services with treatment recommendations and guidelines
Quality of care (outcome)	Medium-term and long-term assessment of outcomes of care	Risk-adjusted: death, readmission after inpatient treatment, adverse events
Need estimates	Prediction of future utilization	Incidence/prevalence estimates in conjunction with demographic prognoses
Evaluation of models of care	Effectiveness and efficiency of new models of care (DMP)	Resource utilization and quality of care in (non) participants

IC integrated care, *DMP* disease management program

Sector-based analyses Pharmaceutical prescription data have been in routine use for many years. The review by Hoffmann (2009) has already been mentioned [25]. Nink et al. (2005) provide a detailed description of the opportunities presented by pharmaceutical data in health services research (information systems, research questions, and selected results) [30]. The Pharmaceutical Prescription Report [*Arzneimittelverordnungsreport*], which has been published annually since 1985, is one of the standard references that provide detailed information about utilization behavior in one of the most important health-care sectors. In the Pharmaceutical Prescription Report, the prescriptions written by SHI-accredited physicians are subjected to a systematic, descriptive analysis and evaluation to improve market and cost transparency. Regular contents of the Prescription Report include the general prescription and market development, the prescription frequency for new active substances, and topics related to indication groups. The 2012 Pharmaceuti-

Table 5.3 Distribution of pharmaceutical costs among insured cases, BARMER GEK, 2010 (in %). (Source: [32])

Percentage of pharmaceutical expenditures	Percentage of members with pharmaceutical prescriptions	Percentage of all members
10	0.15	0.11
20	0.45	0.34
30	1.10	0.84
40	2.46	1.87
50	4.63	3.52
60	7.80	5.93
70	12.53	9.53
80	19.98	15.19
90	33.53	25.49
100	100.00	76.02

cal Prescription Report, for instance, focuses on analyzing the initial results of the early benefit assessment of new active ingredients, where the additional benefit of new medicines is quantified as compared to established medicines, within the context of the Act on the Reorganization of the Pharmaceutical Market (AMNOG: *Arzneimittelneuordnungsgesetz*) [31].

This reference publication is now supplemented by specific health reports published by individual SHIs [32]. The additional reference to a defined population of insured members allows the calculation of epidemiological indices and the identification of foci of care. Targeted analyses seem useful when a high percentage (of costs) of prescribed pharmaceuticals benefit a small percentage of members. For instance, 50 % of all pharmaceutical expenditures were spent on fewer than 4 % of members of the GEK (Gmünder Ersatzkasse; now fused with BARMER to form BARMER-GEK) [32, Table 5.3]. This group primarily consisted of seriously ill patients with multiple morbidities, who are frequently treated with a complex, poorly coordinated medication regimen. Such constellations lend themselves to steering and coordinating measures in the context of disease management programs.

Data of incapacity-to-work are among the most intensively used SHI data to date. Routine reports on the basis of incapacity-to-work reports for the subpopulation of working members have been part of the standard reporting system of all health insurers for many years [33–35]. The annual report on time missed from work published by the AOK Research Institute is merely one example of reports that provide detailed information about the development of sickness figures in the German economy and examine in detail the incapacity-to-work situation in the individual sectors of the economy, with varying focus areas [36]. We will not further discuss these data since the incapacity-to-work situation only indirectly supplies information about HCU. For additional methodological discussions regarding the utilization of data on incapacity to work, please refer to specific publications [16, 37].

The data from the inpatient sector have been used intensively for many years as well. Again, there is an established tradition of regularly published insurance-specific health reports, such as by BARMER GEK or BKK Bundesverband [National Association of Company Health Insurance Funds] (www.bkk.de) [38]. These analyses of the inpatient sector frequently discuss so-called high users of the health-care

Table 5.4 Diagnosis-specific hospitalization frequency for insured members with and without alcohol problems, GEK 2000 through 2003. (cases per 1,000 insured years, age-adjusted). (Source: [39])

Diagnosis category (ICD 10)	Patients with at least one F10 treatment	Members without F10 inpatient treatment
Infectious and parasitic diseases	7.4	2.3
Neoplasms	23.2	18.6
Nutritional and metabolic diseases	11.5	3.9
Mental/behavioral disorders (other than F10)	106.6	4.8
Diseases of the nervous system/sensory organs	30.2	11.9
Diseases of the circulatory system	43.6	24.0
Diseases of the respiratory system	16.2	7.5
Diseases of the digestive system	67.2	18.0
Diseases of the skin and subcutaneous tissue	6.9	2.4
Diseases of the musculoskeletal system and connective tissue	23.7	16.0
Diseases of the genitourinary system	10.9	9.2
Symptoms, signs, abnormal findings not elsewhere classified	21.6	5.2
Injuries and poisonings	65.4	13.0
Total (without F10 cases)	445.0	144.0
Total (with F10 cases)	965.6	144.0

system, meaning members requiring frequent and/or expensive services, who are occasionally referred to as "revolving door" patients. Specific patient groups can be analyzed through specific diagnoses and thanks to the clear member-based information in SHI routine data. Alcoholic patients, for example, are very high users even when they present with other symptoms. After eliminating hospitalizations that are directly related to alcoholism (cases with F10 as main diagnosis), the hospitalization frequency within a 4-year period was still three times higher in alcoholics than in a comparison group of members without alcohol problems (Table 5.4) [39]. Such analyses are made possible by the clear reference to the individual member, which reveals multiple utilizations (in this case, hospitalizations) by the same patient; this reference is not available in other case-based data sources (such as the German federal hospital diagnosis statistics).

Until 2004, it was difficult to identify the health services situation in the outpatient sector because case-based information was not directly transmitted by the service-providing SHI-accredited physicians to the insurances. Until that year, primarily case-based analyses from the outpatient sector could only be created by the Central Research Institute of Ambulatory Health Care [40]. The revision of § 295 SGB V in 2004 enabled case-based or even individual-based analyses of the outpatient care situation using SHI data. The outpatient care sector generates enormously large data sets because about 90 % of all SHI members have at least one outpatient physician contact per year, and an average of 15–20 annual physician contacts per person have been documented through 2008 [28]. In addition, they include data on confirmed diagnoses, tentative diagnoses, and diagnoses by exclusion as well as services according to the EBM (Uniform Value Scale) catalog. While valid contact-based analyses can no longer be performed following the most recent EBM reform in 2008, these data still allow analyses by age, gender, and diagnosis. The available data on the 8.7 million members of BARMER-GEK alone include 74.5 treated cases per quarter, 296 million diagnosis codes, and 498 million billing codes [41].

Prescriptions of non-pharmaceutical therapies and technical aids account for less than 5 % of SHI expenses. However, this sector has been associated with a disproportionate increase in expenses, so that it is increasingly the focus of health services analyses. The National Associations of the SHIs, with support from the AOK Research Institute, have, therefore, created a non-pharmacological therapies information system (*Heilmittel-Informations-System*, HIS) that has been in operation for several years. Schröder et al. (2005) describe the HIS design and structure as well as analysis options [42]. On this basis, annual reports on non-pharmaceutical therapies have been published since 2004; they supply information about the frequency of prescriptions for nonphysician services (e.g., physical, occupational, and speech therapy) [43]. Other insurances now regularly publish reports on non-pharmaceutical therapies and technical aids as well [44].

Morbidity estimates and costs of specific diseases The use of routine data plays a central role in incidence and prevalence estimates of acute and particularly chronic diseases. More precisely, the numbers indicate *treatment* incidence and *treatment* prevalence because secondary data reveal newly arisen or existing diseases only if they become treatment-relevant and are listed as inpatient or outpatient main or secondary diagnoses. SHI secondary data are ideally suited to depict the health services demand as reflected by utilization, show its course over time, and predict future utilization on the basis of population projections. Such uses have been common for several years, for instance for diabetes [45, 46].

Disease-based cross-sector analyses of SHI routine data also allow the calculation of direct disease-related health services costs in the context of health economic analyses. Such analyses can be conducted on a member level and extrapolated to all patients with a specific disease. The disease-related excess costs, when compared with costs for members without the particular disease, can be determined through a case–control approach with matched pairs. For instance, the KoDiM study calculated the total health-care costs for diabetes mellitus in Germany as EUR 45–50 billion per year (2009), which represents a 70 % increase since 2000. A 28 % increase remains, even after the data are standardized by age and gender and inflation-adjusted. This distinct rise results not so much from a growth in per capita costs (approx. EUR 6,000 per year) or excess costs (EUR 2,600 per year) but rather from the increase in diagnosed diabetics to nearly 10 % of all SHI members [47]. This study provides further evidence that controlled study designs can be used with and within SHI routine data.

In the same manner, incidences over time can be estimated in individuals with risk factors, provided the risk factors can be ICD (International Statistical Classification of Diseases and Related Health Problems) operationalized, or in individuals with similar or related diseases; examples include estimates for amputation in diabetes mellitus or endometriosis in patients with related symptoms. [48, 49] Finally, the frequencies of (nonspecific) symptoms and the relationship with potential diagnoses can be determined using routine data, for instance for back pain, an area that is highly relevant in health services [50, 51].

Analyses of specific groups of insured members Beyond pure description, SHI routine data allow a qualitative assessment of the utilization behavior of specific groups of members. For example, recent publications address and quantify the prescription frequencies for pharmaceuticals that are potentially hazardous for older members and are on the so-called PRISCUS list, a listing of medications for which safer alternatives exist from a pharmacological perspective [52]. The work of Schubert et al. (2012) shows that around 1% of retirement-age members receive immediate-release nifedipine, contrary to guidelines [53]. The procedure discussed in that paper can be analogously applied to other specific pharmaceuticals, for instance, to long-term prescriptions following acute myocardial infarction. A prospective analysis of secondary data over an average of 4.2 years showed continuous guideline adherence for 40% of patients [54].

However, patient groups can be defined by more than age, gender, and diagnoses. Regardless of methodological difficulties, SHI routine data are also suitable for analyzing socially disadvantaged groups of members and their typically above-average utilization. This is because occupational biographies in the form of documented employment and unemployment periods are available, at least for working-age members [55]. As example, unemployed members exhibit a higher utilization of inpatient services than employed members in all diagnostic classes; this difference is particularly pronounced in mental illnesses and behavioral disorders, which also includes addictions. Overall, unemployed men accrue about twice as many inpatient days as employed men, a difference that is not as pronounced in women [56].

Cross-sectional analyses of utilization behavior cannot establish causal relationships between unemployment and illness. However, longitudinal designs with the same data set can more specifically investigate potential cause–effect relationships. They show that unemployment is associated not only with poorer health and higher utilization but also with a higher mortality risk. This is found when classifying the insured by degree of unemployment and tracking deaths in each of the four unemployment classes for a 3-year follow-up period. The mortality risk rises with increasing unemployment experience and is three times as high in long-term unemployed members experiencing more than 2 years of unemployment than in those who were never unemployed (Table 5.5) [56]. Hence, SHI routine data can also be used to implement challenging epidemiological study designs.

Subgroup analysis can also focus on specific services that carry high priority in the German health-care system for curative or preventative purposes. This includes services within the German cancer screening program. The SHI catalog of services includes annual fecal occult blood tests (starting at 50 years of age) and colonoscopy (starting at 55 years of age, up to two screenings at least 10 years apart). Analyses of SHI routine data revealed utilization by fewer than 25% of entitled

Table 5.5 Mortality risk of unemployed persons, GEK, 2004. (Source: [55], slightly shortened)

Duration of unemployment in 1993 through 1995	Insured members	Deaths per 100,000 insured, 1996 through 1998	Odds ratio (95 % confidence interval)[a]
No unemployment	254,940	296	1 (reference group)
1–364 days of unemployment	13,815	449	1.8 (1.4; 2.3)
1 year to less than 2 years of unemployment	4,329	554	1.95 (1.3; 2.9)
More than 2 years of unemployment	4,067	959	3.3 (2.4; 4.5)
Total	277,151	318	

[a] adjusted for age and sex; only members less than 50 years of age

members and higher utilization by women due to regular gynecologist visits [57]. In this area, routine data can certainly contribute to quantifying underuse, overuse, and misuse of health services [58].

Quality of care Assessing the outcomes of various treatment alternatives is significant in clinical research. For service providers, patients, and health insurers, an empirically grounded assessment of the quality of care offered by individual service providers is just as important. Internationally, routine data have been commonly used in quality assessments for some time [59–62]. At the same time, external quality assurance measures that have been established for a longer time have proven to be time-consuming and error-prone. The joint project "Quality assurance in inpatient care using routine data (QSR)" of the Federal Association of the AOK, the AOK Research Institute (WIdO), and Helios Kliniken was developed in consideration of this background. In the course of the project, a method was developed to enable the relatively inexpensive, longitudinal, risk-adjusted assessment of the quality of care with the aid of SHI routine data, namely using tracer-specific, outcome-related quality indicators [48, 63]. The validity of the collected data was found to be less affected by quality-relevant biases because the data are not generated in view of a quality assessment, the data are verified by the insurance, and key quality indicators (e.g., hospital readmissions) are documented independently from the institution to be assessed. Even more importantly, unlike most other quality assurance methods in QSR, individual patient-based analysis is possible in addition to case-based analysis. As a result, this procedure enables true longitudinal analyses and ultimately better indicators of the quality of outcomes.

The QSR procedure has been further advanced in the meantime [64]. The AOK hospital navigator now publishes the QSR results for the service areas 'implantation of a hip endoprosthesis in patients with coxarthrosis', 'implantation of a hip endoprosthesis or osteosynthesis in patients with hip fracture', 'implantation of a total knee endoprosthesis', and 'cholecystectomy' (gall bladder removal) (www.qualitaetssicherung-mit-routinedaten.de, as of: May 2012).

Building on the QSR project and in a manner similar to the prospective tracking of myocardial infarction patients, SHI secondary data can be used to present a differentiated picture of the health services situation and medium-term and long-term quality of care in other health-care areas as well, for instance, for osteoarthritis, revisions following endoprosthetic procedures, or initial care dependency [65]. However, this example also demonstrates the (current) limitations of SHI routine data: They reveal (contra)indications to surgical procedures only to a limited degree since they do not include patient-related information (e.g., pain and mobility limitations), and relevant diagnosis-related history information may be missing in case of short observation periods. Notwithstanding their limitations, routine data allow subgroup analyses of members with increased service utilization or of those who are more vulnerable.

Local health services research Typically, most actors within the health-care system have a local perspective and act on the community and district levels (or postal code level). For instance, this applies to the choice of a suitable hospital (from the perspective of the patients and referring physicians), the analysis of hospital catchment areas (from the perspective of service providers), or structural planning (from the perspective of the planning authorities). SHI routine data allow such local health services analyses because they include a clear local reference with the member's place of residence and the location of the service-providing institution (physician's practice and hospital), which potentially permits the resolution of health services structures and processes down to district, community, or postal code.

Local HCU research is important because substantial differences in the utilization of medical services are the rule rather than the exception in Germany, a situation that has been known from other countries for years [1, 12, 66–70]. In the state of Sachsen-Anhalt, there are regions with above-average and below-average utilization persisting over time, even after adjusting for age and gender. When breaking down the total utilization of inpatient services by four-digit postal codes, utilization varies by some 20–30 % above and below the state average, independently of population density and SHI-accredited physician density. In certain (common) diagnoses and surgeries, differences by a factor 2–5 are frequently seen [1] (Fig. 5.2).

Other interesting results of local analyses of the health services situation include: (a) the examination of underuse, overuse, and misuse, and their effects on planning; (b) the quantification of patient migration from and to other service areas, which can affect planning in border regions; (c) the analysis of hospital catchment areas and market shares, which can provide insights into future focus areas of service providers; and (d) the benchmarking of neighboring or structurally similar hospitals using valid process and outcome indicators [58].

Evaluation of new health services models The discussed suitability of SHI routine data for complex, controlled epidemiological studies now enables the evaluation of complex new health-care models, such as disease management programs (DMPs) or integrated care (IC) models. The common self-selection bias generally complicates the evaluation of such programs by simple comparison of participants and nonparticipants. However, advanced methods of secondary data analysis, such as

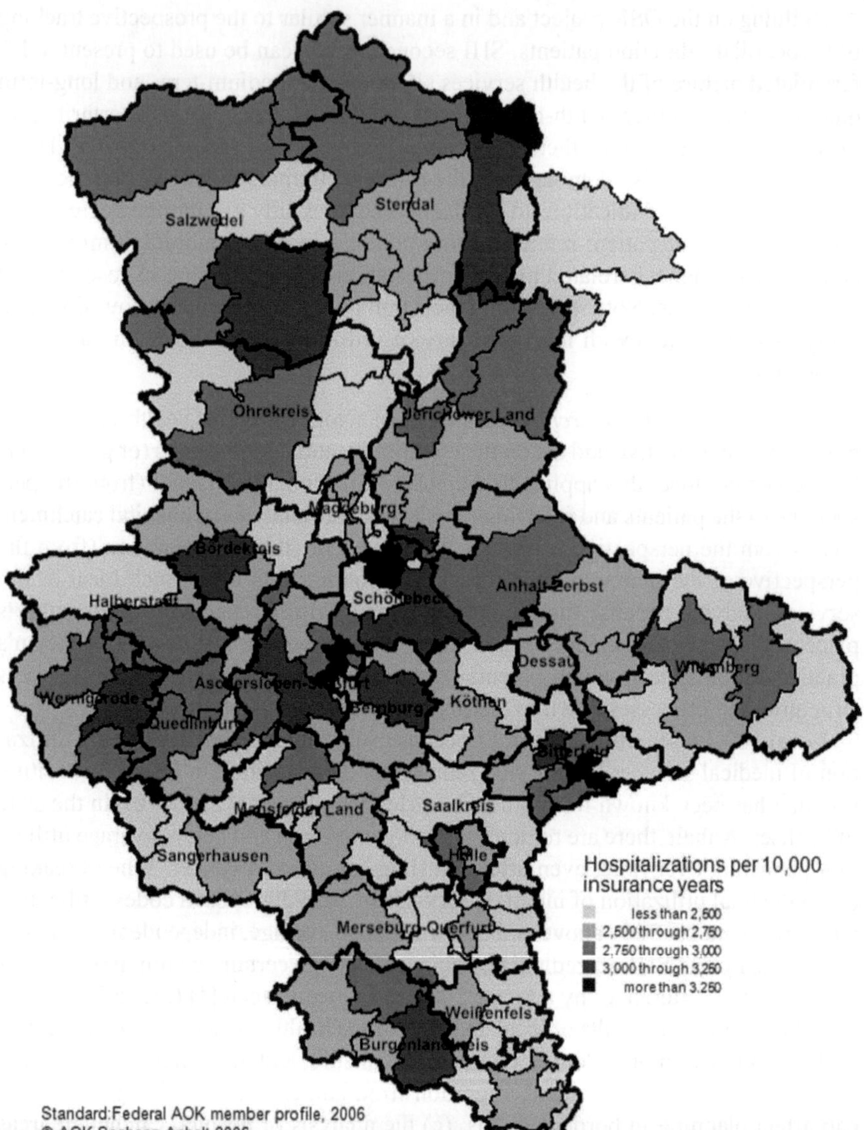

Fig. 5.2 Age-adjusted hospitalization frequency by four-digit postal code areas for members of AOK Sachsen-Anhalt, 2006. (values for the 96 postal code areas vary in a range from 2,080 to 3,832; 10th percentile: 2,275; median: 2,626; 90th percentile: 3,033) (source: [1])

propensity score matching, allow generating control groups that no longer differ from participants in validly operationalizable utilization-influencing factors [71]. Using this approach, an analysis of member data from Techniker Krankenkasse [technicians' health insurance] failed to show a clear proof of effectiveness for the diabetes mellitus DMP: Lower inpatient care costs and fewer emergency admissions, on the one hand, were offset by higher outpatient utilization and more prescriptions on the other [72]. However, such study approaches cannot ensure full structural equivalence because they include only utilization-influencing factors that are expressed by objective socio-demographic characteristics or by documented diagnoses and services.

Some types of controlled studies can also be conducted on the basis of SHI routine data. For instance, an intention-to-treat approach was used in a study of overuse, underuse, and misuse conducted to evaluate the project "Gesundes Kinzigtal" of the AOK and LKK Baden-Württemberg (see Siegel et al. in this issue). The study compares the group of all potential participants in the IC project (of whom some 30 % had decided to participate by late 2011) with a control group that is representative of all other members and is additionally standardized to match the intervention group in all prognostically relevant variables. The intervention is then evaluated using the effect variable 'quality of care' (e.g., extent of guideline compliance) and costs of care (cost development and degree of cost coverage) by comparing the intervention and control groups [73].

Perspectives

The characteristics of SHI routine data and the presented brief examples indicate the wide range of potential uses of these data in HCU research. Twenty years ago, an investigation of surgical treatment quality already recognized this fact: "Insurance claims data are population based, covering all services provided to a defined population regardless of where the care is obtained.... Their low cost and routine availability facilitate their use for monitoring outcomes over long periods. They are free of the reporting bias and inadequate follow-up that afflict case series studies and avoid the high costs required when special registries are organized" [74].

Nevertheless, it is important to keep in mind the limitations of SHI routine data. Two issues are particularly relevant: the validity of diagnostic information and the transferability of the results of secondary data analyses to other populations. A patient-based comparison of diagnostic information in primary physician's patient records with the diagnostic information in SHI billing data revealed considerable underreporting in SHI routine data (in 30 % of cases), particularly for common primary care diagnoses of lesser severity and chronic diseases treated without pharmaceuticals. Simultaneously, permanent diagnoses that were not currently treated were overreported (in 19 % of cases) [75]. A study using SHI data alone also revealed deficits in the continuous documentation of chronic diseases and inconsistencies between diagnosis coding and specific pharmaceutical prescriptions [76]. Nevertheless, these two studies were conducted before the direct transmission of billing information to the SHIs (which started in 2004) and the introduction of the morbidity-oriented risk structure compensation scheme (in 2009).

The validity of diagnosis-based incidence and prevalence estimates has been increased by the availability of outpatient billing data since 2004 and the binding coding of diagnostic confidence. Nevertheless, the diagnosis information in billing data must still be separately validated to supplement the SHI error checks. Depending on the symptoms, confirmed outpatient and inpatient diagnoses and any specific prescriptions are used for validation and identification of so-called epidemiologically confirmed cases. In chronic diseases, documenting a diagnosis alone is typically insufficient [14, 77]. These systematic internal validation approaches increase the quality of the diagnosis-based analysis of SHI routine data.

In case of short observation periods, however, differentiating between incident and prevalent cases of chronic diseases is still a problem because mild cases, such as diagnosed diabetes mellitus not yet requiring drug treatment, may not be regularly documented in billing data. In such cases, billing data should be available for an extended time period if possible, so that initially documented diagnoses as incident cases can be validated throughout several diagnosis-free quarters to avoid overestimating incidence [78]. Provided that incidence and prevalence are validly estimated, SHI routine data allow comprehensive health services monitoring for specific chronic diseases throughout all health-care sectors [79].

The external validity of secondary data analyses generally requires separate examination. Since the employed data sets typically come from a single health insurer, the results are not automatically transferable to members of other SHIs. Particularly, incidence and prevalence estimates depend on the health insurance's member profile. A newer study by Hoffmann and Icks (2011) showed significant differences in member profiles and morbidity structures, even when adjusting for age and gender: "Some morbidity differences remain even after adjusting for relevant health-related variables" [80].

External validity problems could be solved if the so-called data transparency provision act (§ 303a-e SGB V) is consistently implemented to be expected in 2014. The SHI Care Structure Act that came into effect in 2012 now similarly provides that the data reported by the health insurers to the German Federal Insurance Office according to § 268 SGB V for risk structure compensation are combined and made available for further analysis. Although the specific details of the Act are still partly deficient from the perspective of HCU researchers, for the first time the new data pool allows determining members' personal treatment prevalence and indirectly the incidence of treatment-requiring diseases. There have been calls to expand this process to enable more advanced analyses, for instance regarding treatment courses or for small area analyses [81].

In addition to the data pool to be created according to § 303 SGB V, data pools from the Central Research Institute of Ambulatory Health Care in Germany (ZI; www.zi-berlin.de) are already available for cross-insurance analysis. This includes data on billing diagnoses, service ('EBM') codes, and pharmaceutical prescriptions from all physicians in private practice in Germany. This database is primarily used for internal analyses by the Association of SHI Physicians, but it is increasingly made available to health services researchers, and a scientific use file will be set up. The most prominent example is the new health services mapping [*Versorgungsatlas*] project (www.versorgungsatlas.de), which focuses on local variations in utilization on the level of counties and independent towns; successive analyses have been published for various indications since 2011 (e.g., frequency of depression, influenza vaccination rates, and participation rates in bowel cancer screening).

Another cross-insurance data source that may be of interest to HCU researchers is routine data that are directly read out from doctor information systems and processed for secondary use in research. However, this source has only been used in the context of special studies and has not yet been implemented nationwide. Technical issues (such as error-free data transfer from the practice IT systems), logistical difficulties (continuous contact with thousands of physicians in private practice), and methodological challenges (such as cross-practice, consistent patient pseudonymization, or the handling of free text information) currently prevent their routine use; hence, we will not discuss these data in more detail [82].

Members of private health insurance (PHI) have not yet been discussed. The PHI data structure currently does not allow analyses of the described nature. Currently, the research institute of the PHIs largely limits its analyses to topics relevant to health economics and pharmaceutical prescriptions [83, 84]. Therefore, the results of secondary analyses of SHI data cannot be transferred to the privately insured population (which represents about 15 % of the total German population).

SHI Data and the Andersen Model

The utilization of routine data in the context of HCU research is not suitable for investigating individual risk factors that do not immediately require treatment or sociodemographic or socioeconomic factors influencing utilization that are insufficiently documented in routine data. Clinical disease-related factors with direct significance for the type and intensity of utilization (such as degree of severity) are also typically missing from SHI routine data. This limits the modeling of predisposing, enabling, and need factors in the context of the Andersen model of utilization of medical services [85, 86]. Table 5.6 shows which specific factors of the model can be included.

Among the predisposing factors, routine data only include sociodemographic characteristics, which may be of limited use because of the questionable validity of information on education, training, and current occupation [54, 87]. The new version of the occupation code, which SHIs must report at least once yearly for their working members, took effect in December 2011 and could improve this situation [88]. However, the specific health behaviors and attitudes of individual SHI members are generally missing from SHI routine data.

Structural enabling factors, in contrast, are directly available if they are documented through the utilization of SHI-reimbursable medical services and the characterization of the service provider (e.g., primary care physician/ specialist), or they can be retrieved via information on the member's place of residence (postal code, community, or district) for hierarchical analyses. Physician directories of the Associations of SHI Physicians, general hospital plans of the federal states, and an extensive database of socioeconomic variables are available in regional resolution (INKAR,

Table 5.6 Representation of components of the Andersen model in SHI routine data

Factors	Variable	Available in SHI routine data
Predisposing	Age, sex	Yes
	Place of residence	Yes
	Schooling, occupational training	To some degree: for working members: yes; for co-insured family members: no; questionable validity of occupational classification[a]
	Employment status	Yes
	Living with a partner	No
	Migration status	Generally no
	Health behaviors (smoking, alcohol, exercise, nutrition)	Rarely: documentation of obesity (ICD10: E65–68) only if directly relevant to disease
	Health-related attitudes	No
	Social support	No
	Life satisfaction	No
Enabling		
	Primary care physician	Yes, if visited
	Specialist	Yes, if visited
	Insurance status	Yes
	Physician density	Can be determined through place of residence (postal code or administrative district)§
	Hospitals (availability, accessibility)	Can be determined through place of residence (postal code or administrative district)§
	Environmental factors (unemployment, social structure)	Can be determined through place of residence (postal code or administrative district)$
Need	Diseases	Yes
	Self-assessed health status	No
	Health complaints (mental/physical)	To some degree; if they result in utilization and can be ICD coded
	Injuries	Yes
	Pain	To some degree; if it can be operationalized through specific medication
	Disabilities	To some degree; through certifications of incapacity-to-work and incapacity to perform one's usual work as well as disability status
	Limitations in activities of daily living	To some degree; through information about care levels
	Physician findings (e.g., severity of disease)	To some degree; only if included in ICD classification

Factors listed on the basis of [93]

[a] compare [54, 87]; [§] e.g., through Association of SHI Physician's physician register and hospital plans; [$] e.g., INKAR data [indicators and maps on spatial and urban development in Germany and Europe] of the Federal Institute for Research on Building, Urban Affairs and Spatial Development (www.bbsr.bund.de)

Indikatoren und Karten zur Raumentwicklung), indicators and maps on spatial and urban development in Germany and in Europe, available through the Federal Institute for Research on Building, Urban Affairs and Spatial Development; www.bbrs.de).

Some need factors can be identified in SHI routine data. Diseases, injuries, physical and/or mental disorders that lead to the utilization of medical services are represented by the ICD classification and potentially by specific pharmaceutical prescriptions. Symptoms and subjective illnesses that do not lead to contact with professional service providers and do not result in SHI-reimbursable services are problematic. Other methodological issues are the virtual absence of medical findings (e.g., degree of severity) unless they manifest in specific ICD codes as well as the general problem of how nonspecific causes for physician visits are coded in disease diagnoses in the context of ICD and the valid billing regulations.

The limitations of sector-based and particularly insurance-based secondary data, which often fail to fully depict utilization, represent a further problem. For instance, the costs of medical services are not borne by the SHIs alone but often also by other social insurance funds, for instance by the statutory pension insurance in case of medical rehabilitation of employees. Cross-insurance, member-specific analyses may be the primary solution to this problem.

Solution Approach: Individual Linkage

Linkage of primary and secondary data on the individual level could overcome the problem that information on individual health behaviors and specific risk factors, which is typically available in primary data, is missing in SHI routine data. This theoretically ideal solution for epidemiology, and hence HCU research, is fraught with a series of legal, technical, and organizational challenges, and data linkage has, therefore, only been tested in a few cases [76, 89]. Current studies indicate, however, that although often logistically complex, linkage with primary data is technically feasible, legally permissible, and promises novel insights [21, 90].

Specifically, individual data linkage requires obtaining approval for the scientific utilization of social data according to § 75 SGB X from the relevant federal or state supervisory authority, ensuring acceptance of this procedure through the informed consent of study participants, guaranteeing secure data transfer and administration that rule out the reidentification of participations, and collecting SHI data from numerous SHIs based on separate data utilization contracts [21]. On the basis of predominantly positive experiences, individual linkage of primary and secondary data (SHI billing data, cancer registry data, etc.) and the establishment of a secondary data competence center are envisioned for the National Cohort planned to start in 2014 [91]. The National Cohort is expected to provide strong impulses for future health services and HCU research in this respect.

Individual linkage of data also enables the cross-validation of self-reported health-care utilization, particularly in the outpatient sector. No reliable analyses are currently available on the validity of members' self-reported frequency of outpatient physician contacts within a time period of 3 or 12 months (see Swart and Griehl in this volume). These reports can now be compared to health insurance data. Similarly, primary data can be used to estimate the extent to which the introduction of case-based flat rates has led to an underestimated frequency of individual physician contacts in SHI data. Current and future studies will provide important methodological insights in this regard.

The same consideration applies to reported pharmaceutical use. Cross-validation of primary and secondary data can assess the accuracy of self-reported information on prescription-only medications and on the intensity of use of nonprescription medications and hence on the estimate of "utilization bias" [92]. For outpatient physician contacts and prescriptions or drug intake, neither of the two data sources can be considered the gold standard. The situation differs for inpatient stays, where SHI routine data can be assumed to provide complete and accurate documentation (except for inpatient rehabilitation, which is frequently financed through the statutory pension insurance).

References

1. Swart E, Deh U, Robra B-P. Die Nutzung der GKV-Daten für die kleinräumige Analyse und Steuerung der stationären Versorgung. Bundesgesundheitsblatt. 2008; 51:1183–1192.
2. von Ferber L (ed.). Häufigkeit und Verteilung von Erkrankungen und ihre ärztliche Behandlung. Leipzig: ISAB-Verlag; 1994.
3. Robra B-P, Böhlert I, Dembski U, Jakobs P, Leber W-D, Schneider F, Swart E. Krankenhausfallanalyse—Die stationäre Versorgung von Versicherten der AOK Magdeburg. St. Augustin: Asgard-Verlag; 1996.
4. Swart E, Robra B-P. Struktur- und Prozessanalyse des stationären Sektors anhand von GKV-Daten. Frankfurt/M: pmi-Verlagsgruppe; 1998.
5. von Ferber L, Behrens J (eds.). Public Health Forschung mit Gesundheits- und Sozialdaten. Stand und Perspektiven. St. Augustin: Asgard Verlag; 1997.
6. Bormann C, Heller G. Bedarf und Verfügbarkeit von Daten für eine nutzerorientierte Versorgungsforschung in Deutschland. In: Janßen C, Borgetto B, Heller G, editors. Medizinsoziologische Beiträge zur Versorgungsforschung: Theoretische Ansätze, Methoden und Instrumente sowie ausgewählte Ergebnisse. Weinheim: Juventa, 2007. p. 85–92.
7. Swart E, Heller G. Nutzung und Bedeutung von GKV-Routinedaten. In: Janßen C, Borgetto B, Heller G, editors. Medizinsoziologische Beiträge zur Versorgungsforschung: Theoretische Ansätze, Methoden und Instrumente sowie ausgewählte Ergebnisse. Weinheim: Juventa, 2007. p. 93–112.
8. Kurth B-M, editor. Monitoring der gesundheitlichen Versorgung in Deutschland. Köln: Deutscher Ärzteverlag; 2008.
9. Busse R. Konzeptionelle Übersicht über Methoden und Datenquellen in der Versorgungsforschung. Vortrag auf dem 4. Kongress für Versorgungsforschung. Berlin; 23.09.2005. http://mig.tu-berlin.de. Accessed 10 May 2012.
10. Pfaff H, von Pritzbuer E, Kramer M, Driller E. Sozialdatenanalyse als Instrument der Versorgungsforschung. In Swart E, Ihle P, editors. Routinedaten im Gesundheitswesen. Handbuch Sekundärdatenanalyse: Grundlagen, Methoden und Perspektiven. Bern: Huber Verlag, 2005. p. 331–340.
11. Grobe TG, Ihle P. Versichertenstammdaten und sektorübergreifende Analyse. In: Swart E, Ihle P, editors. Routinedaten im Gesundheitswesen. Handbuch Sekundärdatenanalyse: Grundlagen, Methoden und Perspektiven. Bern: Huber Verlag; 2005. p. 17–34.

12. Swart E. Kleinräumige Versorgungsforschung mit GKV-Routinedaten. In: Swart E, Ihle P, editors. Routinedaten im Gesundheitswesen. Handbuch Sekundärdatenanalyse: Grundlagen, Methoden und Perspektiven. Bern: Huber Verlag; 2005. p. 243–252.
13. Hoffmann F, Andersohn F, Giersiepen K, Scharnetzky E, Garbe E. Validierung von Sekundäraten. Grenzen und Möglichkeiten. Bundesgesundheitsblatt. 2008; 51:1118–1126.
14. Schubert I, Ihle P, Köster I. Interne Validierung von Diagnosen in GKV-Routinedaten: Konzeption mit Beispielen und Falldefinition. Das Gesundheitswesen. 2010; 72: 316–322.
15. Gothe H. Pharmakoepidemiologie. Nutzung der Arzneimittelverordnungsdaten. Bundesgesundheitsblatt. 2008; 51:1145–1154.
16. Bödeker W. Gesundheitsberichterstattung und Gesundheitsforschung mit Arbeitsunfähigkeitsdaten der Krankenkassen. In Swart E, Ihle P, editors. Routinedaten im Gesundheitswesen. Handbuch Sekundärdatenanalyse: Grundlagen, Methoden und Perspektiven. Bern: Huber Verlag; 2005. p. 57–78.
17. Swart E, Arbeitsgruppe Erhebung und Nutzung von Sekundärdaten und Arbeitsgruppe Epidemiologische Methoden. GPS—Gute Praxis Sekundärdatenanalyse: Revision nach grundlegender Überarbeitung. Das Gesundheitswesen. 2008; 70: 54–60.
18. Hoffmann W, Latza U, Terschüren C. Leitlinien und Empfehlungen zur Sicherung Guter Epidemiologischer Praxis (GEP)—überarbeitete Fassung nach Revision. Das Gesundheitswesen. 2005; 65: 217–225.
19. Ihle P. Datenschutzrechtliche Aspekte bei der Erhebung von GKV-Routinedaten. In: Swart E, Ihle P, editors. Routinedaten im Gesundheitswesen. Handbuch Sekundärdatenanalyse: Grundlagen, Methoden und Perspektiven. Bern: Huber Verlag; 2005. p. 195–201.
20. Ihle P. Datenschutzrechtliche und methodische Aspekte beim Aufbau einer Routinedatenbasis aus der Gesetzlichen Krankenversicherung zu Forschungszwecken. Bundesgesundheitsblatt. 2008; 51:1127–1134.
21. March S, Rauch A, Thomas D, Bender S, Swart E. Datenschutzrechtliche Vorgehensweise bei der Verknüpfung von Primär- und Sekundärdaten in einer Kohortenstudie: die lidA-Studie. Das Gesundheitswesen. 2012; 74: e122-e129.
22. Glaeske G, Augustin M, Abholz H, Banik N, Brüggenjürgen B, Hasford J, Hoffmann W, Kruse J, Lange S, Schäfer T, Schubert I, Trampisch H-J, Windeler J. Epidemiologische Methoden für die Versorgungsforschung. Das Gesundheitswesen. 2009; 71: 685–693.
23. Pfaff H, Glaeske G, Neugebauer EAM, Schrappe M, Memorandum III: Methoden für die Versorgungsforschung (Teil I). Das Gesundheitswesen. 2009; 71: 505–510.
24. Schubert I, Köster I, Küpper-Nybelen J, Ihle P. Versorgungsforschung mit Routinedaten. Nutzungsmöglichkeiten versichertenbezogener Krankenkassendaten für Fragestellungen der Versorgungsforschung. Bundesgesundheitsblatt. 2008; 51: 1095–1105.
25. Hoffmann F. Review on use of German health insurance medication claims data for epidemiological researchy. Pharmacoepidemiology and Drug Safety. 2009; 18: 349–356.
26. Ihle P, Köster I, Herholz H, Rambow-Bertram P, Schardt T, Schubert I. Versichertenstichprobe AOK Hessen/KV Hessen—Konzeption und Umsetzung einer personenbezogenen Datenbasis aus der Gesetzlichen Krankenversicherung. Das Gesundheitswesen. 2005; 67: 638–645
27. Swart E, Ihle P, editors. Routinedaten im Gesundheitswesen. Handbuch Sekundärdatenanalyse: Grundlagen, Methoden und Perspektiven. Bern: Huber Verlag, 2005.
28. Grobe TG. Arbeiten mit Daten der Gmünder Ersatzkasse. Ein exemplarischer Überblick. Bundesgesundheitsblatt. 2008; 51:1106–1117.
29. Günster C, Klose J, Schmacke N, editors. Versorgungs-Report 2012. Schwerpunkt: Gesundheit im Alter. Stuttgart: Schattauer Verlag, 2012.
30. Nink K., Schröder H., Schubert I. Arzneimittel. In: Swart E, Ihle P, editors. Routinedaten im Gesundheitswesen. Handbuch Sekundärdatenanalyse: Grundlagen, Methoden und Perspektiven. Bern: Huber Verlag, 2005; S- 99–122.
31. Schwabe U, Paffrath D, editors. Arzneiverordnungs-Report 2012. Berlin und Heidelberg: Springer-Verlag, 2012.
32. Glaeske G, Schicktanz C. BARMER GEK Arzneimittelreport 2011. St. Augustin: Asgard-Verlag, 2011.
33. BKK-Bundesverband, editor. BKK-Gesundheitsreport 2011. Essen; 2012.

34. Gerdes S, Marschall J, Nolting H-N. Gesundheitsreport 2012. Heidelberg: medhochzwei.
35. Grobe TG, Dörning H, Mieth I., Held R, Reuther U, Schoppmeyer U. Gesundheitsreport 2011 Sachsen-Anhalt. Wuppertal: BARMER GEK; 2011.
36. Badura B, Ducki A, Schröder H, Klose J, Macco K. Fehlzeitenreport 2011. Heidelberg, Berlin. Springer Verlag; 2011.
37. Zoike E, Bödeker W. Berufliche Tätigkeit und Arbeitsunfähigkeit. Bundesgesundheitsblatt 2008; 51: 1155–1163.
38. Bitzer EM, Grobe TG, Neusser S, Mieth I, Schwartz FW. BARMER GEK Report Krankenhaus 2011. St. Augustin: Asgard-Verlag; 2011.
39. Grobe TG, Dörning H, Schwartz FW. GEK-Gesundheitsreport 2004. Auswertung der GEK-Gesundheitsberichterstattung. Schwerpunkt: Gesundheitsstörungen durch Alkohol. St. Augustin: Asgard-Verlag; 2004.
40. Kerek-Bodden H, Heuer J, Brenner G, Koch H, Lang A. Morbiditäts- und Inanspruchnahmeanalysen mit personenbezogenen Abrechnungsdaten aus Arztpraxen. In: Swart E., Ihle P.(eds.) Routinedaten im Gesundheitswesen. Handbuch Sekundärdatenanalyse: Grundlagen, Methoden und Perspektiven. Bern: Huber Verlag, 2005. p. 35–55.
41. Grobe TG, Dörning H, Schwartz FW. BARMER GEK Arztreport 2012. St. Augustin: Asgard-Verlag, 2012.
42. Schröder H, Schwinger A, Waltersbacher A Heilmittel. In: Swart E, Ihle P, editors. Routinedaten im Gesundheitswesen. Handbuch Sekundärdatenanalyse: Grundlagen, Methoden und Perspektiven. Bern: Huber Verlag, 2005. p. 123–135.
43. Waltersbacher A. Heilmittelbericht 2012. Berlin: Wissenschaftliches Institut der AOK; 2012. www.wido.de. Accessed 24 May 2013
44. Kemper S, Sauer K, Glaeske G. BARMER GEK Heil- und Hilfsmittelreport 2011. St. Augustin; Asgard Verlag; 2011.
45. Hauner H, Köster I, von Ferber L. Prävalenz des Diabetes mellitus in Deutschland. Dt. Med. Wschr. 2003; 128: 2632–2638.
46. Hauner H, Köster I, Schubert. Trends in der Prävalenz und ambulanten Versorgung von Menschen mit Diabetes mellitus. Dtsch Arztebl. 2007; 104: A 2799–2805.
47. Köster I, Schubert I, Huppertz E. Fortschreibung der KoDiM-Studie: Kosten des Diabetes mellitus 2000–2009. Dt. Med. Wschr. 2012; 137: 1013–1016.
48. Heller G. Zur Messung und Darstellung von medizinischer Ergebnisqualität mit administrativen Routinedaten in Deutschland. Bundesgesundheitsblatt. 2008; 51:1173–1182.
49. Abbas S, Ihle P, Köster I, Schubert I. Prevalence and incidence of diagnosed endometriosis and risk of endometriosis in patients with endometriosis-related symptoms: findings from a statutory health insurance-based cohort in Germany. Eur J Obstet Gynecol Reprod Biol. 2012; 160: 79–83.
50. Müller-Schwefe G, Freytag A, Höer A, Schiffhorst G, Becker A, Casser H-R, Glaeske G, Thoma R, Treede R-D. healthcare utilization of back pain patients. Results of a claims data analysis. J Med Economics. 2011; 14: 816–823.
51. Schiffhorst G, Freytag A, Höer A, Häussler B, Gothe H. Schmerztypische Diagnosemuster in Routinedaten—Identifikation mittels Classification and Regression Trees (CART). Das Gesundheitswesen. 2010; 72: 347–355.
52. Holt S, Schmiedl S, Thürmann PA. Potenziell inadäquate Medikation für ältere Menschen: Die PRISCUS-Liste. Deutsches Ärzteblatt. 2010; 107: 543–551.
53. Schubert I, Hein R, Abbas S, Thürmann P. Verordnungshäufigkeiten von nichtretardiertem Nifedipin bei älteren Menschen. Deutsches Ärzteblatt. 2012; 109: 215–219.
54. Küpper-Nybelen J, Hellmich M, Abbas S, Ihle P, Griebenow R, Schubert I. Association of long-term adherence to evidence-based combination therapy after acute myocardial infarction with all-cause mortality. A prospective cohort study based on claims data. European Journal of Clinical Pharmacology. 2012; 68: 1451–1460.
55. Geyer S. Sozialstruktur und Krankheit. Analysen mit Daten der Gesetzlichen Krankenversicherung. Bundesgesundheitsbl 2008; 51: 1164–1172.

56. Grobe TG, Dörning H, Schwartz FW. GEK-Gesundheitsreport 1999. Auswertung der GEK-Gesundheitsberichterstattung. Schwerpunkt: Arbeitslosigkeit und Gesundheit. St. Augustin: Asgard-Verlag; 1999.
57. Stock C, Ihle P, Schubert I, Brenner H. Colonoscopy and fecal occult blood test use in Germany: results from a large insurance-based cohort. Endoscopy. 2011; 771–781.
58. Swart E. Über-, Unter- und Fehlversorgung in der stationären Versorgung—Welche Rückschlüsse lassen sich aus GKV-Routinedaten ziehen? In: Swart E, Ihle P, editors. Routinedaten im Gesundheitswesen. Handbuch Sekundärdatenanalyse: Grundlagen, Methoden und Perspektiven. Bern: Huber Verlag; 2005. p. 253–262.
59. Iezzoni LI. Assessing quality using administrative data. Annals Internal Medicine. 1997; 127: 666–674.
60. Romano PS, Zach A, Luft HS, Rainwater J, Remy LL, Campa D. The California hospital outcomes project: using administrative data to compare hospital performance. Joint Commission J Quality Improvement. 1995; 21: 668–682.
61. Weingart SN, Iezzoni LI, Davis RB, Palmer RH, Chalane M, Hamel MB, Kukamal K, Phillips RS, Davies DT, Banks NJ Use of administrative data to find substandard care. Med Care. 2000; 38: 796–806.
62. Wray NP, Ashton CM, Kuykendall DH, Hollingsworth JC. Using administrative databases to evaluate the quality of medical care: a conceptual framework. Soc Sci Med. 1995; 40: 1707–1715.
63. AOK-Bundesverband, Forschungs- und Entwicklungsinstitut für das Sozial- und Gesundheitswesen Sachsen-Anhalt (FEISA), HELIOS Kliniken, Wissenschaftliches Institut der AOK (WIdO), editors. Qualitätssicherung der stationären Versorgung mit Routinedaten (QSR). Abschlussbericht. Bonn; 2007.
64. Jeschke E, Günster C. Aktueller Stand und Ausbau des QSR-Verfahrens. In: Kuhlen R, Rink O, Zacher J, editors. Jahrbuch Qualitätsmedizin 2011. Berlin: Medizinisch wissenschaftliche Verlagsgesellschaft; 2011; p. 77–87.
65. Willer C, Swart E. Was Routinedaten über Versorgungsumfang und –qualität sagen. Orthopädie und Unfallchirurgie. Mitteilungen, Februar 2012. p. 21–24.
66. Anderson TF, Mooney G, editors. The challenge of medical practice variations. London: Macmillan Press; 1990.
67. Wennberg JE. Dealing with medical practice variations: a proposal for action. Health Affairs. 1984; 3: 6–32.
68. Wennberg JE. Tracking Medicine.New York: Oxford University Press; 2010.
69. Wennberg JE, Gittelsohn A. Small Area Variation in Health Care Delivery. Science. 1973; 182: 1102–1108.
70. Bundesministerium für Gesundheit, editor. Operationshäufigkeiten in Deutschland. Baden-Baden: Nomos-Verlagsgesellschaft; 2000.
71. Hammill BG, Curtis LH, Setoguchi S. Performance of propensity score methods when comparison groups originate from different data sources. Pharmacoepidemiology and drug safety 2012; 21 (S2): 81–89.
72. Linder R, Ahrens S, Köppel D, Heilmann T, Verheyen F. Nutzen und Effizient des Disease Management-Programms Diabetes mellitus Typ 2. Deutsches Ärzteblatt. 2011; 108: 155–162.
73. Siegel A, Stößel U, Schubert I, Erler A. Probleme der Evaluation einer regionalen integrierten Vollversorgung am Beispiel„Gesundes Kinzigtal'. Z. Evid. Fortbild. Qual. Gesundh. Wesen. 2011; 105: 590–596.
74. Wennberg JE, Roos N, Sola L, Schori A. Jaffe R Use of claims data systems to evaluate health care outcomes. JAMA. 1987; 257: 933–936.
75. Erler A, Beyer M, Muth C, Gerlach FM, Brennecke R. Garbage in—Garbage out? Validität von Abrechnungsdiagnosen in hausärztlichen Praxen. Das Gesundheitswesen. 2009; 71: 823–831.
76. Giersiepen K, Pohlabeln H, Egidi G, Pigeot I. Die ICD-Kodierqualität für Diagnosen in der ambulanten Versorgung. Bundesgesundheitsblatt. 50: 1028–1038.

77. Hoffmann W, Bobrowski C, Fendrich K. Sekundärdatenanalyse in der Versorgungsepidemiologie. Bundesgesundheitsblatt. 2008; 51: 1193–1201.
78. Abbas S, Ihle P, Köster I, Schubert I. Estimation of Disease Incidence in Claims Data Dependent on the Length of Follow-Up: A Methodological Approach. Health Services Research. 2012; 47: 746–755.
79. Schubert I, Köster I. Diabetes mellitus: Versorgungsmonitoring auf der Basis von Routinedaten. In: Günster C, Klose J, Schmacke N, editors. Versorgungsreport 2011. Schwerpunkt: Chronische Erkrankungen. Schattauer Verlag, Stuttgart: 2011. p. 129–145.
80. Hoffmann F, Icks A. Unterschiede in der Versichertenstruktur von Krankenkassen und deren Auswirkungen für die Versorgungsforschung: Ergebnisse des Bertelsmann-Gesundheitsmonitors. Das Gesundheitswesen. 2012; 74: 291–297.
81. Mansky T, Robra B-P, Schubert I. Bessere Datenauswertung ermöglichen. Deutsches Ärzteblatt. 2012; 109: 1082–1085.
82. Kersting M, Gierschmann A, Hauswaldt J, Pradier E-H. Routinedaten aus hausärztlichen Arztinformationssystemen—Export, Analyse und Aufbereitung für die Versorgungsforschung. Das Gesundheitswesen. 2010; 72: 323–331.
83. Niehaus F. Alter und steigende Lebenserwartung. Köln: Wissenschaftliches Institut der PKV; 2011.
84. Wild F. Arzneimittelversorgung 2009. Köln: Wissenschaftliches Institut der PKV; 2011.
85. Andersen RM. Revisiting the behavioral model and access to medical care: does it matter? J Health Social Behavior. 1995; 36: 1–10.
86. Andersen RM, Davidson PL. Improving access to care in America: individual and contextual indicators. In: Andersen RM, Rice TH, Kominski GF, editors. Changing the U.S. health care system: key issues in health services, policy, and management. 3rd edition. San Francisco, CA: Jossey-Bass; 2007. p. 3–31.
87. Geyer S. Die Bestimmung der sozioökonomischen Position in Prozessdaten und ihre Verwendung in Sekundärdatenanalysen. In: Swart E, Ihle P, editors. Routinedaten im Gesundheitswesen. Handbuch Sekundärdatenanalyse: Grundlagen, Methoden und Perspektiven. Bern: Huber Verlag; 2005. p. 203–213.
88. Damm K, Lange A, Zeidler J, Braun S, Graf von der Schulenburg JM. Einführung des neuen Tätigkeitsschlüssels und seine Anwendung in GKV-Routinedatenauswertungen. Möglichkeiten und Limitationen. Bundesgesundheitsblatt. 2012; 55: 238–244.
89. John J., Krauth C. Verknüpfung von Primärdaten mit Daten der Gesetzlichen Krankenversicherung in gesundheitsökonomischen Studien: Erfahrungen aus zwei KORA-Studien. In: Swart E, Ihle P, editors. Routinedaten im Gesundheitswesen. Handbuch Sekundärdatenanalyse: Grundlagen, Methoden und Perspektiven. Bern: Huber Verlag, 2005. p. 215–234.
90. Swart E, March S, Thomas D, Salomon T, von dem Knesebeck O. Erfahrungen mit der Datenverknüpfung von Primär- und Sekundärdaten in einer Interventionsstudie. Das Gesundheitswesen. 2011; 73: e126-e132.
91. Wichmann H-E, Kaaks R, Hoffmann W, Jöckel K-H, Greiser KH, Linseisen J. Die Nationale Kohorte. Bundesgesundheitsblatt. 2012; 55: 781–789.
92. Jacobi F. Der Hype um die kranke Seele. Gesundheit und Gesellschaft. 2012, 12 (5). p. 23–27.

Chapter 6
Health Care Utilization: Insights from Qualitative Research

Birgit Babitsch, Claudia Berger, Bernhard Borgetto and Carmen-Cristina Ciupitu-Plath

Health care utilization can be regarded as a complex process influenced by the individual's health status, individual and collective norms and value, the structure of the health care and social welfare system as well as by general societal conditions. It is well known that not only need factors impact the use of health care and medical services. Other aspects, such as enabling and predisposing factors, as defined in Andersen's Behavioral Model of health care Use (Anderson & Davidson 2001), are highly relevant and constitute facilitating or hindering determinants of health care utilization (see Chap. 2 by von Lengerke et al.).

From the (medical) sociological point of view, utilization of professional care is the last step of help seeking. Prior to this, other forms of help seeking mainly in the so-called lay system are used. Furthermore, one's own and other significant persons' health concepts and experiences with the health care system, as well as the perceived urgency of a health problem play a crucial role and contribute to a timely or delayed utilization of health care services.

To date, plenty of empirical studies are available to describe health care utilization in general, as well as for specific diseases or settings, most of whom use quantitative research methods. Furthermore, a substantial evidence base illustrates

B. Babitsch (✉) · C. Berger
Department of New Public Health, School of Human Sciences,
University of Osnabrück, Osnabrück, Germany
e-mail: bbabitsch@uni-osnabrueck.de

C. Berger
e-mail: cberger@uni-osnabrueck.de

B. Borgetto
Faculty of Social Work and Health, HAWK—University of Applied Sciences and Arts,
Faculty of Social Work and Health, Hildesheim, Germany
e-mail: borgetto@hawk-hhg.de

C.-C. Ciupitu-Plath
Berlin School of Public Health, Charité—Universitätsmedizin Berlin,
Berlin, Germany
e-mail: cristina.ciupitu-plath@charite.de

C. Janssen et al. (eds.), *Health Care Utilization in Germany*,
DOI 10.1007/978-1-4614-9191-0_6, © Springer Science+Business Media New York 2014

how health care utilization is influenced by different factors (see Chap. 2 by von Lengerke et al., and other chapters of the book), for which in some cases theoretical models were used as explanatory background. However, the processes of health care utilization are not fully explored so far and there is still a need for in-depth analyses. For this purpose, qualitative approaches provide an excellent opportunity to elaborate on mechanisms of health care utilization and to develop new or rather to develop existing theoretical frameworks.

Qualitative Research in Health Care Services Research

Research in health and health care services is still dominated by quantitative approaches. However, the acceptance of qualitative research has grown immensely over the past years, a fact which can be observed not only in the growing number of relevant publications but also in the existence of specialized journals.

After having overcome the big dispute between the quantitative and qualitative research paradigms, the advantages and disadvantages of the respective methodologies have been brought to the foreground (see, for example, Morse 2011). Nowadays, there is consensus that in health and health care research both approaches are needed and the combination of quantitative and qualitative elements in mixed-method approaches is seen as most appropriate to enhance the understanding in these research fields. In addition, many recent qualitative research publications focus on methodological issues such as the improvement of interview techniques, the establishment of quality criteria, as well as the development of methods for the synthesis of qualitative research, with the aim of improving qualitative research in general, and in health and health care in particular (Hasseler 2007; Kroll et al. 2007; Barnett-Page & Thomas 2009; Kelly 2010; Devers 2011; Merry et al. 2011; Morse 2011; Reynolds et al. 2011)

Using the same approach as applied in the study of Hoff and Witt (2000, cit. in Weiner et al. 2011), Weiner et al. (2011) authored an interesting review focusing on qualitative research in health services and management research over a 10-year period. In total, they selected nine health services and management journals published between 1998 and 2008 and analyzed the quantity, characteristics, and quality of qualitative research studies. The so-called methodological articles were excluded and only research articles were included in the final analysis. For all selected articles a content analysis was performed, retrieving the following information: "(a) the purpose of the article; (b) the data collection method; (c) the study design; (d) the level of methodological detail in the article; (e) the funding source for the research, if any; and (f) the number of pages" (Weiner et al. 2011: 8). In total, 8,377 articles were identified and a final sample of 329 articles fulfilling all inclusion criteria was used for analysis. On average, 9 % of all articles in these nine journals applied qualitative research methods. Compared to the strong increase in quantitative research, the number of qualitative studies remained more or less stable, ranging from 5 to 11 %. However, huge differences could be observed between journals: The highest

Table 6.1 Characteristics of the qualitative research articles (Weiner et al. 2011: 15)

	Current study 1998–2008		Changes from 1995–1997 to present
	Number	Percentage	
Main study purpose			
Description	122	37	+3
Process	89	27	+6
Views/perspectives	60	18	−7
Evaluation	14	4	−2
Cause and effect	44	13	
Study design			
Single case study	36	11	#-#
Multiple case study	193	59	#-#
Ethnography	3	1	#-#
Grounded theory	4	1	#-#
Phenomenological study	1	0	#-#
Biographs	0	0	#-#
General	92	28	#-#
Data collection			
Interviews	155	47	−9
Archival	106	32	−8
Focus group	29	9	−2
Observation	37	11	+5
Mixed methods	70	21	+9
Not specified	2	1	−20

#-# data not available

proportion of qualitative publications was reported for the journal *Health Affair* and the lowest for *Medical Care Research and Review*.

The characteristics of the qualitative research articles are shown in Table 6.1 (Weiner et al. 2011: 15).

The findings show that qualitative research has often been used for description (37 %) and process analysis (27 %). Both areas have increased compared to the former study conducted for the time between 1995 and 1997. More than half of the studies were multi-case studies, whereas ethnography or grounded theory, as well as other qualitative methodological approaches were very rarely used. Data were most often collected via interviews (47 %) and archive searches (32 %); however, both approaches have decreased compared to 1995–1997. In contrast, an increase can be observed regarding the use of observation techniques and mixed-method approaches, which amounted to 11 and 21 %, respectively.

Likewise, the topics addressed in these articles were broad and can be categorized into approximately 600 medical subject heading (MeSH) terms. The six most frequent topics were health services accessibility ($N=28$), Medicaid ($N=26$), efficiency, organizational ($N=25$), organizational innovation ($N=24$), delivery of health care, integrated ($N=23$), and health policy legislation, trends, and economics ($N=22$).

Interestingly, although the number of studies has not increased in the observation period, the citation analysis showed that qualitative research was very well received in the scientific community. The average citation number for the selected qualitative articles was 8.6 (range 0–89) (Weiner et al. 2011). The authors conclude that even if "the publication rate of qualitative articles has not kept pace with that of quantitative research articles, citation analysis suggests that qualitative research articles contribute comparably to the field's knowledge base" (Weiner et al. 2011: 3).

Qualitative Research in Health Care Utilization: Findings of a Systematic Literature Review

The contribution of qualitative studies to health care utilization research was explored by conducting a systematic literature analysis. The literature search was performed in July 2012 (last search on July 3rd 2012), with the aim of identifying all articles using qualitative research methods to investigate health care utilization published between 1998 and 2012 in the German and international context. PubMed was used as the research database. The following search terms were applied:

Concept	Search terms
Qualitative research	Qualitative research [Majr]
	Interviews as topic [Majr]
	Observation [Majr]
	Ethnology [Majr]
	Qualitative [tiab]
	Transcriped [All fields]
Utilization	Health care quality, access, and evaluation [Majr]
	Health services research [Mesh]
	utilization [Subheading]

Limits were set with regard to language (only German or English) and relevant age (only adults). No limitation was set in terms of the qualitative research methods used. The following inclusion and exclusion criteria were applied:

Inclusion criteria:

- Focus on utilization of health care services from patients'/users' point of view
- Use of any qualitative research methods,
- Publication between 1998 and 2012, and
- Focus on adults

Exclusion criteria:

- Methodological articles on qualitative research;
- Focus on specific health problems or areas, specific study population, or specific health care sectors
- Focus on non-Western countries

Eligible articles were selected in three steps: firstly, based on the title, secondly, based on abstracts, and thirdly, based on the full-text publication. In all steps, two researchers (BB and CB) independently screened the publication and included/excluded articles according to a catalogue of a priori set criteria. In cases of disagreement, the selection was discussed and finally a concerted decision was met.

The search yielded 675 articles which were initially screened by title (see Fig. 6.1). In total, 80 articles were regarded as appropriate and these were screened by abstract. Twelve potentially relevant studies were then selected for further review. Finally, two studies were selected after reading the full text. These articles made up the database for the results section.

Description of the Selected Studies

The selected studies were published in 2004 (Cortes et al. 2004) and in 2010 (Berkelmans et al. 2010) (see Table 6.2). The countries covered were the United States of America (Cortes et al. 2004) and the Netherlands (Berkelmans et al. 2010). Both publications were based on a small study sample and applied two different qualitative methodological approaches: focus group (Cortes et al. 2004) and semi-structured interviews (Berkelmans et al. 2010). Cortes et al.'s study sample included asthma patients as well as home-care attendants and health care professionals (physicians and nurse practitioners); participants in Berkelmans et al. (2010)'s research were senior citizens aged 65–91 years. Both studies focus on the use of outpatient health care services.

Main Findings

One of the research aims in the study of Cortes et al. (2004) was to identify cultural barriers to asthma care. The findings of this study were meant to be used in adapting educational and self-management programmes to the specific needs of older minorities. For this purpose, three different focus groups were conducted, including older asthmatic residents ($N=5$), non-licensed caretakers of older asthmatics ($N=7$), and health care professionals ($N=10$), respectively. The first two groups were recruited from two East Harlem community centres and the last group from Mount Sinai Hospital, which belongs to the East Harlem district.

All focus groups participants were asked to report if they encountered difficulties in accessing asthma care and if so, what kind of barriers/problems they faced. The older asthmatics did not mention experiencing any problems with regard to health care access, but rather with the health care utilization itself such as "not enough time to spend with physician," "hurried appointments," and "lack of information" (Cortes et al. 2004: 210). Only two problems/barriers were reported by the home-care attendants: "financial problems, paying for medications" and being "unable to get primary-care provider, need to use the emergency departments" (Cortes

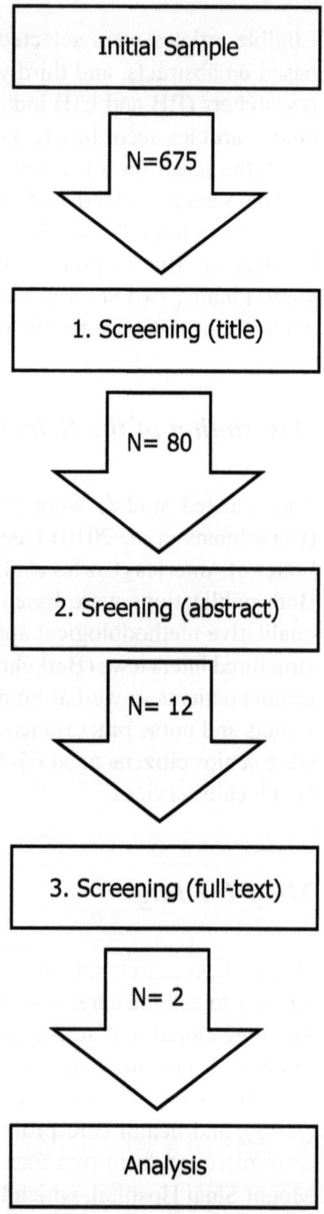

Fig. 6.1 Selection of articles

et al. 2004: 210). On the other hand, a long list of problems concerning access to and quality of health care was suggested by the health care professionals. Most of the aspects mentioned were related to quality of health care. The few reports dealing with inappropriate access referred to "lack of transportation" and in part "low literacy" (Cortes et al. 2004: 210).

Table 6.2 Study description

No.	Author	Title	PY	Country	Sample size	Gender	Age of participants	Population	Setting
1	Berkelmans et al.	Characteristics of general practice care: what do senior citizens value? A qualitative study.	2010	The Netherlands	13	Both	65–91 years and older	General population	GP services
2	Cortes et al.	Using focus groups to identify asthma care and education issues for elderly urban-dwelling minority individuals	2004	United States of America	22	Both	Adult	Asthma patients, home care attendants, health professionals	Asthma care

Berkelmans et al. (2010: 2) interviewed senior citizens to find out their preferences regarding nonmedical services and characteristics of general practitioner (GP) care. Semi-structured interviews were conducted from November 2008 to October 2009 with seven women and six men aged from 65 to 91 years. The participants were selected in four GP practices located in Limburg, Amsterdam, Groningen, and Roden. Nonmedical characteristics and service attributes were defined as follows: "continuity of care giver; distance to the practice; accessibility; expertise and trust; attitude; information; pro-active initiatives; free choice of selecting a caregiver; waiting times" (Berkelmans et al. 2010: 2). All interviewees stated that GP care has to be easy to access. The distance to the practice can emerge as a barrier to access health care services with older age. Accessibility by phone as well as the opportunity to see the GP on the same or the next day when needed were regarded as highly important by the interviewees, especially when the latter had made experiences of not managing to get an appointment with the GP when they were in real need (e.g. out-of-office hours). A free choice of GP was highly appreciated by all interviewees.

Conclusion

The two selected studies give only limited insight into processes of health care utilization as detailed by Andersen's Behavioral Model of health care Use (Andersen & Davidson 2001). The publications are not representative of either health care utilization research or qualitative research methodology. They basically illustrate the kind of findings which can be retrieved from qualitative approaches. Two topics emerged from the selected studies: (1) access and (2) users' preferences. health care utilization is clearly linked with the overall and subgroup-specific access to health care. Even in a system providing full coverage of health care services, subpopulations could face access problems. As shown in the study conducted by Berkelmans et al. (2010), distance can emerge as a barrier to health care in relation to age when GP services are not located in the neighbourhood.

The German Context: Qualitative Methods in Health Services Research

As reported for the international context, an increase of qualitative studies can also be observed in Germany. The fields covered by qualitative research are as broad as described in the review published by Weiner et al. (2011) and an emphasis on interview-based as well as focus group studies can be observed. The importance of qualitative studies in health services research is moreover supported by a recent governmental funding initiative whereby out of two different calls for proposals one area of funding was for qualitative research. Parallel to this development, a working group on qualitative methods was established as a part of the German Network for Health Services Research (see Karbach et al. 2012; Meyer et al. 2012). One result of their activities was the analysis of abstracts submitted to the 8th German Conference on Health Services Research, with a particular focus on abstracts describing qualitative or mixed-methods studies (Karbach et al. 2012). Similar to the review by Weiner et al. (2011), quantitative and qualitative aspects such as study aim and research design were analysed. The authors could identify 74 abstracts of which 47 abstracts used a qualitative approach, mainly representing qualitative research projects. This amounts to 18 % of all abstracts. The most frequent research goals were: needs assessment (41 %), instrument development (36 %), evaluation (22 %), and rarely theorizing (1 %) (Karbach et al. 2012). Interviews (N=45) and focus groups (N=29) were the most frequently applied qualitative research methods. In 46 abstracts the study participants were physicians; 35 abstracts showed data from patients.

In general, the number of studies on health care utilization in Germany is low (see also Babitsch et al. 2012). The few studies which put the main focus on the analysis of health care utilization apply mostly quantitative research methods and use representative survey data. There are only few qualitative health care utilization studies published in peer-reviewed journals; more often, qualitative approaches were used in dissertations.

In a qualitative study, Neumann et al. (2010) explored the presence of barriers in using psycho-oncology services (POS) available at a psycho-oncology institution (POI) in Germany. The authors used focus groups (N=7 with a total of 27 participants) and individual interviews (N=5) and recruited POS users and nonusers, relatives of POS users, and professionals (physicians and nurses) from an affiliated hospital. The study was conducted from May to October 2005. Barriers to POS could be identified and were summarized as follows: (1) information deficits about POI and POS, (2) subjective norms regarding POS, (3) lack of organizational and therapeutic integration, and (4) specific characteristics of cancer patients (Neumann et al. 2010). In regard to the third barrier, the authors found that POS was regarded as not "normal", for which two explanations were offered: (1) there is no regular screening for psychosocial problems (except in case of a crisis) and (2) patients do not perceive POS as a normal service. The lack of information in patients and professionals—another identified barrier—certainly contributes to this finding. Based on these results, the authors developed a model on how the above-mentioned barriers impact POS utilization and derived strategies to overcome them. One simple strategy they proposed was to improve the distribution of information to patients, relatives, and professionals.

To identify ethnic differences in the use of family practitioners in Germany was the research goal in the qualitative study conducted by Bungartz et al. (2001). The authors recruited focus groups participants older than 39 years with a German (N = 11) and Turkish background (N = 17). Two focus groups were conducted with the German natives and three with Turkish immigrants. The study was conducted in the south of Germany and data were collected from April to August 2009. The main aspects asked were amongst others frequency of family practitioners visits, distance to family practitioners, sex, and ethnicity (only asked in focus groups with Turkish immigrants) of family practitioners, and reasons for utilization. The study findings were collapsed into three main categories: "use of family practitioner," "factors for family practitioner's choice," and "interaction between doctor and patient" (Bungartz et al. 2011: 518). Need factors, such as current or long-lasting health problems, were mentioned by all participants as the main reason to utilize the services of their family practitioners, especially when the problem or the request required a personal contact. Many factors influence the choice of family practitioners such as distance, practitioners' age, sex, and ethnicity (only asked from Turkish immigrants), as well as the range of services offered. Interestingly, this qualitative study revealed only minor ethnic differences in health care utilization, which could be largely explained by the high command of German in the study sample.

The influence of patients' subjective concepts on primary health care utilization in Germany and Norway is currently being investigated by Herrmann et al. (2012a). The research project started in 2012 and will be running until 2015 (Herrmann et al. 2012b). The main hypothesis of the project is that "patients" subjective concepts about primary health care utilization play a major role in explaining different health care utilization behavior in different countries" (Herrmann et al. 2012b; website: https://wikis.ovgu.de/spihv/doku.php). Qualitative episodic interviews with 20 patients in Germany and Norway as well as participant observation in each of the four selected German and Norwegian primary-care practices will be conducted.

Conclusion

Qualitative research methodology and its variety of research approaches offer important tools in understanding health care utilization and the underlying processes and attitudes from the patients' and providers' point of view. The results of the review published by Weiner et al. (2011) show that, from a quantitative and—even more so—from a qualitative point of view, qualitative research plays an important role for our understanding of phenomena under study in health services research in general and in health care utilization research in particular. The focus of this chapter was on general health care and therefore limited; further qualitative studies are available in the field nursing research as well as prevention (see Chap. 16).

The number of qualitative studies retrieved from the systematic PubMed literature search was initially high. After applying the inclusion and exclusion criteria, only two studies fulfilled the set requirements. However, health care utilization was only a part of the researchers' interest in these studies, with the consequence that they could only provide insight into few aspects of health care utilization. Nevertheless, they demonstrate the potential of qualitative methods in contributing to our understanding of health care utilization from a patient's and a multi-perspective point of view. Qualitative studies also allow—as a methodological precondition—that contextual aspects and the interconnectedness of factors can be identified.

Overall, qualitative approaches in health care utilization research have not been used to their full potential. Many questions—still unanswered—should be explored in qualitative studies. For instance:

- How do people utilize the health care system? What kind of prior decisions do they meet and how is this affected by sociodemographic and illness-related factors?
- What kind of relationship exists between perceived and observed access to health care and health care utilization?
- How are the factors specified in Andersen's Behavioral Model of health care use interwoven and what role do they play in one's individual decision to utilize health care services?
- How is health literacy linked with health care utilization?

To answer the questions listed above, different qualitative research approaches are appropriate and should be applied. Furthermore, using multiple perspectives including users/patients as well as relatives and professionals will allow health services researchers to get insight in inner processes which can be hardly investigated through quantitative approaches. The future of health services research in general and of health care utilization research thus lies in a clever and appropriate (with regard to the selected research question) mix of qualitative and quantitative research.

References

Andersen RM, Davidson, PL. Improving access to care in America: individual and contextual indicators. In: Andersen RM, Rice TH, Kominski, EF, editors. Changing the U.S. health care system: key issues in health services, policy, and management. San Francisco, CA: Jossey-Bass; 2001. p. 3–30.

Babitsch B, Gohl D, von Lengerke T (2012): Re-revisiting Andersen's Behavioral Model of Health Services Use: a systematic review of studies from 1998–2011. Psychosoc Med 9:Doc11. doi: 10.3205/psm000089.

Barnett-Page E, Thomas J (2009): Methods for the synthesis of qualitative research: a critical review. BMC Medical Research Methodology 9: 59.

Bungartz J, Uslu S, Natanzon I, Joos S (2001): Utilization of the Family Practitioners by Turkish and German Patients—a Qualitative Study. Z All Med 87: 515–522.

Devers KJ (2011): Qualitative methods in health services and management research: pockets of excellence and progress, but still a long way to go. Medical Care Research and Review 68: 41–48.

Hasseler, M (2007): Qualitative Methods: Systematic Reviews in Qualitative Health Care Research as a Basis for Evidence-Based Practice. Gesundheitswesen 69: 297–302.

Herrmann WJ, Haarmann A, Flick U; Bærheim A; Lichte T; Herrmann M (2012a): Patients' Subjective Concepts about Primary Health Care Utilization: a Qualitative Comparative Study Between Norway and Germany. German Congress of General Practice and Familiy Medicine (DEGAM). 21.09.2012. (Abstract).

Herrmann WJ (2012b): Project Homepage. https://wikis.ovgu.de/spihv/doku.php

Karbach U, Stamer M, Holmberg C, Güthlin C, Patzelt C, Meyer T; Arbeitsgruppe Qualitative Methoden des DNVF. (2012): Qualitative research in health services research—discussion paper, Part 2: Qualitative research in health services research in Germany—an overview. Gesundheitswesen 74:510–515

Kelly M (2010): The role of theory in qualitative health research. Family Practice 27: 285.

Kroll T, Barbour R, Harris J (2007): Using focus groups in disability research. Qualitative Health Research 17: 690–698.

Meyer T, Karbach U, Holmberg C, Güthlin C, Patzelt C, Stamer M; Arbeitsgruppe—Qualitative Methoden des DNVF (2012): Qualitative research in health services research—discussion paper, Part 1: What is the idea?. Gesundheitswesen 74: 516–525.

Merry L, Clausen C, Gagnon A, Carnevale F, Jeannotte J, Saucier JF, Oxman-Martinez J (2011): Improving qualitative interviews with newly arrived migrant women. Qualitative Health Research 21: 976–986.

Morse JM (2011): Molding qualitative health research. Qualitative Health Research 21: 1019–1021.

Neumann M, Galushko M, Karbach U, Goldblatt H, Visser A, Wirtz M, Ernstmann N, Ommen O, Pfaff H. (2010): Barriers to using psycho-oncology services: a qualitative research into the perspectives of users, their relatives, non-users, physicians, and nurses. Support Care Cancer 18:1147–1156.

Reynolds J, Kizito J, Ezumah N, Mangesho P, Allen E, Chandler C (2011): Quality assurance of qualitative research: a review of the discourse. Health Research Policy and Systems 9:43.

Weiner BJ, Amick HR, Lund JL, Lee SY, Hoff TJ (2011): Use of qualitative methods in published health services and management research: a 10-year review. Medical Care Research and Review: 68: 3–33.

Part IV
Results: Selected Determinants

Chapter 7
Gender and Utilization of Health Care

Birgit Babitsch, Cornelia Bormann, Daniela Gohl and Carmen Cristina Ciupitu-Plath

Sex/gender plays an important role when it comes to health and illness or health care utilization. It is well known that women and men differ in regard to their well-being, their morbidity and also in their longevity. In most countries of the world, the life expectancy of women exceeds the life expectancy of men. These differences depend on a country's context and are smallest in low-income countries with 1–2 years, and highest in so-called transitioning countries with 8–10 years. In Europe, the gender differences in life expectancies range from 4–7 years; in Germany, women currently reach an average of 82.5 years and men 77.5 years (gender difference = 5 years) (reference period 2008/2010; Statistisches Bundesamt 2012).

There are many reasons for this so-called gender gap. Verbrugge (1985), one of the first authors who provided a comprehensive list of explanatory factors, differentiated these as follows:

1. Biological risks, defined as sex-related intrinsic differences in women and men due to their genes or reproductive physiology.
2. Acquired risks specified as gender differences in living conditions, life styles and health behaviour.
3. Psychosocial aspects of symptoms and care defined as gender differences in the "perception of symptom severity, readiness to tale curative action, and ability to do so" (p. 165).

B. Babitsch (✉)
Department of New Public Health, School of Human Sciences,
University of Osnabrück, Osnabrück, Germany
e-mail: bbabitsch@uni-osnabrueck.de

C. Bormann
Health Sciences, FH Bielefeld—University of Applied Sciences, Bielefeld, Germany
e-mail: cbormann@uni-bremen.de

D. Gohl · C. C. Ciupitu-Plath
Berlin School of Public Health, Charité—Universitätsmedizin Berlin, Berlin, Germany
e-mail: daniela-stefanie.gohl@charite.de

C. C. Ciupitu-Plath
e-mail: cristina.ciupitu-plath@charite.de

C. Janssen et al. (eds.), *Health Care Utilization in Germany*,
DOI 10.1007/978-1-4614-9191-0_7,

4. Health-reporting behaviour specified as gender differences in the openness and the ability to talk about health problems with other persons or professionals.
5. Prior health care and caretakers as causes covers gender differences in the utilization (including made experiences) and satisfaction with the health care system.

This explanatory framework has proved to be a valuable tool in describing gender differences within and between countries. Taking current research findings into account (Luy 2011), it seems that environmental risks and therein health behaviour contribute most to the observed gender gap.

Interestingly, in Verbrugge's framework, two of the risks factor categories are directly related to the health care system and to health care utilization. There are few studies showing that women and men differ in number of physician contacts and in their health-reporting behaviour. It seems that women are more likely to talk about their well-being and their health status with other people and with health professionals than men. This can be partly explained by gender differences in subjective health concepts where women include well-being as an important component of health, whereas men describe their health more in the sense of functioning.

That the health care system is not gender neutral has been shown in many studies. Older studies have identified a medicalisation of women's body, especially with regard to their reproductive health (see for overview: Maschewsky-Schneider 1997; Kuhlmann & Kolip 2005; Babitsch, Ducki & Maschewsky-Schneider 2011). At that time, the grassroots women's health movement and feminist scholars worked together to simultaneously provide evidence designed to emphasize the need for changing the health care system into a more women-friendly one. Current studies have focused mainly on gender bias in the health care system and have identified many problems in regard to diagnosis and therapy, with women being more often disadvantaged compared to men (Rieder & Lohff 2008). One reason, besides many others, is that gender stereotypes on the side of the health care providers, as well as on the side of patients, could lead to a false interpretation of symptoms, as some experimental studies have shown (von dem Knesebeck et al. 2008, 2010). Examples are the diagnoses of myocardial infarction in younger women or depression in men.

The aim of this chapter is to identify gender differences in health care utilization. Due to the huge differences in living circumstances, as well as in health care systems around the world, this chapter will focus on the situation in Europe, and Germany will serve as a case study. Given the complexity of sex/gender influences on health and health care utilization, the explanatory model provided by Verbrugge (1985) will be used as an analytic framework for exploring sex/gender differences in the use of health services. Furthermore, to describe the process of health care utilization, the behavioural model of health care use developed by Andersen and colleagues (Andersen 1995; Anderson & Davidson 2001) will be used (see, for details, Chap. 2 by von Lengerke et al.) and, based on that concept, enabling, predisposing and need factors will be identified. Accordingly, this chapter includes: (1) a brief description of women and men's health in Europe with a particular focus on Germany, (2) the results of a systematic review, (3) an exemplary description of health care utilization in Germany, and (4) a summary and a discussion of gender differences in health care utilization.

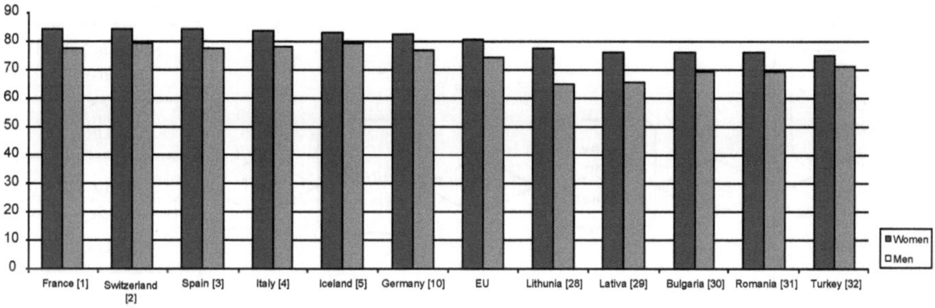

Fig. 7.1 Highest and lowest life expectancy at birth in Europe, by gender, 2005–2007. (OECD 2010)

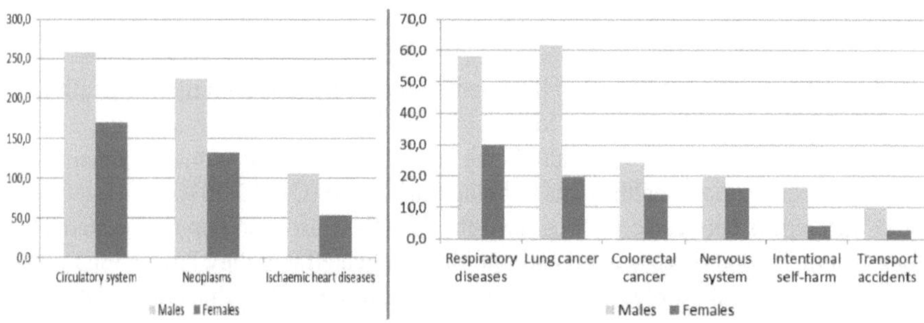

Fig. 7.2 Causes of death, EU-27, 2010 (per 100,000 inhabitants). (Source: Eurostat; http://appsso.eurostat.ec.europa.eu;hlth_cd_asdr)

Women and Men's Health in Europe

Compared to other regions of the world, the life expectancy in Europe is high, although huge differences can be observed between European countries (see Fig. 7.1). Women in France have the highest average life expectancy with 84.4 years, while the lowest can be found in women in Turkey with 75.3 years (difference = 9.1 years). The findings are different in men, where men in Switzerland have the highest life expectancy with 79.1 years and Lithuanian men the lowest with 65.1 years (difference = 14 years). The European average life expectancy is 80.8 years in women and 74.3 years in men. Due to its relatively high life expectancy in both genders, Germany ranks in the upper third among European countries.

The total mortality rates match with the presented life expectancy and highlight the huge differences between European countries. The average total mortality rate in Europe is 696 per 100,000 inhabitants, whereas the gender-specific average rates are 534 per 100,000 inhabitants in women and 912 per 100,000 inhabitants in men. The lowest total mortality rate can be found in Switzerland and the highest in Lithuania. The smallest gender difference exists in Iceland and the biggest in Lithuania, where the total mortality rate is nearly double in men compared to women. The main causes of death in Europe are cardiovascular diseases and cancer (see Fig. 7.2). The

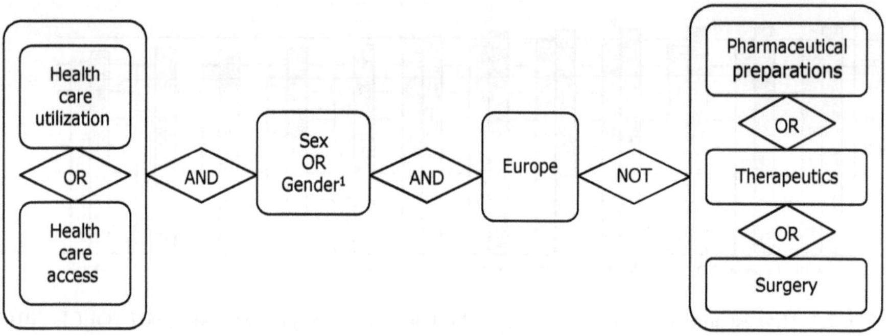

Fig. 7.3 Search strategy

death rates in men are higher in all presented diseases. In Germany, the death rates attributable to these diseases are lower compared to the European average.

An important indicator for health is the self-reported health status. In general, Europeans perceive their health status as being fairly good (OECD 2010), but again with huge differences between countries. Two-thirds of the European population stated that their health is good or very good and one-third indicated that they have a long-standing illness or health problem. In regard to the self-reported health status, Switzerland ranks first and Latvia ranks last. Germany is slightly below the European average, with 65% of its inhabitants reporting their health to be good or very good.

Results of a Systematic Review on Gender Differences in Health Care Utilization in Europe

A systematic review was conducted to investigate gender differences in health care utilization in Europe. The literature search was conducted in July 2011 (last search on 27 July 2011) and updated on 24 January 2012. The search strategy (see Fig. 7.3) aimed at retrieving articles reporting on gender and health care utilization in the European context between 2009 and 2012. Due to the huge number of hits the initially defined time frame from 1998 to 2011 was reduced respectively. PubMed was used as the research database.

The selection of eligible articles was conducted in three steps: firstly, based on the title, secondly, based on abstracts and thirdly, based on the full-text publication. In all steps, two researchers (BB and DG) independently screened the publication and included/excluded articles according to a catalogue of a priori set criteria. In cases of disagreement, the selection was discussed and finally a concerted decision was met. In the first round (selection by title), 22 potentially relevant studies were identified.

The following criteria were applied:

Inclusion criteria:

- Studies related to health care utilization or access to care and gender.
- Studies published between 2009 and 2012.
- Studies on adults.

Exclusion criteria:

- Studies not primarily related to health care, health care utilization, or access to care.
- Focus on health system research, intervention studies, medical/therapy study, screening, etc.
- Focus on specific health problems or areas such as human immunodeficiency virus (HIV), cancer, dental health, etc.
- Specific study population (e.g., disabled, aging people, military personnel, gardeners).
- Studies not conducted in Europe.
- Studies on children.

In the second step (selection by abstract), eight potentially relevant studies were selected. At this stage, further exclusion criteria were introduced since some studies appeared to be too specific and not comparable to other contexts or target groups.

Additional exclusion criteria:

- Focus on ethnicity, financing, health politics, and social support.
- Focus on a specific health care sector (out-of-hours service, walk-in centre).
- Studies on the long-term care of elderly people.

Finally, four studies were selected after reading the fulltext. These articles made up the database for the results section.

Results

An overview of the selected publications is presented in Table 7.1. The studies were published in 2008 (ten Have et al. 2008), 2009 (Gerritsen & Devillé 2009) and in 2010 (Doherty & Kartalova-O'Doherty 2010; Gudmundsdottir & Vilhjalmsson 2010). The countries covered were Ireland (Doherty & Kartalova-O'Doherty 2010), the Netherlands (Gerritsen & Devillé 2009), Iceland (Gudmundsdottir & Vilhjalmsson 2010), and one study referred to the situation in more than one European country (ten Have et al. 2008). All publications included a representative sample of the general population; in addition, one article (Doherty & Kartalova-O'Doherty 2010) included subsamples of the four largest immigrant population groups. All studies included both women and men, and all study participants were older than 18 years. In regard to the health care system, two of the selected publications (Doherty & Kartalova-O'Doherty 2010; Gudmundsdottir & Vilhjalmsson 2010) focused on

Table 7.1 Study description

No.	Author	Title	Year of publication	Country	Sample size	Gender	Age of participants	Population	Setting
1	Doherty & Kartalova-O'Doherty	Gender and self-reported mental health problems: Predictors of help seeking from a general practitioner	2010	Ireland	2,711	Both	18 years and older	General population	GP services
2	Gerritsen & Devillé	Gender differences in health and health care utilization in various ethnic groups in the Netherlands: a cross-sectional study	2009	Netherlands	7,789 persons (Indigenous population) and 1,512 persons (four largest migrant groups)	Both	18 years and older	General population	All sectors
3	Gudmundsdottir & Vilhjalmsson	Group differences in outpatient help seeking for psychological distress: Results from a national prospective study of Icelanders	2010	Iceland	1,924 first wave, 1,592 second wave	Both	18–75 years	General population	Ambulatory care
4	ten Have et al.	Are attitudes towards mental health help seeking associated with service use? Results from the European Study of Epidemiology of Mental Disorders	2008	Belgium, France, Germany, Italy, the Netherlands and Spain	8,796	Both	18 years and older	General population	Not specified

ambulatory care; one (Gerritsen & Devillé 2009) considered all sectors and the other did not specify any sector of the health care system (ten Have et al. 2008). Three of the publications deal with mental health problems (Doherty & Kartalova-O'Doherty 2010; Gudmundsdottir & Vilhjalmsson 2010; 4) and one focused explicitly on gender and ethnicity in health care utilization. All articles are based on nationally representative studies and applied quantitative methods. In one study (Gudmundsdottir & Vilhjalmsson 2010), Andersen's behavioural model of health service use was adopted as theoretical background.

Gender differences in health care utilization were found in all studies, indicating higher rates of use in women compared to men (Doherty & Kartalova-O'Doherty 2010; Gerritsen & Devillé 2009; Gudmundsdottir & Vilhjalmsson 2010; ten Have et al 2008). Against the background of Andersen's behavioural model of health services utilization, Gudmundsdottir and Vilhjalmsson (2010) investigated predictors of outpatient help seeking for psychological distress. They used a random national sample of Icelandic adults and focused on four different forms of distress. Besides gender, other socio-demographic variables such as age and marital status were included. Health care utilization was more frequent in women compared to men. In detail, the findings showed a greater total utilization rate in women, as well as more visits to physicians and complementary and alternative medicine (CAM) providers. After controlling for symptoms, the observed gender differences were reduced, but still significant.

Doherty & Kartalova-O'Doherty (2010) showed that the prevalence of self-reported mental health problems was higher in women than in men (59.4% vs. 40.6%) and women were more likely to have contacted their general practitioner (GP) for such problems in the previous year compared to men (63.2% vs. 54.2%). Additionally, in this study, socio-demographic and psychosocial variables were used as predictors of seeking help from GPs. More of the variables included in the regression model became significant in men than in women. Limitations in social activities were the only significant predictor that increased the probability of help seeking in women. In men, self-reported embarrassment was the strongest predictor. Also, some limitations in physical activities and being married/cohabitating increased men's help-seeking behaviour, whereas secondary education decreased their likelihood to contact a GP. These findings demonstrate that different reasons for seeking help are effective in women and men, seemingly in close connection to societal gender roles.

Reasons for mental health care seeking were also investigated by ten Have et al. (2008). Based on the European Study of Epidemiology of Mental Disorders (ESEMeD), representative data from six European countries (Belgium, France, Germany, Italy, the Netherlands and Spain) were analysed. Female gender increased the probability of accessing mental health care. Other significant predictors were being younger than 65 years of age, higher income and living in Spain or Italy. Women indicated more often than men that they would feel comfortable talking about personal problems. Participants who already had experience with using mental health services were more likely to seek help when faced with a serious health problem and they believed more often that professional help is effective compared to participants without any experiences. These attitudes are significantly associated with health services use. General health care was more likely to be utilized by participants who were open to using professional help in case of a serious emotional problem (ARR = 1.34) and who felt comfortable talking about personal problems (ARR = 1.22). These two attitudes also showed the strongest association to mental health care use (ARR = 2.97 and ARR = 1.88, respectively). Furthermore, the adjusted relative risk ratio was 1.62 for the perceived effectiveness of professional help and 1.31 for feeling embarrassed if friends knew about one receiving professional help. Unfortunately, no gender differentiation of these findings was provided.

The only selected study which is not related to mental health was published by Gerritsen and Devillé (2009). They analysed gender and ethnic differences in health and health care utilization based on data from the second Dutch National Survey of General Practice. Compared to native men, native women reported a poorer health status and consequently used general practice services, physiotherapy, ambulatory mental health care and over-the-counter medication more often. No gender differences were found in this group regarding outpatient medical specialist visits, hospitalization and the use of prescribed medication. However, use of these health services differed between men and women in the four selected immigrant groups (Morocco, Netherlands Antilles, Turkey and Surinam). Although immigrant women assessed their health status similarly to native women (except Netherlands Antilles), a higher utilization among the former group was only found for few health services. Moroccan and Antillean women visited GPs more often than their male counterparts. Turkish women were more often hospitalized than Turkish men and Moroccan women had more contacts to ambulatory mental health care than Moroccan men.

Summary

Against the background of Andersen's behavioural model, the presented studies included mainly predisposing factors (see Table 7.2). As indicated by our search strategy, gender was considered as a horizontal dimension influencing all factors specified in the model. Only one publication (Gudmundsdottir &Vilhjalmsson 2010) explicitly used the Andersen model as its explanatory framework.

The presented studies showed influences in help seeking and health care utilization taking the above-mentioned variables into account. All studies showed a higher utilization rate in women compared to men, which can only partly explained by gender differences in morbidity (need factors) and also by the predisposing and enabling factors. Most commonly used variables were age, marital status and education as predisposing factors and income as an enabling factor. Interestingly, the study conducted by Doherty & Kartalova-O'Doherty (2010) revealed more influencing factors in men compared to women. Referring back to the Verbrugges' explanatory framework it seems very likely that on the one side health-reporting behaviour (ten Have et al. 2008) and on the other side former experiences with the health care system (Doherty & Kartalova O'Doherty 2010) contribute to the observed gender differences in health care utilization (see also Gudmundsdottir & Vilhjalmsson 2010).

Table 7.2 Variables used in studies differentiated according to Andersen's behavioural model

Variables and the studies researching each variable		
Predisposing factors	Enabling factors	Need factors
Age [1, 3, 4]	Income/financial situation [1, 3, 4]	Self-reported/perceived health status [2]
Marital status [1, 3, 4]	Availability of medical services/ inpatient and outpatient care facilities [1]	Self-reported/perceived physical health [1]
Gender/sex [1, 2, 3, 4]	Accessibility to care [1]	Self-reported quality of life [1]
Education [1, 3, 4]	Socioeconomic structure of the neighbourhood [4]	Mental health [1, 3]
Ethnicity/nativity [2]		
Employment status[1, 4]		
Immigrant status [2]		
Region of residence (urban/ rural) [1, 3, 4]		
Health beliefs [4]		
Trust in/familiarity with medical organizations [1, 4]		

[1] Doherty & Kartalova-O'Doherty (2010); [2] Gerritsen & Devillé (2009); [3] Gudmundsdottir & Vilhjalmsson (2010); [4] ten Have et al. (2008)

As three of four articles focused on mental health, the generalization of these findings is limited. However, the frequent focus on mental health care illustrated in our chapter might point to an area of increased gender differences in health service utilization.

Health Care Utilization in Germany—Selected Examples Regarding Contextual Factors

A special focus is put in the following section on Germany, which serves as a case sample to highlight the influence of sex/gender on the process of health care utilization. This allows—as having a defined context—a deeper insight into existing gender differences and similarities. Exemplified on three different areas of the health care system, disease management programmes(DMPs) including guidelines, managed care and cardiovascular diagnostic procedures (intracardiac catheter), the inclusion of gender into political considerations and into decision-making is considered. It will be worked out, if the decisions met influence health care utilization and contribute to a reduction of gender inequality in health care or are provoking the contrary. Other areas of health care delivery where gender differences have been explored intensively, such as preventive programmes, were not taken into account (see, for further details, Chap. 16).

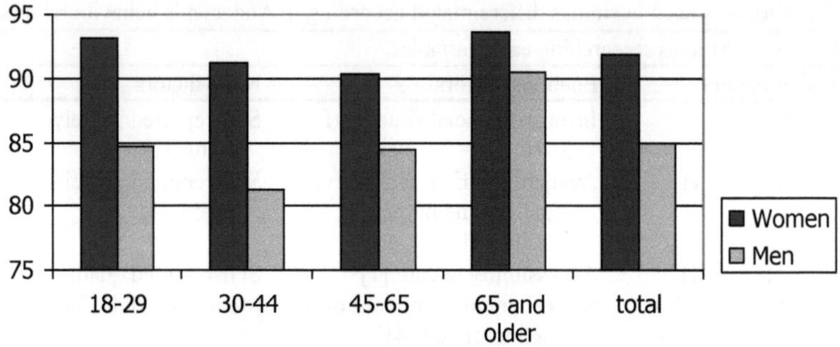

Fig. 7.4 Gender differences in physician contacts during last year. (GEDA 2010; RKI 2012)

Gender and Health Care Utilization: Current Findings

Representative data on health and health care utilization were provided in health reports published by the Robert Koch Institute (RKI). In outpatient care the current data from the German Health Update (GEDA) survey 2010 confirmed—as shown in previous studies—a higher utilization of outpatient health care in women compared to men (RKI 2012; see Fig. 7.4). Overall, the percentage of women who had a physicians' appointment (GP or specialist) in the last year was higher(91.9 %) than men (84.9 %). The observed gender differences are decreasing with age and are consequently most pronounced in the younger age groups (18–44 years; difference around 10 %).The authors argue that probably one reason for the larger gender differences in the younger groups is the routine consultation of a gynaecologist. However, Thode et al. (2005) revealed in a detailed analysis of representative data, that even taking differences in morbidity as well as the utilization of gynaecologist into account, gender differences were reduced but still remain.

Gender Differences in Health Care Utilization: Three Examples

Disease Management Programs (DMP)

In 2000, national disease management programs for selected chronic diseases were introduced into the German health care system. The aim was to improve the quality and effectiveness of outpatient care for chronic ill persons. DMPs are structured and integrated health care programs, in which 1) therapeutic decisions are based on evidence-based clinical practice and treatment guidelines, 2) cooperation among the involved health care professionals (not only medical doctors) are strengthened and 3) patients are educated and involved in the therapeutic process. The participation of health insurance beneficiaries is voluntary. The evaluation and monitoring of DMPs is required by law and hence an obligatory part of the program (BVA 2011).

Sex/gender is one of the evaluation criteria referring to participants in the program. As a consequence, the database only allows comparisons between the programs offered by different statutory health insurances, but not between patients enrolled in DMP programs and patients continuing their treatment in regular outpatient care. This would require additional studies. To date, DMP programs are implemented for: type 1 and 2 diabetes, breast cancer, coronary heart disease, asthma bronchiale and chronic obstructive pulmonary disease (COPD). In September 2011, 10893 programmes with more than 5.9 mio. enrolled health insurance beneficiaries or 6.8 mio. participants were accredited (BVA 2011). The data from one statutory health insurance (AOK) show the following participation rates in women and men (Lente 2011):

DMP	Women (%)	men (%)
Diabetes mellitus Type 2	56.5	43.4
Coronary heart disease	41.3	58.7

The interpretation of these data, as well as drawing conclusions on the adequacy and gender-equity of the health care system is difficult due to the following reasons:

- The data focus on all DMP participants and therefore they do not recognize differences in prevalence rates, nor in indication-specific need;
- No statement can be made regarding the appropriateness and effectiveness of these programs from a gender perspective in the absence of a comparison to regular treatment;
- No research has been conducted on reasons for different participations rates, e.g. interventions provided by the attending physician or by the statutory health insurance;
- It has to be examined whether key components of DMPs such as evidence-based guidelines, training programs, etc., are equally appropriate for women and men, and thus developed and implemented in a gender-sensitive manner (Kuhlmann & Kolip 2005).

Some of these issues were addressed in additional studies, such as ELSID or the KORA study (see Chap. 12). In the ELSID study (Evaluation of a large scale implementation of disease management programs for patients with type 2 diabetes) on diabetic patients insured by the AOK Saxony-Anhalt and Rhineland-Palatinate, DMP was compared with regular care. The analysis showed that the 2-year mortality rate was lower in DMP participants compared to non-participants and the prescription rates for antihypertensives and antilipemics were higher in DMP participants; in contrast, differences in health-related quality of life between participants and non-participants were not clear (Lente 2011, p. 74-77). All in all, the authors came to the conclusion that DMPs have a positive effect. However, the question if this kind of treatment leads to the provision of appropriate and gender-equitable health care for women and men was not assessed based on the available data and remains unanswered.

Integrated health care and medical centers

To reduce problems which often occur in Germany at the transition between health care sectors, e.g. between outpatient and inpatient care, the establishment of integrated care and medical centers (MVZ) was facilitated by the law on the modernization of statutory health insurance, which was passed in 2004. The implementation process has since been continuously evaluated by the National Association of Statutory Health Insurance Physicians (KBV) through MVZ-surveys. The results of these surveys refer mainly to the numbers of newly founded MVZ and involved physicians with their respective sub-specialities and regional aspects, the participation of other health care providers, financial budgets and means of quality assurance (KBV 2009). Only very limited information is available regarding the users and also the effectiveness of such programs. The KBV conducted one survey with health insurance beneficiaries (KBV 2011). The data analysis was stratified by sex/gender, but the general focus lies only on physician consults rather than on the use of medical centers (KBV 2011). Furthermore, the study conducted by the Gemeinsame Registrierungsstelle (2009) only provides estimations regarding the utilization rate of integrated health care without any gender differentiation.

Participation in 'Gesundes Kinzigtal Integrated Care' (GKIC), a regional project of integrated health care developed by two statutory health insurances, is higher in women compared to men: 3,882 men and 4,605 women were enrolled in this program in 2011 (personal communication, Head Office Manager, Nov. 11th, 2011). Only general data are published regarding the participation rates in the provided DMPs, showing that 10.6% of all enrolled participants take part in the DMP for type 2 diabetes, 3.7% in the DMP for coronary heart disease, 1.4% in the DMP for asthma bronchiale and 2.0% in the DMP for COPD (EKIV-Newsletter 3/2011). No information is available for gender. Hence, it has not been investigated so far if both genders profit in the same way from such a project. Such gender-sensitive analyses are not easy to perform and would require considerable additional effort.

Left heart catheterization (coronary angiography)

With the reunification of Germany, the federal government aimed to ensure a uniform health care provision in the old and new federal states. Among other measures, this lead to increased funding for the establishment of left heart catheterization laboratories. The number of such facilities increased by 120% from 1990 to 1999 (SVR-Gesundheit 2001). In 2009, Germany had 830 left heart catheterization laboratories, in which 864,858 left heart catheterizations were performed (Bruckenberg 2010). The advisory council on the assessment of developments in the health care system thus concluded that there was an oversupply of left heart catheterization in Germany compared to other European countries. Moreover, the high number of procedures does not match with the cardiovascular mortality rates in Germany.

In 2009, 65.7% of all cardiac procedures with extracorporeal circulation (ECC) were performed in men and 34.3% in women (Bruckenberg 2010). Minimally invasive diagnostic procedures of the heart carry risks, potential complications being myocardial infarction, cardiac arrhythmias or stroke. Further potential risks are allergic reactions caused by the administration of contrast medium or persistent the puncture site bleeding. Taking these potential complications into account, an oversupply should be avoided. With regard to gender differences many open questions remain, such as:

- Is there an oversupply of cardiac care in men and, if so, why?
- Is the higher rate of minimally invasive diagnostic procedures in men legitimate given the 10-year earlier onset of myocardial infarction in men compared to women?
- Is the provision of cardiac care for women sufficient and adequate?

Conclusion

The concept of gender mainstreaming requires the recognition of gender in all policy aspects and consequences, with the aim of establishing gender equality. Although the federal government adopted gender mainstreaming as a key principle in 1998, the above-mentioned examples showed that gender is not always appropriately considered. Therefore, gender mainstreaming needs to be systematically applied in the health care system, in the provision of health care and in health policy-making. It is problematic when new programs such as DMP consider the patient gender-neutral.

Generally, there are major research gaps in this area, especially on how to ensure that gender is systematically considered in newly developed and implemented health care services.

Summary and Discussion

Although there is enough evidence that women and men differ in health care utilization, it is hardly possible to explain the observed findings. It is quite obvious that health and health care utilization are by itself intricate matters taking sex/gender into account the picture becomes more complex. There are more questions open than answered as shown in both parts of the chapter. Surprisingly, the number of studies explicitly analyzing sex/gender differences in health care utilization is low. In the beginning of the systematic review, we expected much higher number of papers covering this topic. Although we had to reduce the search period due to the overall amount of hits, the number of eligible was rather low.

One main problem which also has been revealed in the examples from Germany is that sex/gender is often treated as a simple variable and, by doing this, the connectedness with other variables, such as education, employment status, income or health beliefs, body awareness and social support, is being disregarded.

Taking this assumption as a prerequisite for doing research there is a huge need for further studies and the (re)-development of theoretical frameworks. As shown for the Andersen's behavioural model, gender is explicitly regarded as a predisposing factor. Whereas sex can indeed be regarded mainly as a predisposing factor, such a restriction in regard to gender is considered too narrow. Given its association with many other elements of the model, gender should rather be integrated in this explanatory framework as a horizontal dimension.

There is no room in this chapter to illustrate an entire research agenda in this area. But along the main topics most relevant research questions will be presented in the following:

1. Help seeking: How do women and men enter the system of professional health care services? How are the processes of help seeking triggered in women and men? What role do the social and societal network play? How are the gender differences influenced by other diversity attributes?
2. Health care utilization: How can the observed gender differences in health care utilization be explained? Are the existent theoretical frameworks sufficient where are potential shortcomings? How is health care utilization influenced by the gender-related structures and roles in a given society?
3. Experiences with the health care system: How do women and men experience and evaluate the utilized (medical) treatments? How are prior experiences linked with further help seeking and health care utilization in women and men?

Many studies in this field are based on the analysis of secondary data which is in our opinion too restricted to elaborate qualitative differences in health care utilization in women and men. To answer these questions preferential primary studies are required.

References

Andersen, R.M. (1995) Revisiting the behavioral model and access to medical care: does it matter? Journal of Health and Social behavior 36:1–10.

Andersen, R.M., Davidson, P.L. (2001) Improving access to care in America: individual and contextual indicators. In: Andersen RM, Rice TH, Kominski EF, editors. Changing the U.S. health care system: key issues in health services, policy, and management. San Francisco, CA: Jossey-Bass. pp. 3–30.

Babitsch, B., Ducki, A., Maschewsky-Schneider, U. (2011). Geschlecht und Gesundheit. In: Hurrelmann, K., Razum, O., Laaser, U. (Hrsg.): Handbuch für Gesundheitswissenschaften, S. 639–660.

Bruckenberger, E. (2010). Herzbericht 2009. 22. Bericht sektorübergreifende Versorgungsanalyse zur Kardiologie und Herzchirurgie in Deutschland sowie vergleichende Daten aus Österreich und den Schweiz, Hannover.
Bundesversicherungsamt (BVA) (2011). Zulassung der Disease Management Programme (DMP) durch das Bundesversicherungsamt. Bonn.
Doherty, D.T., Kartalova-O'Doherty, Y. (2010). Gender and self-reported mental health problems: Predictors of help seeking from a general practitioner. British Journal of Health Psychology 15:213–228.
Evaluation der Integrierten Versorgung Gesundes Kinzigtal. EKIV-Newsletter 3/2011.
Gemeinsame Registrierungsstelle zur Unterstützung der Umsetzung des § 140d SBG V (2009). Entwicklung der integrierten Versorgung in der Bundesrepublik Deutschland 2004–2008. o.O.
Gerritsen, A.A.M., Devillé, W.L. (2009). Gender differences in health and health care utilisation in various ethnic groups in the Netherlands: a cross-sectional study. BMC Public Health 9:109.
Gudmundsdottir, G., Vilhjalmsson, R. (2010). Group differences in outpatient help-seeking for psychological distress: Results from a national prospective study of Icelanders. Scandinavian Journal of Public Health 38:160–167.
Kassenärztliche Bundesvereinigung (KBV) (2009). MVZ-Survey 2008. Die Strategische Positionierung Medizinischer Versorgungszentren. Berlin.
Kassenärztliche Bundesvereinigung (KBV) (2011). Versichertenbefragung der Kassenärztlichen Bundesvereinigung 2011. Berlin.
Kuhlmann, E. (2010). Gender im Mainstream der Medizin. Wohin geht die Reise? In: Kolip, P., Lademann, J. (Hrsg.). Frauenblicke auf das Gesundheitssystem. Frauengerechte Gesundheitsversorgung zwischen Marketing und Ignoranz (S. 239–255). Weinheim und München: Juventa.
Kuhlmann, E., Kolip, P. (2005). Gender und Public Health. Grundlegende Orientierungen für Forschung, Praxis und Politik. Weinheim und München: Juventa.
Lente, E. J. van (2011). Erfahrungen mit strukturierten Behandlungsprogrammen (DMPs) in Deutschland. In: Günster, C., Klose, J., Schmacke, N. (Hrsg.) Versorgungs-Report 2011. Schwerpunkt: Chronische Erkrankungen (S. 55–83). Stuttgart: Schattauer.
Luy, M. (2011) Ursachen der Geschlechterdifferenz in der Lebenserwartung. Erkenntnisse aus der Klosterstudie [Causes of sex differences in life expectancy. Insights from the cloister study], *Swiss Medical Forum* (Schweizerisches Medizin-Forum) 11:580–583.
Maschewsky-Schneider, U. (1997): Frauen sind anders krank. Zur gesundheitlichen Lage der Frauen in Deutschland. Weinheim, München: Juventa Verlag.
OECD (2010) Health at a Glance: Europe 2010, OECD Publishing. http://dx.doi.org/10.1787/health_glance-2010-en.
Rieder, A., Lohff, B. (2008). Gender Medizin: Geschlechtsspezifische Aspekte für die klinische Praxis. Wien: Springer Verlag.
RKI—Robert Koch-Institut (Hrsg.) (2012). Daten und Fakten: Ergebnisse der Studie »Gesundheit in Deutschland aktuell 2010«. Beiträge zur Gesundheitsberichterstattung des Bundes. RKI, Berlin.
Sachverständigenrat für die Konzertierte Aktion im Gesundheitswesen (SVR-Gesundheit) (2001). Bedarfsgerechtigkeit und Wirtschaftlichkeit. Band III: Über-, Unter- und Fehlversorgung. Gutachten 2000/2001. Bonn.
Statistisches Bundesamt (2012). https://www.destatis.de/. Accessed: 24. September 2012.
ten Have, M., de Graaf, R., Ormel, J., Vilagut, G., Kovess, V., Alonso, J.—the ESEMeD/MHEDEA 2000 Investigators (2008). Are attitudes towards mental health help-seeking associated with service use? Results from the European Study of Epidemiology of Mental Disorders. Soc Psychiat Epdeimiol 45:153–163.
Thode, N., Bergmann, E., Kamtsiuris, P. et al. (2005) Einflussfaktoren auf die ambulante Inanspruchnahme in Deutschland. Bundesgesundheitsbl—Gesundheitsforsch—Gesundheitsschutz 48:296–306.

Verbrugge, L.M. (1985): Gender and Health: An Update on Hypotheses and Evidence. Journal of Health and Social Behavior 26:156–182.
von dem Knesebeck, O., Bönte, M., Siegrist, J., Marceau, L., Link, C., Arber, S., Adams, A., McKinlay, J. (2008) Country differences in the diagnosis and management of coronary heart disease—a comparison between the US, the UK and Germany. BMC Health Serv Res 8:198.
von dem Knesebeck, O., Gerstenberger, E., Link, C., Marceau, L., Roland, M., Campbell, S., Siegrist, J., de Cruppé, W., McKinlay, J. (2010) Differences in the diagnosis and management of type 2 diabetes in 3 countries (US, UK, and Germany): results from a factorial experiment. Med Care 48:321–6.

Chapter 8
Socioeconomic Status and the Utilization of Health Services in Germany: A Systematic Review

Jens Klein, Kerstin Hofreuter-Gätgens and Olaf von dem Knesebeck

Introduction

Numerous studies have confirmed the relationship between socioeconomic status (SES), as measured by education, income, and/or occupational status, and morbidity or mortality, for Germany as well as internationally (Mackenbach, 2003, 2006; Marmot & Wilkinson, 2006; Siegrist & Marmot, 2006; Lampert et al., 2007; Mielck, 2008a; Robert Koch-Institut, 2005). These studies found health inequalities between groups of high SES versus low SES as well as a social gradient in morbidity and mortality: The lower a person's social status, the higher the risk to contract a disease or die earlier. One hypothesis to explain these health inequalities is the social causation hypothesis, which states that social status influences health via material, behavioral, and psychosocial factors. Theoretical models to explain this social status gradient also take into account inequalities in medical and health services (Mielck, 2005; Mackenbach, 2006; Mackenbach et al. 2008). Material factors include income, housing situation, residential environment, physical strains at work, and the accessibility, utilization, and quality of medical services. Behavioral factors particularly include behaviors with adverse effects on health, such as smoking, poor nutrition, or sedentary lifestyle, while psychosocial factors take into account psychosocial strains at work and coping resources in the social environment, among other things.

Health care inequalities are the subject of increasing debate in Germany (Tiesmeyer et al., 2008; Geyer, 2008). Discussions about a "two-tier medical system" and unequal chances can be controversial. However, few reviews and overviews on

J. Klein (✉) · K. Hofreuter-Gätgens · O. von dem Knesebeck
Center for Psychosocial Medicine, Department of Medical Sociology, University Medical Center Hamburg-Eppendorf, Hamburg, Germany,
e-mail: j.klein@uke.uni-hamburg.de

K. Hofreuter-Gätgens
e-mail: hofreuter@uke.uni-hamburg.de

O. von dem Knesebeck
e-mail: o.knesebeck@uke.uni-hamburg.de

C. Janssen et al. (eds.), *Health Care Utilization in Germany*,
DOI 10.1007/978-1-4614-9191-0_8,

vertical inequalities in health services are currently available that investigate individual health services sectors for inequalities (Scheffer et al., 2006; Mielck, 2008b; Hofreuter & von dem Knesebeck, 2009; Janßen et al., 2009; Huber & Mielck, 2010; Robert Koch-Institut, 2012).

These papers particularly document inequalities in the utilization of outpatient care, prevention, and health promotion programs. In addition, the studies' large variety of contents and methodological approaches makes it difficult to draw general conclusions about the care situation in Germany. Research in these areas links social epidemiology approaches with topics in health services research and can supply important information to health-policy decision makers.

In light of the complexity of the topic, these questions must be specifically and systematically categorized in a framework for analysis (von dem Knesebeck et al., 2009). Researchers must differentiate between various health services sectors (outpatient care, inpatient care, and prevention) as well as between aspects of access, utilization, and quality of care. Particular overlap exists between health services access versus utilization, and these aspects are difficult to differentiate clearly. Access is primarily considered a supply-side factor, while utilization is more strongly associated with the demand side or patient side (Goddard & Smith, 2001). In addition, differences in utilization levels may be interpreted as indicating either different preferences or different opportunities.

As a result of the growing debate on this topic in Germany, insurance status (private versus statutory health insurance) is becoming an increasingly important issue; in this review, it will be considered in addition to the established vertical status indicators (education, income and occupational status) (Kriwy & Mielck, 2006; Gerlinger, 2008; Geyer, 2008; Lüngen et al., 2008; Huber & Mielck, 2010). In Germany, all employees are required to be insured by one of about 150 statutory health insurances (SHIs) unless their income exceeds a defined upper limit or they are civil servants or self-employed. Private health insurance is available as an alternative or to supplement SHI coverage. Some 90% of the German population is SHI-insured, and the remaining 10% of residents are members of a private health insurance. In SHIs, contributions are calculated based on each member's income, and the offered services are egalitarian, while private health insurances offer various benefit levels at different monthly contribution rates (Deutsche Sozialversicherung, 2012; Gruber & Kiesel, 2009).

In the late 1960s, Ronald M. Andersen started developing a model for describing and analyzing the utilization of health services; this model is now internationally established (Andersen & Newman, 1973; Andersen, 1995, 2008). Among other things, it takes into account specific, individual determinants of utilization, which are classified into "predisposing characteristics", "enabling resources", and "need." Education and occupational status, which are used as indicators of vertical inequality, are considered as predisposing characteristics, while the indicators 'income' and 'insurance status' tend to be classified as enabling resources. The Andersen model has been internationally established as a common reference model for describing and analyzing utilization (Thode et al., 2005).

This study aims to assess systematically the current state of research on the association between SES and the utilization of medical or health-related services in Germany and to document the situation separately for the sectors of care mentioned above.

Assessments of the various results must take into account the data collection period since changes in health policies, such as the introduction of the practice fee (on January 1, 2004) and higher co-payments for various medical services, can have a lasting impact on utilization (Rückert et al., 2008; Mielck et al., 2009, Gerlinger, 2008). In addition, analyzing inequalities in utilization requires controlling for need, such as through pretreatment health status (von dem Knesebeck et al., 2009).

Methods

A systematic review in the PubMed/Medline database was conducted. The search included studies published between January 1, 1998 and June 22, 2012. The following search strategy was applied:

> socioeconomic [Title/Abstract] OR socio-economic [Title/Abstract] OR inequalit* [Title/Abstract] OR income [Title/Abstract] OR education [Title/Abstract] OR occupation* [Title/Abstract] OR "social status" [Title/Abstract] OR "social class" [Title/Abstract] OR "social disparities" [Title/Abstract] OR "insurance status" [Title/Abstract] OR "socioeconomic factors" [MeSH Terms]) AND (usage [Title/Abstract] OR utilisation [Title/Abstract] OR utilization [Title/Abstract] OR uptake [Title/Abstract] OR "health care use" [Title/Abstract] OR "health service use" [Title/Abstract] OR "health services use" [Title/Abstract] OR "utilization" [MeSH Subheading] OR "health services needs and demand" [MeSH Terms]) AND (german [Title/Abstract] OR germany [Title/Abstract] OR german [Language]) AND ("1998" [Date—Publication]:"2012" [Date—Publication])

Inclusion criteria were that the studies (1) investigated the relationship between SES or insurance status and the patients' utilization of medical and health services, (2) were conducted in Germany using a German sample, (3) were published in English or German language, and (4) were published after 1997. Studies that investigated the utilization of health services without adequately taking into account the social status of participants were excluded as well as studies that primarily examined medical service access rather than utilization. Furthermore, studies that focused on migrants living in Germany were excluded because in this group, cultural aspects play a particularly important role aside from socioeconomic factors.

In light of these criteria, first the titles and abstracts of the publications were viewed. Studies that surveyed specific population groups or the general population were included. Education, income, occupational status, as well as various social status indices were taken into account as SES indicators. Moreover, studies that investigated differences in utilization between respondents of different insurance status (private or SHI) were also included. Since it could be expected that some relevant publications may not be listed in PubMed/Medline, the systematic database search was supplemented by viewing the bibliographies of the identified publications and reviews.

Due to inconsistencies in study design and methodological approaches, methodological quality could not be consistently assessed. Not all studies adjusted for need or morbidity, which can directly affect the frequency and duration of utilization. However, most studies were based on established data sets that were designed to be representative. We classified the studies by content using the above-described categories of outpatient care, inpatient care, and prevention. In general, there is a difference between prevention and health promotion, although this differentiation is not consistently applied in the literature. As health promotion includes many services that are not disease specific and are conducted in a wide variety of settings (Schwartz et al., 2003), this systematic review focused on the area of medical prevention, which primarily includes early detection and screening examinations, vaccinations, and dental check-up. However, if in the listed studies, health promotion was assessed in addition to prevention, the results were also documented.

Outpatient care was primarily measured by the frequency of physician visits or differences in the utilization of primary care physicians versus specialists. In the inpatient care sector, studies differentiated between utilization of inpatient rehabilitation, number of surgeries, and the number of hospitalizations and length of stay. These subareas were further categorized by the examined population (general population, children and adolescents, older patients, and those with specific diseases).

Results

The PubMed/Medline search using the described search strategy generated a total of 688 results by June 22, 2012. After an analysis of the titles, 101 contributions were considered to be potentially relevant. The subsequent screening of the abstracts and full texts resulted in the inclusion of 42 publications in the systematic review. When viewing the bibliographies and the associated references, 15 more publications were found, so that a total of 57 publications were taken into account in the further analysis (Tables 8.1–8.3).

Outpatient Care

The studies on the utilization of outpatient care predominantly investigated primary care physician visits and specialist visits (Table 8.1). After adjusting for need, a European comparative study (Lostao et al., 2007) revealed hardly any status-specific differences in the frequency of outpatient care utilization in Germany using relatively old data from the 1990s; the same was found by Smythe et al. (2004). However, a clear relationship between SES and utilization of outpatient care is found across studies when differentiating between visits to primary care physicians versus specialists. Studies examining the general population documented higher utilization of primary care physicians by lower social status groups, while specialists were more frequently utilized by people of higher SES (Or et al., 2008; Röckl-Wiedmann et al., 2002; Baumeister, 2004; Bergmann et al., 2005; Thode et al., 2005; Lüngen et al., 2009; Kürschner et al., 2011; Schnitzer et al., 2011; Stirbu et al., 2011). In

Table 8.1 Socioeconomic status (SES) and the utilization of outpatient care in Germany

Outpatient care				
Author (year)	Sample	Dependent variables	Independent variables	Results
Baumeister et al. (2004)	General population of one federal state (SHIP) (n=4,310)	Frequency of outpatient physician visits (primary care physicians and specialists)	Winkler Index of SES, years of education	Higher number of physician visits (primary care physician and/or internist) for people with lower SES
Bergmann et al. (2005)	Telephone Health Survey 2003 (n=8,318)	Frequency of outpatient physician visits (primary care physicians and specialists)	Winkler Index of SES	The rate of primary care physician visits rises as the SES index drops. Privately insured individuals report less frequent visits to primary care physicians
Bremer and Wübker (2012)	German subsample of the first three waves of SHARE (age > 50 years) (n=2,624)	Frequency of outpatient physician visits (primary care physicians and specialists)	Income	Higher income groups exhibit more frequent specialist visits
Gruber and Kiesel (2010)	German subsample of the first wave of SHARE (age >50 years) (n=2,260)	Utilization of primary care physicians and specialists	Income, years of education, occupational position, and insurance status	Higher utilization of specialists by individuals with higher SES, particularly in men. Education is particularly relevant. Lower utilization of primary care physicians by privately insured individuals
Häuser (2005)	Patients with fibromyalgia syndrome (n=88)	Frequency of outpatient physician visits	Status index as determined by education, income, and occupational status	Social status does not predict utilization
Hessel et al. (2000)	Randomly selected people age 60+ (n=394)	Utilization of primary care physicians and specialists, pharmaceutical consumption	Income	Higher income is associated with more physician visits, but not with primary physician visits or pharmaceuticals' consumption
Huber et al. (2012)	German Health Interview and Examination Survey for Children and Adolescents (KiGGS) (n=17,641)	Physician visits (pediatrician, primary care physician, and alternative medical practitioner)	Insurance status, Winkler Index of SES	SHI-insured children more frequently visit pediatricians or primary care physicians and less frequently visit alternative medical practitioners. The same is true for children of lower SES

Table 8.1 (continued)

Outpatient care				
Author (year)	Sample	Dependent variables	Independent variables	Results
Hullegie and Klein (2010)	Socioeconomic Panel data (SOEP) (1995–2006) (n=45,722)	Frequency of physician visits	Insurance status	Fewer physician visits for privately insured individuals
Kamtsiuris et al. (2007)	German Health Interview and Examination Survey for Children and Adolescents (KiGGS) (n=17,641)	Frequency of outpatient physician visits (primary care physicians and specialists)	Winkler Index of SES	Higher-SES adolescents switch to specialists more rapidly. Primary care physicians are visited more frequently by children of lower SES
Kürschner et al. (2011)	Telephone Health Survey 2006 (n=4,160)	Utilization of the primary care physician model (primary care physician as "gatekeeper")	Winkler Index of SES	Primary care physician model utilized more by people of lower and average SES and less frequently by privately insured people
Lehmann et al. (2012)	Prostate cancer patients (n=242)	Utilization of medical rehabilitation services (inpatient and outpatient)	Status index (consisting of education, occupational status, and income)	No significant associations between SES and utilization
Lostao et al. (2007)	1992 German National Health Survey (n=7,466) and 1998 (n=7,124), European comparison study	Utilization of outpatient care (physician visits)	Educational level and occupational status	Little to no association between SES and utilization
Lüngen et al. (2009)	General population in 2002 (n=75,122) and 2006 (n=60,555)	Utilization of outpatient care (primary care physicians and specialists)	Winkler Index of SES and insurance status	SES-specific frequencies of utilization of outpatient and inpatient care are largely explained by differences in morbidity. Privately insured individuals visit primary care physicians less frequently
Maziak et al. (2004)	Children with asthma between the ages of 5 and 11 from two large cities (n=11,094)	Utilization of medical care due to asthma or wheezing (physician visits)	Highest number of years of schooling of one parent	Children of lower-SES parents visit physicians more frequently

Table 8.1 (continued)

Author (year)	Sample	Dependent variables	Independent variables	Results
Outpatient care				
Or et al. (2008)	1998 German National Health Survey (n=5,371), European comparative study	Frequency of outpatient physician visits (primary care physicians and specialists)	Educational attainment	Compared with participants with higher educational attainment, participants with lower educational attainment visit primary care physicians more frequently and specialists less frequently
Reibling and Wendt (2010)	German subsample of the first wave of SHARE (age >50 years) (n=2,894)	Utilization of specialists	Educational attainment	Patients with higher educational attainment are much more likely to visit a specialist
Röckl-Wiedmann et al. (2002)	General adult population of Bavaria (n=2,051)	Utilization of specialists and alternative medical practitioners	Winkler Index of SES, education, and income	Members of higher social status groups visit more frequently specialists and alternative medical practitioners
Schnitzer et al. (2011)	SHI-insured individuals between the ages of 18 and 79 (n=5,232)	Participation in the primary care physician model (primary care physician as "gatekeeper")	Educational attainment	Participation in the primary care physician model is higher in those with low educational attainment. Lower participation and more frequent utilization of specialists by those with higher educational attainment
Schubert et al. (2011)	Rehabilitation patients in 2004, Socioeconomic Panel (SOEP) (n=19,164)	Participation in rehabilitation (inpatient and outpatient)	Helmert social status index	No influence of social status group on participation in rehabilitation services
Sibold et al. (2011)	Patients with chronic back pain (n=192)	Follow-up care after outpatient rehabilitation	Educational attainment and occupational status	Neither indicator is associated with utilization
Smythe et al. (2004)	Participants in the 1992 German National Health Survey (n=4,428)	Utilization of outpatient care	Social status (derived from income, occupation, and educational level)	No social differences in utilization in chronically ill patients. In patients without chronic illness, utilization is lower in lower social status groups
Stirbu et al. (2011)	Participants in the 1998 German National Health Survey (n=7,124), European comparison study	Utilization of outpatient care (primary care physicians and specialists)	Educational attainment	Participants with low educational attainment utilize primary care physicians more frequently and specialists less frequently

Table 8.1 (continued)

Outpatient care				
Author (year)	Sample	Dependent variables	Independent variables	Results
Thode et al. (2005)	Participants in the 1998 German National Health Survey (n=7,124)	Utilization of outpatient care (primary care physicians and specialists)	Winkler Index of SES and insurance status	Social status does not predict the total number of physician visits. People of high social status visit more frequently specialists; people of low social status consult more often primary care physicians. Insurance status does not significantly influence the frequency of visits
von Lengerke et al. (2005)	Subsample of the KORA survey (n=947)	Utilization of outpatient care by obese and normal-weight adults	Helmert social status index, insurance status	SHI-insured individuals generally utilize primary care physicians more frequently. Social status plays a minor role overall

the study by Lüngen et al. (2009), this social gradient disappears almost completely when controlling for age and morbidity, but privately insured individuals still utilized primary care physicians less frequently. In contrast, the German results of a European comparison study by Stirbu et al. (2011) showed an association between low educational level and higher utilization of primary care physicians when controlling for self-assessed health.

Samples of children and adolescents confirmed the trend that primary care physician visits increase and specialist visits decrease with declining SES (Kamtsiuris et al., 2007; Huber et al., 2012). The study by Huber et al. (2012), which focused on insurance status, showed higher utilization of primary care physicians by SHI-insured children and adolescents, even when controlling for SES.

Studies that consider the older population revealed similar trends (Bremer & Wübker, 2012; Hessel et al., 2000; Reibling & Wendt, 2010; Gruber and Kiesel, 2010; Hullegie & Klein, 2010). Gruber and Kiesel (2010) confirmed the above results for various status indicators, particularly education, as well as for insurance status. Hullegie and Klein (2010) demonstrated that privately insured individuals visit primary care physicians less frequently overall.

Studies that sampled patients with existing illnesses showed that social status was not predictive of utilization (Smythe et al. 2004; Häuser, 2005; von Lengerke et al., 2005; Sibold et al., 2011). However, Smythe et al. (2004) demonstrated that the number of physician visits increased from lowest to highest status group in people without chronic illness, and a second study among obese and non-obese adults (von Lengerke et al., 2005) showed that SHI-insured people more frequently visited primary care physicians. Maziak et al. (2004) demonstrated that asthmatic children of parents with lower social status visited physicians more frequently.

Inpatient Care

The indicators of inpatient care were, chiefly, utilization of rehabilitation services, number of conducted surgeries, and number of hospitalizations and length of stay (Table 8.2).

Seven publications investigated the utilization of rehabilitation services (Altenhöner et al., 2005; Häuser, 2005; Waldmann et al., 2007; Deck, 2008; Geyer & Schlanstedt-Jahn, 2012; Lehmann et al., 2012, Schubert et al. 2011). The association between socioeconomic indicators and utilization was weak to nonexistent, with one exception (Altenhöner et al., 2005), where heart attack patients of higher social status—as measured by education, income, and occupational status—utilized rehabilitation services less frequently. In one study (Waldmann et al., 2007), privately insured individuals tended to participate in fewer rehabilitation services. Deck (2008) reported delayed, but not less frequent, utilization by patients of lower SES.

Two studies that examined large samples of the general population and took into account respondents' morbidity showed little correlation between the number of hospitalizations and social status indicators or indices (Lostao et al., 2007; Lüngen et al., 2009). Hullegie and Klein (2010) also used data of the general population in

Table 8.2 Socioeconomic status (SES) and the utilization of inpatient care in Germany

Inpatient care				
Author (year)	Sample	Dependent variables	Independent variables	Results
Altenhöner et al. (2005)	Myocardial infarction patients ($n=421$)	Participation in cardiological rehabilitation	Winkler Index of SES	Patients of higher social status used rehabilitation services less frequently
Blinkert and Klie (2008)	People between the ages of 40 and 65 ($n=2,000$)	Utilization of home versus inpatient nursing care	Social environment	Family caregivers of lower social status prefer home care (even without professional help)
Deck (2008)	Rehabilitation patients ($n=911$)	Utilization of medical rehabilitation	Status index (consisting of education occupational status, and income)	Utilization largely independent of social status. Trend toward more frequent utilization by patients of higher status groups. Patients with lower status utilize services too late
Geyer et al. (2002)	Children and adolescents ≤15 years of age (SHI data; $n=48,412$)	Hospital admissions and length of stay attributable to acute illnesses	Occupational position of the highest earner in the household	There was no social gradient for hospital admissions attributable to infectious diseases. Children of lower SES had greater length of stay
Geyer and Schlanstedt-Jahn (2012)	Women after primary manifestation of breast cancer ($n=238$)	Utilization of inpatient rehabilitation	Educational attainment, occupational position	Weak to no association between utilization and social indicators
Häuser (2005)	Patients with fibromyalgia syndrome ($n=88$)	Utilization of medical services (hospitalizations due to pain, rehabilitation programs, and surgeries)	Status index as determined by education, income, and occupational status	Social status has no predictive value regarding utilization
Hullegie and Klein (2010)	Socioeconomic Panel data (SOEP) (1995–2006) ($n=45,722$)	Hospital length of stay	Insurance status	No difference regarding length of hospital stay
Icks et al. (2007)	Diabetic children and adolescents <20 years of age ($n=1,277$)	Hospital admissions and length of stay	Parents' professional training	Patients whose parents had a lower level of professional training exhibited more frequent hospitalizations

Table 8.2 (continued)

Inpatient care				
Author (year)	Sample	Dependent variables	Independent variables	Results
Kamtsiuris et al. (2007)	German Health Interview and Examination Survey for Children and Adolescents (KiGGS) ($n=17{,}641$)	Frequency of surgeries	Winkler Index of SES	Children and adolescents from high-SES families received significantly fewer surgeries than children from families of average or low SES
Kiesel and Gruber (2012)	German subsample of the first wave of SHARE (age >50 years) ($n=2{,}453$)	Probability of hospital admission, number of nights in hospital	Insurance status, income, years of education, and occupational status	Higher probability of hospital admission for privately insured individuals. SHI-insured individuals with supplementary private health insurance spend fewer nights in hospital than those without this insurance. Income and years of education play no role
Lehmann et al. (2012)	Prostate cancer patients ($n=242$)	Utilization of medical rehabilitation (inpatient and outpatient)	Status index (consisting of education occupational status, and income)	No significant association between status and utilization
Lostao et al. (2007)	German National Health Survey 1992 ($n=7{,}466$) and 1998 ($n=7{,}124$), European comparison study	Utilization of inpatient care (hospital stays)	Educational attainment, occupational status	Little to no association between SES and utilization
Lüngen et al. (2009)	General population in 2002 ($n=75{,}122$) and 2006 ($n=60{,}555$)	Utilization of inpatient care (hospital stays)	Winkler Index of SES and insurance status	SES-specific frequencies of utilization of outpatient and inpatient care are largely explained by differences in morbidity
Maziak et al. (2004)	Children with asthma between the ages of 5 and 11, from two large cities ($n=11{,}094$)	Utilization of medical care due to asthma or wheezing (emergency admissions and hospital admissions)	Highest number of years of schooling of one parent	Children of patients with lower social status show more frequently emergency and hospital admissions

Table 8.2 (continued)

Inpatient care				
Author (year)	Sample	Dependent variables	Independent variables	Results
Schnabel et al. (2009)	Children up to age 2 (n=3,097)	Hospitalizations (accidental injuries, respiratory and digestive diseases)	Parents' educational status	Higher percentage of inpatient admissions attributable to digestive diseases in children of parents with low or average educational level
Schubert et al. (2011)	Rehabilitation patients in 2004, Socioeconomic Panel (SOEP) (n=19,164)	Participation in rehabilitation (inpatient and outpatient)	Helmert social status index	No influence of social status on participation
von Lengerke et al. (2005)	Subsample of the KORA survey (n=947)	Utilization of inpatient care by obese and normal-weight adults	Helmert social status index	Social status plays a minor role overall
Waldmann et. al. (2007)	Patients with colorectal tumors (n=245)	Utilization of inpatient rehabilitation	Years of education and insurance status	No relationships between the number of years of education and utilization. Privately insured individuals participated less frequently

a study with a health economic focus to demonstrate that the length of stay was not associated with insurance status. In contrast with the number of physician visits, which was also assessed in the study, length of stay is not easily influenced by patients. The need-adjusted study by Kiesel and Gruber (2012) revealed that privately insured individuals are more likely to be hospitalized, but income and years of education were insignificant.

A more differentiated picture emerges for children and adolescents. One study showed no social gradient for the frequency of hospital admissions attributable to acute illness (Geyer et al., 2002). However, the length of stay increased with declining SES, which the authors explained with likely differences in the severity of disease. Kamtsiuris et al. (2007) found that children and adolescents from high-SES families underwent surgery less frequently, while Icks et al. (2007) found more frequent hospitalizations in diabetic children and adolescents from lower status groups. Schnabel et al. (2009) reported that young children of parents with low or average education levels were more frequently hospitalized for digestive tract disorders. After adjusting for severity of disease, asthmatic children with parents of lower social status exhibited more frequent emergency admissions and hospitalizations (Maziak et al., 2004). Social status played only a minor role in patients with fibromyalgia or obesity (Häuser, 2005; von Lengerke et al., 2005).

Very little is known about the relationship between utilization and vertical inequality in German inpatient and outpatient long-term care. Blinkert and Klie (2008) documented a relationship between the type of long-term care (home versus institutional, with versus without professional support) and the social environment of the affected families. Accordingly, people of lower social status groups preferred home care.

Prevention

Inequalities in the utilization of preventive services have been comparatively well researched. The trends regarding status-specific utilization vary by type of preventive service and by surveyed population. One can roughly distinguish early detection and screening examinations, vaccinations, and dental check-up (Table 8.3).

Early detection examinations can be categorized into cancer screening and early detection check-up for children and adolescents. On the basis of general population data, two studies using relatively old data sets showed few status-specific differences in the utilization of cancer screening services (Röckl-Wiedmann et al., 2002; Lostao et al., 2007). The screening mammography survey by Albert et al. (2011) even found that nonparticipants were characterized by a higher educational level, higher income, and more frequently carried private insurance. However, the majority of studies documented an association between higher utilization of cancer screening (breast, colon, prostate, skin, ovarian, and cervical cancer) and higher SES (Bremer & Wübker, 2012; Kahl et al., 1999; Richter et al., 2002; Bergmann et al., 2005; Klug et al., 2005; Rückinger et al., 2008; Seidel et al., 2009; Sieverding et al., 2008; von dem Knesebeck & Mielck, 2009; Lüngen et al., 2009; Kuitto et

Table 8.3 Socioeconomic status (SES) and the utilization of prevention in Germany

Prevention				
Author (year)	Sample	Dependent variables	Independent variables	Results
Albert et al. (2012)	Female population in 10 federal states (n=3,226)	Participation in screening mammography program	Educational attainment, income, and insurance status	Non-participants had a higher educational level and a higher net household income and were twice as likely to be privately insured
Bergmann et al. (2005)	Telephone Health Survey 2003 (n=8,318)	Utilization of flu vaccination, "Health Check-Up" and cancer screenings	Winkler Index of SES	Less frequent utilization of flu vaccine by privately insured individuals and members of the highest status groups. Few status-specific differences for the "Health Check-Up". Willingness to participate in cancer screening increases with social status
Born et al. (2006)	General population of one federal state (SHIP) (n=4,310)	Dental check-up	Educational attainment, occupational status, income, and insurance status	More frequent utilization by privately insured individuals and those with higher educational attainment. No association with income and occupational position
Böhmer et al. (2011)	GEDA 2009 Telephone Health Survey (n=21,262)	Utilization of flu vaccination	Educational status and income	Higher income is associated with higher vaccination status; no association with education
Bremer and Wübker (2012)	German subsample of the first three waves of SHARE (age > 50 years) (n=2,624)	Utilization of preventive services from primary care physicians and specialists	Income	Higher-income groups more frequently utilized preventive services offered by specialists. Few income-related inequalities in preventive services offered by primary care physicians

Table 8.3 (continued)

Prevention				
Author (year)	Sample	Dependent variables	Independent variables	Results
Freund et al. (2010)	Patients in German primary care physician practices ($n=178$)	Utilization of "Health Check-Ups"	Educational attainment	Failure to utilize services is reported less frequently by participants with lower or middle-level secondary school degree but no completed vocational training, more frequently by participants with completed vocational training
Geyer and Micheelis (2012)	Dental patients (three surveys, $n=500$, $n=655$, $n=921$)	Check-up or visits due to pain	Educational attainment, income	Low income and low educational attainment are associated with lower utilization
Huber et al. (2012)	German Health Interview and Examination Survey for Children and Adolescents (KiGGS) ($n=17{,}641$)	Utilization of preventive services (early detection check-up, allergy testing, vaccinations, dental check-up)	Insurance status and Winkler Index of SES	SHI-insured children utilize dental check-up more regularly, more frequently utilize prick tests, and are more commonly fully vaccinated (MMR). Higher utilization of early detection check-up in privately insured children
Kahl et al. (1999)	Participants in the German National Health Survey ($n=7{,}124$)	Utilization of screening and health promotion services	Social status and insurance status	Higher participation in cancer screening and "Health Check-Up" by higher status groups (SHI-insured individuals only). Participation in health promotion services also higher in higher status groups, lower participation particularly in SHI-insured men
Kamtsiuris et al. (2007)	German Health Interview and Examination Survey for Children and Adolescents (KiGGS) ($n=17{,}641$)	Utilization of early detection check-up	Winkler Index of SES	Utilization of early detection check-up and the completeness of the program drops with social status

Table 8.3 (continued)

Prevention				
Author (year)	Sample	Dependent variables	Independent variables	Results
Klug et al. (2005)	Randomly selected women in a large city (n=532)	Utilization of breast and cervical cancer screening	Educational attainment, income, and Winkler social status index	Younger age at first mammography and at first pap smear for women of higher social classes
Knopf et al. (2008)	German Health Interview and Examination Survey for Children and Adolescents (KiGGS) (n=17,641)	Dental check-up	Winkler Index of SES	Less frequent utilization of check-up for lower-SES patients
Koller et al. (2009)	Mothers residing in Bavaria (n=3,426)	Utilization of prenatal check-up	Mother's occupation	Lower participation by mothers of lower occupational status
Kriwy (2012)	Parents (n=464), children and adolescents (n=9,270), physicians (n=136)	MMR vaccination status	Parents' educational level	Lower parent education is associated with a higher probability of vaccination
Kuitto et al. (2010)	Randomly selected women between the ages of 14 and 65 (n=760)	Participation in screening and HPV vaccinations (cervical cancer)	Educational attainment and social status	Higher participation in screening by women with higher SES, but higher vaccination rate in lower-SES women
Lostao et al. (2007)	German National Health Survey 1992 (n=7,466) and 1998 (n=7,124), European comparison study	Utilization of cancer screening	Educational attainment and occupational status	Little to no association between SES and utilization
Lüngen et al. (2009)	General population in 2002 (n=75,122) and 2006 (n=60,555)	Utilization of cancer screening	Winkler Index of SES and insurance status	Lower status groups utilize cancer screening less frequently. Privately insured individuals utilize screening more frequently
Mielck et al. (2006)	MONICA study participants with type 2 diabetes (n=378)	Utilization of diabetes management classes	Educational attainment	Participation in diabetes management classes is lower in those with lower educational attainment

Table 8.3 (continued)

Prevention				
Author (year)	Sample	Dependent variables	Independent variables	Results
Poethko-Müller et al. (2007)	German Health Interview and Examination Survey for Children and Adolescents (KiGGS) (n=16,460)	Vaccination status of children and adolescents	Winkler Index of SES	Status-specific differences in vaccination rates are inconsistent and hardly suggest disparities
Richter et al. (2002)	North Rhine-Westphalian Health Survey (n=1,920)	Utilization of cancer screening, "Health Check-Up", and health promotion activities	Winkler Index of SES	Lower participation in cancer screening with lower SES; for women, the same applies for health promotion activities. No disparities regarding "Health Check-Up"
Ringwald et al. (2006)	General population (16–68 years of age) (n=6,812)	Hepatitis B vaccination status	Occupation	Lower vaccination rate in those with low occupational status
Röckl-Wiedmann et al. (2002)	General adult population of Bavaria (n=2,051)	Utilization of cancer screening, vaccinations (polio, tetanus, and hepatitis A+B) and HIV testing	Winkler Index of SES, education, and income	Higher-SES individuals have a better vaccination status and more frequently take HIV tests. No status-specific differences in cancer screening
Rückinger et al. (2008)	Female patients in Bavaria ≥20 years of age (aggregate data, n=2,223,135)	Utilization of cancer screening	Average household income	Districts with lower average income exhibit particularly low utilization rates
Schneider et al. (2005)	Working individuals aged 18 to 69 (n=3,313)	Participation in back exercises within 1 year	Occupational status, education, and income	In bivariate analyses, only low occupational status was associated with lower participation. In need-adjusted multivariate analyses, this relationship is no longer identifiable
Schönberger et al. (2009)	Data from children's vaccination passports (n=2,116)	Utilization of measles vaccination	Income and educational attainment of parents	Status indicators do not significantly predict vaccination rate
Schultze-Lutter et al. (2008)	Initial contact to the psychological crisis center (n=872)	Utilization of psychological crisis center	Educational attainment	Higher participation in people with higher educational attainment

Table 8.3 (continued)

Prevention				
Author (year)	Sample	Dependent variables	Independent variables	Results
Seidel et al. (2009)	Randomly selected women between the ages of 35 and 65 (n=13,612)	Utilization of cervical cancer screening	Educational attainment and occupational status	Lower educational attainment is associated with lower utilization; no association with occupational status
Sieverding et al. (2008)	Randomly selected men aged 45–70 (n=10,659)	Utilization of prostate cancer screening	Income, educational attainment, and insurance status	Higher participation with higher educational attainment, higher income, and private health insurance. However, relatively little variance is explained by SES variables
Simoes et al. (2006, 2009)	Perinatal data of pregnant women (n=556,948)	Utilization of prenatal examinations	Occupational status	Lower utilization by those with low occupational status
von dem Knesebeck and Mielck (2009)	German subsample of the first wave of SHARE (age >50 years) (n=1,921)	Utilization of screening examinations (mammography, colonoscopy, and eye examinations)	Education, income, and financial wealth	People of higher SES more frequently participate in screening

al., 2010) or private insurance (Bergmann et al., 2005; Lüngen et al., 2009). The same applies to health promotion activities that were analyzed in parallel by two studies (back exercise, stress management, healthy nutrition, weight reduction, and cessation programs) (Kahl et al., 1999; Richter et al., 2002). The need-adjusted study by Bremer and Wübker (2012) notably found that the utilization of specialist preventive services was associated much more strongly with SES than prevention provided by primary care physicians.

A social gradient in the form of lower participation by lower status groups was also found for other preventive check-ups, such as prenatal examinations (Koller et al. 2009; Simoes et al. 2006, 2009), eye examinations (von dem Knesebeck & Mielck, 2009), and the utilization of early detection centers for mental disorders (Schultze-Lutter et al., 2008). No status-specific inequalities were found for the German "Health Check-Up" preventive service (Kahl et al., 1999; Richter et al., 2002; Bergmann et al., 2005; Freund et al., 2010). A relationship between occupational status and participation in back exercises resolved when adjusting for need (Schneider et al. 2005). Again, early detection check-ups in children and adolescents were less frequently and less completely utilized by lower-SES and SHI-insured individuals (Kamtsiuris et al., 2007; Huber et al., 2012). Patient participation in diabetes-related classes is also associated with higher educational level (Mielck et al., 2006).

No consistent relationship could be identified between social status and vaccination rate. For child and adolescent vaccinations against measles, mumps, and rubella (MMR), higher status groups and privately insured individuals exhibited a slightly lower vaccination rate (Poethko-Müller et al., 2007; Kriwy, 2012; Huber et al., 2012, Schönberger et al. 2009). No social gradients have been found for the flu vaccine regarding income (Bremer & Wübker, 2012) and for various other vaccines (tetanus, diphtheria, polio, hepatitis B, Hib, and pertussis) (Poethko-Müller et al., 2007). Only the booster rates for tetanus and diphtheria were slightly lower in lower social status groups. However, other publications reported that higher-SES members exhibited a better vaccination status (tetanus, polio, and hepatitis A and B) (Röckl-Wiedmann et al., 2002; Ringwald et al., 2006). Another study showed the same for the flu vaccine when measured against income but not education (Böhmer et al., 2011). Kuitto et al. (2010) found higher participation in human papillomavirus (HPV) vaccinations against cervical cancer in lower status groups.

Four studies investigated dental check-up (Born et al., 2006; Knopf et al., 2008; Geyer & Micheelis, 2012; Huber et al., 2012). In the general population of one federal state (Mecklenburg-Western Pomerania), more regular dental check-ups were found for those with a higher educational level and private health insurance (Born et al., 2006). Geyer and Micheelis (2012) also documented a lower number of dentist visits (both routine-based and problem-based) in the group with the lowest education and income. Lower-SES children and adolescents received insufficient caries prevention (Knopf et al., 2008). For the same sample, Huber et al. (2012) calculated that respondents with lower SES and SHI (mutally adjusted) take care of dental hygiene les regularly. Surprisingly, participation in check-up was significantly less regular in privately insured individuals than in the SHI-insured population.

Discussion

This systematic review offers an overview of published study results on the association between SES and the utilization of medical and health-related services in Germany. Indicators of social inequality were education, income, and occupational status, and these indicators were supplemented by insurance status.

We differentiated health services utilization from health services access. The sectors of utilization were classified into outpatient care, inpatient care, and prevention (von dem Knesebeck et al., 2009). According to Andersen's model of utilization behavior (Andersen & Newman, 1973; Andersen, 1995, 2008), the above indicators of social inequality are categorized as "predisposing characteristics" (education and professional status) and "enabling factors" (income and insurance status).

For the period between January 1, 1998 and May 16, 2012, we found a total of 57 relevant publications for this review. Differences in methodology, sampling, and the outcome variables required a differentiated interpretation of results. Since not all studies were adjusted for need for care, the extent to which documented differences are caused by dissimilar needs is unclear in some instances. The year in which the data were collected also plays an important role since ongoing developments in German health policies can have a major effect on patients' utilization behavior (Gerlinger, 2008; Mielck, 2008b; Rückert et al., 2008). However, most studies were conducted on the basis of established, high-quality surveys. Regarding insurance status, it must be taken into account that it is somewhat more difficult to interpret than the established inequality factors of education, income, and occupational status. In addition, different subgroups and service offers are found within SHI-insured and privately insured groups.

Our results confirm those of the most recent reviews that also took into account vertical inequalities in utilization of health services in Germany (Mielck, 2008b; Janßen et al., 2009). Furthermore, this review provides a detailed overview of the current state of research in various medical service sectors.

In outpatient care, social inequalities manifest particularly in the form of differences in the utilization of specialists versus primary care physicians. Patients with lower social status or SHI visit primary care physicians significantly more frequently and specialists significantly less frequently than patients of higher SES. Otherwise, differences in outpatient care are rather minor and can in part be explained by greater need in lower social status groups. The documented socioeconomic differences in the utilization of primary care physicians versus specialists suggest differences in awareness of available health services. Establishing initial contact through the primary care physician in case of illness (the gatekeeper model) is a German health policy goal; therefore, increasing the rate of specialist visits in lower social groups is not a pressing concern. The higher specialist contact rate by higher-SES individuals might be explained by the EUR10 practice fee, which was payable for each initial specialist visit without referral from a primary physician, for instance, and might be a less significant issue for this group. Higher-SES patients might be more willing to pay another practice fee to allow them to directly visit the specialist without getting a referral from the physician last visited. At the beginning of 2013, 9 years after its introduction, the government abolished the practice fee again. Nevertheless, the question remains whether the demonstrably higher morbidity in lower SES groups (Mielck, 2005, 2008a) should not result in higher rates of specialist visits by the respective at-risk groups. This could suggest underprovision of medical care for disadvantaged social groups.

The fewest studies were available for inpatient care, but our search revealed comparatively consistent results in this sector. With a few exceptions, social status plays a fairly minor role in inpatient care, particularly in inpatient rehabilitation. Few results are currently available for long-term care, making it difficult to draw conclusions in this area. Overall, the research on status-specific utilization behavior in the inpatient sector is fragmented, so that conclusions must be treated with caution, and additional studies are required. It is conceivable that access rules and financing or coverage through SHI benefits may have a leveling effect.

Most publications as well as the largest social differences were found in the sector of prevention. This overview differentiates by the type of preventive service and by the surveyed population. With a few exceptions, most studies reveal social inequalities in the utilization of various cancer screenings. Higher SES and private health insurance are associated with higher utilization. A similar pattern is found for early detection check-ups in children and adolescents. This trend also applies to other programs, such as prenatal examinations, but less so to the "Health Check-Up" offered in Germany. However, the benefits of such early detection and screening examinations are not without controversy, which must be borne in mind when interpreting these results (e.g., Gomella et al., 2011; Kalager et al., 2012).

Far fewer disparities were found in the area of vaccinations. Results differ slightly by vaccination type, but status-specific differences play only a minor role. In contrast, studies on dental check-up revealed that higher-SES children and adolescents took advantage of these services more regularly. Surprisingly, one study documented less regular check-up in privately insured children and adolescents. In some sectors, awareness may therefore need to be raised, regardless of educational or occupational status. For instance, information about the purpose of vaccinations should be addressed equally to all residents without regard to SES.

Overall, social inequalities in the utilization of health services differ by health care sector. In inpatient and outpatient care, inequalities are absent or limited to certain aspects, while socioeconomic differences are greatest in preventive services. Results also suggest differences in utilization between SHI-insured and privately insured individuals, but comparatively little research is currently available in this area.

References

Albert, U.S., Kalder, M., Schulte, H., Klusendick, M., Diener, J., Schulz-Zehden, B., Kopp, I., Nass-Griegoleit, I., 2011. Das populationsbezogene Mammografie-Screening-Programm in Deutschland: Inanspruchnahme und erste Erfahrungen von Frauen in 10 Bundesländern [The population-based mammography screening Programme in Germany: uptake and first experiences of women in 10 federal states]. Das Gesundheitswesen 74, 61–70.

Altenhöner, T., Leppin, A., Grande, G., Romppel, M., 2005. Social inequality in patients' physical and psychological state and participation in rehabilitation after myocardial infarction in Germany. International Journal of Rehabilitation Research 28, 251–257.

Andersen, R.M., 1995. Revisiting the behavioral model and access to medical care: does it matter? Journal of Health and Social Behavior 36, 1–10.

Andersen, R.M., 2008. National health surveys and the behavioral model of health services use. Medical Care 46, 647–653.

Andersen, R.M., Newman, J.F., 1973. Societal and individual determinants of medical care utilization in the United States. The Milbank Memorial Fund Quarterly. Health and Society, 51, 95–124.

Baumeister, S.E., Alte, D., John, U., 2004. Inanspruchnahme medizinischer Leistungen: Welche Rolle spielt die soziale Unterstützung?—Ergebnisse der Study of Health in Pomerania (SHIP) [Medical services utilisation: which role does social support play?—Results from the Study of Health in Pomerania (SHIP)]. Das Gesundheitswesen 66, 175–179.

Bergmann, E., Kalcklösch, M., Tiemann, F., 2005. Inanspruchnahme des Gesundheitswesens [Health care utilisation. Initial results of the Telephone Health Survey 2003]. Bundesgesundheitsblatt—Gesundheitsforschung—Gesundheitsschutz 48, 1365–1373.

Blinkert, B., Klie, T., 2008. Soziale Ungleichheit und Pflege. Aus Politik und Zeitgeschichte 12/13, 25–33.

Böhmer, M.M., Walter, D., Müters, S., Krause, G., Wichmann, O., 2011. Seasonal influenza vaccine uptake in Germany 2007/2008 and 2008/2009: Results from a national health update survey. Vaccine 29, 4492–4498.

Born, G., Baumeister, S.E., Sauer, S., Hensel, E., Kocher, T., John, U., 2006. Merkmale von Risikogruppen einer unzureichenden Inanspruchnahme zahnmedizinischer Leistungen—Ergebnisse der Study of Health in Pomerania (SHIP) [Characteristics of risk groups with an insufficient demand for dental services—results of the Study of Health in Pomerania (SHIP)]. Das Gesundheitswesen 68, 257–264.

Bremer, A., Wübker, P., 2012. Soziale Ungleichheit und Inanspruchnahme medizinischer und präventiver Leistungen, in: Kirch, W., Hoffmann, T., Pfaff, H. (Eds.) Prävention und Versorgung, Thieme, Stuttgart/New York, pp. 226–249.

Deck, R., 2008. Soziale Ungleichheit in der medizinischen Rehabilitation [Social inequality in medical rehabilitation]. Das Gesundheitswesen 70, 582–589.

Deutsche Sozialversicherung, 2012. [homepage on the internet]. Available from: http://www.deutsche-sozialversicherung.de/en/health/index.html (accessed 16 October 2012)

Freund, T., Lekutat, C., Schwantes, U., Szecsenyi, J., Joos, S., 2010. Gesundheitsuntersuchung und Impfstatus—Ergebnisse einer Patientenbefragung in deutschen Hausarztpraxen [Health screening and vaccination status—results from a patient survey in German general practices]. Das Gesundheitswesen 72, 804–807.

Gerlinger, T., 2008. Gesundheitspolitik und die Frage der sozialen Ungleichheit in der gesundheitlichen Versorgung, in: Tiesmeyer, K., Brause M., Lierse, M., Lukas-Nülle M, Hehlmann, T. (Eds.) Der Blinde Fleck. Ungleichheiten in der Gesundheitsversorgung, Verlag Hans Huber, Bern, pp. 39–52.

Geyer, S., 2008. Ein,- Zwei,- oder Mehrklassenmedizin? Soziale Ungleichheiten in der gesundheitlichen Versorgung., in:, Weber, A. (Ed.) Gesundheit- Arbeit- Rehabilitation, Roderer Verlag, Regensburg, pp. 136–146.

Geyer, S., Micheelis, W., 2012. Changes in problem-based and routine-based healthcare attendance: a comparison of three national dental health surveys. Community dentistry and oral epidemiology 40, 459–467.

Geyer, S., Schlanstedt-Jahn, U., 2012. Gibt es soziale Ungleichheiten in der Inanspruchnahme der onkologischen Rehabilitation bei Mammakarzinompatientinnen? [Are there social inequalities in the utilisation of oncological rehabilitation by breast cancer patients?] Das Gesundheitswesen 74, 71–78.

Geyer, S., Peter, R., Siegrist, J., 2002. Socioeconomic differences in children's and adolescents' hospital admissions in Germany: a report based on health insurance data on selected diagnostic categories. Journal of Epidemiology and Community Health 56, 109–114.

Goddard, M., Smith, P., 2001. Equity of access to health care services: theory and evidence from the UK. Social Science & Medicine 53, 1149–1162.

Gomella, L.G., Liu, X S., Trabulsi, E.J., Kelly, W.K., Myers, R., Showalter, T., Dicker, A., Wender, R. (2011). Screening for prostate cancer: the current evidence and guidelines contro-versy. The Canadian journal of urology, 18(5), 5875–5883.

Gruber, S., Kiesel, M., 2009. Wer konsultiert den Allgemeinarzt in Deutschland? Eine Analyse zum Einfluss von Versicherung und anderen sozialen Merkmalen auf die Inanspruchnahme allgemeinmedizinischer Leistungen im Alter, in: Engelhardt, H (Ed.) Altern in Europa. Empirische Analysen mit dem Survey of Health, Ageing and Retirement in Europe, University of Bamberg Press, pp. 94–143.

Gruber, S., Kiesel, M., 2010. Inequality in health care utilization in Germany? Theoretical and empirical evidence for specialist consultation. Journal of Public Health 18, 351–365.

Häuser, W., 2005. Das Fibromyalgiesyndrom in der Sozialgerichtsbarkeit—psychosoziale Risikofaktoren und Prädiktoren der Inanspruchnahme medizinischer Leistungen [Fibromyalgia in the legal procedures of the German Sozialgericht—psychosocial risk factors and predictors of health care utilization]. PPmP—Psychotherapie · Psychosomatik · Medizinische Psychologie 55, 72–78.

Hessel, A., Gunzelmann, T., Geyer, M., Brähler, E., 2000. Inanspruchnahme medizinischer Leistungen und Medikamenteneinnahme bei über 60jährigen in Deutschland—gesundheitliche, sozialstrukturelle, sozio-demographische und subjektive Faktoren [Utilization of medical services and medication intake of patients over 60 in Germany–health related, social structure related, socio-demographic and subjective factors]. Zeitschrift für Gerontologie und Geriatrie 33, 289–299.

Hofreuter, K., von dem Knesebeck, O., 2009. Soziale Ungleichheit und gesundheitliche Versorgung, in: Wesenauer, A., Sebinger, S. (Eds.) Soziale Ungleichheit und Gesundheit. Gesundheitliche Versorgung und Gesundheitsförderung—Eine Frage der sozialen Gerechtigkeit? (2nd Ed.), Mabuse, Frankfurt am Main, pp. 25–39.

Huber, J., Mielck, A., 2010. Morbidität und Gesundheitsversorgung bei GKV- und PKV-Versicherten. Forschungsstand empirischer Studien [Morbidity and healthcare differences between insured in the statutory ("GKV") and private health insurance ("PKV") in Germany. Review of empirical studies]. Bundesgesundheitsblatt—Gesundheitsforschung—Gesundheitsschutz 53, 925–938.

Huber, J., Lampert, T., Mielck, A., 2012. Unterschiede bei Gesundheitsrisiken, Morbidität und gesundheitlicher Versorgung zwischen Kindern GKV- bzw. PKV-versicherter Eltern: Ergebnisse aus dem Kinder- und Jugendgesundheitssurvey (KiGGS) [Inequalities in health risks, morbidity and health care of children by health insurance of their parents (statutory vs. private health insurance): results of the German KiGGS Study.]. Das Gesundheitswesen 74, 627–638.

Hullegie, P., Klein, T.J., 2010. The effect of private health insurance on medical care utilization and self-assessed health in Germany. Health Economics 19, 1048–1062.

Icks, A., Rosenbauer, J., Strassburger, K., Grabert, M., Giani, G., Holl, R.W., 2007. Persistent social disparities in the risk of hospital admission of paediatric diabetic patients in Germany-prospective data from 1277 diabetic children and adolescents. Diabetic Medicine 24, 440–442.

Janßen, C., Grosse-Frie, K., Dinger, H., Schiffmann, L., Ommen, O., 2009. Der Einfluss von sozialer Ungleichheit auf die medizinische und gesundheitsbezogene Versorgung in Deutschland, in: Gesundheitliche Ungleichheit—Grundlagen, Probleme, Perspektiven (2nd Ed.), VS Verlag, Wiesbaden, pp. 150–165.

Kahl, H., Hölling, H., Kamtsiuris, P., 1999. Inanspruchnahme von Früherkennungsuntersuchungen und Maßnahmen zur Gesundheitsförderung [Utilization of health screening studies and measures for health promotion]. Das Gesundheitswesen 61 Spec No, S163–168.

Kalager, M., Adami, H.O., Bretthauer, M., Tamimi, R.M., 2012. Overdiagnosis of invasive breast cancer due to mammography screening: results from the Norwegian screening program. Annals of Internal Medicine 156, 491–499.

Kamtsiuris, P., Bergmann, E., Rattay, P., Schlaud, M., 2007. Inanspruchnahme medizinischer Leistungen. Ergebnisse des Kinder Jugendgesundheitssurveys (KiGGS). [Use of medical services. Results of the German Health Interview and Examination Survey for Children and

Adolescents (KiGGS)]. Bundesgesundheitsblatt—Gesundheitsforschung—Gesundheitsschutz 50, 836–850.

Kiesel, M., Gruber, S., 2012. Sozioökonomische Determinanten der stationären Versorgung in Deutschland, in: Kirch, W., Hoffmann, T., Pfaff, H. (Eds.) Prävention und Versorgung, Thieme, Stuttgart/New York, pp. 696–711.

Klug, S.J., Hetzer, M., Blettner, M., 2005. Screening for breast and cervical cancer in a large German city: participation, motivation and knowledge of risk factors. The European Journal of Public Health 15, 70–77.

Knopf, H., Rieck, A., Schenk, L., 2008. Mundhygiene. Daten des KiGGS zum Karies-präventiven Verhalten [Oral hygiene. KIGGS data on caries preventative behaviour]. Bundesgesundheitsblatt—Gesundheitsforschung—Gesundheitsschutz 51, 1314–1320.

Koller, D., Lack, N., Mielck, A., 2009. Soziale Unterschiede bei der Inanspruchnahme der Schwangerschafts-Vorsorgeuntersuchungen, beim Rauchen der Mutter während der Schwangerschaft und beim Geburtsgewicht des Neugeborenen. Empirische Analyse auf Basis der Bayerischen Perinatal-Studie [Social differences in the utilisation of prenatal screening, smoking during pregnancy and birth weight—empirical analysis of data from the Perinatal Study in Bavaria (Germany)]. Das Gesundheitswesen 71, 10–18.

Kriwy, P., 2012. Similarity of parents and physicians in the decision to vaccinate children against measles, mumps and rubella. International Journal of Public Health 57, 333–340.

Kriwy, P., Mielck, A., 2006. Versicherte der gesetzlichen Krankenversicherung (GKV) und der privaten Krankenversicherung (PKV): Unterschiede in Morbidität und Gesundheitsverhalten [Persons insured with the German statutory sickness funds or privately insured: differences in health and health behaviour]. Das Gesundheitswesen 68, 281–288.

Kürschner, N., Weidmann, C., Müters, S., 2011. Wer wählt den Hausarzt zum "Gatekeeper"? [Who enrolls in a general practitioner model? The behavioral model of health services use and general practitioner-centered care in Germany]. Bundesgesundheitsblatt—Gesundheitsforschung—Gesundheitsschutz 54, 221–227.

Kuitto, K., Pickel, S., Neumann, H., Jahn, D., Metelmann, H.R., 2010. Attitudinal and sociostructural determinants of cervical cancer screening and HPV vaccination uptake: a quantitative multivariate analysis. Journal of Public Health 18, 179–188.

Lampert, T., Kroll L.E., Dunkelberg, A., 2007. Soziale Ungleichheit der Lebenserwartung in Deutschland. Aus Politik und Zeitgeschichte 42, 11–18.

Lehmann, C., Beierlein, V., Hagen-Aukamp, C., Kerschgens, C., Rhee, M., Frühauf, S., Otto, J. et al. 2012. Psychosoziale Einflussfaktoren für die Inanspruchnahme medizinischer Rehabilitationsmaßnahmen bei Patienten mit einer Prostatakrebserkrankung [Psychosocial predictors of utilization of medical rehabilitation services among prostate cancer patients]. Die Rehabilitation 51, 160–170.

Lostao, L., Regidor, E., Geyer, S., Aïach, P., 2007. Patient cost sharing and social inequalities in access to health care in three western European countries. Social Science & Medicine 65, 367–376.

Lüngen, M., Stollenwerk, B., Messner, P., Lauterbach, K.W., Gerber, A., 2008. Waiting times for elective treatments according to insurance status: A randomized empirical study in Germany. International Journal for Equity in Health 7, 1.

Lüngen, M., Siegel, M., Deabik, A., Büscher, G., von Törne, I., 2009. Ausmaß und Gründe für Ungleichheiten der gesundheitlichen Versorgung in Deutschland. Studien zu Gesundheit, Medizin und Gesellschaft, Köln, 5/2009.

Mackenbach, J.P., 2003. Widening socioeconomic inequalities in mortality in six Western European countries. International Journal of Epidemiology 32, 830–837.

Mackenbach, J.P., 2006. Health Inequalities: Europe in Profile. An independent expert report commissioned by the UK presidency of the EU. London, Department of Health.

Mackenbach, J.P., Stirbu, I., Roskam, A.J.R., Schaap, M.M., Menvielle, G., Leinsalu, M., Kunst, A.E., 2008. Socioeconomic inequalities in health in 22 European countries. The New England Journal of Medicine 358, 2468–2481.

Marmot, M., Wilkinson, R.G., 2006. Social Determinants of health (2nd Ed.). Oxford University Press; Oxford/New York.

Maziak, W., von Mutius, E., Keil, U., Hirsch, T., Leupold, W., Rzehak, P., Behrens, T., Weiland, S.K., 2004. Predictors of health care utilization of children with asthma in the community. Pediatric Allergy and Immunology 15, 166–171.

Mielck, A., 2005. Soziale Ungleichheit und Gesundheit. Einführung in die aktuelle Diskussion. Verlag Hans Huber, Bern.

Mielck, A., 2008a. Soziale Ungleichheit und Gesundheit in Deutschland—Die internationale Perspektive [Health inequalities in Germany. The international perspective]. Bundesgesundheitsblatt—Gesundheitsforschung—Gesundheitsschutz 51, 345–352.

Mielck, A., 2008b. Zum Zusammenhang gesundheitlicher Ungleichheit und gesundheitlicher Versorgung, in: Tiesmeyer, K, Brause M., Lierse, M., Lukas-Nülle M, Hehlmann, T. (Eds.) Der Blinde Fleck. Ungleichheiten in der Gesundheitsversorgung, Verlag Hans Huber, Bern, pp. 21–38.

Mielck, A., Reitmeir, P., Rathmann, W., 2006. Knowledge about Diabetes and Participation in Diabetes Training Courses: The Need for Improving Health Care for Diabetes Patients with Low SES. Experimental and Clinical Endocrinology & Diabetes 114, 240–248.

Mielck, A., Kiess, R., von dem Knesebeck, O., Stirbu, I., Kunst, A.E., 2009. Association between forgone care and household income among the elderly in five Western European countries—analyses based on survey data from the SHARE-study. BMC Health Services Research 9, 52.

Or, Z., Jusot, F., Yilmaz, E., 2008. Impact of health care system on socioeconomic inequalities in doctor use. Institut de recherche et documentation en économie de la santé, Paris.

Poethko-Müller, C., Kuhnert, R., Schlaud, M., 2007. Durchimpfung und Determinanten des Impfstatus in Deutschland [Vaccination coverage and predictors for vaccination level. Results of the German Health Interview and Examination Survey for Children and Adolescents (KiGGS)]. Bundesgesundheitsblatt—Gesundheitsforschung—Gesundheitsschutz 50, 851–862.

Reibling, N., Wendt, C., 2010. Bildungsniveau und Zugang zu Gesundheitsleistungen. Eine vergleichende Analyse von Zugangsregulierung und Inanspruchnahme fachärztlicher Leistungen in Europa [Access to health care by level of education. A comparative analysis of access regulation and utilisation of specialist health care in Europe]. Das Gesundheitswesen 72, 447–454.

Richter, M., Brand, H., Rössler, G., 2002. Sozioökonomische Unterschiede in der Inanspruchnahme von Früherkennungsuntersuchungen und Maßnahmen der Gesundheitsförderung in NRW [Socio-economic differences in the utilisation of screening programmes and health promotion measures in North Rhine-Westphalia, Germany]. Das Gesundheitswesen 64, 417–423.

Ringwald, J., Mertz, I., Zimmermann, R., Weisbach, V., Rabe, C., Strasser, E., Seyboth, S., Eckstein, R., 2006. Hepatitis B vaccination status among healthy adults in Germany. Health Policy 79, 306–312.

Robert Koch-Institut, 2005. Beiträge zur Gesundheitsberichterstattung des Bundes. Armut, soziale Ungleichheit und Gesundheit. Robert Koch-Institut, Berlin.

Robert Koch-Institut, 2012. Beiträge zur Gesundheitsberichterstattung des Bundes. Daten und Fakten: Ergebnisse der Studie "Gesundheit in Deutschland aktuell 2010". Robert Koch-Institut, Berlin.

Röckl-Wiedmann, I., Meyer, N., Fischer, R., Laubereau, B., Weitkunat, R., Uberla, K., 2002. Schichtspezifische Inanspruchnahme medizinischer Leistungen und Vorsorgeverhalten in Bayern: Ergebnisse einer repräsentativen Bevölkerungsbefragung [The use of medical services and the utilization rate in screening programs in relation to social class: results of a representative survey in Bavaria]. Sozial- und Präventivmedizin/Social and Preventive Medicine 47, 307–317.

Rückert, I.-M., Böcken, J., Mielck, A., 2008. Are German patients burdened by the practice charge for physician visits ('Praxisgebuehr')? A cross sectional analysis of socio-economic and health related factors. BMC Health Services Research 8, 232.

Rückinger, S., Kries, R. von, Pauli, S., Munte, A., Mielck, A., 2008. Die Krebsfrüherkennungsuntersuchung für Frauen wird in Regionen mit niedrigerem Haushaltseinkommen seltener in Anspruch genommen—Analyse von Daten der Kassenärztlichen Vereinigung Bayerns [Cancer

screening for women is less frequently visited in regions with lower household income—analysis of data from health insurances in Bavaria]. Das Gesundheitswesen 70, 393–397.
Scheffer, S., Dauven, S., Sieverding, M., 2006. Soziodemografische Unterschiede in der Teilnahme an Krebsfrüherkennungsuntersuchungen (KFU) in Deutschland—Eine Übersicht [Sociodemographic differences in the participation in "early detection of cancer examinations" in Germany—a review]. Das Gesundheitswesen 68, 139–146.
Schnabel, E., Sausenthaler, S., Liese, J., Herbarth, O., Borte, M., Schaaf, B. et al. 2009. Hospital admissions in children up to the age of 2 years. European Journal of Pediatrics 168, 925–931.
Schneider, S., Hauf, C., Schiltenwolf, M., 2005. Nutzerstruktur und Korrelate der Teilnahme an Rückenschulen: eine repräsentative Studie an der bundesdeutschen erwerbstätigen Bevölkerung [Attendance at back care programmes: a representative study of the working population in Germany]. Sozial- und Präventivmedizin/Social and Preventive Medicine 50, 95–106.
Schnitzer, S., Balke, K., Walter, A., Litschel, A., Kuhlmey, A., 2011. Führt das Hausarztmodell zu mehr Gleichheit im Gesundheitssystem? Ein Vergleich der Versorgungssituation von Hausarztmodellteilnehmern und Nichtteilnehmern [Do gatekeeping programs increase equality of health care in Germany? A comparison of the health care situation of participants and nonparticipants]. Bundesgesundheitsblatt—Gesundheitsforschung—Gesundheitsschutz 54, 942–950.
Schönberger, K., Grote, V., von Kries, R., Kalies H., 2009. Risikofaktoren für eine verspätete oder nicht erfolgte Masernimpfung bei Kleinkindern [Risk factors for delayed or missed measels vaccination in young children]. Bundesgesundheitsblatt - Gesundheitsforschung - Gesundheitsschutz 52, 1045-1052.
Schubert, M., Behrens, J., Becker, C., Zimmermann, M., 2011. Die Teilnehmerstruktur medizinischer Rehabilitationsmaßnahmen in Deutschland [Participant structure of medical rehabilitation measures in Germany]. Rehabilitation 50, 372–378.
Schultze-Lutter, F., Picker, H., Ruhrmann, S., Klosterkötter, J., 2008. Das Kölner Früh-Erkennungs- & Therapie-Zentrum für psychische Krisen (FETZ). Evaluation der Inanspruchnahme [The Cologne Early Recognition and Intervention Center for mental crises (FETZ). Evaluation of service use]. Medizinische Klinik 103, 81–89.
Schwartz, F.W., Badura, B, Busse, R., Leidl R, Raspe, H., Siegrist, J., Walter, U., 2003. Public Health. Urban & Fischer Verlag, München, pp. 181–214.
Seidel, D., Becker, N., Rohrmann, S., Nimptsch, K., Linseisen, J., 2009. Socio-demographic characteristics of participation in the opportunistic German cervical cancer screening programme: results from the EPIC-Heidelberg cohort. Journal of Cancer Research and Clinical Oncology 135, 533–541.
Sibold, M., Mittag, O., Kulick, B., Müller, E., Opitz, U., Jäckel, W.H., 2011. Prädiktoren der Teilnahme an einer Nachsorge nach ambulanter Rehabilitation bei erwerbstätigen Rehabilitanden mit chronischen Rückenschmerzen [Predictors of participation in medical rehabilitation follow-up in working patients with chronic back pain]. Die Rehabilitation 50, 363–371.
Siegrist, J., Marmot, M., 2006. Siegrist J, Social inequalities in health. New evidence and policy implications. Oxford University Press; Oxford/NewYork.
Sieverding, M., Matterne, U., Ciccarello, L., Luboldt, H.-J., 2008. Prostatakarzinomfrüherkennung in Deutschland. Untersuchung einer repräsentativen Bevölkerungsstichprobe. [Early detection of prostate cancer in Germany. A study of a representative random sample of the population]. Der Urologe 47, 1233–1238.
Simoes, E., Münnich, R., Kunz, S., Schmahl, F., 2006. Association between maternal occupational status and utilization of antenatal care. International Archives of Occupational and Environmental Health 79, 75–81.
Simoes, E., Kunz, S., Schmahl, F., 2009. Inanspruchnahmegradienten in der Schwangerenvorsorge fordern zur Weiterentwicklung des Präventionskonzepts auf [Utilisation gradients in prenatal care prompt further development of the prevention concept]. Das Gesundheitswesen 71, 385–390.
Smythe, J., Abholz, H.H., Alves, B., Blane, D., Borgers, D., 2004. Soziale Ungleichheit im Zugang zur ambulanten Behandlung in England und Deutschland [Social differences to outpatient care in England and Germany]. ZFA—Zeitschrift für Allgemeinmedizin 80, 58–62.

Stirbu, I., Kunst, A.E., Mielck, A., Mackenbach, J.P., 2011. Inequalities in utilisation of general practitioner and specialist services in 9 European countries. BMC Health Services Research 11, 288.

Thode, N., Bergmann, E., Kamtsiuris, P., Kurth, B.-M., 2005. Einflussfaktoren auf die ambulante Inanspruchnahme in Deutschland [Predictors for ambulatory medical care utilization in Germany]. Bundesgesundheitsblatt—Gesundheitsforschung—Gesundheitsschutz 48, 296–306.

Tiesmeyer, K, Brause M., Lierse, M., Lukas-Nülle M, Hehlmann, T. (Eds.), 2008. Der Blinde Fleck. Ungleichheiten in der Gesundheitsversorgung, Verlag Hans Huber, Bern.

von Lengerke, T., Happich, M., Reitmeir, P., John, J., 2005. Utilization of out- and inpatient health services by obese adults: a population-based study in the Augsburg region, Germany. Das Gesundheitswesen 67 Suppl 1, 150–157.

von dem Knesebeck, O., Mielck, A., 2009. Soziale Ungleichheit und gesundheitliche Versorgung im höheren Lebensalter [Social inequality and health care among the aged]. Zeitschrift für Gerontologie und Geriatrie 42, 39–46.

von dem Knesebeck, O. von dem, Bauer, U., Geyer, S., Mielck, A ., 2009. Soziale Ungleichheit in der gesundheitlichen Versorgung—ein Plädoyer für systematische Forschung Social Inequality in Health Care—a plea for systematic research. Das Gesundheitswesen 71, 59–62.

Waldmann, A., Lautz, E., Hampe, J., Schreiber, S., Schafmayer, C., Katalinic, A., 2007. Popgen-Darmkrebs: Reha-Inanspruchnahme von jüngeren Patienten mit kolorektalem Tumor [Utilization of inpatient rehabilitation of younger Patients with colorectal neoplasms—results of the project "Popgen-Colorectal Cancer". Die Rehabilitation 46, 349–355.

Chapter 9
Migration and Health Care Utilization in the European Context

Carmen Cristina Ciupitu-Plath, Daniela Gohl, Christopher Kofahl and Birgit Babitsch

Introduction

Migration is a social phenomenon with extensive implications on a cultural, demographic, economic, and political level. Defined as a geographical movement from one location to another, with the aim of establishing a new residence (Goodman, 1992), the migration process entails essentially a status modification for the mobile individual. This change in status, however, is inherently accompanied by an alteration in the individual's sociocultural environment, often requiring an intense adaptation process. This is particularly the case for international migration, where the adjustment to a new normative system is often accompanied by stress and uncertainty, against a background of limited social support networks to facilitate the adaptation process (Kirkcaldy et al., 2006). In association with specific migration-triggering experiences such as poverty, discrimination, or war-related trauma, post-migration stressors contribute to shaping the health challenges and opportunities of migrants in the receiving country.

Throughout the past six decades, as a consequence of larger scale geopolitical transformations (e.g., the fall of the Iron Curtain, globalization, and armed conflicts

C. C. Ciupitu-Plath (✉)
Charité – Universitätsmedizin Berlin,
Berlin School of Public Health, Berlin, Germany
e-mail: cristina.ciupitu-plath@charite.de

D. Gohl
e-mail: daniela-stefanie.gohl@charite.dec

C. Kofahl
Center for Psychosocial Medicine, Department of Medical Sociology,
University Medical Center Hamburg-Eppendorf, Hamburg, Germany
e-mail: kofahl@uke.uni-hamburg.de

B. Babitsch
Department of New Public Health, University of Osnabrück,
School of Human Sciences, Osnabrück, Germany
e-mail: bbabitsch@uni-osnabrueck.de

C. Janssen et al. (eds.), *Health Care Utilization in Germany,*
DOI 10.1007/978-1-4614-9191-0_9,

generating large numbers of asylum seekers), many Western European countries experienced a shift in status from being traditional emigration countries to increasingly receiving significant immigrant inflows themselves. An important driving force in the European migration process, however, was the increased demand on the labor market in postwar Western countries, which attracted labor migrants either from former colonies (e.g., in Great Britain and France) or from partner states with which specific bilateral agreements had been established (e.g., in Germany, Austria, Switzerland, the Netherlands, Belgium, Denmark, and Sweden) (Hansen, 2003). Although restrictions were imposed on these labor migration waves starting in the early 1970s, they resulted in an increasing ethnic diversification of the local population in receiving countries. However, because labor migration was assumed to be only temporary, efforts to integrate the new ethnic groups into the broader social structure were limited and often inadequate (Hansen, 2003). Migration-related changes in the population structure thus found the health- and social-care systems in most of the new receiving countries unprepared to adequately respond to the specific health care needs and challenges of migrant groups.

Currently, the migration phenomenon at a European level is mostly characterized by East–West population movements, driven primarily by the most recent European Union (EU) extension waves, which greatly facilitated cross-border mobility between former socialist, Southeast European countries, and old member states. Although they have the legal right to travel to and reside in any EU country, labor market restrictions still apply for the citizens of new member states in many Western European countries, limiting their access to legal employment and consequently local health insurance schemes. For instance, this is the case in Germany, where many migrants from new EU member states were reported to access health care services in settings essentially designed for undocumented migrants (Castaneda, 2009; Schlopker et al., 2009).

Such examples point to the stark necessity for European health care systems exposed to migration phenomena to be able to identify and respond in a timely manner to the new demographic and cultural challenges posed by the inflow of different ethnic groups. In order to achieve this structural flexibility, more research is required to provide the evidence to support appropriate reform and health services development.

European Research on Migrant Health and Use of Health Services

In European research on the interplay between migration and health care use, the criteria most often employed in differentiating between ethnic groups are related to country of birth, nationality, and citizenship (Baglio et al., 2010; Jimenez-Rubio and Hernandez-Quevedo, 2011; Suurmond et al., 2011; Terraza-Nunez et al., 2010). The participants' mother tongue has also been used as a classification criterion by some scholars in research on the general migrant population (Jensen et al., 2010; Ruppen et al., 2010).

On the other hand, more specific migrant groups, such as undocumented migrants, asylum seekers, or refugees, are primarily defined on the basis of their legal residence status in the receiving country (Castaneda, 2009; Razavi et al., 2011; Schoevers et al., 2010). These definitions, however, may vary according to the particular legislative systems of individual European countries.

Regardless of the various classification criteria, epidemiological data show that migrants are in poorer health than the local populations in several European countries (Germany, Great Britain, and the Netherlands) (Stanciole and Huber, 2009; Zeeb and Razum, 2006). This suggests an interplay between deprivation, health care need, and limitations in access to adequate care among migrants (Stanciole and Huber, 2009), despite an initial relative health status advantage associated with voluntary migration, often described as the "healthy migrant effect" (Kirkcaldy et al., 2006). A similar trend also emerges from migrants' own assessments of their health status, but the existing literature does not consistently show significant differences between migrant and native groups in this respect (Kirkcaldy et al., 2006).

Generally, migrants are confronted with a set of specific individual-level, provider-level, and system-level barriers to accessing health care services in their host countries (Scheppers et al., 2006). Within the scope of European health care systems, where some health insurance coverage is often granted to migrant residents, these barriers emerge mostly from unfamiliarity with the new environment, particularly patient–provider language differences, lack of knowledge of available health services, as well as diverging health beliefs, practices, and explanatory models (Lindert et al., 2008; Stanciole and Huber, 2009). Even in the absence of significant language barriers, many migrants may face both individual and system-related challenges in accessing care, such as

- difficulties in gaining residential registration and health insurance documents,
- increased vulnerability on the labor market preventing them from using health care in a timely manner or taking sick leave when necessary, and
- insufficient access to information regarding the health care system and different expectations from the health care provision process (Terraza-Nunez et al., 2010).

In addition to acting as a barrier to access, the latter can also impact migrants' evaluation of quality of care, as can inadequate patient–provider communication and perceived discrimination (Suurmond et al., 2011).

In terms of actual utilization of health services among migrants, evidence at a European level is inconsistent. This is assumed to derive from variation in the samples used in available studies, and also from differences in the characteristics, needs, beliefs, and practices between and within different ethnic and migrant groups. However, recent research in European countries points to a tendency toward lower rates of health care use in adult migrants compared to local populations (Berchet and Jusot, 2012), particularly in terms of preventive services such as screening examinations (Norredam et al., 2009). Although some authors reported lower specialist- and outpatient-care use in migrants (Deville et al., 2011; Jimenez-Rubio and Hernandez-Quevedo, 2011; Huber et al., 2008), others found equal or higher utilization levels than in the native population (Norredam et al., 2009).

Although in some studies, migrants were found to make greater use of primary care services (Norredam et al., 2009; Huber et al., 2008), this was not found in all studies (Jimenez-Rubio and Hernandez-Quevedo, 2011). Depending on the study context, migrant use of inpatient care was reported as lower (Baglio et al., 2010), equal to, or higher than that of nonmigrants (Norredam et al., 2009). The same was the case for emergency care services (Borde and David, 2007; Huber et al., 2008; Jimenez-Rubio and Hernandez-Quevedo, 2011; Norredam et al., 2009). Concerning mental health problems, migrants appear to have a higher burden of disease (Kirkcaldy et al., 2006); however, their use of specific services like psychiatric treatment or psychotherapy does not always match this increased need for care (Huber et al., 2008). Irrespective of their legal residence status in their host country, migrant women appear to be more prone to seeking care associated with reproductive events, either in inpatient (Baglio et al., 2010; Huber et al., 2008) or in outpatient settings (Castaneda, 2009; Schlopker et al., 2009).

Although traditional immigration countries, such as the USA or Australia, have already acquired substantial expertise in catering to the health care needs of ethnically diverse groups, their good practice examples could hardly be directly transferred to European countries, given their different sociocultural backgrounds and health system structures.

Therefore, efforts have been directed toward identifying best practices based on European experiences in health care provision to migrant patients (Deville et al., 2011; Jensen et al., 2010). However, their implementation still requires action on a broad scale, from increasing financial allocations for migrant health at a system level to improving communication and mutual understanding between providers and patients in the individual health care encounter, both from a linguistic and a cultural viewpoint (Eshiett and Parry, 2003; Jensen et al., 2010).

This chapter will further address specific issues in health care use among migrants in Europe based on the application of Andersen's theoretical model of health services utilization (Andersen, 1995; Andersen & Davidson, 2007) to a sample of original articles reporting on relevant research in the European context. The aim of this review is to gain a better understanding of the health care utilization process, against a background of conflicting evidence in the available literature.

Literature Search Strategy

In order to identify recent research on factors that influence migrants' utilization of health services in European receiving countries, we have conducted a systematic search of literature published in Medline/PubMed based on the strategy depicted in Fig. 9.1.

In order to increase its specificity, the search was restricted to retrieving only English- and German-language studies with human adult subjects (PubMed limits: age 19 and older), published between January 2008 and July 2011.

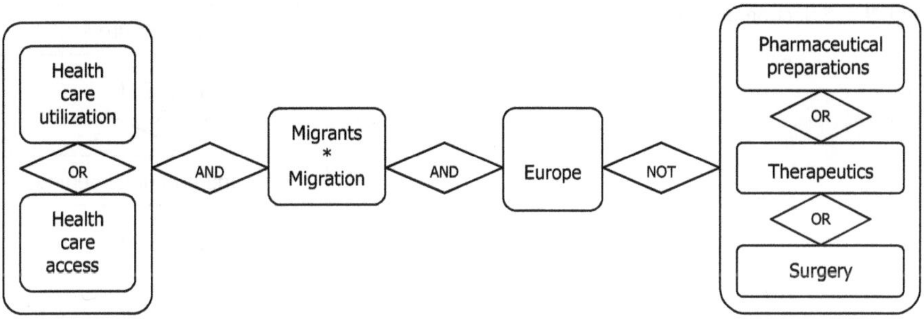

Fig. 9.1 Search strategy

The initial search identified 93 studies published in English and German. Prior to the selection process, criteria for study inclusion and exclusion were established, as follows.

Inclusion criteria:

- Studies related to health care utilization or access to care
- Studies on the adult migrant population living in European countries

Exclusion criteria:

- Studies whose main focus was not related to health care, health care utilization, or access to care
- Focus on specific health problems or areas (e.g., cancer, human immunodeficiency virus (HIV), tuberculosis, hepatitis, specific infectious and parasitic diseases, heart conditions, severe mental disorders, dementia, screening, and genetics)
- Focus on specific interventions/programs
- Specific study population (e.g., inmates, farm workers, international travelers, and men having sex with men)
- Specific health care sectors (e.g., palliative care, home care, reproductive health, and oral health)
- Studies not conducted in Europe
- Studies on children

Based on the above criteria, two researchers independently performed three review rounds in which retrieved articles were screened by title and author, abstract, and, ultimately, full-text publication. After each review round, the researchers compared and discussed their article selection and came to a concerted decision.

In this process, additional exclusion criteria emerged, as some previously retained studies were found to be too specific and hardly comparable to other contexts or target groups.

Additional exclusion criteria: Pharmaceutical studies were included under the exclusion criteria.

The final article selection comprised eight studies, as illustrated in Fig. 9.2.

Fig. 9.2 Selection process

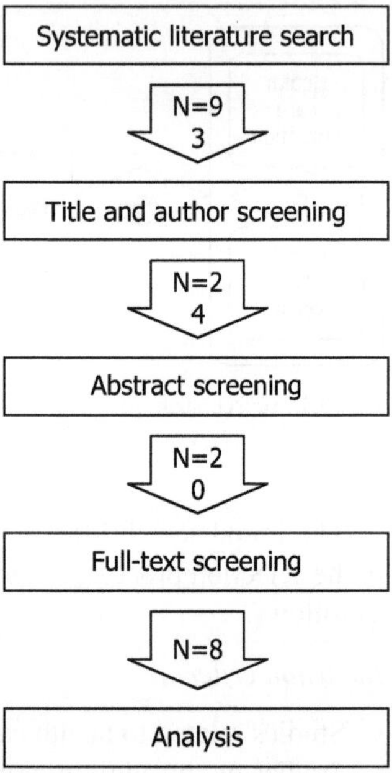

Results

Description of Sampled Articles

Of the eight studies selected for review, five originated from the Netherlands (Fassaert et al., 2009a; Fassaert et al., 2009b; Fassaert et al., 2009c; Lanting et al., 2008; Schoevers et al., 2010) and the remaining three articles report on migrant health care use in Swiss (Maier et al., 2010), Irish (Toar et al., 2009), and Portuguese (Dias et al., 2008) settings. Only three of the articles included in our final selection, all of which were based on research conducted in the Netherlands, referred explicitly to Andersen's model as the theoretical framework for their study design and implementation (Fassaert et al., 2009a; Fassaert et al., 2009b; Fassaert et al., 2009c). Partly resulting from the application of the Andersen model, all selected studies had a quantitative research component, which additionally allows the formal assessment of associations between predisposing, enabling, and need factors on the one hand and health services utilization on the other. Regarding the type of services considered in the selected articles, a strong focus on the areas of mental health and primary care was observed. Additionally, use of oral health services was mentioned in one study. Although most studies focused on the general migrant population or the most prominent ethnic minority groups, three articles reported on health care utilization in the more specific categories of undocumented migrants, asylum seekers, and refugees. The main characteristics of the selected studies are presented in Table 9.1.

Table 9.1 Research characteristics of the selected studies

Country of origin		
The Netherlands	5	(Fassaert et al., 2009a; Fassaert et al., 2009b; Fassaert et al., 2009c; Lanting et al., 2008; Schoevers et al., 2010)
Switzerland	1	(Maier et al., 2010)
Ireland	1	(Toar et al., 2009)
Portugal	1	(Dias et al., 2008)
Study type		
Quantitative	7	(Dias et al., 2008; Fassaert et al., 2009a; Fassaert et al., 2009b; Fassaert et al., 2009c; Lanting et al., 2008; Maier et al., 2010; Toar et al., 2009)
Mixed methods	1	(Schoevers et al., 2010)
Health services type		
Primary care/general practice	5	(Dias et al., 2008; Fassaert et al., 2009b; Maier et al., 2010; Schoevers et al., 2010; Toar et al., 2009)
Specialist care	4	(Fassaert et al., 2009b; Maier et al., 2010; Schoevers et al., 2010; Toar et al., 2009)
Hospital outpatient	3	(Dias et al., 2008; Lanting et al., 2008; Toar et al., 2009)
Hospital inpatient	2	(Dias et al., 2008; Toar et al., 2009)
Mental health	6	(Fassaert et al., 2009a; Fassaert et al., 2009b; Fassaert et al., 2009c; Maier et al., 2010; Schoevers et al., 2010; Toar et al., 2009)
Oral health	1	(Schoevers et al., 2010)
Study population		
General migrant population	5	(Dias et al., 2008; Fassaert et al., 2009a; Fassaert et al., 2009b; Fassaert et al., 2009c; Lanting et al., 2008)
Undocumented migrants	1	(Schoevers et al., 2010)
Asylum seekers/refugees	2	(Maier et al., 2010; Toar et al., 2009)

Definitions of Migrants as Study Participants

Under the assumption of consistency in the criteria used to classify specific migrant categories, the definitions reported in the studies selected for our review are presented below according to their target group.

When distinguishing between different ethnic groups in research on the general migrant population, studies conducted in the Netherlands consistently refer to the definition of the Dutch national statistics office (Statistics Netherlands), using individual and parental country of birth as classification criteria (Fassaert et al., 2009a; Fassaert et al., 2009b; Fassaert et al., 2009c; Lanting et al., 2008). This algorithm assigns Dutch ethnicity to an individual whose parents were both born in the Netherlands. Similarly, first-generation migrants are those who were born outside of Dutch borders and who have at least one parent born abroad. Second-generation migrants are those who were born in the Netherlands but who have at least one parent who was born abroad and has immigrated to the Netherlands. In the Portuguese study (Dias et al., 2008), no explicit definition for migrants was provided. Instead, participants were recruited through a migration state agency, which implies both an a priori self-identification and external classification as a migrant, most likely based on nationality or citizenship.

Using a strategy similar to that employed by Dias et al. (2008), studies focusing on asylum seekers and refugees did not explicitly define their study population but recruited participants from state agencies on the basis of their legal residence status. As such, Maier, Schmidt, and Mueller (2010) identified their study participants through the Swiss Federal Office for Migration, using application for asylum as a selection criterion. Along the same lines, Toar, O'Brian, and Fahey (2009) gained access to their study population (i.e., asylum seekers and refugees in Ireland) through state agencies where residence status is formally recorded: direct provision centers for asylum seekers and community welfare offices for refugees.

In their study on undocumented female migrants in the Netherlands, Schoevers and colleagues (2010) defined undocumented migrants as people who do not have any residence permit that would authorize their stay in the country where they temporarily live.

Study Samples

Dias and colleagues (2008) conducted a cross-sectional survey on 1513 immigrants visiting the National Immigrant Support Centre throughout a month (response rate = 86 %). Participants were on average 33 years old (standard deviation (sd) = 8.9) and originated mostly from Portuguese-speaking countries in South America (50.5 %) and Africa (34.8 %). Their average length of stay in Portugal was 6.6 years (sd = 0.8), and 53 % were male. Most participants (64.7 %) had completed more than 10 years of schooling, and 80 % were employed.

The three studies authored by Fassaert and colleagues relied on data collected within the scope of the 2004 Amsterdam Health Monitor, a general public health survey organized by the Amsterdam municipality. Depending on the specific focus of each report, however, the samples drawn from the original study population varied, ranging in size between 580 and 646 participants. Two studies focusing on mental health services included both ethnic Dutch and migrants (Fassaert et al., 2009a; Fassaert et al., 2009b), whereas one other study only focused on the general utilization of health services among migrant respondents (Fassaert et al., 2009c). All three studies included only Turkish and Moroccan migrants. In both studies comparing ethnic Dutch with migrants, the latter were significantly younger than their native peers ($p < 0.001$), had a lower education level ($p < 0.001$), and were more likely to have public health insurance ($p < 0.001$). Relative to the other gender, more Dutch and Turkish women and more Moroccan men were included in studies on mental health care (Fassaert et al., 2009a; Fassaert et al., 2009b). In the study focusing on the impact of acculturation on health service use, the overall gender distribution was relatively equal, with 49.4 % of the respondents being female (Fassaert et al., 2009c).

Lanting et al. (2008) recorded data on 1,332 patients attending the internal medicine outpatient clinic of the Erasmus Medical Centre in Rotterdam, including ethnic Dutch as well as Surinamese, Turkish, Moroccan, Antillean/Aruban, and Cape Verdean migrants. More women than men attended the outpatient clinic in all ethnic groups, with the exception of the Cape Verdean migrants. Migrants mostly belonged to the first generation residing in the Netherlands (93.5 %) and had a lower socioeconomic status level when compared to ethnic Dutch (71 % vs. 33 % belonged to the lowest socioeconomic status category, respectively).

In their study on mental health status and health care utilization, Maier and colleagues (2010) recruited 78 adult asylum seekers originating from 18 countries, mainly located in Asia (47 %) and Africa (27 %). Participants were mostly male (73 %), unmarried (56 %), and most of their applications for asylum were still unresolved (91 %). The mean age in the sample was 29.9 years (sd = 8.4).

Schoevers et al. (2009) conducted a mixed-method study on a sample of 100 undocumented women living in the Netherlands. Among the participants, 53 % lived in an urban area, 73 % had children, and 53 % had a partner. On average, participants were 36.4 years old, and the majority had come to the Netherlands for political reasons (57 %). Most of the women (80 %) were unemployed, and only 19 % reported difficulties in reading and writing. Interpretation was required in 37 % of cases and was provided by a professional interpreter for only 13 % of the women.

The study of Toar et al. (2009) focused on differences in health care utilization between 60 asylum seekers and 28 refugees living in Ireland. Compared to refugees, asylum seekers displayed lower educational attainment and had been residing in Ireland for a shorter time. Study participants were mostly married males, with an average age of 36.2 for refugees and 32.8 for asylum seekers.

Predisposing Factors

Predisposing factors were the most prominently mentioned pathways for analyzing utilization in the selected studies. Specific to our review, all articles needed to include migration status as a main component of the conducted research. Beyond the mere classification of the study population in migrants and nonmigrants, all studies also included a qualitative distinction between and within study participant groups based on attributes like country of origin, nationality, ethnicity, and mother tongue. Four studies also recorded residence status (legal/illegal; asylum seeker/refugee) as a migration-specific factor influencing health services utilization (Dias et al., 2008; Fassaert et al., 2009a; Maier et al., 2010; Toar et al., 2009). Similarly, information on migrants' length of stay in the receiving country was recorded in three studies (Dias et al., 2008; Schoevers et al., 2010; Toar et al., 2009). Some studies further reported on the following migration-related indicators: reasons for migration, proficiency in the language spoken in the receiving country (Schoevers et al., 2010), and migration-associated stress (Toar et al., 2009).

Reports on participants' age were included in all articles, and all eight quantitative and/or mixed-method studies included age as a variable in their statistical analyses. Information on sex/gender was also reported and analyzed in all eight articles included in our sample. Given the specific vulnerability of this subgroup, Schoevers et al. (2010) focused their research solely on undocumented migrant women.

Social structure as a predisposing factor for health care utilization (Andersen, 1995; Andersen & Davidson, 2007) was operationalized in the sampled studies through indicators such as level of education (Dias et al., 2008; Fassaert et al., 2009a; Fassaert et al., 2009b; Fassaert et al., 2009c; Toar et al., 2009) and occupation or employment status (Dias et al., 2008; Schoevers et al., 2010), which were included in five and two articles, respectively. Although we acknowledge the validity of Andersen's classification of income as an enabling factor for health care utilization, Lanting et al. (2008) used standardized household income quintiles to define socioeconomic status, which in our view was a measure of social stratification.

Given their specificity, studies on the influence of genetic factors on health services utilization were not included in the present review. Moreover, health beliefs and issues of mental dysfunction and autonomy as predisposing factors were not mentioned in any of the selected articles.

Although it may be argued that parenthood may be an indicator of social relationships, which Andersen places in the category of enabling factors, in our view, having children was used by Schoevers et al. (2010) as a factor predisposing individuals to using health care services.

Enabling Factors

Health insurance as a factor enabling the utilization of health services was included in two articles (Fassaert et al., 2009a; Fassaert et al., 2009b). Against the background of extensive insurance coverage in the Dutch health care system, both studies focused on type of health insurance (public/private), which displays important associations with income, as an enabler in accessing health care at different levels of quality.

Income was not additionally referred to as an enabling factor in any of the reviewed articles. Dias, Severo, and Barros (2008) recorded housing conditions and self-rated economic situation as indicators of wealth. However, these factors were not included as explanatory variables in their analysis of health services use among migrants.

Health services availability was estimated in one study (Lanting et al., 2008) through referral area. This proxy regional indicator stands for the specific density of health care facilities in a particular geographic area, which ultimately influences the physical dimension of access to care.

Data on marital status, as an indicator of social relationships, were collected and reported in three studies (Maier et al., 2010; Schoevers et al., 2010; Toar et al., 2009). However, marital status was mostly used as a simple sociodemographic descriptor of the study sample, without being included in further, more detailed analyses relating it to health services utilization.

Need Factors

Most studies in our analysis included measures to estimate need, with the exception of one article, which was nonspecific in this sense (Dias et al., 2008). Two studies reported on health care use based on evaluated need (Lanting et al., 2008; Maier et al., 2010), whereas four studies included both evaluated and perceived need assessment tools (Fassaert et al., 2009a; Fassaert et al., 2009b; Fassaert et al., 2009c; Toar et al., 2009). Only one article focused exclusively on perceived need for health care (Schoevers et al., 2010). Evaluated need was common not only in studies conducted in health care settings (Lanting et al., 2008), where need was established based on expert evaluation as suggested by Andersen (Andersen, 1995; Andersen & Davidson, 2007), but also in surveys conducted outside of health care-provision settings. The latter also included objective measurements of need, such as diagnostic tests assessing specific disease symptoms and manifestations (Fassaert et al., 2009a; Fassaert et al., 2009b; Fassaert et al., 2009c; Maier et al., 2010; Toar et al., 2009). Often, study participants were asked to report on the number of chronic conditions they were suffering from as a proxy indicator of previous expert evaluation (Fassaert et al., 2009c; Toar et al., 2009).

On the other hand, subjective need for health care utilization was assessed through self-rated health status (Fassaert et al., 2009c; Schoevers et al., 2010; Toar et al., 2009) or specific tools, such as the Perceived Need for Care Questionnaire (PNCQ) (Fassaert et al., 2009a).

Health Care Need

In the study of Fassaert et al. (2009a), the prevalence of diagnosed common mental health disorders as well as age-adjusted and sex-adjusted perceived need for mental health care and perceived discordance (unmet or partially met need for care) were significantly higher in Turkish migrants than in ethnic Dutch or Moroccan respondents. Levels of unmet need appeared to be high, especially regarding social interventions. However, bivariate analyses of variance (ANOVA) pointed to higher symptom levels in terms of somatization, anxiety, depression, and agoraphobia for both migrant groups when compared to the ethnic Dutch (Fassaert et al., 2009a).

Turkish respondents also displayed significantly higher rates of mental health morbidity compared to both their Dutch and Moroccan peers ($p<0.001$) in a second study based on the Amsterdam Health Monitor survey (Fassaert et al., 2009b). The same study also found that migrants experience higher levels of psychological distress than their Dutch counterparts do.

In another study, Fassaert et al. (2009c) found that 55.4 % of the Turkish and Moroccan migrants included in the sample perceived their health to be moderate or bad. On average, participants had 1.8 chronic conditions, within a total range from 0 to 11 chronic ailments.

In the study conducted by Maier et al. (2010), 41 % of included asylum seekers had at least one clinically relevant mental disorder at the time of the study, mostly related to traumatic stress, with the most frequently identified disorders being major depression, posttraumatic stress disorder, and somatoform pain disorder. Whereas 29 % of participants had at least two mental disorders, 11 % had three or more mental health conditions at the time of the study (Maier et al., 2010).

In the research by Lanting et al. on use of outpatient internal medicine services, migrants had a higher likelihood to be referred to the Erasmus Medical Centre for gastrointestinal symptoms; however, they were less likely to be referred for nonspecific symptoms such as general weakness, tiredness, or memory problems. No further differences were noted in terms of vascular disease or other symptoms. Overall, compared to ethnic Dutch, migrants had a higher risk of being diagnosed with liver disease and a lower risk of not receiving a diagnosis following extensive analysis. However, when presenting with abdominal pain, migrants were more likely not to receive a diagnosis (Lanting et al., 2008).

In the study conducted by Schoevers et al. (2010), a total of 80 % of undocumented female migrants reported having had health complaints during their undocumented stay in the Netherlands. Almost half did not receive medical attention for their ailments.

Toar et al. (2009) conducted a detailed analysis on differences in health care needs between refugees and asylum seekers in Ireland, revealing that compared to refugees, asylum seekers had higher levels of pre-migration and post-migration stressors ($p=0.05$ and $p<0.01$, respectively), as well as a higher risk of both posttraumatic stress disorder and anxiety and depression symptoms (odds ratio (OR) = 6.3 and OR = 5.8, respectively). General self-reported health was not associated with any of the following factors: residence status, presence of chronic conditions, pre-migration stressors and symptoms of posttraumatic stress disorder, anxiety, and depression. However, high levels of post-migration stressors were associated with a higher risk of poor self-rated general health status. The presence of chronic conditions also increased the risk of posttraumatic stress disorder and symptoms of depression and anxiety. Gender, duration of stay in Ireland, and education level were not associated with mental health symptoms. When controlling for pre-migration and post-migration stressors, no association was observed between residence status and mental health symptoms. Post-migration stressors in particular, and also pre-migration stressors and the presence of chronic conditions, emerged as risk factors for posttraumatic stress disorder and symptoms of depression and anxiety (ORs = 17.3, 3.9, and 12.3, respectively). Although residence status had no direct association with mental health symptoms, its association with post-migration and pre-migration stressors suggests that residence status might be a marker for these risk factors (Toar et al., 2009).

Barriers to Access

In their study, Dias et al. (2008) also explored factors limiting access to health care services among immigrants in Portugal. Reported barriers to accessing health care in this context referred to waiting times, providers' attitudes, cost, distance/transportation, and language. Women complained more than men about waiting times and providers' attitudes as barriers to accessing health care. Waiting times were more often mentioned as a barrier by African men and women as well as by Eastern European women. As a possible consequence, dissatisfaction rates with care provided by the Portuguese National Health System was higher among migrants from Eastern Europe than among those from Africa or South America (30.3 % vs. 20.1 % and 21.4 %, respectively; $p=0.001$).

When considering barriers to accessing mental health services in the Netherlands, Fassaert et al. (2009a) found that the preference for self-reliance in solving mental health issues played a major role in reducing access to mental health care in both ethnic Dutch and migrants. In addition, migrants tended to be pessimistic about the potential benefits of mental health therapy and also lacked information on where to seek help. Among migrant participants, 20.7 % reported that they had solicited professional help but did not receive any (Fassaert et al., 2009a).

Of the undocumented migrant women who participated in the study conducted by Schoevers et al. (2010), 69 % reported having encountered barriers in accessing health services. Among these, 29 % mentioned institutional barriers, 22 % referred to personal obstacles, and 18 % named both types of health access limitations. Institutional barriers consisted of financial issues and refusal of services, whereas personal barriers mostly referred to fear and shame or lack of information (Schoevers et al., 2010).

Use of Health Services

Dias et al. (2008) found that 3.6 % of the migrants included in their study were not aware of where they could access health care if needed. Among those who had a better understanding of the health system, 61.7 % would use the services of a Health Centre. Approximately 20 % of respondents, of which significantly more were men ($p=0.001$), had never accessed care provided by the National Health Service (NHS). Most NHS users had used both Health Centre and hospital services (54.4 %). However, men tended to only make use of just one type of service (Health Centre or hospital), as opposed to women, who were more likely to have used both. In logistic regression analyses, the ORs of accessing health care in both genders increased with a longer stay in Portugal and with origin from African countries versus Eastern Europe. Additionally, in men, legal residence status was predictive of increased use of health care services (Dias et al., 2008).

Consistent with the higher levels of mental health morbidity among Turkish migrants in the study sample, the regression analyses conducted by Fassaert et al. (2009a) revealed that, when controlling for age and gender, perceived need and discordance (unmet or partially met need) were significantly higher among Turkish respondents. However, when including the prevalence of common mental health disorders and symptom intensity levels in the regression model, ORs dramatically decreased, suggesting a lower perceived need for mental care in migrants compared to ethnic Dutch at similar levels of mental morbidity. Turkish migrants reported unmet or partially met need significantly more often than ethnic Dutch ($p=0.001$). However, in regression analyses, ethnic differences could again be explained by differences in levels of morbidity and symptom intensity. Socioeconomic status was not a significant predictor, neither for perceived need for care nor for discordance (Fassaert et al., 2009a).

When looking into associations between acculturation and use of health care services in Turkish and Moroccan migrants in Amsterdam (Fassaert et al., 2009c), no relationship between acculturation and general practitioner care uptake could be established. Instead, primary care use was driven by health care-need factors like the number of chronic illnesses and self-reported health status. In terms of specialist care use, better communication in Dutch was related to lower utilization among Turkish migrants ($p=0.032$). In Moroccan men ($p=0.044$), a higher degree of emancipation was related to lower use of specialist health care. In addition, better Dutch communication skills triggered an increased uptake of mental health services in Turkish men ($p=0.003$) and a decreased use of mental health care in Moroccan men ($p=0.033$). Among Turkish women, higher levels of social interaction with ethnic Dutch was associated with higher use of mental health services ($p=0.02$). Overall, the associations between acculturation and health care use were rather moderate. Language skills, however, played a significant role in the observed associations.

In analyzing ethnic differences in uptake of mental health care, Fassaert et al. (2009b) found that among the 50.9% of respondents who reported visiting a health care provider for mental health problems, 35% accessed specialist care, whereas almost 16% consulted a primary care provider. Initial regression analyses indicated that Turkish respondents were more likely than ethnic Dutch to have accessed primary care for mental health issues. Inclusion of mental health morbidity in the model reduced the ORs for Turkish and Moroccan ethnicities, without revealing significant differences when compared to the ethnic Dutch. When also considering psychological distress, it appeared that Moroccan respondents used mental health services in primary care less frequently than ethnic Dutch ($p=0.025$). In terms of specialist mental health care, no differences between migrants and Dutch respondents were apparent when considering age, gender, and mental health morbidity. With the inclusion of psychological distress in the model, uptake of specialist mental health care appeared to be lower among migrants; however, the differences did not reach statistical significance. Socioeconomic status could not explain differential usage of mental health care by migrants compared to ethnic Dutch, neither in primary nor in specialist care (Fassaert et al., 2009b).

In the study of Lanting et al. (2008), immigrants displayed higher utilization of outpatient internal medicine services than ethnic Dutch patients, both when the Erasmus Medical Center referral area and the Rotterdam municipal region were considered, with the highest rates reported among Turkish migrants (RR of 1.82 and 1.97, respectively). Differences in health services use were mostly attributable to first-generation migrants since no differences in use were observed between second-generation migrants and ethnic Dutch patients.

When assessing the health care use of asylum seekers in Switzerland, Maier et al. (2010) looked at both their health care visits and costs compared to the local population. The average yearly expenditure for health services provided to asylum seekers in the study sample was 1.8 times higher than the average expenditure for the Swiss population ($p=0.022$). The mean number of doctor visits among the study participants (10.7, sd = 15.4) was twice as high as the local population average. Participants with mental disorders had, on average, significantly more appointments and accounted for significantly higher health care costs than participants without mental conditions ($p=0.025$, $p=0.043$, respectively). Only 26 % of the study participants had received mental health care in the 12 months preceding the study, although 41 % suffered from mental conditions. On average, the annual costs for mental health care accounted for 14 % of the total annual health care costs, which is comparable to the general average annual expenditure for mental health care in the Swiss health care system (16 %). Analysis of health services use for physical health issues suggests that serious medical events (e.g., surgery) did not play a major role in the health care use reported for the study sample.

Although 80 % of women in the sample of Schoevers et al. (2010) had experienced health problems during their undocumented stay in the Netherlands, 56 % received no care for their health complaints and 5 % reported receiving only partial care. Among the study participants, 13 % had not accessed any health services, and 19 % had at least one contact with a mental health care provider within the previous year. Almost half of the women had visited a general practitioner in the previous 2 months, one-third had visited a specialist while undocumented, and one-third had seen a dentist in the previous year. Higher health care utilization was reported by women who had come to the Netherlands for political reasons. Lack of Dutch language skills was associated with fewer general practitioner visits (OR = 0.28). "Poor" self-rated health was, on the other hand, associated with more general practitioner visits (OR = 4.89) but fewer specialist contacts (OR = 0.26) when compared with women who considered their health to be "good."

In terms of differences in health care utilization between asylum seekers and refugees in Ireland, Toar et al. (2009) found that asylum seekers visited their general practitioner at a significantly higher rate than refugees. Otherwise, no intergroup differences were noted regarding use of medication or dental, mental, or hospital care.

Table 9.2 provides an overview of the selected studies and their main findings.

Concluding Discussion

After conducting a comprehensive search for literature published in Europe on health care use among migrants within the past 3 years, we identified eight studies fulfilling all inclusion criteria that were established for the purpose of our analysis. All publications originated from traditional emigration countries that have become receiving countries throughout the past five decades. The eight publications selected for review covered all types of health services and focused on both general and specific migrant groups (i.e., undocumented migrants, asylum seekers, and refugees). Migrant participants in the selected studies tended to be

Table 9.2 Overview of selected studies and their main results

Authors, (Publication year), Country	Sample	Data source	Predisposing factors	Enabling factors	Need factors	Utilization indicators	Major findings
Dias, Severo & Barros (2008), Portugal	$N=1{,}513$ immigrants attending the National Immigrant Support Centre	Survey	Nationality Country of origin Age Gender Length of stay in Portugal Employment status Immigration status Education	Housing conditions Economic situation	Nonspecific	Knowledge of where to seek health care Use of the National Health Service and type of services used Satisfaction with care Access barriers	Women had a higher and more varied use of health services than men ($p=0.001$) For both genders, a longer stay in Portugal and African versus Eastern European descent were significant predictors of increased used of health services. Additionally in men, legal residence status significantly predicted higher health care utilization rates.
Fassaert, de Wit, Tuinebreijer, Verhoeff, Beekman & Dekker (2009), The Netherlands	$N=626$ ethnic Dutch, Moroccan, and Turkish participants in the 2004 Amsterdam Health Monitor	Survey	Ethnicity Age Gender Education	Health insurance type	Perceived and evaluated need for mental health care	Perceived need for care and discordance (unmet or partially met need) Access barriers	When controlling for age, gender, prevalence of common mental health disorders, and symptom intensity levels, migrants displayed a lower perceived need for mental health care compared to ethnic Dutch. At similar levels of mental distress, there is no evidence that the need for mental health care is less often met in migrants than in ethnic Dutch

Table 9.2 (continued)

Authors, (Publication year), Country	Sample	Data source	Predisposing factors	Enabling factors	Need factors	Utilization indicators	Major findings
Fassaert, Hesselink & Verhoeff (2009), The Netherlands	$N=646$ ethnic Moroccan and Turkish participants in the 2004 Amsterdam Health Monitor	Survey	Sex Age Ethnicity SES (education level)		Perceived and evaluated need	Self-reported use of general practitioner, specialist, and mental health care in the previous 2 months	Moderate associations between acculturation and use of health services were observed. No association between acculturation and primary care use was identified. Specialist care use decreased with beter Dutch communication skills in Turkish migrants, ($p=0.032$) and with a higher degree of emancipation in Moroccan men ($p=0.044$). Mental health care use increased with better Dutch communication skills in Turkish men ($p=0.003$) and with greater social interaction with ethnic Dutch among Turkish women ($p=0.02$). In Moroccan men, mental health care use decreased with better Dutch communication skills ($p=0.033$)
Fassaert, de Wit, Verhoeff, Tuinebreijer, Gorissen, Beekman & Dekker (2009), The Netherlands	$N=580$ ethnic Dutch, Moroccan, and Turkish participants in the 2004 Amsterdam Health Monitor	Survey	Ethnicity Age Gender Education	Health insurance type	Perceived and evaluated need	Self-reported use of mental health services	The study findings indicate an equal use of specialist mental health services based on objective need (mental health diagnosis). When considering perceived need (psychological distress), migrants had a lower use of primary mental health care

Table 9.2 (continued)

Authors, (Publication year), Country	Sample	Data source	Predisposing factors	Enabling factors	Need factors	Utilization indicators	Major findings
Lanting, Bootsma, Lamberts, Mackenbach & Joung (2008), The Netherlands	N=1,332 new patients of the outpatient internal medicine clinic of Erasmus Medical Centre Rotterdam between 2002 and 2003	Hospital records	Ethnicity Age Sex Socioeconomic status (standardized household income)	Referral area	Evaluated need	Use of outpatient hospital health services Reasons for referral Diagnosis	Use of outpatient internal medicine services was higher in first-generation migrants and equal in second-generation migrants, when compared to the ethnic Dutch population
Maier, Schmidt & Mueller (2010), Switzerland	N=78 asylum seekers in the canton of Zürich	Diagnostic interviews and insurance records	Age Sex Marital status Residence status Region of origin		Evaluated need for mental health care	Use of primary, specialist, and mental health services Cost of health care use	Asylum seekers display a higher use of health services, generating significantly higher costs compared to the local population. However, they receive less specific mental health care than needed based on their higher levels of mental health morbidity
Schoevers, Loeffen, van den Muijsenbergh & Lagro-Janssen (2010), The Netherlands	N=100 undocumented migrant women living in the Netherlands	Structured questionnaires, semi-structured interviews	Age Marital status Having children Country of origin Employment status Dutch skills Duration of undocumented stay Reason for staying in the Netherlands		Perceived need	Use of primary, specialist, mental, and oral health services Access barriers	Fifty-six percent of respondents reported an unmet need for health care. Health care use was higher in women who had immigrated to the Netherlands for political reasons and lower in women with poor Dutch language skills. Lower perceived health status was associated with higher rates of primary care use and lower rates of specialist care use

Table 9.2 (continued)

Authors, (Publication year), Country	Sample	Data source	Predisposing factors	Enabling factors	Need factors	Utilization indicators	Major findings
Toar, O'Brien & Fahey (2009), Ireland	N=88 asylum seekers and refugees in Sligo and Leitrim	Survey	Residence status Pre- and post-migration stressors Gender Age Marital status Duration of residence in Ireland Education		Perceived and evaluated need	Use of primary, specialist, hospital, mental, and oral health services	Asylum seekers display higher rates of primary care use compared to refugees

younger and more economically deprived than their ethnic majority counterparts. In both studies on asylum seekers and refugees, respondents were predominantly young, married men.

Beyond need factors such as perceived health status, symptom levels, or number of chronic conditions, migration-specific predisposing factors such as residence status, region of origin, duration of stay in the receiving country, migrant generation, communication skills in the local language, level of interaction with the local population, adherence to the value system of the host culture, and reason for migration were identified as explanatory variables for health services utilization in our review. Enabling factors were seldom included in the statistical analyses, and those that were considered did not significantly predict health care use in the reviewed studies.

Migrants appear to prefer accessing health services within primary care (Dias et al., 2008). This is illustrated by their high rates of primary care utilization, which are at times higher than those of the local population, as often described in the literature (Huber et al., 2008; Norredam et al., 2009). In case of undocumented migrants or asylum seekers, general practitioners might be the most easily accessible point of health care delivery (Schoevers et al., 2010; Maier et al., 2010). Moreover, primary care use appears to be need-driven, irrespective of migrants' levels of acculturation (Fassaert et al., 2009c) or their legal residence status (Toar et al., 2009). Maier et al. (2010) report a significantly higher number of doctor appointments in migrants than in the Swiss population in Zürich, but they do not distinguish between primary and specialist care visits.

Interestingly, use of specialist health services in migrants appears to moderately decrease with higher levels of acculturation (Fassaert et al., 2009c) and is not influenced by residence status (asylum seekers vs. refugees) (Toar et al., 2009). With only 19 % of women in their sample having accessed specialist care while undocumented, Schoevers et al. (2010) suggest low utilization of such services in this vulnerable group. In terms of the utilization of oral health care, we only found data indicating that 33 % of the undocumented women studied by Schoevers et al. (2010) had had contact with a dentist in the year preceding the study.

The only reports on the utilization of hospital services indicate that gender but not legal residence status might play a role (Dias et al., 2008; Toar et al., 2009). In this sense, higher and more varied use of health services (including hospital care) was found among women (Dias et al., 2008), which might be a natural consequence of women's reproductive role, as suggested in the literature (Baglio et al., 2010; Castaneda, 2009). Regarding outpatient hospital services, Lanting et al. (2008) reported migrant generation to be a significant predictor of increased use, with first-generation migrants having higher rates of use than the native Dutch, whereas no difference was observed between the latter and second-generation migrants.

A high objective need for mental health care was identified in the migrant samples evaluated in the reviewed studies—whether they were general migrant groups or asylum seekers (Fassaert et al., 2009a; Fassaert et al., 2009b; Maier et al., 2010; Toar et al., 2009). Although more detailed research suggests relatively equal use of mental health services in migrant and native residents when considering objective need for care (Fassaert et al., 2009a; Fassaert et al., 2009b), the high absolute levels of unmet needs in migrants cannot be ignored and call for urgent action. Maier et al. (2010) particularly pointed to potential health services misuse in asylum seekers, who make extensive use of primary care, generating high health costs, but do not receive adequate mental health care as would be necessary given their high burden of mental conditions. Lower perceived need for mental health care, despite high levels of objectively evaluated symptoms, appears to play a major role in reducing the use of mental health services in migrants, as illustrated by Fassaert and colleagues (2009a, b). This issue could be addressed through the development of culturally tailored therapy programs and awareness-raising campaigns targeting migrant communities with a known risk for increased psychological distress.

None of the selected studies were conducted in Germany, which might be explained by the selection criteria and the primary focus on utilization of health care. As pointed out in the introduction, an increasing interest in migration and health, and accordingly a growing number of publications on this topic can also be observed in Germany. Although these publications also touch on health utilization issues, their main focus lies on either more general questions or very specific aspects of immigrants' health (see, for example, RKI 2008a/b, Boral et al. 2012) as well as specific health care settings (e.g., emergency departments (Borde & David 2007), rehabilitative care (Bronzka et al. 2012), and obstetrics (Borde et al. 2008)). The results show that in Germany, as reported for the broader European context, immigrants face more and different health problems than native Germans do and also experience difficulties in accessing the right health service at the right time. An interesting, life-course oriented model has been developed by Spallek et al. (2011), summarizing key assumptions on explanatory factors regarding the observed ethnic differences. This model allows not only to identify health threats along the process of immigration, but also to develop specific and appropriate approaches to enhance immigrants' health. Additionally, the proposed theoretical framework could be used to explain ethnic differences in health care utilization, a perspective that has been mentioned but so far not conceptualized as an integral part of the model.

An important step in addressing the health of migrants in Germany has been the integration of specific immigrant status and migration background indicators in the German health reporting system, which allows the identification of specific health problems and health care needs in the immigrant population. Two main nationally representative reports are available in this sense, one focusing particularly on children and adolescents (RKI 2008a) and one for all age groups (RKI 2008b). Beyond a detailed health status description, revealing a relatively disadvantaged situation in immigrants compared to native Germans, these reports provide rather limited information on health care utilization. The presented findings, however, indicate lower utilization rates, especially in preventive services (see also Razum & Spallek, 2009).

In conclusion, in both Europe and Germany in particular, more research should be devoted to identifying the role of patient–provider ethnic matching in shaping migrants' preferences in terms of the type of health services they use. In this sense, it would be useful to know if the increased use of primary care services among migrants is associated with a greater number of professionals with migration background among general practitioners than among specialists and if ethnic matching prevails over objective health care need in determining the choice of health care provider. The latter is particularly relevant in the case of mental health care utilization, as suggested by Kirkcaldy et al. (2006).

Furthermore, efforts should be directed toward reducing barriers in accessing health care, which, as reported in the reviewed studies and exemplified for the German context, are still prevalent among migrant groups and consequently impact their use of health services and perceptions of quality of care. Consistent with the findings of other studies (Stanciole and Huber, 2009; Terraza-Nunez et al., 2010), studies included in our analysis reported barriers to the utilization of health care among migrants. These included lack of information on where to seek help and limited proficiency in the local language, provider attitudes, cost issues, the organization of health care (e.g., waiting times), as well as specific health-related beliefs and expectations regarding the health provision process (Dias et al., 2008; Fassaert et al., 2009a; Schoevers et al., 2010; RKI 2008b; Spallek et al. 2011). Particularly worrisome, however, are reports of refused care (Fassaert et al., 2009a; Schoevers et al., 2010). Although in the case of undocumented migrants, refusal of services was triggered by their lack of insurance coverage as a result of their residence status (Schoevers et al., 2010), no explanation was found for refusing help to migrant groups described in the study of Fassaert et al. (2009a). From the viewpoint of health being a human right, however, refusal of care is problematic, and current evidence should stimulate efforts aimed at improving health care provision for undocumented migrants and similar marginal groups.

At a political level, recommendations for measures aimed at reducing barriers to access and improving the health of migrants in multicultural societies in the European Union have been in place since 2006 (Council of Europe, 2006; Council of Europe, 2011). Nevertheless, current evidence shows that efforts to implement culturally tailored health services (interpretation, cultural competency training of health professionals, increasing transparency on available health services and access to the health care system, provision of translated educational materials, etc.) are still lagging behind. Novel approaches, such as the German concept of "intercultural opening" (Penka et al. 2012), might offer promising solutions in achieving equitable access to health care for immigrants in the future.

The generalizability of our results to a broader European context is somewhat limited by the narrow selection criteria for studies included in the review. In addition, although most studies were representative at a local level, it is unclear to what extent they adequately illustrate the migrant health care utilization process in their respective countries of origin or broader regions. Despite small sample sizes in some studies (Toar et al., 2009), however, first insights on specific migrant health issues were reported, laying an important foundation for further research in the field.

Our review reflected, perhaps on a small scale, the challenges faced by European research on migrants' health care utilization. The great diversity of target migrant populations, study designs (intragroup vs. intergroup comparisons), as well as differences in the way ethnicity and migrant background are conceptualized and operationalized in various health care systems and research projects might explain the wide variations in the current evidence base, which to date does not allow drawing an unequivocal, general conclusion regarding the health care use of migrant groups at a European level. Moreover, in view of the cultural and legislative heterogeneity of European countries, it seems unlikely that such generalizable conclusions will be brought about by health services research in the near future.

References

Andersen, R. M. & Davidson, P. L. (2007). Improving access to care in America: individual and contextual indicators. In: R. M. Andersen, T. H. Rice & G. F. Kominski editors, Changing the U.S. health care system: key issues in health services, policy, and management (p. 3–31). 3rd edition. San Francisco, CA: Jossey-Bass.

Andersen, R. M. (1995) Revisiting the behavioral model and access to medical care: does it matter? *J Health Soc Behav*, 36, 1–10.

Baglio, G., Saunders, C., Spinelli, A. & Osborn, J. (2010) Utilisation of hospital services in Italy: a comparative analysis of immigrant and Italian citizens. *J Immigr Minor Health*, 12, 598–609.

Berchet, C. & Jusot, F. (2012) Immigrants' Health Status and Use of Healthcare Services: A Review of French Research. *Questions d'économie de la santé.*

Boral, S., Borde, T., Kentenich, H., Wernecke, K.D. & David, M. (2012) Migration and symptom reporting at menopause: a comparative survey of migrant women from Turkey in Berlin, German women in Berlin, and women in Istanbul. *Menopause*, (in press).

Borde, T. & David, M. (2007) [Treatment of immigrants in emergency clinics]. *MMW Fortschr Med*, 149, 38–9.

Borde, T., Dudenhausen, J.W. & David, M. (2008) [Migrants in obstetrics–psychosomatic aspects in the context of acculturation]. Psychother Psychosom Med Psychol., 58 (3–4), 183–188.

Brzoska, P., Voigtländer, S., Spallek, J. & Razum, O. (2012) [The use of routine data to study rehabilitative care in populations with a migrational background: potential and limitations]. Gesundheitswesen, 74(6), 371–378.

Castaneda, H. (2009) Illegality as risk factor: a survey of unauthorized migrant patients in a Berlin clinic. *Soc Sci Med*, 68, 1552–60.

Council of Europe (2006) Recommendation Rec (2006) 18 of the Committee of Ministers to member states on health services in a multicultural society IN MINISTERS, C. O. (Ed.).

Council of Europe (2011) Recommendation CM/Rec (2011) 13 of the Committee of Ministers to member states on mobility, migration and access to health care IN MINISTERS, C. O. (Ed.).

Deville, W., Greacen, T., Bogic, M., Dauvrin, M., Dias, S., Gaddini, A., Jensen, N. K., Karamanidou, C., Kluge, U., Mertaniemi, R., Riera, R. P., Sarvary, A., Soares, J. J., Stankunas, M., Strassmayr, C., Welbel, M. & Priebe, S. (2011) health care for immigrants in Europe: is there still consensus among country experts about principles of good practice? A Delphi study. *BMC Public Health*, 11, 699.

Dias, S. F., Severo, M. & Barros, H. (2008) Determinants of health care utilization by immigrants in Portugal. *BMC Health Serv Res*, 8, 207.

Eshiett, M. U. & Parry, E. H. (2003) Migrants and health: a cultural dilemma. *Clin Med*, 3, 229–31.

Fassaert, T., De Wit, M. A., Tuinebreijer, W. C., Verhoeff, A. P., Beekman, A. T. & Dekker, J. (2009a) Perceived need for mental health care among non-western labour migrants. *Soc Psychiatry Psychiatr Epidemiol*, 44, 208–16.

Fassaert, T., De Wit, M. A., Verhoeff, A. P., Tuinebreijer, W. C., Gorissen, W. H., Beekman, A. T. & Dekker, J. (2009b) Uptake of health services for common mental disorders by first-generation Turkish and Moroccan migrants in the Netherlands. *BMC Public Health*, 9, 307.

Fassaert, T., Hesselink, A. E. & Verhoeff, A. P. (2009c) Acculturation and use of health care services by Turkish and Moroccan migrants: a cross-sectional population-based study. *BMC Public Health*, 9, 332.
Goodman, N. (1992) Population. *Introduction to Sociology*. New York, HarperCollins Publishers, Inc.
Hansen, R. (2003) Migration to Europe since 1945: Its History and its Lessons. *The Political Quarterly*, 74, 25–38.
Huber, M., Stanciole, A. E., Wahlbeck, K., Tamsma, N., Torres, F., Jelfs, E. & Bremner, J. (2008) Quality in and Equality of Access to Healthcare Services. European Commission.
Jensen, N. K., Nielsen, S. S. & Krasnik, A. (2010) Expert opinion on "best practices" in the delivery of health care services to immigrants in Denmark. *Dan Med Bull*, 57, A4170.
Jimenez-Rubio, D. & Hernandez-Quevedo, C. (2011) Inequalities in the use of health services between immigrants and the native population in Spain: what is driving the differences? *Eur J Health Econ*, 12, 17–28.
Kirkcaldy, B., Wittig, U., Furnham, A., Merbach, M. & Siefen, R. G. (2006) [Health and migration. Psychosocial determinants]. *Bundesgesundheitsblatt Gesundheitsforschung Gesundheitsschutz*, 49, 873–83.
Lanting, L. C., Bootsma, A. H., Lamberts, S. W., Mackenbach, J. P. & Joung, I. M. (2008) Ethnic differences in internal medicine referrals and diagnosis in the Netherlands. *BMC Public Health*, 8, 287.
Lindert, J., Schouler-Ocak, M., Heinz, A. & Priebe, S. (2008) Mental health, health care utilisation of migrants in Europe. *Eur Psychiatry*, 23 Suppl 1, 14–20.
Maier, T., Schmidt, M. & Mueller, J. (2010) Mental health and healthcare utilization in adult asylum seekers. *Swiss Med Wkly*, 140, w13110.
Norredam, M., Nielsen, S. S. & Krasnik, A. (2009) Migrants' utilization of somatic healthcare services in Europe–a systematic review. *Eur J Public Health*, 20, 555–63.
Penka, S., Kluge, U., Vardar, A., Borde, T. & Ingleby, D. (2012) The concept of "intercultural opening": the development of an assessment tool for the appraisal of its current implementation in the mental health care system. Eur Psychiatry, 27 (2), 63–69.
Razavi, M. F., Falk, L., Bjorn, A. & Wilhelmsson, S. (2011) Experiences of the Swedish healthcare system: an interview study with refugees in need of long-term health care. *Scand J Public Health*, 39, 319–25.
Razum, O. & Spallek, J. (2009) Zugangsbarrieren zur gesundheitlichen Versorgung. Bundeszentrale für politische Bildung. http://www.bpb.de/gesellschaft/migration/dossier-migration/57307/barrieren-praevention.
RKI—Robert-Koch-Institut (2008a) Gesundheit von Kindern und Jugendlichen mit Migrationshintergrund. Beiträge zur Gesundheitsberichterstattung des Bundes.
RKI—Robert-Koch-Institut (2008b) Migration und Gesundheit. Schwerpunktbericht der Gesundheitsberichterstattung des Bundes.
Ruppen, W., Bandschapp, O. & Urwyler, A. (2010) Language difficulties in outpatients and their impact on a chronic pain unit in Northwest Switzerland. *Swiss Med Wkly*, 140, 260–4.
Scheppers, E., Van dongen, E., Dekker, J. & Geertzen, J. (2006) Potential barriers to the use of health services among ethnic minorities: a review. *Fam Pract*, 23, 325–48.
Schlopker, K., Herrmann, M., Grosser-Kaya, C., Robra, B. P., Dippelhofer-Stiem, B., Schutze, F. & Heintze, C. (2009) [Unresolved problems of undocumented migrants in Germany: an analysis of medical consultations in Berlin, Cologne and Bonn]. *Gesundheitswesen*, 71, 839–44.
Schoevers, M. A., Loeffen, M. J., Van den Muijsenbergh, M. E. & Lagro-Janssen, A. L. (2010) health care utilisation and problems in accessing health care of female undocumented immigrants in the Netherlands. *Int J Public Health*, 55, 421–8.
Spallek, J., Zeeb, H. & Razum, O. (2011) What do we have to know from migrants' past exposures to understand their health status? a life course approach. *Emerg Themes Epidemiol.*, 8:6.
Stanciole, A. E. & Huber, M. (2009) Access to Health Care for Migrants, Ethnic Minorities, and Asylum Seekers in Europe. *Policy Brief.* European Centre.

Suurmond, J., Uiters, E., DE Bruijne, M. C., Stronks, K. & Essink-Bot, M. L. (2011) Negative health care experiences of immigrant patients: a qualitative study. *BMC Health Serv Res*, 11, 10.

Terraza-Nunez, R., Toledo, D., Vargas, I. & Vazquez, M. L. (2010) Perception of the Ecuadorian population living in Barcelona regarding access to health services. *Int J Public Health*, 55, 381–90.

Toar, M., O'Brien, K. K. & Fahey, T. (2009) Comparison of self-reported health & healthcare utilisation between asylum seekers and refugees: an observational study. *BMC Public Health*, 9, 214.

Zeeb, H. & Razum, O. (2006) [Epidemiological research on migrant health in Germany. An overview]. *Bundesgesundheitsblatt Gesundheitsforschung Gesundheitsschutz*, 49, 845–52.

Chapter 10
How Do Socioeconomic Factors Influence the Amount and Intensity of Service Utilization by Family Caregivers of Elderly Dependents?

Daniel Lüdecke, Eva Mnich and Christopher Kofahl

Introduction

As in nearly all European countries, demographic developments in Germany have led to both a relative and an absolute increase in the country's elderly population. Reasons for this trend include increased life expectancy, thanks to lower infant mortality rates, medical advancements, overall better living conditions in terms of nutrition and hygiene, and lower birth rates resulting in steadily increasing old-age dependency ratios. Germany's age dependency ratio (the ratio between the retirement-age population and the working-age population) is currently around 34 %,[1] but is projected to increase to 62 % in 2040 and to 67 % in 2060 (Statistisches Bundesamt 2009).

Increasing longevity and an aging population mean an increase in both the number of elderly citizens in need of long-term care and the length of time between when care is initially needed and death. In Germany, the number of people in need of long-term care is predicted to increase from 2.34 million in 2009 to 3.4 million in 2030. At the same time, the number of people over age 80 is expected to nearly double from 3.6 million to an estimated 6.3 million (DESTATIS 2008; Statistisches Bundesamt 2011).

---

[1] The German Federal Statistical Office (Statistisches Bundesamt) defines "working age" as 20–64 years when calculating the old-age dependency ratio. Population calculations in other countries often use an age range of 15–64 years.

D. Lüdecke (✉) · E. Mnich · C. Kofahl
Center for Psychosocial Medicine, Department of Medical Sociology,
University Medical Center Hamburg-Eppendorf, Hamburg, Germany
e-mail: d.luedecke@uke.uni-hamburg.de

E. Mnich
e-mail: emnich@uke.uni-hamburg.de

C. Kofahl
e-mail: kofahl@uke.uni-hamburg.de

C. Janssen et al. (eds.), *Health Care Utilization in Germany*,
DOI 10.1007/978-1-4614-9191-0_10,

Both in Germany and in the rest of Europe, the care and support needed by these people is primarily provided by relatives or friends and close acquaintances within the home environment (Mestheneos and Triantafillou 2005). As numerous studies have shown, these responsibilities are often sources of great physical and mental burdens for caregivers (Di Rosa et al. 2011; Schulz and Beach 1999). Caring for elderly people with cognitive impairments, in particular, places extraordinary demands on caregivers and takes a significant toll on their health (Barinaga 1998; Gräßel 1998; Gräßel 1996; Kofahl et al. 2009; MacDonald and Dening 2002; Pinquart and Sorensen 2003). Those with multimorbidity or a form of dementia often require full-time, round-the-clock care. At the same time, not only has the age of those in need of care been increasing, there has also been an increase in the age of the relatives caring for them (Kofahl et al. 2007; Lamura et al. 2008). Because of their age, these older caregivers are more liable to become ill themselves. On the other hand, younger family caregivers who are still gainfully employed are often faced with multiple burdens when forced to juggle work, caregiving, and family responsibilities.

In Germany, 69 % of all people in need of long-term care receive care at home (Pfaff 2011). In over 90 % of these cases, care and assistance are provided by family members. Home care provided by family is provided by the family alone, that is, without the help of professional care services, in 71 % of cases. Only 29 % of family home-care arrangements involve the use of such services (Pfaff 2011). Most family caregivers are women, especially daughters and daughters-in-law. However, the number of male caregivers is rising. Whereas in 1991 men represented a mere 17 % of primary caregivers, the proportion of male caregivers increased to 27 % in 2002 (Schneekloth and Wahl 2005), and according to data from the German Socio-economic Panel, it has reached 35 % in 2006 (Rothgang et al. 2008). As most male caregivers tend to be caring for their elderly wives, they themselves are already advanced in age at the time of caregiving, and their age statistically far surpasses the average age of female caregivers (Rothgang et al. 2008).

Most care recipients wish to be cared for at home for as long as possible. Given the enormous costs associated with residential care, this is also a goal of social policy and of long-term care insurance. In order to achieve this, it is crucial that family caregivers are provided with situation-specific services that support them and relieve their burden of care. Unfortunately, however, family caregivers usually take better care of their needy relatives than of themselves and, as a result, often put off or fail to make timely use of health promotion, prevention, and relief services for their own well-being. A mere one-third of all family caregivers turn to ambulatory services for support (Haug et al. 1999; Rauch 2000).

Informal caregiving networks, on the other hand, have been gaining in significance, and the development of more need-based services is becoming increasingly important for at-home care. The major challenges for society are therefore to sustain, promote, and support informal resources and to provide the opportunity to use services aimed at assisting and relieving the burden of family caregivers. Consequently, the main social policy goals of the current German long-term care insurance reform are to promote self-help, civic engagement, and the balance between career and caregiving. The reasons for this are obvious. Caregivers who experience less of a burden and less of a decrease in their income and pensions provide care at home for a longer time. Since the main reasons for care facility placement are that primary caregivers feel overburdened and/or experience problems with their own health, reducing caregiver burden may make it possible to shorten the length of a stay in a care facility or avoid a stay altogether (Barinaga 1998; Barusch 1988; Gräßel 2000).

This is particularly true for family caregivers of those with dementia. Various studies have demonstrated the positive effects of counseling and training programs for family caregivers, including a significant delay in care facility placement (Brodaty et al. 1997; Kurz 2011; Mittelman et al. 1996). Caregivers were able to provide care at home for up to twice as long as in the studies' control groups. Other positive effects of such programs include less mental stress and improved health knowledge among family caregivers as well as improvements in the mood of those suffering from dementia —though not in the burden on caregivers (Brodaty et al. 2003).

Objectives

The EUROFAMCARE[2] project provides an overview of the situation of family caregivers of elderly dependents in Europe in terms of the existence, awareness, availability, use, and acceptance of support services. The project comprised two large substudies. As part of one substudy, national background reports on the current situation of family caregivers were generated in 23 European countries based on secondary data analyses. For the other substudy, approximately 1,000 family caregivers were surveyed in each of six countries (Germany, Greece, Italy, Poland, Sweden, and the United Kingdom) considered representative of the different cultural and welfare systems in Europe.

In this chapter, we aim to analyze the utilization of support services regarding the impact of different socioeconomic factors of family caregivers as well as care situation characteristics on service utilization. Two different models have been calculated, distinguishing between the frequency of service use (units per 6 months) on the one hand and the number of service types on the other. To reveal the underlying structure and detect the most influential factors on service utilization, a regression-tree algorithm has been conducted for data analysis.

[2] The EUROFAMCARE project was funded by the European Union (EU) (contract no.: QLK6-CT-2002-02647) and coordinated by the Department of Medical Sociology at the University of Hamburg (www.uke.de/eurofamcare).

Methods

Sampling

In 2004, 5,923 family caregivers from the six countries named above were interviewed at home about their experiences. Included in the study were primary caregivers providing at least 4 h of personal care or support per week to a relative aged 65 years or older. Subjects providing solely financial support were excluded. The unique aspect of the study's sampling approach was that family caregivers were recruited directly and not through those in need of care and assistance, thereby avoiding preselection bias based on the particular care needs or level of dependency ("care level," CL) of care recipients.

Data were collected using a mixed recruitment strategy. Various means of contacting potential interview partners were chosen including making contacts through social and health services, physicians, pharmacies, Alzheimer's associations, advertisements in newspapers, and word of mouth. This sampling procedure was chosen based on cultural and religious aspects and the fact that available services vary between sites. The spectrum of recruitment strategies should be as broad as possible to ensure that all types of care situations are found in our sample. For this purpose, all EUROFAMCARE partners agreed to employ a common saturation method, i.e., the sampling strategy aimed at covering all facets of family caregiving rather than taking a representative sample in a strict statistical sense. Sampling was conducted at least in predefined chosen sample communities or, if possible, nationwide by parallel or consecutive application of any suitable recruitment strategy covering the three types of areas: "metropolitan," "urban," and "rural."

The interviews were conducted by interviewers from our university centers and from a social research institute with a nationwide network of interviewers to achieve a population-based sample. In the end, the interviewers achieved a total sample size of 1,003 family caregivers (Lüdecke et al. 2008). The comparison of the socioeconomic indicators, the care situations, and the caregiver and care recipient characteristics of the German EUROFAMCARE data with those of the representative MUG III Study of 2002 ("Potential and Limitation of Independent Living in Private Households in Germany") (Schneekloth and Wahl 2005) showed strong consistencies in both studies (Lüdecke et al. 2008).

Measures

When developing the survey questionnaire, we preferred scales that had already proven reliable and valid in international studies. To systematically assess care recipients' need of support, instruments from the Geriatric Assessment were used (McKee et al. 2008). Activities of daily living (ADL) status was measured with the Barthel Index (Mahoney and Barthel 1965), and instrumental activities of daily living (IADL) were measured using selected items from the Older American Resources and Services Questionnaire (OARS; Fillenbaum and Smyer 1981). The total dependency of the cared-for person is a sum-score of the Barthel Index and the IADL score of each cared-for person with a range from 0 (physically independent) to 17 (severely dependent). Cognitive impairments were assessed through questions asking whether the dependent has memory problems or has been diagnosed with dementia. Data on behavioral disturbances were collected using a three-item short version of the Behavioural and Instrumental Stressors in Dementia (BISID; Keady and Nolan 1996).

Caregiver burden was measured using the Carers of Older People in Europe Index (COPE Index), which is available in several different languages and contains three subscales: one assessing the negative impact of caregiving, one assessing the positive value of caregiving, and one assessing the quality of the support received during caregiving (Balducci et al. 2008; McKee et al. 2008; McKee et al. 2003). Information on caregiver well-being and subjective quality of life were obtained using the WHO-5 Well-Being Index (Bech 2008; World Health Organization 1998) and two items from the SF-36 (Health-Related Quality of Life; Brazier et al. 1992).

Data Entry and Analyses

To better determine which factors influence family caregivers' use of support services, we implemented a conditional graphical model, a so-called conditional inference tree (Hothorn et al. 2006a; Hothorn et al. 2006b) based on a learning tree algorithm which embeds tree-structured regression models. The conditional inference-tree algorithm is predicated on recursive binary partitioning embedded in a framework of permutation tests introduced by Strasser and Weber (1999). At each node, a global null hypothesis $H_0 : f(Y \mid X_j) = f(Y)$ is tested on a prespecified α level of 0.05. In case of acceptance, the tree algorithm interrupts and no further data split will be performed, which means the algorithm has detected all significant impact factors on the dependent variable for this certain group of cases represented by the tree branch. Otherwise, the covariate X_j with the strongest influence on Y will be selected as a new node, and the null hypothesis will be tested in each subset of the tree again, which means *all* covariates are tested for the strongest influence on the dependent variable Y again, including the selected covariate X_j. Due to this recursive approach, covariates may appear several times in the course of a tree branch via a new data split in the "subranges" of a scale,[3] for instance, when subgroups, as characterized by a certain covariate, are differentiated into further sub-subgroups, depending on the answer categories or values of the covariate. The distribution in each terminal node is shown as a boxplot.

[3] For example: If a scale ranging from 0 to 10 points is split into a = 0–5 and b = 6–10, the subranges a and b may be split again, for example, into c (0–2) and d (3–5) as well as e (6–8) and f (9–10).

Table 10.1 Variables included in the model and their related Andersen categories

Variable	Andersen category
Variables characterizing the family caregivers	
Age of the family caregiver	Predisposing
Gender of the family caregiver	Predisposing
Job demands (work hours) per week (in hours)	Predisposing
Restrictions in employment as a result of caregiving	Predisposing
Level of education attained by the caregiver (1 = low, 3 = high)	Predisposing
Degree of relationship between caregiver and care recipient	Predisposing
Subjectively perceived burden of care (COPE Index (negative impact), higher score = heavier burden)	Need
Self-reported health (SF-36)	Need
Subjectively perceived positive effects of caregiving (COPE Index (positive value), higher score = more positive perception)	Enabling
Feeling well supported as caregiver	Enabling
Variables characterizing the care situation	
Time spent on caregiving per week (in hours)	Need
Care recipient's need of assistance and support (dependency) as assessed by the Barthel Index and IADL Score (0–17, higher score = greater need of care and higher dependency)	Need
Length of caregiving (time since the caregiver took on caregiving responsibilities)	Need
Locality (metropolitan, urban, rural)	Enabling

Tree-based models are recommended as an alternative to logistic regression analyses (Nagy et al. 2010) in order to detect the underlying structure and most influential variables on the dependent variable "service utilization." Furthermore, they allow detecting nonlinear relationships and interactions between the factors (independent variables).

The variables for calculating the tree model were chosen according to the following criteria: on the one hand, the variables should characterize both the family caregivers and the care situation to provide a comprehensive picture of the care settings. On the other hand, the chosen variables should reflect contextual and individual factors that influence service utilization (Andersen and Davidson 2001). The variables included in the model are shown in Table 10.1.

Caregiver household income was not included in the analyses because of too many missing responses for that variable and lack of adequate imputation criteria for a flawless substitution of these missing data.

Data entry was performed using Data Entry™ 3.0. Descriptive statistics were performed with SPSS™ 20, while the tree-based model was computed using the R statistics tool (R Development Core Team 2009) using the *party* package (Hothorn and Zeileis 2009).

Table 10.2 Sample characteristics of the German sample

Characteristic	Percentage/mean
Total caregivers	N=1,003 (100%)
Female caregivers	76%
Female cared-for elderly	69%
Average age of caregiver	53.8 years (SD=13.4 years)
Average age of cared-for elderly	79.7 years (SD=8.3 years)
Elderly with classified care level	60% (n=602)
Thereof Care Level 1	33%
Thereof Care Level 2	42%
Thereof Care Level 3	25%
Memory problems (undiagnosed)	22%
Diagnosed dementia	34%

Results

The following section presents the results of the interviews carried out with the 1,003 family caregivers in the German substudy.

Description of the German Sample

At the time of interview, the average age of the surveyed family caregivers was 54 years (standard deviation (SD) = 13.4 years). Three-quarters were women (76%), and a large percentage was working; these employed family caregivers worked an average of 32 h per week (42%). The average age of the elderly care recipients was 80 years (SD=8.3 years), and 69% of them were women. Although 72% of family caregivers considered their elderly dependents to be in moderate-to-severe need of assistance (operationalized by limitations in ADLs and IADLs), only 60% of these dependents were receiving long-term care insurance benefits.[4] Of these, 33% were classified as CL 1, 42% as CL 2, and 25% as CL 3. In a good 30% of cases, benefits had not yet been applied for, and in approximately 10% of cases, the application had been rejected or was still being processed (Lüdecke et al. 2008). Dementia had been diagnosed in 34% of care recipients, and another 22% suffered from memory problems that had not (yet) been formally diagnosed (see Table 10.2).

[4] Long-term care insurance is a type of social insurance which covers the risk of a future need for care. The majority of the German population has statutory long-term care insurance coverage. In the event that care is needed, covered individuals may obtain cash benefits for the "informal" caregivers and/or benefits-in-kind like professional care from the long-term care insurance funds. However, eligibility depends on the level of need for care. Following an assessment to determine an individual's level of dependency, he or she is then classified under one of three care levels (CLs) needed.

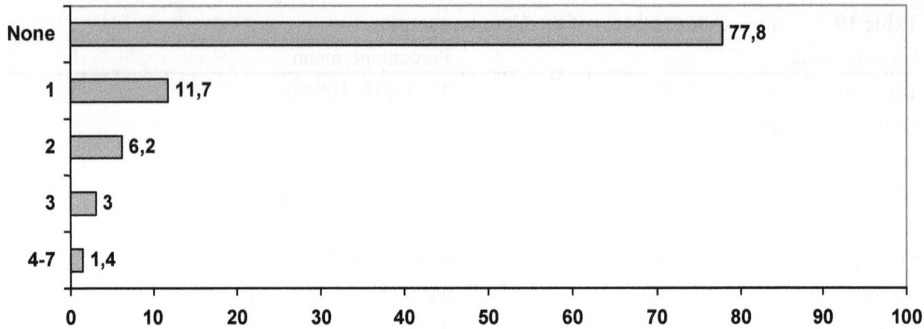

Fig. 10.1 How many special services for family caregivers are being utilized? (Number of services specifically for caregivers, in %, N=1,003)

Utilization of Professional Services

As part of the study, family caregivers were surveyed about their use of different support services, with a distinction being made between services aimed directly at caregivers (e.g., self-help groups, support groups for family caregivers, counseling services, and caregiving courses) and services primarily directed at those in need of care (e.g., primary care physicians and physician specialists, ambulatory care services, inpatient and semi-inpatient care facilities, and meals on wheels). Below, we will examine the types of support services used by caregivers that can help ease their burden of care.

Looking solely at services specifically for family caregivers, we notice that the overall utilization level of this type of services is very low. Nearly 78 % do not make use of any of these services at all, about 12 % use at least one service, and only a small portion (approximately 10 %) use two services or more (see Fig. 10.1).

Although certain support offers and services are aimed primarily at those in need of care (e.g., outpatient care services or semi-inpatient facilities), it can be assumed that these types of services also directly or at least indirectly ease the burden of caregivers. Figure 10.2 presents the results for the use of both types of services—that is, both services specifically aimed at caregivers and services whose main target group is those in need of care.

Even after expanding the range of potential services by services primarily addressing the dependent elderly, nearly half of the surveyed caregivers were found to make no use of any (professional) support services. While only one-third of those surveyed used one service, approximately one-fourth were found to take advantage of two services or more (see Fig. 10.2).

The support services reportedly used by family caregivers can be broken down into the following areas (multiple responses possible):

- Ambulatory care: 26 %
- Household help: 11 %
- Meals on wheels: 11 %

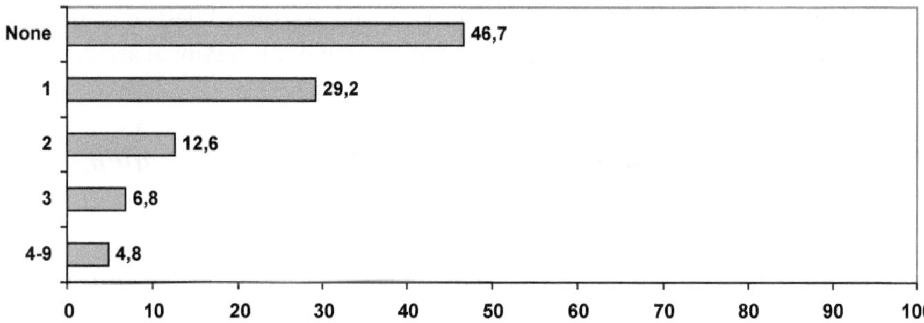

Fig. 10.2 How many services that ease the burden of care are being used by family caregivers? (Services for caregivers and for those in need of care, in %, $N=1{,}003$)

Table 10.3 Utilization of professional services by care level of the care recipients (only those collecting long-term care insurance benefits, $n=579$, $\chi^2=1.77$, df=2, $p=0.413$)

Utilization of professional services	CL 1 ($n=193$, 33.3 %)	CL 2 ($n=240$, 41.5 %)	CL 3 ($n=193$, 25.2 %)	Total ($N=579$, 100 %)
Yes (%)	67.4	65.4	71.9	67.7
No (%)	32.6	34.6	28.1	32.3
Total (%)	100	100	100	100

- Medical counseling: 8 %
- Counseling on social laws: 6 %
- Advisory centers, adult day-care centers, and private in-home caregivers/nurses: each 4 %
- Support groups for family caregivers and Internet-based information: each 3 %
- Self-help groups, caregiving courses, assistance services, and home visits by social service providers: each 2 %

Service Use by Dependency Care Level

Family caregivers may be in need of support when their responsibilities become too great and physically demanding. Their use of assistance or support services is presumed to vary depending on the level of care needed by their dependents, since a greater need of care increases the likelihood that benefits-in-kind from the long-term care insurance will be used. Of all surveyed family caregivers, 58 % are caring for a relative who is collecting long-term care insurance benefits. Whereas a good two-thirds of these caregivers (68 %) make use of professional support services, the other one-third do not use any such services (see Table 10.3). No significant differences in support service utilization were found by the CL of the care recipients. Among the care recipients receiving long-term care insurance benefits, one-third had been classified into CL 1, about 42 % into CL 2, and 25 % into CL 3.

As evidenced by these results, dependent CL and associated degree of need of care do not have a significant impact on the utilization of professional services.

Determinants on Amount and Intensity of Service Utilization

In this section, we distinguish two models of service utilization.

First, we used the tree algorithm to analyze impact factors on the *intensity* of service utilization. We asked the family caregivers which kind of services they or their dependent elderly had utilized in the last 6 months and how often this service was utilized (daily, weekly, etc.) or how many units of a service had been received in the preceding 6 months. Answers have been recoded into the following categories:

- Daily
- More than once a week but less than daily
- Once a week
- Twice a month
- Once a month
- Less than once a month

A count variable was computed to indicate the total number of units of all services utilized in the preceding 6 months. This measure was used as a dependent variable for the first model, where we looked for factors influencing the intensity of service utilization.

Then, we used the same tree algorithm to analyze impact factors influencing the amount of different services used. This variable and its characteristics have already been described above (see above, Utilization of professional services).

Factors Influencing the Intensity of Service Utilization (Used Units per 6 Months)

The first tree-based model[5] reveals the structure of factors that influence the intensity of service utilization for relieving the burden on family caregivers. The algorithm found three different service utilization groups. Only two characteristics have been identified as significant predictors of service utilization (see Fig. 10.3).

Group 1: Less-Educated Caregivers with Lower Perceived Burden (Node 3) Negative impact of care (node 1, $p<0.001$) generates the first split and divides the sample into one group with lower (negative impact score of 14 or less) and another group with higher perceived burden (negative impact score of above 14). At a lower negative impact, the next significant determinant on the intensity of service utilization is education status (node 2, $p<0.001$). Less-educated family caregivers with lower

[5] Including the listed variables in Table 10.1 as independent variables and intensity of service utilization as dependent variable.

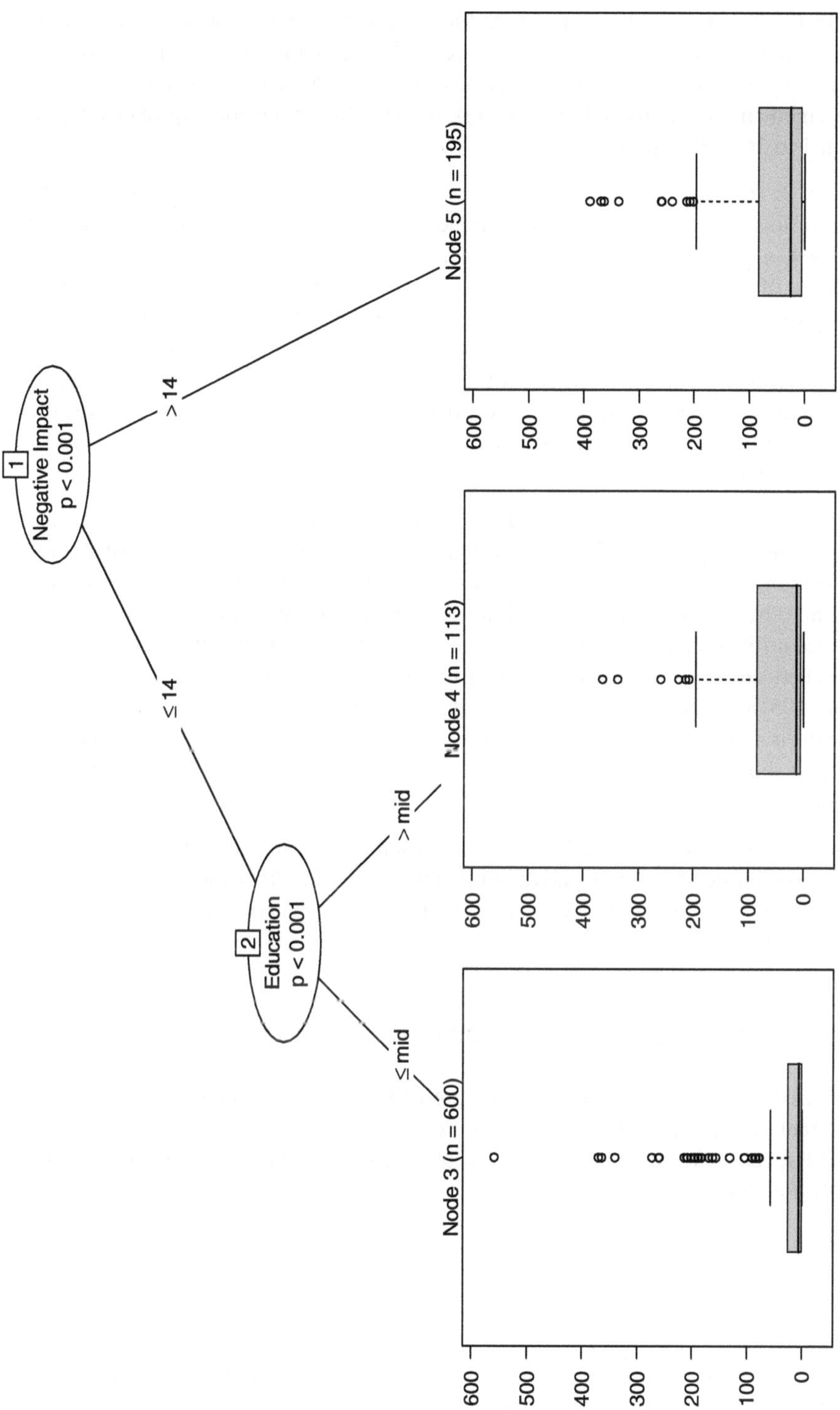

Fig. 10.3 How many times were services that ease the burden of care utilized in the preceding 6 months? (n=911)

subjectively perceived burden of care (node 3, $n=600$) have a lower service utilization rate than the other groups. On average, these family caregivers utilized 33 "service units" in the last 6 months. Looking at the boxplot for this group, we can see a median score of 6 used service units, with the lower and upper quartile ranging from 1 to 26 service units.

Group 2: Higher Educated Caregivers with Lower Perceived Burden (Node 4) In case of lower negative impact and a higher educational status of family caregivers (node 4, $n=113$), service utilization increased in comparison to Group 1 up to an average of 60 "service units" used in the last 6 months. That means while family caregivers with lower educational status tend to use services less frequently when they perceive a lower subjective burden, caregivers with higher educational status use services more frequently even if they perceive the same burden of care as less-educated caregivers. For this group, we find a median score of 13 service units, the lower quartile beginning with 6 service units and the upper quartile ranging to 85 service units.

Group 3: High-Burdened Caregivers (Node 5) Subjectively perceived high burden of care (node 1, $p<0.001$) is a strong, significant predictor of the intensity of service utilization, independent of all other variables included in our model. That means that no other variable had a more significant impact to explain a high frequency of service utilization, i.e., the tree algorithm did not find any more significant interactions between negative impact and intensity of service utilization. This group (node 5, $n=195$) with an average of 60 "service units" that have been used in the last 6 months is simply characterized by a high subjectively perceived burden of care. The boxplot shows a median score of 26 service units, with the lower and upper quartile ranging from 6 to 8 service units.

Summary To summarize, higher educational status of family caregivers and/or high perceived burden of care (negative impact) predict higher frequency of service utilization. Less-educated family caregivers with a lower negative impact tend to utilize services less frequently.

Factors Influencing the Number of Different Services Used

This tree-based model[6] reveals a structure of factors that influence the number of different services used to relieve the burden on family caregivers. The algorithm found seven different types of service utilization (see Fig. 10.4), which are described in detail below.

[6] Including the same variables as in the first model as independent variables and *number of different services utilized* as a dependent variable.

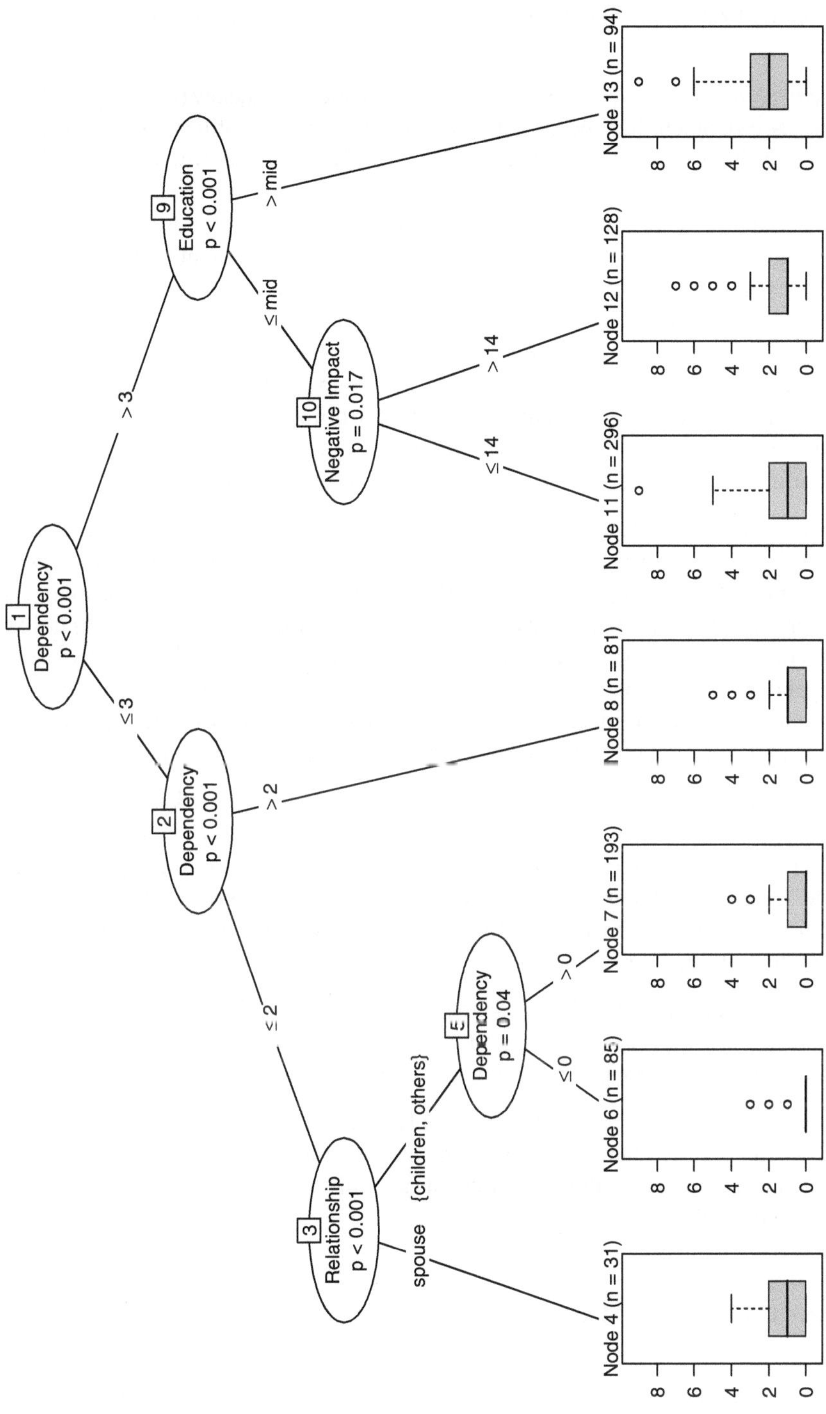

Fig. 10.4 How many different services that ease the burden of care are being utilized by family caregivers? ($n = 908$)

Service Utilization for Slightly Dependent or Physically Independent Elderly

Group 1: Slight Dependency (Node 8) First of all, the dependency (node 1, $p < 0.001$) of the care recipient has the strongest influence on service utilization. The performed split divides the sample into a group of family caregivers who care for elderly persons with a low dependency score (dependency score less than 4 (range from 0 to 17)) and another group of those who care for elderly with a moderate or high score (dependency score at least 4). If the elderly person is slightly dependent, the dependency (node 2, $p < 0.001$) again predicts the service utilization. At a dependency value of exactly 3 (which means the elderly are slightly dependent), we found a group (node 8, $n = 81$) that we may call "slight dependency" with an average of 0.9 utilized services. The resulting boxplot for this group shows a median score of 1 and the lower and upper quartile ranging from 0 to 1 utilized service. According to our results, only the characteristic "slight dependency" of the cared-for persons predicts service utilization for this group, independent from other (socioeconomic) variables.

Group 2: Married Older Caregivers in Need of Support (Node 4) If the elderly person is (almost) physically independent, the relationship between the family caregiver and care recipient (node 3, $p < 0.001$) influences service utilization. Caregivers and care recipients who are married or have live-in partners (node 4, $n = 31$) utilize an average of 1.2 services, even though the cared-for person is (almost) physically independent. The boxplot shows a median score of 1 and the lower and upper quartile range from 0 to 2 utilized services. This shows that especially older family caregivers are using support services even if the care dependency is comparatively low.

Groups 3 and 4: Relatives Caring for Physically Independent or Slightly Dependent Elderly (Nodes 6 and 7) If the family caregivers are relatives other than spouses or partners, services were only utilized when the care recipient was slightly dependent (node 7, $n = 193$, with an average service utilization of 0.5 services). The boxplot for this group shows a median score of 0 and the lower and upper quartile ranging from 0 to 1 utilized service.

If the elderly person is physically independent, family caregivers other than spouses or partners have an average utilization of 0.2 services (node 6, $n = 85$). According to the boxplot for this group, the median as well as the lower and upper quartile are 0.

Summary To summarize, we found an interaction between dependency and the relationship between family caregiver and care recipient in terms of service utilization in those cases where the care recipients are only slightly (physically) dependent or even not at all.

Service Utilization for Moderately or Highly Dependent Elderly

Group 5: Higher Educated Family Caregivers (Node 13) If the elderly person is moderately or severely dependent, the educational status of the family caregiver (node 9, $p < 0.001$) is the strongest predictor of service utilization. If the caregivers are higher educated, we find an average of 2 utilized services (node 13, $n = 94$), independent from the subjectively perceived burden as measured with the negative impact scale of the COPE Index.[7] The boxplot shows a median score of 2, with the lower and upper quartiles ranging from 1 to 3 used services.

Groups 6 and 7: Less-Educated Family Caregivers with Low and High Subjectively Perceived Burden of Care (Nodes 11 and 12) Only when the family caregiver is less educated (node 9, $p < 0.001$) is the negative impact of care (node 10, $p < 0.017$) a relevant predictor of service utilization. Less-educated family caregivers who care for moderately or severely dependent elderly persons tend to use fewer services when they feel less burdened by the care work (node 11, $n = 296$). On average, this group uses about 1.1 services, while the median score is 1 and the lower and upper quartiles range from 0 to 2.

Service utilization increases when less-educated family caregivers perceive a high subjective burden of care (node 12, $n = 128$). In this case, the average amount of utilized services is about 1.6, the median score for this group is 1, and the lower and upper quartiles range from 1 to 2 services.

Summary In case of moderate or severe dependency of care recipients, we found interactions between higher dependency and higher education as predictors for service utilization, independent of whether the higher educated caregivers perceive a higher or lower burden of care. The negative impact only interacts with lower education: moderate or severe dependency, combined with lower education status, leads to increased service utilization if the perceived burden is higher.

Discussion

We have chosen the partition-tree algorithm because this method—compared to traditional analytical methods—facilitates the presentation of highly dimensional data and allows direct interpretation. Furthermore, missing values could be integrated in the analysis instead of using complex multiple imputation algorithms. The tree algorithm allows "the construction of interpretable tree structures not suffering a systematic tendency towards covariates with many possible splits or many missing values" (Hothorn et al. 2006b) and thus "is applicable to any kind of data—whether it does or does not contain missing values" (Hapfelmeier et al. 2012).

The utilization of support services aimed directly at family caregivers is very low. According to Brodaty et al. (2005), this is true even if the caregiver is aware

[7] As a reminder: If there were an interaction between higher educational level, (higher or lower) subjectively perceived burden of care and service utilization, the covariate "negative impact" would have been significant and split the tree path from node 9 to 13 into two more subgroups. Thus, we can assume that services are utilized by higher educated caregivers, regardless of the negative impact of care.

of the services. Including certain services not only aimed primarily at those in need of care but also often served as a source of relief for family caregivers slightly increased the percentage of caregivers using support services.

Among socioeconomic characteristics, we mainly found *need* and *predisposing* factors, as defined by the Andersen model, as predictors for service utilization.

Looking at the *number of service units used*, only two factors were relevant to explain service utilization. The higher educational status of family caregivers (predisposing factor) and/or the high perceived burden of care (negative impact, need factor) are predictors of a higher frequency of service utilization.

Regarding the *number of different services used,* a more differentiated picture is revealed. In case of lower dependency of the cared-for person, service utilization is very low. However, there seems to be an interaction between dependency and the relationship between family caregiver and care recipient in terms of service utilization. In cases where the care recipients and caregivers are married or live-in partners (which is associated with a higher age of the caregivers), services are used independently of whether the cared-for persons are only slightly (physically) dependent or even not at all dependent. This might indicate that elderly family caregivers have trouble managing the care due to their own age-related deterioration of physical health even if the frail, cared-for person is almost independent. Thus, *older* family caregivers can be seen as a vulnerable subgroup among family caregivers, with special needs for assistance and support (Bolin et al. 2008; Lee 2011; Shahly et al. 2012; Taggart et al. 2012).

In case of moderate or severe dependency of care recipients, interactions have been found between higher dependency and higher education as predictors for service utilization. Higher educated caregivers tend to use more services even when their perceived burden of care is low, while family caregivers with lower educational level only seem to use services in case of higher perceived burden of care. Thus, the negative impact only interacts with lower education: moderate or severe dependency combined with lower education status leads to increased service utilization if the perceived burden is higher.

In addition to older caregivers, *less-educated caregivers* are a vulnerable group. According to the education level of family caregivers, it seems that better educated caregivers can more easily access services due to better information about available help, for instance, how or where to find and access the necessary services or how to manage bureaucratic barriers when applying for such help (Chiu and Eysenbach 2011; Lamura et al. 2006). Another explanation is the high costs of services (Lamura et al. 2006), which can be seen as a barrier for service utilization by lower educated family caregivers. Taking opportunity costs into account (Carmichael and Charles 2003; Heitmueller and Inglis 2007), higher educated people are more likely to occupy well-paid jobs and prefer to pay for services instead of reducing career advancements.

To summarize, four important factors mainly impact service utilization:

- Need factors: dependency of elderly person and negative impact
- Predisposing factor: educational level of family caregiver and (high) age of family caregiver (or relationship)

Policymakers can particularly address predisposing factors to support informal care structures. Among less-educated family caregivers, increased service utilization is likely when available information and support services are more easily accessible. In addition, not only the availability of support services but also their advantages and benefits for the affected caregivers must be emphasized to increase the motivation for service utilization.

References

Andersen RM, Davidson PL (2001) Improving access to care in America: individual and contextual indicators. In: Andersen RM, Rice TH, Kominski EF (eds) Changing the U.S. health care system: key issues in health services, policy, and management. Jossey-Bass, San Francisco, CA, pp 3–30.

Balducci C, Mnich E, McKee K, et al. (2008) Negative Impact and Positive Value in Caregiving: Validation of the COPE Index in a Six-Country Sample of Carers. The Gerontologist 48:276–286.

Barinaga M (1998) Caregivers need healing, too. Science 282:1031–1032.

Barusch AS (1988) Problems and coping strategies of elderly spouse caregivers. Gerontologist 28:677–685.

Bech P (2008) Measuring the dimensions of psychological general well-being by the WHO-5. Quality of Life Newsletter 32:15–16.

Bolin K, Lindgren B, Lundborg P (2008) Your next of kin or your own career? Caring and working among the 50+ of Europe. J Health Econ 27:718–738. doi: 10.1016/j.jhealeco.2007.10.004.

Brazier JE, Harper R, Jones NM, et al. (1992) Validating the SF-36 health survey questionnaire: new outcome measure for primary care. BMJ 305:160–164.

Brodaty H, Gresham M, Luscombe G (1997) The Prince Henry Hospital dementia caregivers' training programme. Int J Geriatr Psychiatry 12:183–192.

Brodaty H, Green A, Koschera A (2003) Meta-Analysis of Psychosocial Interventions for Caregivers of People with Dementia. J Am Geriatr Soc 51:657–664.

Brodaty H, Thomson C, Thompson C, Fine M (2005) Why caregivers of people with dementia and memory loss don't use services. Int J Geriatr Psychiatry 20:537–546. doi: 10.1002/gps.1322.

Carmichael F, Charles S (2003) The opportunity costs of informal care: does gender matter? J Health Econ 22:781–803. doi: 10.1016/S0167–6296(03)00044–4.

Chiu TML, Eysenbach G (2011) Theorizing the health service usage behavior of family caregivers: a qualitative study of an internet-based intervention. Int J Med Inform 80:754–764. doi: 10.1016/j.ijmedinf.2011.08.010.

DESTATIS (2008) Pressemitteilung Nr. 121.

Di Rosa M, Kofahl C, McKee K, et al. (2011) A typology of caregiving situations and service use in family carers of older people in six European countries: The EUROFAMCARE study. GeroPsych 24:5–18.

Fillenbaum GG, Smyer MA (1981) The development, validity, and reliability of the OARS multidimensional functional assessment questionnaire. J Gerontol 36:428–434.

Gräßel E (1996) Körperbeschwerden und Belastung pflegender Familienangehöriger bei häuslicher Pflege eines über längere Zeit hilfsbedürftigen Menschen. Psychother Psychosom med Psychol 46:189–193.

Gräßel E (1998) Häusliche Pflege dementiell und nicht dementiell Erkrankter. Teil II: Gesundheit und Belastung der Pflegenden. Z Gerontol Geriat 31:57–62.

Gräßel E (2000) Warum pflegen Angehörige? Ein Pflegemodell für die häusliche Pflege im höheren Lebensalter. Zeitschrift für Gerontopsychologie & -psychiatrie 13:85–94.

Hapfelmeier A, Hothorn T, Ulm K, Strobl C (2012) A new variable importance measure for random forests with missing data. Stat Comput. doi: 10.1007/s11222-012-9349-1.

Haug MR, Ford AB, Stange KC, et al. (1999) Effect of giving care on caregiver's health. Research on Aging 21:515–538.

Heitmueller A, Inglis K (2007) The earnings of informal carers: wage differentials and opportunity costs. J Health Econ 26:821–841. doi: 10.1016/j.jhealeco.2006.12.009.

Hothorn T, Zeileis A (2009) partykit: A Toolkit for Recursive Party-tioning. http://R-forge.R-project.org/projects/partykit/.

Hothorn T, Hornik K, van de Wiel MA, Zeileis A (2006a) A Lego System for Conditional Inference. The American Statistician 60:257–263. doi: 10.1198/000313006X118430.

Hothorn T, Hornik K, Zeileis A (2006b) Unbiased Recursive Partitioning: A Conditional Inference Framework. Journal of Computational and Graphical Statistics 15:651–674. doi: 10.1198/106186006X133933.

Keady J, Nolan M (1996) Behavioural and instrumental stressors in Dementia (BISID): refocussing the assessment of caregiver need in dementia. J Psychiatr Ment Health Nurs 3:163–172.

Kofahl C, Arlt S, Mnich E (2007) "For Better or for Worse…" Differences and Similarities of Caring Spouses and Other Family Caregivers in the German Survey of the Project EUROFAMCARE. Zeitschrift für Gerontopsychologie & -psychiatrie 20:211–225.

Kofahl C, Lüdecke D, Döhner H (2009) Der Einfluss von Betreuungsbedarf und psychosozialen Determinanten auf Belastung und Wohlbefinden von pflegenden Angehörigen alter Menschen. Ergebnisse aus der deutschen Teilstichprobe des Projekts EUROFAMCARE. Pflege & Gesellschaft 3:236–253.

Kurz A (2011) Psychosoziale Interventionen bei demenziell Erkrankten und deren Angehörigen. Versorgungsforschung für demenziell erkrankte Menschen.

Lamura G, Döhner H, Kofahl C (2008) Family Carers of Older People in Europe. A Six-Country Comparative Study. LIT Verlag, Hamburg.

Lamura G, Mnich E, Wojszel B, et al. (2006) The experience of family carers of older people in the use of support services in Europe: selected findings from the EUROFAMCARE project. Z Gerontol Geriatr 39:429–442. doi: 10.1007/s00391-006-0416-0.

Lee R (2011) The outlook for population growth. Science 333:569–573. doi: 10.1126/science.1208859.

Lüdecke D, Mnich E, Kofahl C (2008) Characteristics of the sample. In: Döhner H, Kofahl C, Lüdecke D, Mnich E (eds) Family Care for Older People in Germany. Results from the European Project EUROFAMCARE. LIT Verlag, Hamburg, pp 107–124.

MacDonald A, Dening T (2002) Dementia is being avoided in NHS and social care. BMJ 324:548.

Mahoney FI, Barthel DW (1965) Functional Evaluation: The Barthel Index. Md State Med J 14:61–65.

McKee K, Philp I, Lamura G, et al. (2003) The COPE Index—a first stage assessment of negative impact, positive value and quality of support of caregiving in informal carers of older people. Aging & Mental Health 7:39–52.

McKee K, Balducci C, Krevers B, et al. (2008) The EUROFAMCARE Common Assessment Tool (CAT)—Item and scale development and description. In: Lamura G, Döhner H, Kofahl C (eds) Supporting Family Carers of Older People in Europe. Empirical Evidence, Policy Trends and Future Perspectives. LIT Verlag, Hamburg, pp 49–73.

Mestheneos E, Triantafillou J (2005) Supporting Family Carers of Older People in Europe—The Pan-European Background Report. LIT Verlag, Münster.

Mittelman MS, Ferris SH, Shulman E, et al. (1996) A family intervention to delay nursing home placement of patients with Alzheimer disease. A randomized controlled trial. JAMA 276:1725–1731.

Nagy K, Reiczigel J, Harnos A, et al. (2010) Tree-Based Methods as an Alternative to Logistic Regression in Revealing Risk Factors of Crib-Biting in Horses. Journal of Equine Veterinary Science 30:21–26. doi: 10.1016/j.jevs.2009.11.005.

Pfaff H (2011) Pflegestatistik 2009. Pflege im Rahmen der Pflegeversicherung—Deutschlandergebnisse. 31.

Pinquart M, Sorensen S (2003) Associations of stressors and uplifts of caregiving with caregiver burden and depressive mood: A meta analysis. J Gerontol B Psychol Sci 58B:453–460.

R Development Core Team (2009) R: A language and environment for statistical computing. R Foundation for Statistical Computing, Vienna, Austria.

Rauch U (2000) Unnahbare Helfer: Pflegende Angehörige. Pflegen ambulant 11:24–28.

Rothgang H, Borchert L, Müller R, Unger R (2008) GEK-Pflegereport 2008: Schwerpunktthema: Medizinische Versorgung in Pflegeheimen. Asgard, Sankt Augustin.

Schneekloth U, Wahl H-W (2005) Möglichkeiten und Grenzen selbständiger Lebensführung in privaten Haushalten (MuG III). Integrierter Abschlussbericht. Bundesministerium für Familien, Senioren, Frauen und Jugend, Berlin.

Schulz R, Beach SR (1999) Caregiving as a risk factor for mortality: the Caregiver Health Effects Study. Journal of the American Medical Association 282:2215–2219.

Shahly V, Chatterji S, Gruber MJ, et al. (2012) Cross-national differences in the prevalence and correlates of burden among older family caregivers in the World Health Organization World Mental Health (WMH) Surveys. Psychol Med 1–15. doi: 10.1017/S0033291712001468.

Statistisches Bundesamt (2009) Bevölkerung Deutschlands bis 2060: 12. koordinierte Bevölkerungsvorausberechnung. Wiesbaden.

Statistisches Bundesamt (2011) Pflegestatistik 2009. Statistisches Bundesamt, Wiesbaden.

Strasser H, Weber C (1999) On the Asymptotic Theory of Permutation Statistics. Mathematical Methods of Statistics 8:220–250.

Taggart L, Truesdale-Kennedy M, Ryan A, McConkey R (2012) Examining the support needs of ageing family carers in developing future plans for a relative with an intellectual disability. J Intellect Disabil 16:217–234. doi: 10.1177/1744629512456465.

World Health Organization (1998) WHO Info Package: Mastering depression in primary care (Version 2.2). WHO, Geneva.

Part V
Results: Selected Diseases

Chapter 11
Health Services Utilization by Community-Dwelling Dementia Patients and Their Family Caregivers

Carolin Donath, Gudrun Ulbrecht, Hannes Grau, Elmar Graessel, Larissa Schwarzkopf, Petra Menn, Simone Kunz and Rolf Holle

Introduction

Dementia is one of the most common and serious disorders in the elderly and is a main cause for institutionalization (Aguero-Torres et al. 2001). Most elderly people would like to live with their families for as long as possible (Goldsmith 1996), but patients with progressive dementia may require institutional care because providing care at home can present a heavy physical and mental burden for family caregivers (Sörensen et al. 2006).

The authors belong to the "Working Group on Dementia Health Services Research."

C. Donath (✉) · G. Ulbrecht · H. Grau · E. Graessel
Friedrich-Alexander-Universität Erlangen-Nürnberg, Clinic of Psychiatry and Psychotherapy, Center for Health Services Research in Medicine, Erlangen, Germany
e-mail: carolin.donath@uk-erlangen.de

G. Ulbrecht
e-mail: gudrun.ulbrecht@uk-erlangen.de

H. Grau
e-mail: Hannes.Grau@uk-erlangen.de

E. Graessel
e-mail: elmar.graessel@uk-erlangen.de

L. Schwarzkopf · P. Menn · S. Kunz · R. Holle
Helmholtz Zentrum München—German Research Center for Environmental Health (GmbH), Institute of Health Economics and Health Care Management, Neuherberg, Germany
e-mail: l.schwarzkopf@helmholtz-muenchen.de

P. Menn
e-mail: petra.menn@helmholtz-muenchen.de

S. Kunz
e-mail: simone.kunz@helmholtz-muenchen.de

R. Holle
e-mail: holle@helmholtz-muenchen.de

C. Janssen et al. (eds.), *Health Care Utilization in Germany*,
DOI 10.1007/978-1-4614-9191-0_11, © Springer Science+Business Media New York 2014

In a review of 42 international studies, Luppa et al. (2008) used the behavioral model by Andersen (Andersen and Davidson 2001) to predict institutionalization of dementia patients and arrived at various results. For instance, higher age of the dementia patient and of the family caregiver increase the probability of institutionalization or reduce the time to institutionalization. In addition, advanced dementia is directly linked to the probability of institutionalization.

Regarding the health services available to community-dwelling patients, the following questions arise: What are the predictors of the utilization of care and support services by dementia patients and their family caregivers? What are the predictors of the utilization of non-pharmacological therapies (NPTs)? How does the utilization of health insurance and long-term care insurance (LTCI) benefits differ by the stage of dementia? We conducted two studies to answer these questions. Applying the model by Andersen (2001), this chapter presents the results of these studies

- Regarding the utilization of care services for the patient as well as caregiver support services
- Regarding the patients' utilization of NPTs as well as the utilization of health insurance and long-term care insurance benefits depending on the stage of dementia

Utilization of Care Services and Caregiver Support Services

The study presented below investigated significant predictors of utilization of care and support services by German family caregivers and community-dwelling dementia patients. In addition, we created a general overview of the data on ten care and support services as regards awareness, utilization, need, and accessibility.

Care and Support Services Available to Patients and Their Family Caregivers

Professional Home Care

Professional home care involves professional nursing staff visiting the patient at home to provide care services (Zhu and Sano 2006). In Germany, these services can be billed through the LTCI if the patient has been assigned to a Care Level[1].

[1] Care levels are composed according to § 15 as follows: Definite care dependent are in need for help at least once daily in two care areas and more than once a week for home help (Care Level 1); Strong care dependent (Care Level 2) are in need for help at least three times a day for different times in at least two care areas and more than once a week for home help; Very strong care dependent (Care Level 3) are in need for help around the clock (including at night) and more than once a week for home help;

Pursuant to § 36 (SGB XI), nursing services are provided to community-dwelling, care-dependent patients in the form of nursing benefits-in-kind.

The nursing benefits-in-kind cover the expenses for general care and home help. Home care services are one of the best known and most commonly utilized services to support family caregivers in Germany.

Short-Term Institutional Care

Short-term institutional care provides temporary inpatient care to patients who require assistance in activities of daily living and are normally cared for at home by family caregivers. Section 42 (SGB XI) provides that care-dependent people are entitled to short-term institutional care in the event that home care is temporarily unavailable, not yet provided, or not provided to the required extent. Further, the combination of home care and semi-inpatient care (during the day or night) must be insufficient. Short-term institutional care is provided on an inpatient basis.

Furthermore, § 39 (SGB XI) provides that patients are entitled to short-term institutional care if the caregiver is temporarily impeded due to illness, vacation, or for other reasons; the patient then becomes entitled to respite care. For each calendar year, respite care is limited to a maximum of 4 weeks (28 days). Since January 1, 2012, the maximum benefit amount is EUR 1,550. Pursuant to § 39 sentence 2 (SGB XI), respite care can only be claimed if the family caregiver has provided care to the care-dependent person in the patient's home environment for at least 6 months before the initial utilization of this benefit.

Adult Day Care

In *adult day care*, patients are placed in a group with other dementia patients and receive care from professional care providers (typically trained nurses) at an external facility for up to 8 h per day. Most patients are picked up and dropped off at home by a transport service. Therapeutic services are not necessarily included in day care. NPT, such as training of specific skills, can be offered on a voluntary basis. Medical care by a physician is not part of this service. This is a semi-inpatient service to supplement home care. Costs are covered by the social LTCI if the patient is considered care-dependent. § 41 (SGB XI) sets out the entitlement of care-dependent people to day care or night care. The entitlement is unlimited in time and can be claimed if home care cannot be ensured to an adequate extent or if the service is necessary to supplement or support home care.

Day Hospitals

Like adult day care, *day hospitals* offer group care to patients for several hours during the daytime. However, day hospitals also offer pharmacological therapy and NPT through a team of various health professionals under medical supervision. In addition to therapeutic interventions, diagnostic procedures are regularly performed (Jolley et al. 2006; Schunk and Steinwachs 2003; Woods et al. 2005). The legal bases for the entitlement to day hospital benefits are the same as those for adult day care. Day hospitals are also considered semi-inpatient services, and patients are entitled to these services if they are care-dependent and home care cannot be ensured to an adequate extent or if this service is necessary to supplement or support home care.

Care Groups

Care groups are a low-threshold service and provide temporary, hourly relief to family caregivers. In these small groups, dementia patients receive care outside of their homes on an hourly basis (Jost et al. 2006; Krauß 2006). The family caregiver must independently organize or provide transport to the care group. These services are typically offered once weekly for 2–3 h. While the patients are attending the group, family caregivers can choose to exchange experiences with other caregivers in a parallel caregiver group. Such services are typically offered by associations, community consulting centers, and self-help organizations. The Nursing Care Reform Act [*Pflege-Weiterentwicklungsgesetz*] that came into effect in 2008 envisions a further expansion of such "low threshold" services.

Caregiver Counseling

Classic *caregiver counseling* is offered at counseling centers that family caregivers visit. In contrast, actively approaching (outreach) counseling is provided at the caregiver's home upon request, or meetings can take place at a neutral location. In addition, telephone counseling is offered by groups such as self-help organizations, and advice is also available on Internet forums, and on information pages of ministries of health or their associations, and self-help organizations. Classic caregiver counseling at counseling centers supplies information and offers interventions to strengthen mental and material resources. Caregiver counseling thereby provides tangible as well as informational and emotional components of social support (Gallagher-Thompson and Coon 2007; Selwood et al. 2007). Pursuant to § 45a (SGB XI), "low threshold" services also include agencies that arrange contacts between care services and care-dependent people. Caregiver counseling centers are considered as such agencies and are therefore considered "low threshold" services.

Support Groups for Dementia Caregivers

In *support groups for dementia caregivers*, family caregivers attend meetings led by an experienced caregiver (peer-led self-help group) or a professional (professional-led caregiver support group).

Pursuant to § 45d (SGB XI), self-help groups are "voluntary, neutral, independent, not-for-profit associations of individuals." In support groups for dementia caregivers, caregivers who provide home care to a significantly care-dependent person meet to exchange experiences. These groups serve to discuss burdens and problems and offer tangible support (information, "tips") as well as emotional support. Support groups are considered "low threshold" services.

Home Help

This support service helps care-dependent patients to maintain their own housekeeping (e.g., cleaning, shopping, and food preparation). *Home help* can be ensured through in-kind services provided by a nursing care service § 36 (SGB XI) or through a nursing care allowance § 37 (SGB XI). According to § 36 (SGB XI), care-dependent patients who receive home care are entitled to general care and home help as benefits-in-kind. These services are provided by qualified care providers. This staff is employed by the long-term care insurance or by professional home care services with which the long-term care insurance has entered into a health service agreement. Hence, home help is a form of direct relief for family caregivers.

Caregiver Skill Training

Pursuant to § 45 (SGB XI), caregiver skill training aims to promote the involvement in care provision, facilitate care and assistance, and reduce the care-related physical and mental burden. In caregiver skill training, professional nurses teach family caregivers the skills and abilities needed to perform care-giving tasks and to specifically interact with dementia patients and handle symptoms (cognitive decline, behavioral disorders, and associated affective symptoms) (Bower et al. 2002). Pursuant to § 45 (SGB XI), caregiver skill training is free of charge, and family caregivers can apply to the LTCI to receive this benefit. LTCIs may offer the classes independently or in cooperation with other LTCIs or contract them out to other suitable institutions.

Voluntary Help

Voluntary help is an hourly relief service for the family caregiver at the patient's home. The voluntary help is a "low-threshold" service that is financed through the social LTCI and provided by volunteers. The volunteers must be trained to offer this service, but training courses vary by federal state [*Bundesland*]. They range from short introductions that last a few hours to 40-h training programs that particularly cover handling dementia-specific behaviors and offering suitable activities. In most cases, the trained volunteers visit the patients once a week for 2–3 h. During this time, family caregivers can pursue their own interests or take care of other tasks.

The volunteers are predominantly middle-aged women. In about one-third of cases, they have some previous experience with dementia patients and wish to provide a meaningful social service (Gräßel and Schirmer 2006).

Methods

Design and Execution

The results presented in Chap. 2 summarize a study conducted on the basis of a written, anonymous survey of family caregivers of community-dwelling dementia patients (Donath et al. 2009a; Donath et al. 2009b; Donath et al. 2011; Donath et al. 2009c; Graessel et al. 2011; Gräßel et al. 2010a; Gräßel et al. 2010b; Gräßel et al. 2009; Gräßel et al. 2010c). The study on the care of dementia patients focused on a total of ten "low threshold" outpatient and semi-inpatient services plus one temporary inpatient service. In addition to exploring quality features that such services should offer from the family caregivers' perspective, the study aimed to determine the awareness of and subjective need for individual services. The study was conducted in the form of a survey questionnaire in four German regions: in Erlangen and the district of Erlangen-Höchstadt (south), in Dortmund and surroundings (west), in the city and district of Kassel (north–central), and in the state of Brandenburg, particularly the area around Potsdam (north–east). The study was cross-sectional. The survey documents were distributed through the Medical Service of the Health Insurance (Medizinischer Dienst der Krankenkassen (MDK)), the regional Alzheimer societies, caregiver counseling centers, and professional home care services. A total of 2,000 questionnaires were distributed, and 404 were returned.

The survey documents consisted of a letter, the questionnaire, a return envelope, and an information brochure. The enclosed letter discussed the aim of the survey, the four researcher groups, the financial support by the German Alzheimer Society, the free return envelope, and the anonymous nature of the survey and analyses. Before conducting the survey, we estimated a response rate of 20 %. We therefore distributed a total of 500 forms in each study region to meet our goal of 100 completed questionnaires per region. The recruitment period was set to 6 months. The estimated response rate was based on previous surveys of family caregivers of dementia patients, which achieved a response rate of 25 % (Gräßel 1998). The survey and the study aimed to reach family caregivers without experience with the services ("nonusers") as well as caregivers who have already utilized support services ("users"). We intended to distribute the questionnaire to 200 "nonusers" and 300 "users." Nonusers were to be reached through the MDK. The MDK staff was asked to distribute the survey documents during the initial review (for social LTCI purposes). According to German law, the initial review by the social LTCI is conducted when the patient first applies to be assigned to a Care Level and hence to receive insurance benefits in the form of monetary benefits or benefits-in-kind. With this approach, we planned to reach family caregivers of dementia patients in an early stage of disease. The assumption was that most of these caregivers had not yet utilized any relief services. The MDK staff was requested to give the survey documents to family caregivers and ask them to participate if one of the nursing care diagnoses in the MDK review was "dementia."

We aimed to reach the 300 "users" in each region through the offices of the regional Alzheimer societies, caregiver counseling centers, and professional home care services. The involved institutions distributed the questionnaires, including the letter and brochure. With this recruitment method, the dementia patients were more likely to have suffered from the disease for an extended time period, and the family caregivers were more likely to have had some experience with various relief and support services.

Of the total 2000 distributed questionnaires, $N = 404$ were returned, which equals to a national response rate of 20 %, as expected. The response rate varied by region as follows: $N = 152$ (of 500) for the Brandenburg region (30 %); $N = 87$ (of 500) for the Dortmund region (17 %); $N = 83$ (of 500) for the Kassel region (17 %); and $N = 82$ (of 500) for the Erlangen region (16 %).

Sample Characteristics

On average, the surveyed family caregivers were 61.3 years old (standard deviation 11.9). About three-fourths of them (73 %) were women. Nearly half (48 %) had completed 9 years of education, and about one-fifth (21 %) had finished 12 years of schooling. Slightly more than one-fourth (29 %) of family caregivers were still employed, and 75 % lived together with the patient. Nearly half (44 %) of the participants lived in large cities with at least 100,000 inhabitants. Among the family caregivers, about half (48.9 %) were the patient's child and almost half (44 %) were the patient's spouse. Two-thirds (65 %) of the respondents were supported by others in care provision. The patients who received care from family caregivers were mostly women (64 %) and on average 78.8 years old (standard deviation 9.1). On average, 5.1 net hours of care were required (standard deviation 4.7), and the mean time since diagnosis was 50.8 months (standard deviation 39.4).

Instruments and Statistical Analyses

The nine-page questionnaire was piloted with family caregivers to test the comprehensibility and acceptability of questions.

The questionnaire collected the socio-demographic data of the family caregivers and the dementia patients as well as characteristic data on the care situation, such as the time required for care activities per day (in hours). Thereafter, a total of ten support services were briefly described (to enable respondents unfamiliar with the service to answer further questions). Questions on the utilization of specific services followed. The questions “Are you aware of the service?” and “Do you use the service?” were to be answered dichotomously (yes/no). A 5-point Likert scale was used to measure the caregivers’ perceived need for the respective service in their specific care situation (from 0 = “I don’t need it” to 4 = “I need it urgently”), with the additional note “regardless of whether you were previously aware of the service or have previously used it.” The accessibility of the service was assessed using three categories such as “don’t know,” “not easily accessible to me,” and “accessible to me.” Finally, we asked the following open question: “Regardless of whether you have already used the service, what would you personally expect from a good “service?”” The term “service” was then replaced by one of the ten care and support services. The below summary of results does not include an analyses of the open question.

Quantitative data are available for 97 % of respondents. To determine which variables predict the utilization of the respective service, we conducted ten service-specific binary logistic regression analyses with utilization/nonutilization as the dependent variable. Before conducting the regression analyses, a multicollinearity analysis was performed. Its goal was to reduce highly correlated variables to simplify the model. We decided to exclude variables at a mean correlation of $r = 0.4$ and above. Following an analysis of associations between the respective variables, the expert panel excluded specific variables such as degree of kinship, living together in one household, employment status of the family caregiver, and care level. For some of the ten services, accessibility was also highly correlated with other variables. Details are presented in the results tables below.

The methods used in this study have already been described elsewhere since individual results of the study have been previously published (Donath et al. 2009a; Donath et al. 2009b; Donath et al. 2011; Donath et al. 2009c; Graessel et al. 2011; Gräßel et al. 2010a; Gräßel et al. 2010b; Gräßel et al. 2009; Gräßel et al. 2010c).

Results

The above study reveals that family caregivers’ awareness of *professional home care services* is very high, with 84 % of respondents knowing about them (Graessel et al. 2011). About half (47 %) of the respondents actually use this service (Graessel et al. 2011). The subjective need assessment for professional home care shows that about two-fifths (41 %) of responding family caregivers need professional home care very urgently (21 %) or urgently (20 %), while nearly one-fifth (22 %) state that they do not need or hardly ever need (16 %) it.

In our study, the utilization rate of *short-term institutional care* was 27 % (Donath et al. 2009c). With 76 % of family caregivers knowing about it, the awareness of this service is very high in Germany (Donath et al. 2009c). In part, this may be due to the financial support of this service by the LTCI for patients assigned to a care level. In the subjective need assessment of this service, two-thirds of German family caregivers subjectively need short-term institutional care urgently (26 %) or very urgently (23 %) (Donath et al. 2009c).

Our study shows a 32 % utilization rate of *adult day care* (Donath et al. 2011). Seventy-eight percent of family caregiver reported being aware of the service. Fewer than half of family caregivers of dementia patients (42 %) reported urgently or very urgently needing this service (Donath et al. 2011).

In Germany, the utilization rate of *day hospitals* is 8 % (Donath et al. 2009a). One factor for the low utilization is certainly the comparatively low awareness of the service, with only 46 % of family caregivers knowing about it (Donath et al. 2009a). In addition, day hospitals may not be sufficiently accessible in every region—particularly in rural areas—as they are typically linked to large, specialized treatment centers. Nevertheless, more than half (53 %) of the family caregivers need support through a day hospital very urgently (24 %) or urgently (29 %) (Donath et al. 2009a).

In Germany, 12 % of family caregivers of dementia patients utilize *care groups* (Gräßel et al. 2009). Certainly, this low utilization level is in part the result of low awareness. Fewer than half (43 %) of the respondents knew about this service at all (Gräßel et al. 2009). On the basis of this relatively low awareness, the family caregivers' responses regarding the subjective need for the service (all respondents) make sense: About one-fourth (26 %) of caregivers report needing a care group very urgently (10 %) or urgently (16 %), while more than half of respondents state that they do not need (33 %) or hardly ever need (20 %) care groups (Gräßel et al. 2009).

Caregiver counseling is a relief service for family caregivers. With 59 % of respondents knowing about it, the awareness of caregiver counseling is relatively high (Gräßel et al. 2010b). Caregiver counseling is used by more than one-third (39 %) of the respondents (Gräßel et al. 2010b). An assessment of the perceived need for this service reveals that more than one-third (40 %) of responding caregivers need this form of counseling very urgently (10 %) or urgently (29 %) (Gräßel et al. 2010b).

Family caregivers' awareness of *support groups for dementia caregivers* is high, with 70 % of respondents knowing about them (Gräßel et al. 2010c). Slightly fewer than half (42 %) of respondents used the service (Gräßel et al. 2010c). About one-third (30 %) of responding family caregivers subjectively need this service very urgently (11 %) or urgently (19 %) (Gräßel et al. 2010c).

The surveyed respondents are less aware of *home help*, with only 52 % of respondents knowing about the service (Graessel et al. 2011). About one-fifth of respondents (19 %) use the service, and about one-fourth (27 %) need it urgently or very urgently (Graessel et al. 2011).

The awareness of *caregiver skill training* is relatively low, with 43 % of family caregivers knowing about it (Donath et al. 2009b). Only 13 % use caregiver skill training (Donath et al. 2009b). In our study, 15 % of family caregivers report needing caregiver skill training urgently, and 6 % need it very urgently (Donath et al. 2009b).

In our study, 52 % of respondents knew about *voluntary help* and 18 % use it (Gräßel et al. 2010a). The survey shows that almost one-third (30 %) of respondents very urgently (12 %) or urgently (18 %) need this service (Gräßel et al. 2010a).

Predictors of Service Utilization

The Andersen model (2001) classifies the predictors for the utilization of health-care services into three categories: predisposing factors, enabling factors, and need factors (subjective and objective need). A study by Toseland (2002) showed that predisposing factors and enabling factors more strongly predict utilization than do need factors. However, this study suffered from two limitations in terms of the predictability of service utilization by family caregivers of dementia patients: (1) Toseland's sample was not dementia-specific and (2) the analyses were not service-specific but were analyzed collectively as "community offers" and "health service offers."

Therefore, this study examines the utilization of specific services. It aims to clarify which of the three types of factors from the Andersen model is predictive of utilization. In addition, we wanted to determine whether the importance of the three factors varies among services.

Regardless of the type of service, all regression analyses confirm the importance of the need factor, specifically the subjective conviction of the caregiver that a service is needed (perceived need) (see Tables 11.1 and 11.2). This is the strongest predictor for the utilization of a service. The only significant enabling factor, applicable to these services, is service accessibility in the sense that family caregivers who do not know about the accessibility of the nearest short-term institutional care (or adult day care) use this service significantly less frequently (or tend to use it less frequently). Similarly, family caregivers who know nothing about the accessibility of the nearest caregiver counseling service use this service significantly less frequently. Among predisposing factors, two variables are particularly significant predictors of utilization: age of the patient and caregiver and the latter's educational level. The family caregiver's age predicts utilization of professional home care and adult day care, with higher age being associated with more frequent utilization. This association is also found between patient age and the utilization of professional home care. The same relationship exists for two other care-related services: higher patient age predicts the utilization of "home help" and "caregiver skill training." This association with advanced age may be caused by the growing acceptance of external assistance through specific nursing services as a result of the patient's increasing frailty and comorbidities.

For care groups and caregiver skill training, utilization levels are influenced by the education level of the family caregiver, as family caregivers with a low educational level tend to use this service more frequently for themselves or the patient than relatives with a higher education level. In general, however, predisposing factors are not as highly predictive and not as consistently predictive for all services as are need factors (need for a service).

Table 11.1 Binary-logistic regression analyses with utilization of the respective service as the dependent variable (N=404)

Variable	Professional home care		Short-term institutional care		Day care		Day hospital		Care groups		Andersen category
	β	*p*	*β*	*p*	*β*	*p*	*β*	*p*	*β*	*p*	
Caregiver sex[a]	−0.801	0.055	−0.416	0.253	0.174	0.702	1.095	0.153	0.204	0.762	Pre-disposing
Caregiver age	−0.043	0.006	−0.007	0.599	0.035	0.048	−0.010	0.715	0.022	0.438	Pre-disposing
Caregiver educational level[b]	0.738	0.077	−0.415	0.185	0.241	0.615	0.398	0.575	1.908	0.025	Pre-disposing
Patient sex[a]	−0.636	0.109	−0.030	0.393	−0.056	0.899	0.804	0.234	0.535	0.394	Pre-disposing
Patient age	0.097	0.001	0.033	0.054	0.004	0.854	−0.034	0.247	−0.014	0.587	Pre-disposing
Duration of illness	0.005	0.284	0.007	0.121	0.000	0.971	−0.003	0.645	0.008	0.202	Need
Hours of care/day	0.023	0.569	0.055	0.172	−0.041	0.372	0.067	0.320	−0.011	0.834	Need
Need for service	0.986	<0.001	0.406	0.001	1.071	<0.001	0.410	0.023	0.858	<0.001	Need
Others' help in care provision[c]	−0.101	0.760	−0.154	0.625	−0.445	0.249	0.746	0.156	1.012	0.055	Enabling
Place of residence: urban/rural[d]	0.103	0.746	−0.450	0.147	−0.099	0.782	−0.282	0.574	−0.515	0.297	Enabling
Awareness of the service[e]	−21.682	0.997	−20.087	0.997	−20.206	0.997	−19.803	0.995	−20.460	0.995	Enabling
Accessibility of the service[f]	–	–	−0.779	0.040	−0.748	0.072	0.137	0.793	–	–	Enabling

Previously published results of our own studies (Donath et al. 2009a; Donath et al. 2011; Donath et al. 2009c; Graessel et al. 2011; Gräßel et al. 2009)
β regression coefficient
[a] Sex: female, reference value: male
[b] Family caregiver's education level:
-Professional home care/day care/day hospital/care groups: lower-level secondary school, reference value: higher-level secondary school
-Short-term institutional care: middle-level or higher-level secondary school; reference value: lower-level secondary school or no degree
-Short-term institutional care: middle-level or higher-level secondary school; reference value: lower-level secondary school or no degree
[c] Others' help in care provision: no, reference value: yes
[d] Place of residence: rural, reference value: urban
[e] Awareness of the service: no, reference value: yes
[f] Accessibility of the service: short-term institutional care/day care/day hospital: unknown accessibility, reference value: accessible to me

Table 11.2 Binary-logistic regression analyses with utilization of the respective service as a dependent variable (N=404)

Variable	Caregiver counseling		Support groups		Home help		Caregiver skill training		Voluntary help		Andersen category
	β	p	β	p	β	p	β	p	β	p	
Caregiver sex[a]	−0.398	0.421	−0.294	0.522	−0.130	0.790	0.749	0.234	−0.231	0.611	Pre-disposing
Caregiver age	<0.001	0.993	0.001	0.956	0.019	0.319	−0.013	0.580	0.004	0.801	Pre-disposing
Education of caregiver[b]	0.451	0.267	0.421	0.256	−0.595	0.275	−1.639	0.001	0.154	0.746	Pre-disposing
Patient sex[a]	−0.157	0.759	−0.461	0.251	0.342	0.498	−0.104	0.855	−0.0188	0.658	Pre-disposing
Patient age	0.007	0.831	−0.011	0.592	0.100	0.001	0.068	0.012	0.022	0.297	Pre-disposing
Duration of illness	−0.003	0.543	0.004	0.376	−0.011	0.058	−0.002	0.794	−0.004	0.390	Need
Hours of care/day	−0.070	0.099	0.039	0.367	−0.035	0.499	−0.065	0.318	0.083	0.056	Need
Need for service	0.566	<0.001	1.292	<0.001	1.000	<0.001	0.495	0.004	0.419	0.003	Need
Others' help in care provision[c]	−0.209	0.585	0.071	0.842	−0.097	0.833	−0.009	0.984	0.372	0.324	Enabling
Place of residence: rural vs. urban[d]	−0.003	0.993	−0.334	0.346	−0.452	0.269	−0.814	0.082	0.198	0.601	Enabling
Awareness of the service[e]	−21.529	0.995	−21.489	0.996	−20.421	0.995	−20.077	0.995	−20.497	0.995	Enabling
Accessibility of the service[f]	−1.152	0.007	–	–	–	–	–	–	–	–	Enabling

Previously published results of our own studies (Donath et al. 2009b; Graessel et al. 2011; Gräßel et al. 2010a; Gräßel et al. 2010b; Gräßel et al. 2010c)

β Regression coefficient

[a] Sex: female, reference value: male

[b] Family caregiver's education level Caregiver counseling: lower/upper level secondary school, reference value: less than 10 years of schooling Support groups for dementia caregivers/caregiver skill training: middle-level or higher-level secondary school; reference value: lower-level secondary school or no degree-Home help/voluntary help: middle-level secondary school, reference value: higher-level secondary school.

[c] Others' help in care provision: no, reference value: yes

[d] Place of residence: rural, reference value: city

[e] Awareness of the service: no, reference value: yes

[f] Accessibility of the service: unknown accessibility, reference value: accessible to me

Discussion and Conclusions About the Utilization of Care Services, Relief Services, and Support Services

Our results (Graessel et al. 2011) agree with other studies (dello Buono et al. 1999; Roelands et al. 2008; Toseland et al. 1999) that report a relatively high awareness of *professional home care*, at 69 % and 92 % of respondents. According to international studies, the utilization level of professional home care is between 23 and 47 % (Brodaty et al. 2005; Lamura et al. 2006; Philip and Ghosh 1992; Toseland et al. 1999), levels that are equal to or lower than in our study (Graessel et al. 2011). It is likely that cost coverage, which varies internationally as a result of different insurance systems, is a significant influencing factor and in part explains differences between countries. Subjective need is much higher in our study than in US studies, with Toseland (1999) reporting 9 % and Brodaty et al. reporting (2005) 8 %. However, the percentage of family caregivers who state that they do not need professional home care is also higher in our study than in the literature (15 %) (dello Buono et al. 1999).

The utilization level of *short-term institutional care* ranges from 3 to 26 % in international studies (Gräßel 1997; Lamura et al. 2006; Philip and Ghosh 1992; Toseland et al. 1999; van Exel et al. 2006); the higher value corresponds to the results found in our study (Donath et al. 2009c). Awareness levels reported in the international literature vary greatly, with results ranging from 7 to 90 % (Roelands et al. 2008; Toseland et al. 1999; van Exel et al. 2006). The perceived need for this service is considerably higher in our study than the 8 % reported by Toseland (US) (Toseland et al. 1999) and higher than the 13 % reported by van Exel (Netherlands) (van Exel et al. 2006).

Internationally, awareness and knowledge about *adult day care* range between 33 and 94 % (dello Buono et al. 1999; Roelands et al. 2008; Toseland et al. 1999; van Exel et al. 2006). Our results were in the middle of this range (Donath et al. 2011). Adult day care utilization rates are reported as between 4 and 61 % in international studies (Kosloski and Montgomery 1993; Lamura et al. 2006; Toseland et al. 1999; van Exel et al. 2006). However, not all of these rates are dementia-specific. The utilization rate found in our study is in the middle of this range (Donath et al. 2011). However, particularly in Europe, relatively low utilization rates (4 %) can be assumed.(Lamura et al. 2006). Compared to our study (Donath et al. 2011), a much lower need for day care is reported internationally, at 10 % in the USA and 19 % in the Netherlands (Toseland et al. 1999; van Exel et al. 2006).

The *day hospital* utilization rate in our study (Donath et al. 2009a) is similar to the rates in international studies, which are reported as only between 3 and 18 % (Chow et al. 2000; dello Buono et al. 1999; Toseland et al. 1999). Older US studies (1999) report an awareness rate of 71 %, which is much above the rate found in our study (Donath et al. 2009a). However, this difference could result from insufficient differentiation between the terms "day care" and "day hospital," which are separate concepts in Germany but are not always differentiated as clearly internationally. The perceived need for day hospitals distinctly differs as well. Only 3 % of family caregivers answer affirmatively in the US study by Toseland et al. (1999), whereas our study found a much higher percentage (Donath et al. 2009a).

According to North American data, the average utilization rate of *care groups* is only 5% (Chow et al. 2000; Toseland et al. 1999), lower than in our study (Gräßel et al. 2009). Our results for the awareness of the service were comparable to the 50% in the Toseland study (1999). The percentage of family caregivers who "need" the service is much higher in our study (Gräßel et al. 2009) than the 11% reported by a US study (Toseland et al. 1999).

The high awareness of *caregiver counseling* in our study (Gräßel et al. 2010b) is comparable with North American results (awareness rates of between 56 and 63%) (Toseland et al. 1999). In Italy, awareness is much higher at 91% (dello Buono et al. 1999). The results regarding the need for the service (Gräßel et al. 2010b) are comparable with the results of a study by Colantonio et al. (2001), where 40% of respondents stated that they need professional caregiver counseling. However, the results reported by Toseland et al. (1999) are much lower (4–7%). The utilization level in our study (Gräßel et al. 2010b) is higher or equal to utilization levels reported from international studies, which range from 4 to 31%. (Chow et al. 2000; dello Buono et al. 1999; Lamura et al. 2006; Toseland et al. 1999).

Family caregivers' awareness of *support groups for dementia caregivers* is high (Gräßel et al. 2010c). The same was found by Toseland et al. (1999), at awareness levels of 59%. In our study, almost half of the respondents used the service (Gräßel et al. 2010c). Other studies reported values of between 5 and 14% (Chow et al. 2000; Lamura et al. 2006; Toseland et al. 1999). As regards the perceived need for this service, our results (Gräßel et al. 2010c) are three times higher than those reported by Toseland (1999) at 9% and about twice as high as those by Colantonio (2001) at 18%.

Other studies report the awareness level for *home help* as between 27% and 55% (Roelands et al. 2008; Toseland et al. 1999). Some of these values are higher and some lower than in our study (Graessel et al. 2011). The same is true in the comparison of utilization levels (Graessel et al. 2011). According to international studies, the utilization of home help ranges between 4 and 35% (Brodaty et al. 2005; Chow et al. 2000; dello Buono et al. 1999; Lamura et al. 2006; Toseland et al. 1999). Regarding the need for the service, the results of Brodaty et al. (2005) were similar (23%) to those in our study (Graessel et al. 2011). Toseland (1999) reports a much lower value at 9%.

Our study (Donath et al. 2009b) supports the assumption that the utilization level of *caregiver skill training* is generally low (between 1% and 24%). The utilization rate is particularly low in Germany and Europe (2% or 10%) (Lamura et al. 2006; Toseland et al. 1999). Awareness rates are slightly higher in other studies. Toseland et al. (1999) report 58% for "educational programs" and 49% for "home modification assistance."

Awareness of *voluntary help* ranges between 53% and 57% in other studies (Toseland et al. 1999; van Exel et al. 2006), and these values are comparable with those found in our study (Gräßel et al. 2010a). However, the level of awareness was much lower (19%) in Belgium (Cooke et al. 2001). According to international studies, the utilization level of voluntary help ranges from 1 to 50% (Chan 2007; Kosloski and Montgomery 1993; Lamura et al. 2006; Toseland et al. 1999;

van Exel et al. 2006). For Germany and Europe, reported utilization rates are between 1 and 2%, which is lower than in our study (Gräßel et al. 2010a).

In summary, the utilization of many of the care and support services for family caregivers is comparatively low. Even awareness of some services is relatively low in international comparison. Low awareness is a fundamental cause of relatively low utilization levels since only known services can be used. However, Brodaty et al. (2005) report low utilization of services by family caregivers even when these services are well known and even when the services are free of charge (Kosloski and Montgomery 1993). That means that other significant determinants of utilization must exist. In our study, caregivers' assessment of the need for the respective service (as in "I personally need it") is a significant predictor of utilization for all support and care services.

As an apparently contradictory result, the study by Toseland et al. (2002) showed that this perceived "need" is not a significant predictor of utilization for the entire range of utilization of health and human services (Toseland et al. 2002). However, it must be borne in mind that this study did not differentiate between individual services but investigated collective categories of services. In fact, awareness-dependent utilization is significantly moderated by perceived need if analyzing the utilization rates of individual services—as we did in our study. The findings by Monahan et al. (1992) and Burks et al. (1991) agree with the results of the regression analyses presented here. In both studies, family caregivers' assessment of their personal need for the services (in this case support groups for dementia caregivers) was a significant predictor of utilization by these caregivers of dementia patients. In addition, the results of the regression analyses presented here agree with the findings by Kosloski and Montgomery (1993) and Montoro-Rodriguez et al. (2003), who also identified perceived need (i.e., personal need for) a service as a significant predictor of utilization.

We can therefore draw the following practical conclusions: to increase the utilization of care and support services, family caregivers should not only be made aware of the service or the available services, but also the advantages of using these services should be pointed out to them. In addition, every family caregiver should be informed about the location and accessibility of the nearest support services that are not provided at the patient's home.

Utilization of Non-Pharmacological Therapie (NPTs) by Stage of Dementia; Utilization of Health Insurance and Long-Term Care Insurance Benefits by Stage of Dementia

The dementia care initiative in primary practice (IDA) study was conducted as a health services study to investigate the care situation of community-dwelling dementia patients and their family caregivers. The research question was how training of general practitioners in guideline-compliant diagnostics and treatment and the recommendation of support services (support groups for dementia caregivers,

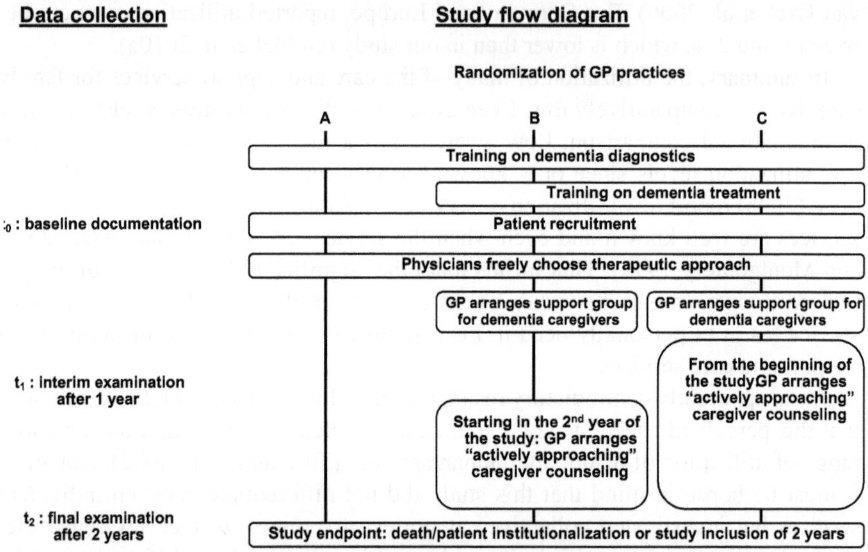

Fig. 11.1 IDA study design (with permission from Medizinisch Wissenschaftliche Verlagsgesellschaft)

actively approaching caregiver counseling) affect the progression of disease, the burden on family caregivers, and their quality of life. In particular, we aimed to determine whether the described interventions can delay institutionalization and to assess the health economic effects of the study interventions. In addition, the IDA study data were used to create a comprehensive estimate of the cost of care for community-dwelling dementia patients.

Methods

IDA is a unique model project in Germany that aims to improve the quality of care of dementia patients and to relieve and support their family caregivers. The study was conducted in the region of Middle Franconia. All members of AOK Bavaria aged 65 or above were eligible to participate if they had a Mini Mental State Examination (MMSE) score of 10 through 24 and received a family member's help in activities of daily living (Holle et al. 2009). Patients with severe dementia were excluded from the study. Figure 11.1 depicts the IDA study design. The study protocol has been previously published (Holle et al. 2009). Using a general practitioner-based health services structure with pharmacological and non-pharmacological interventions, the study offered a model with additional support for family caregivers and patients. Thanks to the active participation of 129 general practitioners, 390 patients with their family caregivers participated in the three-arm, cluster-randomized comparative study. Following initial training (in groups, from June 2005 through September 2006), the general practitioners of Group A provided evidence-based "usual care" in the 2-year observation period (from July 2005 to December 2008); general practitioners of Groups B and C additionally recommended participation in professional-led support groups for dementia caregivers. In Group C, physicians could additionally offer actively approaching caregiver counseling by a trained nurse (IDA counselor) starting in the first year. In Group B, this service was available starting in the second year of the study. For this purpose, the project hired four counselors who kept in regular contact with the primary caregivers and visited the patients and family caregivers in their home environment. The goal was to offer advice and to support the family caregivers in their daily (care-related) tasks on the basis of case and care management.

The study primarily aimed to determine whether actively approaching caregiver counseling can delay permanent institutionalization. So far, the IDA study has been unable to demonstrate statistically significant differences in effect between usual medical care and care plus counseling and support services as regards institutionalization (Menn et al. 2012). The key results of the study and a detailed description and process evaluation of the intervention have been published (Donath et al. 2010; Grossfeld-Schmitz et al. 2010).

Using a dichotomous scaled item (yes/no), respondents were asked at the start of the study (T0) whether the patient receives non-pharmacological treatment. If yes, the survey asked about the type of therapy. In addition to the patient description, the general practitioner recorded the MMST, DemTect (another dementia screening method), mental and behavioral disorders, ICD10 comorbidities, type of dementia, and the patient's age and sex. The mean patient age was 80.3 (SD=6.8), and 68% of the patients were women. The mean MMST score was 19 (SD=3.8). Among the patients, 65% suffered from mild dementia (MMST score of 18–24), and 35% from moderate dementia (MMST score of 10–17). The mean DemTect score was 5.9 (SD=3.6) (values ≤ 8 are classified as suspected dementia). The diagnosis was Alzheimer disease in 37% of the cases, vascular dementia in 27%, and mixed type in 5%. In 30% of patients, "unspecified dementia" was reported. In total, 69% of patients exhibited mental or behavioral disorders. Some 95% of patients suffered from additional diseases (ICD diagnoses). The most common comorbidity was hypertension (56%), followed by diabetes mellitus (40%), and ischemic heart disease (23%). The average age of the patients' family caregivers was 59.4 years (SD=13.4), three-fourths were women, and one-third were patients' spouses. Two-thirds of family caregivers (65%) held a degree from a lower secondary school, and about one-third were employed.

The IDA study further aimed to document the service utilization of study participants in the various service sectors as well as the associated costs.

The latter analyses were based on health insurance data of the study participants, which were available for the entire intervention period. Since the IDA study focused on the living conditions of community-dwelling dementia patients, it only took into account services that were provided before the endpoint (death or institutionalization). Seven subjects withdrew their consent and were excluded from the analyses, so that the data from 383 dementia patients were analyzed.

Table 11.3 General practitioners' prescriptions of non-pharmacological therapies to community-dwelling patients with mild to moderate dementia ($n=385$)

Type of non-pharmacological therapy	Patients with mild dementia[a] ($n=251$) n (n%)	Patients with moderate dementia[b] ($n=134$) n (n%)	P^c (two-tailed)	Total sample n (n%)
Physical therapy	13 (5.2)	16 (11.9)	0.024	29 (7.5)
Occupational therapy	6 (2.4)	3 (2.2)	1.000	9 (2.3)
Memory training	7 (2.8)	1 (0.7)	0.347	8 (2.1)
Other NPT	15[d] (6.0)	3[e] (2.2)	0.204	18 (4.7)

[a] Mini Mental State Examination (MMSE) score of 18–24

[b] Mini Mental State Examination (MMSE) score of 10–17

[c] Fisher's exact test

[d] 5x therapeutic exercise; 3x integration into daily life; 3x mobilization; 2x memory training; 1x massage; 1x compression bandages

[e] 1x social facilitation; 1x speech therapy; 1x diabetes mellitus diet

Results

Predictors of NPT Utilization

Community-dwelling dementia patients receive few NPT (see Table 11.3). Our data were collected before the start of the IDA project through a survey of the general practitioners. Occupational therapy and memory training, relatively specific treatments of dementia symptoms, are only prescribed in 2 % of cases. In contrast, physical therapy, which is not dementia-specific, is the most common non-pharmacological treatment for 8 % of cases, and it is prescribed significantly more frequently for patients with moderate dementia than for those with mild dementia. According to the Andersen model (2001), the diagnosis of mild or moderate dementia is among the 'need category' predictors (evaluated need, factors of objective need) of NPT utilization.

Annual Utilization of Services by Stage of Dementia

To calculate an "IDA year," the observed data were modified as follows:

First, the data were adjusted on an annual basis. For this purpose, the observed data were divided by the time spent in the home environment. For instance, the cumulative data of a study participant who still lived at home after 2 years were divided by 2, while the data of a patient who moved to a nursing home after 6 months were divided by 0.5.

Then, patients were weighted by the percentage of time spent living at home. For instance, data of a study participant who lived at home for the entire 2 years entered into all analyses with a weight of one, while those of a patient who moved to a nursing home after 6 months were weighted 0.25.

The data were then adjusted for age and sex.

Table 11.4 Annual utilization by community-dwelling patients—adjusted for age and sex ($n=383$)

Service sector	Mean utilization volume	Number of service users	Percentage (%)
General practitioner contacts	34.4	382	99.7
Specialist contacts	10.1	343	91.1
Pharmaceutical prescriptions	36.2	380	99.2
Hospital stays	1.2	262	68.4
Hospital length of stay	12.8		
Prescriptions of NPT	2.1	140	36.6
Prescriptions of technical aids	3.0	288	75.2
Number of days entitled to SHI-financed professional home care	67.2	142	37.1
Inpatient rehabilitation stays	0.1	40	10.4
Rehabilitation length of stay	1.4		

NPT non-pharmacological therapies, *SHI* statutory health insurance

Table 11.4 presents the utilization volume and user groups within an "IDA year." These data have not yet been published in such detailed analysis. Only the total costs to the insurance have been previously published (Schwarzkopf et al. 2011).

Clearly, nearly all study participants utilized outpatient medical care and pharmaceutical prescriptions, while rehabilitation services were less relevant.

On the basis of the assumption that progressing dementia is associated with increasing service utilization (Quentin et al. 2009), Table 11.5 lists utilization in all sectors separately for patients with moderate dementia (MMSE score of 10–17; $n=135$) versus mild dementia (MMSE score of 18–24; $n=248$).

Study participants with moderate dementia tended to utilize more statutory health insurance (SHI) benefits than those with mild dementia. Exceptions are inpatient treatment and rehabilitation, which were utilized more frequently by participants with mild dementia. However, none of the observed sectors exhibited a significant difference in utilization frequency.

In the two subgroups, the percentage of service users was generally comparable for the individual service sectors. A statistically significant difference ($p=0.02$) was only found for (SHI-financed) professional home care, which was prescribed significantly more frequently to patients with moderate dementia than to those with mild dementia.

Note that the insurance data only reveal the number of days of professional home care to which the patient was entitled. They do not reveal the scope of services provided by the care staff within this timeframe (time per day, frequency of visits, types of services, etc.). Therefore, the utilization volume of the professional home care services does not allow clear conclusions to be drawn regarding differences in nursing care needs.

Table 11.5 Annual service utilization by community-dwelling patients by stage of dementia (adjusted for age and sex)

	Mild dementia (n=248)			Moderate dementia (n=135)		
Service sector	Volume	Users		Volume	Users	
General practitioner contacts	33.7	247	99.6%	35.7	135	100%
Specialist contacts	10.5	233	94.0%	9.2	116	85.9%
Pharmaceutical prescriptions	34.5	247	100%	39.7	133	98.5%
Hospital stays	1.2	167	67.3%	1.2	95	70.4%
Hospital length of stay	13.6			11.5		
Prescriptions of NPT	2.0	96	38.7%	2.5	44	32.6%
Prescriptions of technical aids	2.9	184	74.2%	3.4	104	77.0%
Number of days entitled to professional home care	57.9	81	32.7%*	85.7	61	45.2%*
Inpatient rehabilitation stays	0.1	28	11.3%	0.1	12	8.9%
Rehabilitation length of stay	1.5			1.2		

* p-values significant on 5 % level in χ^2 test

Morbidity Spectrum and Types of Utilized Services

It is generally assumed that dementia patients suffer from multiple other chronic diseases. These comorbidities are typically not caused by dementia but by a general age-related deterioration in health (Thorpe et al. 1994; Zekry et al. 2008). However, comorbidities often affect dementia patients more severely than patients without dementia since the former have greater difficulty communicating their condition to the outside world and exhibit limited treatment compliance (Chassagne et al. 2008).

In our study population, 226 people (59 %) suffered from hypertension. Other important comorbidities were hypercholesterolemia with 138 patients (36 %), heart failure with 136 patients (36 %), and type II diabetes with 130 patients (34 %). The distribution of these diseases was similar in patients with mild versus moderate dementia. The identified comorbidities supported the hypothesis that the range of illnesses does not significantly differ between dementia patients and people without dementia.

In light of this background, the studies focused on identifying dementia-specific factors affecting the types of utilized services. Prescriptions associated with the general aging process were deemed less relevant.

Within the study period, 167 participants with mild dementia and 95 participants with moderate dementia received inpatient treatment. When analyzing the three most common discharge diagnoses—relative to the total population of 383 dementia patients—18 mild dementia patients (7 %) were *hospitalized* at least once for cardiac insufficiency, 13 (5 %) for somatoform disorders, and 12 (5 %) for stroke. Among patients with moderate dementia, 18 people (13 %) were hospitalized for heart failure, 10 patients (7 %) for femoral neck fractures, and 8 (6 %) for pneumonia.

Pneumonia was significantly more common in patients with moderate dementia (p=0.05). In addition, this group exhibited about twice as many diagnoses of femoral neck fracture as the mild dementia group. Although the difference was not significant (p=0.10), this observation may indicate that progressive dementia can be associated with reduced mobility and hence an elevated risk of falls.

In terms of *pharmacological treatment*, a relationship can be drawn between the stage of dementia and the type of drug prescription. Among those with mild dementia, 112 patients (45 %) received nonsteroidal anti-inflammatory and anti-rheumatic drugs, 98 patients (40 %) received pure ACE inhibitors, and 96 participants (39 %) were prescribed mild analgesics and antipyretics. Among patients with moderate dementia, antipsychotics were the most commonly prescribed to 64 patients (47 %), followed by mild analgesics and antipyretics to 54 patients (40 %), and loop diuretics to 49 patients (37 %).

This means that significantly ($p < 0.0001$) more patients with moderate dementia than patients with mild dementia were prescribed antipsychotics (70 people, 28 %). The preferred prescription was for butyrophenone derivatives, which are used to treat disorders such as psychoses. This supports the hypothesis that progressive dementia is associated with increased behaviors (such as aggressiveness) on the basis of psychotic symptoms (such as delusions), which in turn are pharmaceutically treated.

However, the percentage of patients receiving anti-dementia drugs was identical in the two groups (mild dementia: $n=77$; 31 %; moderate dementia: $n=42$; 31 %).

In the area of *NPT and technical aids*, no relationship was found between stage of dementia and the types of utilized services. Among *NPT*, physical therapy, massage, and occupational therapy were the most common services. The most frequently prescribed *technical aids* were walkers and incontinence products.

Hence, the range of services chiefly included therapies and products that would be intuitively expected for this age group.

Rehabilitation services were primarily provided following hospitalization for femoral neck fractures. Neurological rehabilitation was another common service in patients with mild dementia. In the course of the study, rehabilitation services were only utilized by about 10 % of participants, so the analysis was not statistically reliable.

Utilization of Long-Term Care Insurance Benefits

At the start of the study, 33 % of patients (81 people) with mild dementia were assigned to a care level; more than half of them to Care Level I. Among the study participants with moderate dementia, 62 % received LTCI benefits. Most of them were in Care Level II.

Among the patients with moderate dementia, 81 people (60 %) were still living at home at the end of the study, compared to 175 mild dementia patients (70 %). The former group included 68 (71 %) recipients of LTCI benefits and the latter group included 69 (43 %).

A total of 141 patients with mild dementia (56 %) and 114 with moderate dementia (84 %) received LTCI benefits at some time during the study. This difference in the percentages of beneficiaries is statistically significant ($p<0.0001$).

Nursing care allowance (239 users) was claimed more frequently than benefits-in-kind (126 users).

Table 11.6 Insurance expenditures per average study year (adjusted by age and sex)

Service sector	Total population (n=383)	Mild dementia (n=248)	Moderate dementia (n=135)
Hospital costs	3,045 €	3,198 €	2,746 €
Physician costs	1,068 €	1,093 €	1,021 €
Pharmaceutical costs	1,584 €	1,487 €	1,758 €
Costs of NPT	246 €	220 €	301 €
Costs of technical aids	303 €	268 €	369 €
Costs of SHI-financed professional home care	653 €	509 €	940 €
Costs of rehabilitation treatment	209 €	233 €	162 €
Costs covered by health insurance	7,194 €	7,184 €	7,215 €
Costs covered by LTCI	2,491 €	2,017 €*	4,759 €*
Total costs**	10,169 €	9,216 €	12,033 €

NPT non-pharmacological therapies, *SHI* statutory health insurance, *LTCI* long-term health insurance

* p-values significant at the 5 % level in the generalized linear two-part model

** Costs from the model estimate do not correspond to the sum of the mean costs in the individual sectors

In the group with moderate dementia, 53 people received only nursing care allowance (47 %), 4 people only benefits-in-kind (4 %), and 39 people only combined benefits (34 %). The remaining 18 patients switched between nursing care allowance and combined benefits in the course of the study.

Among the participants with mild dementia, 64 received only nursing care allowance (45 %), 4 only benefits-in-kind (3 %), and 42 only combined benefits (30 %). Among the remaining 31 patients, 29 switched between nursing care allowance and combined benefit, and one person each switched between nursing care allowance and benefits-in-kind and between benefit-in-kind and combined benefits.

Hence, the percentage of LTCI beneficiaries with combined benefit was significantly higher in the group with moderate dementia than in those with mild dementia (p=0.01). The differences regarding the nursing care allowance were just below the significance level (p=0.06).

Costs of Utilization

The same method was used to adjust cost data as for benefit utilization data. Assuming that the actual expenses incurred by the insurance are of primary interest, we did not discount or inflation-adjust the costs to a common reference year.

The health insurances' service expenditures largely paralleled the utilization data. In areas where patients with moderate dementia exhibited a higher utilization volume, their costs were correspondingly higher.

For the LTCI, the differences in expenditures were strongly correlated with the stage of disease: the expenditures for nursing care services were almost 2.5 times higher for patients with moderate dementia than for those with mild dementia ($p \leq 0.0001$). In all other areas, the differences in cost were not significant (see Table 11.6).

Table 11.7 Predictors of the utilization of insurance benefits by stage of dementia

Variable	Mild dementia (n=248) n (n %) (evaluated need)	Moderate dementia (n=135) n (n %) (evaluated need)	p
Number of days entitled to SHI-financed professional home care	81 (32.7%) volume 57.9	61 (45.2%) volume 85.7	0.02
Antipsychotics (administration)	70 (28.2%)	64 (47.4%)	<0.0001
Utilization of LTCI benefits	140 (56.4%)	113 (83.7%)	<0.001
Costs of LTCI benefits	2,017 €	4,759 €	<0.001

SHI statutory health insurance, *LTCI* long-term care insurance

LTCI benefits were the main cost factor in the care of patients with moderate dementia; they equaled to about 4,750 € or approximately 40% of total costs. In patients with mild dementia, costs of hospital care exceeded LTCI benefits, which were in second place but "only" equaled about 22% of total costs.

Summary and Discussion of the Utilization of Health Insurance and Long-Term Care Insurance Benefits

According to the Andersen model (2001), the diagnosis of mild versus moderate dementia is a need-category predictor of the utilization of health insurance and LTCI benefits (evaluated need, objective need).

In our study population, the reasons for utilizing benefits were largely comparable between the two groups. Particularly in terms of NPT and technical aids, prescriptions tended to be caused by growing age-related physical limitations rather than by dementia itself. In contrast, a direct relationship seems to exist between pharmaceutical prescriptions and the stage of dementia. While the percentage of patients with anti-dementia drug prescriptions was the same in mild and moderate dementia, patients with moderate dementia received anti-psychotic drugs much more frequently (see Table 11.7).

In the inpatient sector, the significant accumulation of pneumonia diagnoses in patients with moderate dementia was difficult to interpret in the absence of information about their general condition. Although not statistically significant, the relative accumulation of femoral neck fractures in this group was interpreted as an indication of deteriorating dementia symptoms.

The simple model of more severe dementia symptoms resulting in higher utilization frequency and a higher percentage of users was still inadequate to explain the utilization behavior of patients in all service sectors: significant differences in LTCI benefits (utilization and costs) and SHI benefits (prescription of domiciliary care) were all to the disadvantage of patients with moderate dementia, and there was a general trend toward higher costs and utilization volumes. However, patients with mild dementia had more specialist visits and longer hospital and rehabilitation stays—although these results were not statistically significant.

In terms of expenses, the slightly higher costs for patients with mild dementia were attributed to more frequent specialist visits since reimbursement rates are higher for specialists than for general practitioners. In the hospital sector, the higher expenditures for patients with mild dementia were associated with more treatment days but not with more treatment episodes (i.e., more admissions). Presumably, longer treatment duration and higher costs are caused by long-term semi-inpatient and full inpatient treatments at gerontopsychiatric facilities that were reimbursed outside of the DRG system. Services outside of the DRG system play only a minor role in patients with moderate dementia.

Insurance data revealed that in general, community-dwelling dementia patients utilize increasing levels of health-care services financed by the social insurance system over time. This development is caused by the combined effect of age-related morbidity and the progression of dementia.

This results in increasing expenditures within the social insurance system, but progressing dementia was a clear cost-driver only for the LTCI. For the SHI, in contrast, increased expenditures in some sectors were nearly balanced out by reduced expenditures in others. However, additional studies with larger samples are required to determine whether these results can be generalized to all community-dwelling dementia patients or whether they were caused by specific characteristics of the IDA study population.

Summary of Results of the Predictor Analyses in View of the Andersen Model

One factor in the need category is a particularly significant predictor of utilization of the services examined in our study: all services are used more frequently if the caregivers subjectively believe that they need them. Service accessibility, one of the enabling factors, predicts the utilization of three services. Family caregivers who do not know about accessibility exhibit significantly (or tendentially) less frequent utilization of the nearest short-term institutional care (or adult day care) and caregiver counseling. Predisposing factors that predicted utilization of the individual services included patient age and the age and educational level of the family caregiver. Specifically, a lower educational level is associated with less frequent utilization of support groups for dementia caregivers. The age of the family caregiver predicts the utilization of two services: professional home care and adult day care are used more frequently by older family caregivers. This relationship is also found for patient age. Higher patient age is associated with more frequent utilization of professional home care, home help, and caregiver skill training. Overall, the utilization of all services is more clearly and more consistently predicted by the need factor (need for the service) than by predisposing factors (age of family caregiver, educational level of family caregiver, and patient age).

In one of our described studies, a factor in the evaluated need category (diagnosis of mild versus moderate dementia) is a significant predictor of the utilization of certain types of non-pharmacological treatments.

References

Aguero-Torres H, von Strauss E, Viitanen M, Winblad B, Fratiglioni L (2001) Institutionalization in the elderly: the role of chronic diseases and dementia. Cross-sectional and longitudinal data from a population-based study. J Clin Epidemiol 54:795–801

Andersen RM, Davidson PL (2001) Improving access to care in America: individual and contextual indicators. In: Andersen RM, Rice TH, Kominski GF (eds) Changing the U.S. health care system: key issues in health services, policy, and management. John Wiley & Sons Inc., San Francisco, pp 3–30

Bower F, McCullough C, Pille B (2002) Synthesis of research findings regarding Alzheimer´s disease: part IV, education of family and staff caregivers. Online Knowl Synth Nurs 9:1–7

Brodaty H, Thomson C, Thompson C, Fine M (2005) Why caregivers of people with dementia and memory loss don't use services. Int J Geriatr Psychiatry 20:537–546

Burks V, Lund D, Hill R (1991) Factors associated with attendance at caregiver support group meetings. Act Adapt Aging 15:93–108

Chan J (2007) Carers' perspective on respite for persons with acquired brain injury. Int J Rehabil Res 30:137–146

Chassagne P, Idrissi-Kassimy F, Rigal O (2008) Comorbidite et syndromes dementiels [Comorbidity and dementia]. Psychol Neuropsychiatr Vieil 6:43–48.

Chow T, Ross L, Fox P, Cummings J, Lin K-M (2000) Utilization of Alzheimer's disease community resources by Asian-Americans in California. Int J Geriatr Psychiatry 15:838–847

Colantonio A, Kositsky A, Cohen C, Vernich L (2001) What support do caregivers of elderly want? Results from the Canadian Study of Health and Aging. Can J Public Health 92:376–379

Cooke D, McNally L, Mulligan K, Harrison M, Newman S (2001) Psychosocial interventions for caregivers of people with dementia: a systematic review. Aging Ment Health 5:120–135

dello Buono M, Busato R, Mazzetto M, Paccagnella B, Aleotti F, Zanetti O, Bianchetti A, Trabucchi M, de Leo D (1999) Community care for patients with Alzheimer's disease and non-demented elderly people: use and satisfaction with services and unmet needs in family caregivers. Int J Geriatr Psychiatry 14:915–924

Donath C, Bleich S, Gräßel E (2009a) Gerontopsychiatrische Tageskliniken—Prädiktoren der Inanspruchnahme und Qualitätserwartungen aus Sicht pflegender Angehöriger von Demenzpatienten. Psychiatr Prax 36:175–181

Donath C, Luttenberger K, Gräßel E (2009b) Pflegekurs—Prädiktoren der Inanspruchnahme und Qualitätserwartungen aus Sicht pflegender Angehöriger eines Demenzpatienten . Gesundheitswesen 71:291–292

Donath C, Winkler A, Gräßel E (2009c) Short-term residential care for dementia patients:predictors for utilization and expected quality from a family caregiver's point of view. Int Psychogeriatr 21:703–710

Donath C, Gräßel E, Großfeld-Schmitz M, Lauterberg J, Wunder S, Marx P, Ruckdäschel S, Mehlig H, Holle R (2010) Effects of general practitioner training and family support services on the care of home-dwelling dementia patients—results of a controlled cluster-randomized study. BMC Health Serv Res 10:314

Donath C, Winkler A, Graessel E, Luttenberger K (2011) Day care for dementia patients from a family caregiver's point of view: a questionnaire study on expected quality and predictors of utilisation—Part II. BMC Health Serv Res 11:76

Gallagher-Thompson D, Coon D (2007) Evidence-based psychological treatments for distress in family caregivers of older adults. Psychol Aging 22:37–51

Goldsmith M (1996) Hearing the voice of people with dementia. Opportunities and obstacles. Jessica Kingsley, London

Graessel E, Luttenberger K, Bleich S, Adabbo R, Donath C (2011) Home nursing and home help for dementia patients: predictors for utilization and expected quality from a family caregiver's point of view. Arch Gerontol Geriatr 52:233–238

Gräßel E (1997) Temporary institutional respite in dementia cases: who utilizes this form of respite care and what effect does it have? Int Psychogeriatr 9:437–448

Gräßel E (1998) Häusliche Pflege dementiell und nicht dementiell Erkrankter Teil I: Inanspruchnahme professioneller Pflegehilfe []. Z Gerontol Geriatr 31:52–56

Gräßel E, Schirmer B (2006) Freiwillige Helferinnen und Helfer zur Entlastung der Angehörigen demenzkranker Menschen []. Z Gerontol Geriatr 39:217–226

Gräßel E, Römer H, Donath C (2009) Betreuungsgruppen—Prädiktoren der Inanspruchnahme und Qualitätserwartungen aus Sicht pflegender Angehöriger eines Demenzkranken. Z Gerontol Geriatr 42:394–401

Gräßel E, Luttenberger K, Römer H, Donath C (2010a) Ehrenamtlicher Betreuungsdienst bei Demenz—Prädiktoren der Inanspruchnahme und Qualitätserwartungen aus Sicht pflegender Angehöriger. Fortschr Neurol Psychiatr 78:536–541

Gräßel E, Luttenberger K, Trilling A, Donath C (2010b). Counselling for dementia caregivers—predictors for utilization and expected quality from a family caregiver's point of view. Eur J Ageing 7:111–119

Gräßel E, Trilling A, Donath C, Luttenberger K (2010c) Support groups for dementia caregivers – Predictors for utilisation and expected quality from a family caregiver´s point of view: a questionnaire survey PART I*. BMC Health Serv Res 10:219

Grossfeld-Schmitz M, Donath C, Holle R, Lauterberg J, Ruckdäschel S, Mehlig H, Marx P, Wunder S, Gräßel E (2010) Counsellors contact dementia caregivers – predictors of utilisation in a longitudinal study. BMC Geriatr 10

Holle R, Gräßel E, Ruckdaschel S, Wunder S, Mehlig H, Marx P, Pirk O, Butzlaff M, Kunz S, Lauterberg J (2009) Dementia care initiative in primary practice – study protocol of a cluster randomized trial on dementia management in a general practice setting. BMC Health Serv Res 9:91

Jolley D, Benbow S, Grizzell M (2006) Memory clinics. Postgraduate Medical Journal 82:199–206

Jost E, Voigt-Radloff S, Hüll M, Dykierek P, Schmidtke K (2006) Fördergruppe für Demenzpatienten und Beratungsgruppe für Angehörige. Zeitschrift für Gerontopsychologie & -psychiatrie 19:139–150

Kosloski K, Montgomery R (1993) Perceptions of respite services as predictors of utilization. Res Aging 15:399–413

Krauß A (2006) Ehrenamtliche Hilfen zur Unterstützung pflegender Angehöriger demenziell erkrankter Menschen Engagementförderung und –qualifizierung.Fachhochschule Erfurt, Erfurt

Lamura G, Mnich E, Wojszel B, Nolan M, Krevers B, Mestheneos L, Döhner H (2006) Erfahrungen von pflegenden Angehörigen älterer Menschen in Europa bei der Inanspruchnahme von Unterstützungsleistungen: Ausgewählte Ergebnisse des Projektes EUROFAMCARE. Z Gerontol Geriatr 39:429–442

Luppa M, Luck T, Braehler E, Koenig HH, Riedel-Heller SG (2008). Prediction of institutionalisation in dementia. A systematic review. Dement Geriatr Cogn Disord 26:65–78

Menn P, Holle R, Kunz S, Donath C, Lauterberg J, Leidl R, Marx P, Ruckdäschel S, Vollmar HC, Wunder S et al (2012) Dementia care in the general practice setting: a cluster randomized trial on the effectiveness and cost Impact of three management strategies. Value in Health 15:851–859

Monahan D, Greene V, Coleman P (1992) Caregiver support groups: factors affecting use of service. Soc Work 37:254–260

Montoro-Rodriguez J, Kosloski K, Montgomery R (2003) Evaluating a practice-oriented service model to increase the use of respite services among minorities and rural caregivers. Gerontologist 43:916–924

Philip I, Ghosh U (1992) Community care services: views of patients attending a geriatric day hospital. Health Bull 50:296–301

Quentin W, Riedel-Heller SG, Luppa M, Rudolph A, Konig HH (2009) Cost-of-illness studies of dementia: a systematic review focusing on stage dependency of costs. Acta Psychiatr Scand 121:243–59

Roelands M, Van Oost P, Depoorter A (2008) Service use in family caregivers of persons with dementia in Belgium: psychological and social factors. Health Soc Care Community 16:42–53

Schunk M, Steinwachs K (2003) Strukturen und Veränderungen im multimodalen Behandlungskonzept der Gerontopsychiatrischen Tagesklinik des Klinikums am Europakanal Erlangen. Psychiatr Prax 30:203–206

Schwarzkopf L, Menn P, Kunz S, Holle R, Lauterberg J, Marx P, Mehlig H, Wunder S, Leidl R, Donath C et al (2011) Costs of care for dementia patients in community setting: an analyses for mild and moderate disease stage. Value in Health 14:827–835

Selwood A, Johnston K, Katona C, Lyketsos C, Livingston G (2007). Systematic review of the effect of psychological interventions on family caregivers of people with dementia. J Affect Disord 101:75–89

Sozialgesetzbuch (SGB XI)— Soziale Pflegeversicherung, zuletzt geändert durch Art. 2c des Gesetzes vom 21.07.2012 [] (BGBl. I S. 1601)

Sörensen S, Duberstein P, Gill D, Pinquart M (2006). Dementia care: mental health effects, intervention strategies, and clinical implications. Lancet Neurol 5:961–973

Thorpe J, Widman LP, Wallin A, Beiswanger J, Blumenthal HT (1994) Comorbidity of other chronic age-dependent diseases in dementia. Aging (Milano) 6:159–66

Toseland R, McCallion P, Gerber T, Dawson C, Gieryic S, Guilamo-Ramos V. (1999) Use of health and human services by community-residing people with dementia. Soc Work 44:535–548

Toseland R, McCallion P, Gerber T, Banks S (2002) Predictors of health and human services use by persons with dementia and their family caregivers. Soc Sci Med 55:1255–1266

van Exel J, Morée M, Koopmanschap M, Schreuder Goedheijt T, Brouwer W (2006) Respite care—an explorative study of demand and use in Dutch informal caregivers. Health Policy 78:194–208

Woods B, Spector AE, Jones CA, Orrell M, Davies SP (2005) Reminiscence therapy for dementia. Cochrane Database Syst Rev:DC001120

Zekry D, Herrmann FR, Grandjean R, Meynet MP, Michel JP, Gold G, Krause KH (2008) Demented versus non-demented very old inpatients: the same comorbidities but poorer functional and nutritional status. Age Ageing 37:83–89

Zhu C, Sano M (2006) Economic consideration in the management of Alzheimer´s disease. Clin Interv Aging 1:143–154

Chapter 12
Utilization of Primary Care Physicians by Obese Men and Women: Review for Germany and Results from the MONICA/KORA Cohorts S3/F3 and S4/F4

Thomas von Lengerke, Petra Menn, Rolf Holle, Andreas Mielck, Christa Meisinger and Silke B. Wolfenstetter

Introduction

In Germany, the prevalence of obesity is increasing. Data from the Federal Health Reporting (GBE) by the Robert KochInstitute show that in 1998, 18.9% of men and 22.5% of women among those aged 18–79 years were obese, compared to 23.3% and 23.9%, respectively, in 2008–2011 [1]. Obesity, or excess body fat accumulation, is therefore a significant issue in the German and other health care systems, although it remains unclear which classes of obesity do and should cause health-care utilization (a similarassertion holds for preobesity and risk factors for becoming overweight). The issue is particularly relevant given evidencethat the prevalence of severe obesity (i.e., body mass index [BMI]≥35) is rising more strongly than that of moderate obesity. While the latter increased from 13.2% in 1985 to

T. von Lengerke (✉)
Center for Public Health and Health Care, Medical Psychology Unit,
Hannover Medical School, Hannover, Germany
e-mail: lengerke.thomas@mh-hannover.de

P. Menn · R. Holle · A. Mielck · S. B. Wolfenstetter
Helmholtz Zentrum München—German Research Center for Environmental Health (GmbH),
Institute of Health Economics and Health Care Management, Neuherberg, Germany
e-mail: petra.menn@helmholtz-muenchen.de

R. Holle
e-mail: holle@helmholtz-muenchen.de

A. Mielck
e-mail: mielck@helmholtz-muenchen.de

C. Meisinger
Helmholtz Zentrum München—German Research Center for Environmental Health (GmbH),
Institute of Epidemiology II, Neuherberg, Germany
e-mail: christa.meisinger@helmholtz-muenchen.de

S. B. Wolfenstetter
e-mail: silke.wolfenstetter@helmholtz-muenchen.de

C. Janssen et al. (eds.), *Health Care Utilization in Germany*,
DOI 10.1007/978-1-4614-9191-0_12,

16.5 % in 2002 among adults aged 25–64 years, severe obesity more than doubled (from 3 to 6.5 %) [2]. In a recent study on this age group using representative population samples from the Augsburg region (Southern Germany) from 2004 to 2008, 7.2 % of the surveyed population was severely obese [3].[1] According to the hitherto existing German evidence-based obesity guideline, the family doctor plays a key role in the long-term care of overweight/obese patients [4]. The call for primary care physicians (PCPs) to act preventively in regard to obesity stresses the relevance of primary care in this context as well [5]. Against this background, the goals of this chapter are the following:

- Based on population studies, provide a review on the obesity-associated utilization of outpatient PCP care by adults in Germany.[2,3]
- Against this background, analyze the associations between moderate and severe obesity on the one hand and the utilization of outpatient PCP care on the other hand using data of two population surveys in the Augsburg region.
- Finally, systematize the results of these analyses using the behavioral model of health services use by Ronald M. Andersen [7, 8], and discuss possible shortcomings and potential future research on health services utilization associated with adult obesity.

We focused on population studies because of their important advantages over claims data, routine data, care process data, and patient studies when scrutinizing obesity-associated utilization of care (and other determinants of utilization). Population studies facilitate using nonusers as a reference group for users of care as well as normal-weight and nonobese persons as reference groups for obese groups (in claims data, underrepresentation of obesity is highly probable because its reporting in German primary care is generally low [9, 10], at least in nondiabetic patients [11, 12]).

Obesity and Utilization of PCPs: Review for Germany

To gain an overview of the obesity-associated utilization of outpatient care provided by PCPs in Germany using population studies, we conducted the following literature search on December 1, 2012 in PubMed (www.pubmed.gov) for the print publication period of January 1, 1998 to December 31, 2012, and adults as the target group:

---

[1] The GBE does not report separate prevalencesfor moderate and severe obesity.

[2] "Obesity-associated utilization of care" is not limited to instances where people use services explicitly because of their obesity, but more generally excess utilization by obese people compared to nonobese people (excess burden of disease). Accordingly, Hurley et al. have proposed a method to consider "baseline health care costs" (in terms of costs of illness observable in the subpopulation not affected by a condition) in order to determine attributable (and in this sense"specific") costs of the condition [6].

[3] Underweight and associated health disorders are not the topic of this chapter.

("utilization"[ti] OR "utilisation"[ti] OR "use"[ti] OR "access"[ti] OR "health care"[ti]) AND (body weight OR obesity OR overweight OR adiposity OR adipose OR obese) AND (Germany) Filters: English or German, Abstract available, From 1998/01/01 to 2012/12/31, Humans, Adult: 19+ years (10/31/2012 9:11 AM)

To identify health care utilization and obesity as study topics and Germany as the national context, we combined title and/or full-text searches of these and related expressions. The search resulted in the identification of 22 publications. Via a manual search, two papers were added, resulting in an initial list of 24 publications. The first author assessed these publications by screening titles, abstracts, and, if necessary, full texts. Only studies (or parts of studies) that met the following criteria were included:

- Compared obese individuals to at least one nonobese group including normal-weight people, and outcomes include a measure of PCP utilization (basic criterion of relevance).
- Adult study population ($\geq$19 years).
- Primary study.
- Population-based study.

By these criteria, five studies were selected for an obligatory full-text review [3, 13–17], which revealed that all five studies met the above inclusion criteria and thus were included in this review. Their main results are described below. Unless stated otherwise, the normal-weight group served as a reference group in each of the respective studies.

In a 1994 Infratestsurvey, Schneider found that in all examined age groups (14–29, 30–49, and $\geq$50 years), obese participants most frequently reported high PCP utilization, defined as a minimum of eight contacts per annum (15.7 %, 13.2 %, and 34.7 % versus 4.4 %, 7.5 %, and 23.2 % in the preobese group and 3.6 %, 3.7 %, and 23.5 % in the normal-weight group) [13]. In addition, the utilization of weight-reduction programs was strongly correlated with BMI (highest rate of 17 % for obese women aged 30–49 years).

In a study with data from the 1998 German National Health Interview and Examination Survey (the most comprehensive German health survey, not only for obesity) on determinants of outpatient care utilization, Thode et al. presented a model adjusted for numerous other factors and found that obesity was associated with 1.1 times higher PCP consultation [14, 15]. They found no excess utilization for overall physician visits, contacted specialists, or internist visits.

In the Monitoring of Trends and Determinants in Cardiovascular Disease (MONICA) Augsburg Survey 1994/1995, Meisinger et al. found that among women aged 50–74 years, the obese group had a 1.6 times higher probability of consulting a PCP at least four times within a 12-month period [16]. However, this indicator was problematic because it pooled nonusers and low users as well as PCP and internist visits. This study also showed that obese participants had a comparatively high tendency to postpone cancer screenings.

In contrast to the above studies, von Lengerke et al. distinguished between moderate and severe obesity in an analysis of the Cooperative Health Research in the

Region of Augsburg (KORA) Survey S4 1999–2001 in the Augsburg region [17]. They found that the odds for any utilization of PCPs were significantly higher for adults with moderate obesity than for those with normal weight (odds ratio: 1.8), while severe obesity was associated with a higher number of visits when compared to normal weight among users (incident rate ratio: 1.6), and with high utilization in terms of being in the top 5 % of the distribution (odds ratio: 3.6). Utilization of inpatient care as measured by the number of days in hospital was elevated in the severe obesity group only.

Finally, in a longitudinal study using data from the MONICA/KORA cohorts S3/F3 and S4/F4 with a 7- to 10-year follow-up period, Wolfenstetter et al. found that compared to the group of participants that had maintained normal weight from baseline to follow-up, the following groups reported significantly more PCP visits: weight gain from normal weight (+36 %), weight loss from preobesity (+39 %), maintained preobesity (+34 %), weight gain after preobesity (+43 %), maintained moderate obesity (+48 %), weight gain from moderate obesity (+107 %), weight loss from severe obesity (+114 %), and maintained severe obesity (+83 %) [3]. Moreover, these associations of weight development with PCP visits were stronger and more consistent than associations with utilization of internists and other physicians.

In sum, all five studies found significantly higher utilization of PCPs in obese versus nonobese groups in terms of number of visits per annum. While two of the studies stratified the analysis of PCP utilization by age [13, 16], none of them presented their results of PCP use in any systematic fashion stratified for gender. This represents a limitation in this research field because gender is a key predisposing factor for health care use in general [7, 8] and because of sex differences in obesity and energy homeostasis regulation ([18]). For instance, physical exercise has been shown to be less effective for weight loss in women than in men [19], and weight loss tends to produce a greater reduction in serum glucose, insulin, and lipids in men than in women [20]. Since such differences may affect utilization, the following analysis of associations between PCP utilization and preobesity, moderate obesity, and severe obesity (compared to normal weight) will be stratified by sex to provide empirical insights on whether these associations differ between women and men.

Obesity and Utilization of PCPs by Women and Men: Results of the MONICA/KORA Cohorts S3/F3 and S4/F4

This analysis uses data formerly analyzed with a different focus by Wolfenstetter et al. [3]. Thus, information provided in the following sections on study design, population, sampling (Sect. 12.3.1), and measures (Sect. 12.3.2) will be limited to material useful to understanding the present analysis (Sects. 12.3.3 and 12.3.4). For more information, see the above-mentioned publication [3].

Study Design, Population, and Sampling

The MONICA/KORA Surveys S3 (1994/1995) and S4 (1999/2001) are population-based health surveys. Participants in each survey were randomly selected from all registered citizens of German nationality aged 25–74 years with permanent residence in Augsburg or its two surrounding counties. The follow-up studies were conducted for S3 after 10 years (F3) and for S4 after 7 years (F4). Samples of 4,856 participants (S3) and 4,261 participants (S4) took part in the baseline surveys. Of these, 3,006 (F3) and 3,080 (F4) adults also participated in the follow-up studies. For the present analyses, data from both surveys were combined. Since data on PCP utilization were not collected from participants aged 65 years and older in S3, all subjects aged 65 and above at baseline were excluded ($n=833$). Individuals were also excluded if data on BMI at baseline were missing ($n=34$), if no information on school education was available ($n=5$), or if diabetes was present at baseline but not at follow-up ($n=9$). Also, participants with a BMI$\leq$18.5 kg/m^2 at baseline ($n=30$) were excluded due to small numbers. Of the remaining 5,175 participants, data were missing on the end-point variable (PCP utilization) in four. In sum, the two longitudinal surveys provided complete data for 5,171 individuals (2,608 from S3/F3; 2,563 from S4/F4). Written informed consent was obtained from all participants, and the studies were approved by the responsible ethics committee (Bavarian Medical Association, Munich).

Measures

PCP Utilization. PCP utilization was assessed in F3 by the following item: "How often did you visit a primary care physician in the past 12 months?" In F4, participants were asked, "How often did you visit a primary care physician in the past 3 months?" To achieve comparable 1-year time horizons, all F4 utilization data were extrapolated to 12 months.

Obesity. Trained medical staff measured body weight and height anthropometrically as part of the standardized medical examination. Calibration of measuring instruments was ensured through weekly or daily inspections using standard weights. BMI was calculated for each participant as weight in kilograms/(height in meters)^2. In accordance with the World Health Organization (WHO) [21], the following classification was used for the analysis: normal weight: $18.5\leq\text{BMI}<25$, preobesity: $25\leq\text{BMI}<30$, moderate obesity (obesity class 1): $30\leq\text{BMI}<35$, and severe obesity (obesity classes 2–3): BMI$\geq$35. Our analyses used BMI status at the respective baseline survey.

Diabetes. Incident diabetes between baseline and follow-up (i.e., between S3 and F3 or S4 and F4) was assessed by checking if the follow-up self-report variable 'age at diagnosis of diabetes' fell into the time period between the two surveys. Prevalent diabetes was coded if the self-report variables indicated diabetes at both baseline and follow-up.

Sociodemographic and Socioeconomic Factors. We used information on sex, age, and school education from the baseline surveys. Education was assessed by professionally trained medical staff during an extensive, standardized face-to-face interview [22] and was used as an operationalization of socioeconomic status because in Germany, the association with obesity is stronger for education than for income or occupational status [23]. Respondents indicated their highest education level as follows: primary or secondary general school (German "Grundschule" or "Hauptschule"), intermediate secondary ("Realschule"), or grammar/upper secondary school ("Gymnasium").

Statistical Analysis

IBM SPSS Statistics Version 20 was used. Sociodemographic and socioeconomic characteristics as well as the diabetes status of baseline BMI groups were compared using an analysis of variance for continuous variables and a chi-squared test for categorical variables. For PCP visits, a generalized linear regression analysis was conducted to account for their typically skewed distribution (GENLIN, the SPSS procedure fitting generalized linear models and generalized estimating equations). A negative binomial distribution was chosen since data showed signs of overdispersion. The model included the factors sex and BMIgroup at baseline, their interactionand age (at baseline), dummy variables for education (reference: primary or secondary general school) and diabetes status (reference: diabetes neither at baseline nor at follow-up), and a dummy variable indicating whether the subject participated in the S3/F3 or the S4/F4 study as covariates. Wald chi-squared statistics are reported as model effects tests, with *p*-values of 0.05 or less considered to be statistically significant. For the estimated mean number of PCPvisits in the different BMI groups among both women and men, 95 % Wald confidence intervals are reported. By the GENLINalgorithm, these are asymmetric, a quality that has been argued to have advantages over symmetric confidence intervals in cases of asymmetry of the relative likelihood regions relative to the location of the maximum likelihood estimate [24].

Results

Table 12.1 describes the sample both overall and by BMI status in terms of sociodemographics/socioeconomics and diabetes status. In the severely obese subgroup, a majority of 57.3 % were participants of the S4/F4cohort. The rate of severe obesity was 5.5 % in this cohort versus 4.1 % in the S3/F3cohort (not shown). In the nonobese range, almost two-thirds of normal-weight people were women (65.6 %), while an almost reversed pattern was found in the preobese group, of whom about six out of ten were men (60.3 %). Within the obese range, gender was approximately equally distributed in the moderate obesity group, while in the severely obese group-

Table 12.1 Sample description by BMI categories at baseline

		BMI categories[a] at baseline										
		Overall		Normal weight		Pre-obesity		Moderate obesity		Severe obesity		χ^2 (or F)/*p*-value
		N	col %	*N*	col % row %	*N*	col % row %	*N*	col % row %	*N*	col % row %	
		5,171	100%	1,925	37.2	2,256	43.6	742	14.3	248	4.8	
Cohort/ surveys	S3/F3	2,608	50.4	999	51.9	1,145	50.8	358	48.2	106	42.7	9.0/0.029
					38.3		43.9		13.7		4.1	
	S4/F4	2,563	49.6	926	48.1	1,111	49.2	384	51.8	142	57.3	
					36.1		43.3		15.0		5.5	
Sex	Women	2,685	51.9	1,262	65.6	895	39.7	359	48.4	169	68.1	308.9/<0.001
					47.0		33.3		13.4		6.3	
	Men	2,486	48.1	663	34.4	1,361	60.3	383	51.6	79	31.9	
					26.7		54.7		15.4		3.2	
Age (years)	Baseline mean (SD)	45.2 (11.0)		41.1 (10.4)		46.9 (10.8)		49.3 (10.1)		49.0 (10.2)		(166.7)/<0.001
	Follow-up mean (SD)	53.7 (11.0)		49.6 (10.4)		55.4 (10.9)		57.7 (10.1)		57.3 (10.3)		(160.2)/<0.001
Schooleducation	Primary/secondary general	2,763	53.4	757	39.3	1,302	57.7	532	71.7	172	69.4	298.5/<0.001
					27.4		47.1		19.3		6.2	
	Intermediate secondary	1,257	24.3	594	30.9	504	22.3	112	15.1	47	19.0	
					47.3		40.1		8.9		3.7	
	Grammar/upper secondary	1,151	22.3	574	29.8	450	19.9	98	13.2	29	11.7	
					49.9		39.1		8.5		2.5	
Diabetes status	No diabetes	4,844	93.7	1,899	98.6	2,128	94.3	645	86.9	172	69.4	389.1/<0.001
					39.2		43.9		13.3		3.6	
	Incident (follow-up only)	207	4.0	13	0.7	80	3.5	66	8.9	48	19.4	
					6.3		38.6		31.9		23.2	
	Prevalent (at both surveys)	120	2.3	13	0.7	48	2.1	31	4.2	28	11.3	
					10.8		40.0		25.8		23.3	

[a] Normal weight: $18.5 \leq BMI < 25$, preobesity: $25 \leq BMI < 30$, moderate obesity (obesity class 1): $30 \leq BMI < 35$, severe obesity (obesity classes 2–3): $BMI \geq 35$
SD standard deviation

Table 12.2 Tests of model effects in the generalized linear regression analysis

Source of variation	Wald-χ^2	df	Sig.
Constant	99.5	1	$p<0.001$
Sex (factor)	34.0	1	$p<0.001$
BMI group (factor)	58.7	3	$p<0.001$
Age (at follow-up)	40.8	1	$p<0.001$
No diabetes	Ref.		
Incident diabetes	30.7	1	$p<0.001$
Prevalent diabetes	17.5	1	$p<0.001$
Primary/secondary general school education	Ref.		
Intermediate secondary school education	4.8	1	$p=0.029$
Grammar/upper secondary school education	46.8	1	$p<0.001$
Sex (factor) by BMI group (factor) (*interaction term*)	13.4	3	$p=0.004$
Survey (F4 vs. F3)	39.0	1	$p<0.001$

almost seven out of ten people were women (68.1 %). Mean age increased fairly linearly from normal weight to moderate obesity, both at baseline and at follow-up, with the mean age of the severely obese group being on the level of the moderately obese group. The moderate and the severe obesity groups had approximately the same pattern of school education, with nearly 70 % holding a primary or secondary general school degree (71.7 % and 69.4 %, respectively). At the same time, higher schooling was more often found in the preobese and especially the normal-weight group, with around 30 % of participants in the latter group holding intermediate secondary or grammar/upper secondary degrees (30.9 % and 29.8 %, respectively). Finally, the probability of being affected by diabetes monotonically increased with BMI. Namely, diabetes prevalence and incidence were 0.7 % in normal-weight individuals, but this rate increased to 11.3 % prevalent diabetes and 19.4 % incident diabetes among the severely obese. The latter rates were also notably higher than those in the moderate obesity group, which remained in the single-digit range with a 4.2 % prevalence and 8.9 % incidence of diabetes.

The generalized linear regression analysis (Table 12.2) shows that women reported one more PCP visit on average (per year) than men (4.2 vs. 3.2, Wald-χ^2 of main effect=34.0, $p<0.001$). Also, there was a strong gradient regarding the main effect of the BMIfactor in that number of PCP visits increased with BMI (normal weight: 2.8, pre-obesity: 3.4, moderate obesity: 3.8, and severe obesity: 4.7; Wald-χ^2=58.7, $p<0.001$). In terms of the hypothesis of differential effects of body-weight status on PCP utilization in women versus men, Fig. 12.1 presents the key result of the analysis, i.e., the number of PCP visits in the year before follow-up by body mass category at baseline and by sex(Wald-χ^2 of interaction term =13.4, $p=0.004$). Among women, all overweight groups differ from the normal-weight group in that they reported significantly more PCP visits (preobesity: 4.3, moderate obesity: 4.5, and severe obesity: 5.0, vs. 3.1 in the normal-weight group). In

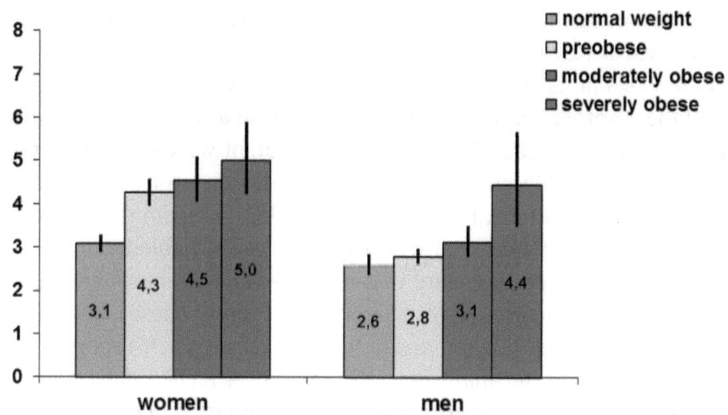

Fig. 12.1 Number of PCP visits in the year before follow-up by body mass category at baseline and sex (means with 95 % confidence intervals, adjusted for age at baseline and survey cohort, school education, and diabetes status [dummy variables])

contrast, the group standing out from the rest among men are those with severe obesity, who reported 4.4 PCP visits, significantly more than their normal-weight (2.6 visits) and preobese counterparts (2.8 visits), and marginally more than the moderately obese group in statistical terms (3.1 visits). The means of the preobese and the moderately obese group were not significantly higher than the mean of the normal-weight group.

Regarding the covariates, PCP visits were positively associated with age (Wald-$\chi^2=40.8$, $p<0.001$; no change in results when entering age at baseline versus follow-up), both incident and prevalent diabetes (Wald-$\chi^2=30.7$ and 17.5, respectively, $p<0.001$), primary or secondary general school education (Wald-$\chi^2=4.8$, $p=0.029$ for intermediate secondary and 46.8, $p<0.001$, for grammar/upper secondarydegree as one's highest grade), and belonging to the S4/F4 cohort (Wald-$\chi^2=39.0$, $p<0.001$).

Discussion

The present analyses produced the following overall results: First, the review of population-based studies on obesity-associated PCP utilizationfound significantly higher use in obese than in nonobese groups as measured by the number of visits per annum. Second, an analysis of data from the MONICA/KORA cohorts S3/F3 and S4/F4 showed that women had almost one-third (31.3 %) more PCP visits than men, and PCP visits linearly increased with the BMI group, with the highest mean number of PCP visits in severely obese individuals (4.7 vs. 2.8 in normal weight). Third, among women, all overweight groups had more PCP visits than the normal-weight group; among men, those with severe obesity reported higher utilization than the other three BMIgroups.

Before interpreting these findings and drawing conclusions, strengths and limitations of the present research have to be considered. While the strength of the systematic review lies in its specificity (PCP utilizationby obesity status in Germany), strengths of the empirical part are that data come from a survey using rigorous quality assurance procedures [22], body weight and height were measured (rather than self-reported), and sample size allowed for stratification for both BMIstatus and gender. Regarding limitations, first the review makes no claim to be meta-analytic. Second, including only population-based studies is justifiable as noted at the end of the introductory section to ensure that normal-weight persons can be used as a reference group for obese groups (especially the severely obese), but this excluded claims data and patient studies and meant that we relied on self-reported utilization. The latter also applies to the analyses of the MONICA/KORA data.

Third, our analyses modeled utilization in the year before the follow-up surveys, i.e., a single time period, by BMIstatus at baseline. This implies that changes in utilization from baseline to follow-up could not be modeled and tested for their association with body-weight status. Thus, we could not control for utilization habits, which may be only partially related to need factors—and may be especially relevant to PCP utilization. However, we did control for proxy variables for such habits (sex, age, and education), and our results suggested that the effects of BMI status are specific and alternative explanations (e.g., aging leading to both weight gain and higher use) are unlikely.

Fourth, utilization may be underestimated since baseline nonresponse is, and follow-up surveynonresponse may be, associated with higher burdens of morbidity. For instance, a nonresponse analysis comparing participants in the S4 survey with 49 % of its nonresponders showed that nonresponders more often had a lower level of education (German Hauptschule, i.e.,general secondary school: 65 % vs. 54 %) and fair or poor self-rated health (28 % vs. 21 %) were more often unmarried (34 % vs. 29 %) and smokers (29 % vs. 26 %), and more frequently reported physician visits in the last 4 weeks (46 % vs. 38 %), myocardial infarction (6 % vs. 3 %), and diabetes (7 % vs. 4 %) [25]. It is possible that similar patterns may be found for the 3,031 baseline participants who dropped out of the follow-up surveys in the present analysis. For example, among baseline participants 64 years of age or younger (n=7,296), 37.3 % fell into the normal-weight range, 42.3 % were preobese, 15.2 % were moderately obese, and 5.3 % were severely obese. At follow-up, dropout was slightly higher among the moderate obesity and severe obesity groups (14.4 and 4.8 %) than among those in the normal-weight group. On the whole, it is likely that the obese groups (especially the severely obese) are more affected by utilization underestimates. If so, however, the above-reported differences to the normal-weight group represent rather conservative tests, and real differences may even be greater.

Fifth, utilization data in follow-up surveys F3 and F4 were assessed retrospectively over time horizons of 12 and 3 months, respectively. Thus, inaccuracies in the self-reported data cannot be excluded. Patient recall of physician visits over a time period as long as 12 months is subject to uncertain validity, potentially resulting in underestimates. In addition, the 3-month F4 data were extrapolated to 12 months. Again, underestimates are possible since a response of "no utilization" was coded as zero for 1 year, although the patient may have visited a physician 4 months ago, for instance (with no data being available to estimate how often this was the case). This may also explain significant effects of the study sample in terms of lower outpatient utilization in F4 than in F3. On the other hand, if a patient visited a physician 10 times in the last 3 months due to acute illness, this number was extrapolated to 40 visits in the year preceding the survey, so that overestimates cannot be excluded. As for the procedure employed in F3, underestimates again cannot be excluded given evidence that having taken part in this survey positively correlates with the actual number of recalled visits [26] (also note the discussion on this in Swart & Griehl, this volume). However, there are no indications that these limitations have biased utilization differentials between the groups as defined by maintenance of or changes in BMI category. Also, the 3-month timeslot in F4 was not at the same time of the year for all participants of the survey since it was conducted over a time period of 18 months.

Sixth, diseases other than diabetes (e.g., cancers and gastrointestinal disorders) were not taken into account. However, the role of a wider range of physical (co) morbidities will be investigated using the Physical Functional Comorbidity Index (PFCI) [27], which is not yet available for the S3/F3 and S4/F4 longitudinal cohorts.

Seventh, in January 2004, a German health care reform introduced a € 10 fee for the first outpatient visit to a physician in each quarter for all adults covered by statutory health insurance(this fee was abolished in January 2013). Since utilization data for the present study were collected in 2004/2005 (F3) and 2006/2008 (F4), after the introduction of the €10 fee, this fee may have had some impact on participants' visits to physicians, at least at the beginning of the observation period. One analysis concerning differences by socioeconomic status has demonstrated that avoiding a physician visit due to this fee is comparatively common among low-income groups [28]. However, contrary to expectations and public opinion, the effects of this new co-payment on decisions to visit physicians have been shown to be rather limited [29, 30], so potential bias should be minorand may not have affected the differences between BMI development subgroups. It should also be noted that this study did not analyze the reasons for utilization and did not focus on the referral system from PCPs to medical specialists (as one characteristic of the German outpatient healthcare system).

Finally, the present surveys are restricted to participants with German citizenship. Since studies have repeatedly shown that obesity is more prevalent in the migrant population [31], our results cannot be extrapolated to the total resident population of Germany without making further assumptions.

Bearing this in mind, the present results can be interpreted as follows: Besides the self-evident positive association of PCP utilization with age, the finding that women had more visits to PCPs than men is largely consistent with previous results and may be explained by the finding that communication and shared decisionmaking are more preferred by female patients and at the same time more common in primary care practice [32]. Consistent with previous findings [14, 15, 33], significantly more general practitioner (GP)visits were reported by lower socioeconomic groups, defined as people with low education levels in this study.

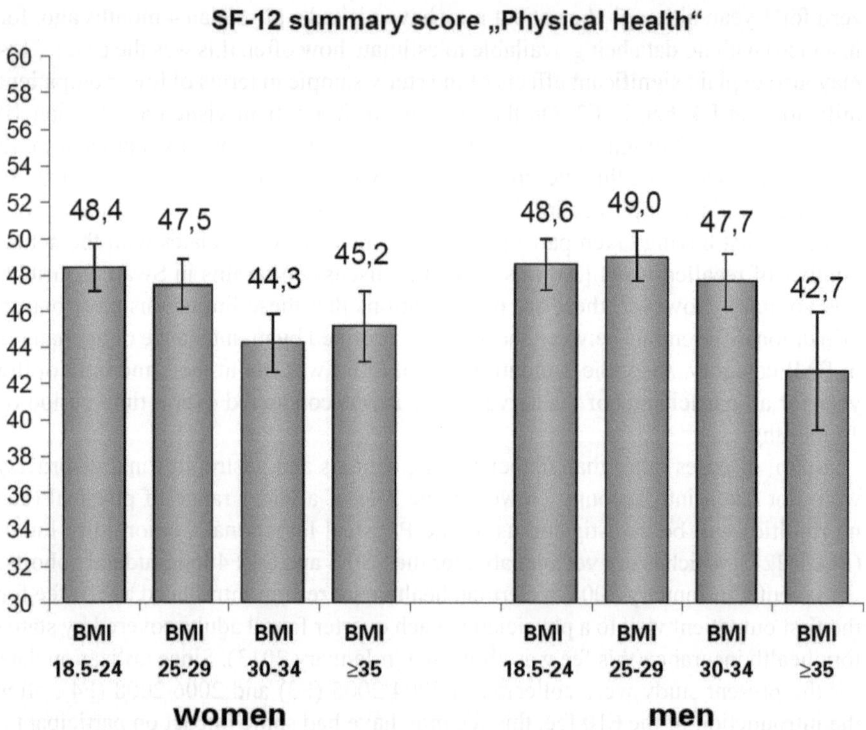

Fig. 12.2 Physical health-related quality of life (SF-12 summary score) by BMI for women and men (means and 95% confidence intervals adjusted for age and socioeconomic status). (Reproduced from [34])

Concerning the focal independent variable of the present analysis, the differences in the number of PCP visits across the four BMI categories (in terms of the latter's main effect) indicated that while all three overweight groups reported higher utilization than those in the normal-weight range, the moderate obesity group did not report significantly more visits than the preobese group, but fewer visits than the severely obese group (adjustment for diabetes, as a major comorbidity of obesity, did not diminish these effects). However, this pattern held only overall but neither for women nor for men separately, which highlights the limitations of previous research that did not differentiate between women and men. In particular, while among women, all three overweight groups showed excess PCP utilization, among men neither the preobese nor the moderately obese group had significantly more visits than the normal-weight group, leaving the severely obese group as the only one with excess utilization.

Interestingly, these results largely parallel the pattern found for physical health-related quality of life among women and men of different BMI status in the KORA population [34] (see Fig. 12.2). In that study, among men the severely obese group was also the only overweight group with significantly lower physical health-related quality of life than normal-weight men. In contrast, among women both obese groups had an impaired physical health-related quality of life. Given that impaired physical health-related quality of life has been shown to determine the utilization of PCPs in the KORApopulation [35, 36], the parallelism of patterns in Figs. 12.1 and 12.2 supports the validity of the present results and may explain the identified gender pattern.

The only diverging aspect is that preobese women did not differ significantly in physical health-related quality of life from those in the normal-weight range [34], but in the present analysis, preobese women nevertheless had excess PCP visits. This might be due to the higher probability of preobese women being dissatisfied with their body weight when compared to preobese men (58.1 % vs. 32.2 % in the KORApopulation [37]). This holds despite the fact that body-weight dissatisfaction did not predict PCP use in another KORA paper [27]; due to lack of statistical power, those analyses could not be stratified by women and men and thus failed to rule out gender-specific patterns in findings.

Lastly, we will look at how the present analysis fits into Andersen's behavioral model of health services use [7, 8] as the overarching framework of the present volume. First of all, we must note that our empirical analysis included only a small number of selected individual predisposing factors (sex, age, education) and need factors (obesity, diabetes) as determinants of PCP utilization and thus excluded both individual enabling factors and all contextual factors (for details, see Babitsch, Gohl, and von Lengerke, this volume). While these restrictions may be viewed as a limitation, they were made deliberately to meet our analytical goal of testing gender differences in the association between moderate and severe obesity on the one hand and PCP utilization on the other. In our view, it is possible to relate a given analysis to themodel *and* to restrict it to a (small) number of selected variables in order to take an in-depth account of the complexity potentially inherent even in such a small set of variables. In other words, in our view testing Andersen's model may not (only) be pursued by studies including all kinds of variables in one statistical model (with potentially associated problems such as over-adjustment for or overlooking of effect modifications), but (rather) by incremental strategies looking at individual paths of the explanatory process or causal ordering via step-by-step, i.e., consecutive, analyses.

A principally independent but related issue highlighted by the present empirical analysis is the question how predisposing versus enabling factors should be (statistically) modeled in accordance with Andersen's concept of their effects on utilization. While need factors denote conditions that are conceived as requiring medical treatment and must be defined for utilization to actually take place, enabling factors facilitate (or, in case of scarcity or absence, impede) utilization [7–8]. In our view, it makes sense to model them as modifiers of the effect of a given need factor and thus test the interaction between the need factor and the enabler in terms of moderation analysis [38–39]. Against this background, it may be instructive that our analysis shows that sex, as a basic variable usually categorized as a predisposing factor in the model, *moderates* the association of obesity and the utilization of PCPs in the gender-specific manner described above (excess use only in severe obesity for men and excess use in all three overweight groups for women). Note that the opposite idea, i.e., moderation of the effect of sex on utilization by obesity status, is not a viable option if one accepts that predisposing factors are conceptualized as "notdirectly responsible for use" ([8], in press). In other words, while the distinction between predisposing versus enabling factors may be useful conceptually, and certainly has been one of the key features in the adoption of the behavioral model of health services use by health care utilization researchers for decades, it does not precisely imply how they should be modeled when empirically applying the theoretical framework. Also, the open question remains whether sex (and, for that matter, gender in terms of the psychosocial realities of being female or male in a society) may also be associated with features that enable people to utilize services (similarly, one could ask whether income is "only" an enabler or "also" predisposes to use certain services).

Concluding Summary

In population-based studies in Germany, obesity is associated with excess utilization of PCPs in terms of number of visits, holding especially for severe obesity. No data have yet been published on the reasons for and content of the consultations. Excess PCP utilization is associated only with severe obesity among men but with all three overweight groups among women. This pattern parallels obesity-associated reduction in physical health-related quality of life. Future studies should replicate these findings and examine the roles of enabling and contextual factors in this context, for instance, income as an effect modifier and the gender-specific impact of regional PCP density.

References

[1] Kurth B-M. Erste Ergebnisse aus der „Studie zur Gesundheit Erwachsener in Deutschland" (DEGS). In German. Bundesgesundheitsblatt Gesundheitsforschung Gesundheitsschutz. 2012;55:980–90.
[2] Helmert U, Strube H. [The development of obesity in Germany in the period from 1985 until 2000]. In German. Gesundheitswesen. 2004;66:409–15.
[3] Wolfenstetter SB, Menn P, Holle R, Mielck A, Meisinger C, von Lengerke T. Body weight changes and outpatient medical care utilisation: Results of the MONICA/KORA cohorts S3/F3 and S4/F4. Psychosoc Med. 2012;9:1–14.
[4] Hauner H, Buchholz G, Hamann A, Husemann B, Koletzko B, Liebermeister H, et al. Evidenzbasierte Leitlinie: Adipositas—Prävention und Therapie. Version 2007. 2013. In German. www.adipositas-gesellschaft.de/fileadmin/pdf/leitlinien/adipositas-leitlinie-2007.pdf. Accessed 5 June, 2013
[5] Metz U, Welke J, Esch T, Renneberg B, Braun V, Heintze C. Perception of stress and quality of life in overweight and obese people—implications for preventive consultancies in primary care. Med Sci Monit. 2009;15:PH1–6.
[6] Hurley SF, Bond LM, Carlin JB, Evans DB, Kaldor JM. A method for estimating baseline health care costs. J Epidemiol Community Health. 1995;49:525–31.

[7] Andersen RM. Revisiting the behavioral model and access to medical care: does it matter? J Health Soc Behav 1995;36:1–10.

[8] Andersen RM, Davidson PL, Baumeister SE. Improving access to care in America. In: Kominski EF, editor. Changing the U.S. health care system: Key issues in health services, policy, and management. San Francisco, CA: Jossey-Bass; 2013. p. 33–69.

[9] Hauner H, Bramlage P, Losch C, Steinhagen-Thiessen E, Schunkert H, Wasem J, et al. Prevalence of obesity in primary care using different anthropometric measures–results of the German Metabolic and Cardiovascular Risk Project (GEMCAS). BMC Public Health. 2008;8:282.

[10] Hauner H, Koster I, von Ferber L. Frequency of 'obesity' in medical records and utilization of out-patient health care by 'obese' subjects in Germany. An analysis of health insurance data. Int J Obes Relat Metab Disord. 1996;20:820–4.

[11] Bramlage P, Wittchen HU, Pittrow D, Kirch W, Krause P, Lehnert H, et al. Recognition and management of overweight and obesity in primary care in Germany. Int J Obes Relat Metab Disord. 2004;28:1299–308.

[12] von Lengerke T, Hagenmeyer EG, Gothe H, Schiffhorst G, Happich M, Haussler B. Excess health care costs of obesity in adults with diabetes mellitus: a claims data analysis. Exp Clin Endocrinol Diabetes. 2010;118:496–504.

[13] Schneider R. Relevanz und Kosten der Adipositas in Deutschland. In German. Ernährungs-Umschau. 1996;43:369–74.

[14] Thode N, Bergmann E, Kamtsiuris P, Kurth B-M. Einflussfaktoren auf die Inanspruchnahme des deutschen Gesundheitswesens und mögliche Steuerungsmechanismen. In German. Berlin: Robert Koch Institut; 2004.

[15] Thode N, Bergmann E, Kamtsiuris P, Kurth BM. [Predictors for ambulatory medical care utilization in Germany]. In German. Bundesgesundheitsblatt Gesundheitsforschung Gesundheitsschutz. 2005;48:296–306.

[16] Meisinger C, Heier M, Loewel H. The relationship between body weight and health care among German women. Obes Res. 2004;12:1473–80.

[17] von Lengerke T, Happich M, Reitmeir P, John J. Utilization of out- and inpatient health services by obese adults: a population-based study in the Augsburg region, Germany. Gesundheitswesen. 2005;67 Suppl 1:S150–7.

[18] Lovejoy JC, Sainsbury A. Sex differences in obesity and the regulation of energy homeostasis. Obes Rev. 2009;10:154–67.

[19] Hollis JF, Gullion CM, Stevens VJ, Brantley PJ, Appel LJ, Ard JD, et al. Weight loss during the intensive intervention phase of the weight-loss maintenance trial. Am J Prev Med. 2008;35:118–26.

[20] Perreault L, Ma Y, Dagogo-Jack S, Horton E, Marrero D, Crandall J, et al. Sex differences in diabetes risk and the effect of intensive lifestyle modification in the Diabetes Prevention Program. Diabetes Care. 2008;31:1416–21.

[21] WHO. Obesity: Preventing and managing the global epidemic. Geneva: WHO; 2000.

[22] Holle R, Happich M, Lowel H, Wichmann HE. KORA—a research platform for population based health research. Gesundheitswesen. 2005;67:S19–25.

[23] Nocon M, Keil T, Willich SN. Education, income, occupational status and health risk behaviour. J Public Health. 2007;15:401–5.

[24] Williamson, T.S.: Log-binomial models: maximum likelihood and failed convergence [Dissertation]. http://hdl.handle.net/1880/48526 (2011). Accessed 5 June, 2013.

[25] Hoffmann W, Terschuren C, Holle R, Kamtsiuris P, Bergmann M, Kroke A, et al. [The problem of response in epidemiologic studies in Germany (Part II)]. In German. Gesundheitswesen. 2004;66:482–91.

[26] Wallihan DB, Stump TE, Callahan CM. Accuracy of self-reported health services use and patterns of care among urban older adults. Med Care. 1999;37:662–70.

[27] von Lengerke T, John J. Use of medical doctors, physical therapists, and alternative practitioners by obese adults: does body weight dissatisfaction mediate extant associations? J Psychosom Res. 2006;61:553–60.

[28] Ruckert IM, Bocken J, Mielck A. Are German patients burdened by the practice charge for physician visits ('Praxisgebuehr')? A cross sectional analysis of socio-economic and health related factors. BMC Health Serv Res. 2008;8:232.

[29] Augurzky B, Bauer T, Schaffner S. Copayments in the German health system—Do they work? Essen: Rheinisch-Westfälisches Institut für Wirtschaftsforschung; 2006.

[30] Schreyögg J, Grabka MM. Copayments for ambulatory care in Germany: a natural experiment using a difference-in-difference approach. Berlin: DIW, 2008.

[31] Apfelbacher CJ, Loerbroks A, Cairns J, Behrendt H, Ring J, Kramer U. Predictors of overweight and obesity in five to seven-year-old children in Germany: results from cross-sectional studies. BMC Public Health. 2008;8:171.

[32] van den Brink-Muinen A, Verhaak PF, Bensing JM, Bahrs O, Deveugele M, Gask L, et al. Communication in general practice: differences between European countries. Fam Pract. 2003;20:478–85.

[33] van Doorslaer E, Masseria C, Koolman X. Inequalities in access to medical care by income in developed countries. CMAJ. 2006;174:177–83.

[34] von Lengerke T, Janssen C, John J. Sense of coherence, health locus of control, and quality of life in obese adults: physical limitations and psychological normalcies. Int J Public Health. 2007;52:16–26.

[35] von Lengerke T, John J. Excess use of general practitioners by obese adults: does health-related quality of life account for the association? Psychol Health Med. 2007;12:536–44.

[36] von Lengerke T, John J. General practitioners' opportunities for preventing ill health in healthy vs morbid obese adults: a general population study on consultations. J Public Health. 2007;15:71–80.

[37] Mönnichs G, von Lengerke T. [Dissatisfaction with body weight after reduction dieting in women and men: Results of the KORA-Survey 2000]. In German. Z Gesundheitspsychol. 2004;12:116–30.

[38] Baron RM, Kenny DA. The moderator-mediator variable distinction in social psychological research: conceptual, strategic, and statistical considerations. J Pers Soc Psychol. 1986;51:1173–82.

[39] Hayes AF. Introduction to mediation, moderation and conditional process analysis: A regression-based approach. New York, NY; Guilford; 2013.

Chapter 13
Utilization of Physiotherapy by Patients with Rheumatic Diseases

Holm Thieme and Bernhard Borgetto

Introduction

Rheumatic disorders are among the most common diseases of the musculoskeletal system. In its Report on Rheumatic Disorders, the German government estimates that about one-third of early retirement cases, one-fifth of hospital days, and a high percentage of all physician visits are caused by rheumatic disorders (Rheumabericht der Bundesregierung 1997). The most common diagnoses are rheumatoid arthritis (RA; International Classification of Diseases (ICD)-10: M05-06), psoriatic arthritis (PsA; ICD-10: M07), osteoarthritis (OA; ICD-10: M15-M19), systemic lupus erythematosus (SLE; ICD-10: M32), fibromyalgia (FM; ICD-10: M79), and ankylosing spondylitis (AS; ICD-10: M45).

This chapter analyzes the factors influencing the utilization of physical therapy (PT) by patients with rheumatic disorders in Germany. After providing an overview of the epidemiological importance of rheumatic disorders and the effectiveness of PT, we will therefore present and discuss the results of a current review on the prevalence of PT utilization and its predictors in rheumatism patients in Germany and a secondary data analysis of rheumatism-related health services data on the utilization of PT services and their potential predictors.

Epidemiology

In Germany, the adult lifetime prevalence of inflammatory rheumatic disorders is 3.4 % (Schneider et al. 2006). One out of 100 persons under 30 and every 16th person aged 70+suffer from a rheumatic disorder. Starting at age 40, the

H. Thieme (✉) · B. Borgetto
HAWK—University of Applied Sciences and Arts,
Faculty of Social Work and Health, Hildesheim, Germany
e-mail: agf_thieme@hawk-hhg.de

B. Borgetto
e-mail: borgetto@hawk-hhg.de

C. Janssen et al. (eds.), *Health Care Utilization in Germany*,
DOI 10.1007/978-1-4614-9191-0_13, © Springer Science+Business Media New York 2014

prevalence is higher for women than for men, and more than twice as many women than men over age 70 suffer from rheumatism (Schneider et al. 2006). The prevalence of RA is about 0.5–1%, with women being affected twice as commonly as men (Symmons 2002). Kaipiainen-Seppänen and Aho (2000) report a PsA prevalence of 0.1%. Sun et al. (2007) found OA incidence rates of 1,103 new cases per 100,000 inhabitants for women and 934/100,000 for men. Bernatsky et al. (2007) calculated an SLE prevalence of 51/100,000 inhabitants. In Germany, an FM prevalence of 0.4% for women and 0.05% for men has been calculated (Sauer et al. 2011).

Effectiveness of PT

Rheumatic disorders result in a high burden of disease. In addition to reducing functional ability and quality of life (Carmona et al. 2001), they are the most common cause of chronic health limitations (~40%) and long-term disability (~50%) among the most epidemiologically relevant disorders (Andrianakos et al. 2005).

Alongside pharmacological therapy and specialist care, PT is one of the most important treatment elements for patients with RA according to current guidelines (Schneider et al. 2011). Clinical and experimental studies confirm the effectiveness of PT in RA patients (Baillet et al. 2012, 2010). On the basis of randomized controlled trials, a systematic literature search found a high level of evidence that therapeutic interventions consisting of functional strengthening and low-intensity and high-intensity exercise therapy reduce pain and increase patients' general functional abilities (Ottawa Panel Members 2004). The review by van den Ende et al. (2000) arrived at similar results and supports the effectiveness of therapeutic exercises in increasing aerobic capacity and strength. Alongside these positive results on the effectiveness of active exercises, literature reviews on the effects of passive interventions (thermotherapy, balneotherapy, and electrotherapy) revealed a more complex picture: while electrotherapy was shown to be effective in terms of increasing strength and resistance to fatigue (Brosseau et al. 2002), thermotherapy was not associated with any significant effects on objectively measured parameters (Robinson et al. 2002).

FM patients benefit from exercise therapy for increasing global well-being (Kelley and Kelley 2011), from hydrotherapy for the alleviation of pain (McVeigh et al. 2008), and from both therapies for reducing disability and alleviating pain (Dziedzic et al. 2008).

Experimental studies also suggest a number of PT recommendations for OA patients. For instance, systematic literature reviews consider exercise therapy, particularly group therapies, aquatic therapy, electrotherapy, manual therapy, and strengthening exercises as effective components of PT in OA patients (Thomas et al. 2009, Lange et al. 2008, Jamtvedt et al. 2008).

For AS patients, PT in the form of individualized and group therapy and aquatic therapies are considered effective as well (Vliet and Li 2009, Dagfinrud et al. 2008).

Utilization of PT

Alongside these results of experimental clinical studies that clarify PT effectiveness under ideal trial conditions, current practices in the prescription and utilization of PT should be examined in an effort to identify and counteract underuse, overuse, and misuse. The provision of PT services in Germany is an interesting topic and the subject of current discussion. In Germany, PT is typically provided on the basis of a physician's prescription. The number, frequency, and type of PT sessions are diagnosis dependent as specified by the catalog of non-pharmacological therapies [*Heilmittelkatalog*]. Hence, PT utilization is indirect, with the physician acting as a gatekeeper. Direct access to PT services without requiring a physician visit has been the subject of recent debate in Germany. This option is currently being tested through pilot studies (IFK 2012, Scheel 2012). At this time, self-regulated utilization is only an option through physical therapists who are also licensed alternative medical practitioners [*Heilpraktiker*] (Bundesverwaltungsgericht 2009).

A study by Zink et al. (2001) on the basis of a German national register revealed great inter-practice variations in the prescription frequencies for active and passive PT at outpatient rheumatology care facilities. Only a small part of this variation was explained by the case mix.

Prevalence of PT utilization in Germany

In a current systematic literature review (Thieme and Borgetto 2012), we examined PT utilization in Germany and its potential predictors and determinants. The methods and results of the review are described in detail in the original publication. It shows that between 25 % and 59 % of patients with rheumatic disorders receive PT. The results of different studies varied widely, based on the rheumatological diagnoses and other factors.

RA patients received or were prescribed PT in 25 % (Thieme et al. 2009, Zink et al. 2006) to 55 % (Thieme and Borgetto 2011) of cases. Studies on outpatient services (Thieme et al. 2009, Mau and Müller 2008) found lower rates than studies on PT in general (Zink et al. 2006, Zink et al. 2003, Zink et al. 2001). Two studies examined FM patients. On the basis of statutory health insurance (SHI) data, Sauer et al. (2011) found that 59 % of patients were prescribed outpatient PT. Thieme and Borgetto (2011) used the data of a questionnaire survey to conduct a secondary data analysis and found that 53 % of FM patients utilized therapeutic exercises. Another study found that the utilization of PT rose by 7 % between 1994 and 1999 (Zink et al. 2003). Two studies examined data of AS patients. One study found a prescription rate of 48 % for outpatient individualized PT (Mau and Müller 2008). The other study determined that 64 % of respondents utilized individualized PT and 13.7 % utilized group PT (Zink et al. 2006).

Determinants of PT utilization in Germany

As described in Chap. 2, determinants and predictors of utilization can be described as individual and contextual factors using Andersen's model (Andersen 2008).

Several studies report individual factors that may influence the provision, prescription, and utilization of PT services in Germany. For patients with RA, Thieme and Borgetto (2011) found that patients who received exercise therapy were significantly younger than those who did not. Their data further demonstrated that the time since diagnosis in these patients was longer and that they experienced greater pain intensity and reported lower quality of life in some items of the Short Form-36 Health Survey. On the basis of a questionnaire survey, Mau and Müller (2008) also found that utilization clearly depended on the severity of disease. Among RA patients, PT was received by 31 % of the most disabled versus 14 % of the least disabled. In addition, they reported that patients in active stages of RA, with severe fatigue, and greater functional disability were more likely to receive PT. In the study by Waltz (2000), the best predictors of PT utilization in RA patients were severe fatigue and more severe functional limitations. In addition, the authors found a weak relationship with active stages of RA. For patients with FM, it was found that those using PT services were younger and had more pain than those who did not use PT (Thieme and Borgetto 2011;Table 13.1).

Regarding the contextual factors influencing RA patients' utilization of PT services, Thieme et al. (2009) reported that prescription rates of PT services varied considerably according to medical specialty of the prescribing practitioners. Primary care physicians prescribed more outpatient PT services than did orthopedic specialists. Zink et al. (2003, 2001) found equally wide variations in PT utilization between 26 different rheumatology centers. Mau and Müller (2008) reported variations in PT utilization from 10 to 45 % between different rheumatologists (Table 13.1)

Prevalence of PT utilization in international comparison

The reported prevalence of PT utilization by RA patients in Austria is 50 %, similar to German numbers (Wagner et al. 2005). In two studies from the Netherlands, the prevalence of utilization varied between one-third and one-half of examined patients (Jacobi et al. 2004, Waltz 2000). In the USA, 6 % and 17 % of examined patients reported having received individualized PT within the past 12 and 6 months, respectively (Kahn et al. 2007, Berkanovic et al. 1991). In Canada, some 83 % reported having participated in individualized or group PT (Li et al. 2004).

For the USA, Hsieh et al. showed that only 11 % of OA patients took advantage of PT (Hsieh and Dominick 2003).

Determinants of PT utilization in international comparison

When comparing Germany and the Netherlands, Waltz (2000) found that the prevalence of utilization by RA patients depends on disease activity, with patients in ac-

Table 13.1 Characteristics and results of the reviewed studies on PT service utilization in Germany (from: Thieme et al. 2012)

Reference	Diagnosis	Sample size	Setting	Study design	Date of evaluation	Method of evaluation	Results[1]
Sauer et al. 2011	FM	n=2857	Health insurance records	Cross-sectional	2007	Document analysis	59 % received outpatient PT services
Thieme et al. 2011	RA, FM	n=570	Patients were revcruited from self-help groups, PT practices, rheumatology practices and clinics	Longitudinal	2001–2004	Questionnaire survey	PT use: 55 % with RA, 53 % with FM Differences between users and non-users: RA+FM: users were younger, had more pain; RA: time since diagnosis in users was longer, users had more pain and reduced health related quality of life
Thieme et al. 2009	RA	n=18056	Health insurance records	Cross-sectional	2007	Document analysis	Approximately 25 % received outpatient PT services; variations by medical specialty
Mau and Müller 2008	RA, AS	RA: n=204 AS: n= 47 Rheumatologists: n= 117	10 rheumatology practices Rheumatologists recruited from the German Society for Rheumatology	Cross-sectional	2007	Questionnaire survey	Outpatient individual PT prescribed to 25 % (25th to 75th percentile: 10–45 %) of RA patients and 48 % (25th to 75th percentile: 20–81 %) of AS patients with wide variation between rheumatologists; RA: 31 % with an FFbH < 50, 22 % with an FFbH > 50–≤ 70 and 14 % with an FFbH > 70 received individual outpatient PT; general practitioners prescribed more nonmedical treatments than rheumatologists

Table 13.1 (continued)

Reference	Diagnosis	Sample size	Setting	Study design	Date of evaluation	Method of evaluation	Results[1]
Zink et al. 2006	RA AS	RA: $n=9{,}627$ AS: $n=1{,}378$ PsA: $n=1{,}863$	24 arthritis centers, over 80 individual inpatient and outpatient institutions	Cross-sectional	2002	National database of routine data	Prescription rates: RA: 41.8% for individual PT, 9.2% for group PT, PsA: 46% for individual PT, 9.5% for group PT; AS: 64% for individual PT, 13.7% for group PT
Zink et al. 2003	RA	1993: $n=23{,}103$ 1999: $n=28{,}939$	24 arthritis centers	Longitudinal	1993–1999	National database of routine data	1993: 34% used individual PT, 1999: 41% used individual PT; in 29 rheumatology centers PT use 1999 varied between 18 and 76 %
Zink et al. 2001	RA	$n=7{,}326$	24 arthritis centers including 71 single outpatient and inpatient institutions	Cross-sectional		National database of routine data	Prescription rates: 41% (25th to 75th percentile: 34–54%) for individual PT, 27% (25th to 75th percentile: 19–37%) for group PT; prescription rates varied substantially between different types of practice patterns (use of combination therapy) in clinics
Waltz 2000	RA	$n=200$	1 German and 1 Dutch outpatient clinic	Longitudinal	1994–1996	Questionnaire survey	50% of patients in Germany and the Netherlands used PT, no national differences Predictors for PT use: strong associations with severe fatigue and more functional limitations, weak association with high disease activity (DAS)

[1] Target variables were the ratio of patients who used or were prescribed PT interventions and the identified determinants or influencing factors of PT interventions.

tive stages of arthritis more frequently taking advantage of PT. Severe fatigue and more severe functional problems were additional important predictors of PT utilization in that study. There were no national differences between the two countries (Waltz 2000). Berkanovic et al. (1991) arrived at a similar result in the USA. In this publication, patients with more severe functional disability, more severe limitations in activities of daily life, and poorer self-reported health more commonly received PT services. In addition, white skin color was found to be a negative predictor of PT utilization, while a greater tendency to use medical and therapeutic services was a positive predictor. A study in Belgium found a distinct association between utilization and time of diagnosis. PT was utilized by 8 % of patients in early stages of RA and 26 % of those in late-stage RA (Westhovens et al. 2005). Li et al. (2004) calculated predictors and found that moderate to high family income increases the utilization of active PT exercises in Canada. In a US study with almost 800 included RA patients, Iversen et al. (2011) showed that high disease activity, stronger social networks, and more severe disability increase the utilization of PT, while not holding a college degree reduces it.

For other diagnostic groups, few data on the determinants of PT utilization were found in the literature. Hsieh and Dominick (2003) demonstrated that higher severity of disease, stronger belief in the benefits of therapy, and physician recommendation are associated with greater PT utilization by OA patients in the USA.

Research problem

The analysis reveals that relatively little is known about PT utilization by patients with rheumatic disorders in Germany. While particularly the 'core documentation' [*Kerndokumentation*] provides a good basis for determining the prevalence of utilization (Zink et al. 2003), influencing factors have rarely been investigated. In the analysis of overuse, misuse, and underuse, health services data can suggest positive as well as negative influencing factors, and these factors can then be specifically targeted if action is required. On this basis, a secondary analysis of the RheumaDat Panel (Borgetto und Stößel 2011, Borgetto et al. 2008) has been conducted. It aimed to determine the prevalence of PT utilization and its potential predictors in patients with RA or FM.

Methods

The secondary data analysis was conducted using a questionnaire-based survey (RheumaDat) by the University of Freiburg. In the observation study, a cohort of rheumatism patients were surveyed for a time period of 2 years using standardized questionnaires. The questionnaires were administered to patients every half year at four survey times (t_1–t_4).

To ensure that the widest possible range of services is represented in the study, the participants were recruited through various occupational groups (rheumatologists, general practitioners, physical therapists, etc.) and in various sectors (outpatient, acute inpatient, rehabilitation, and self-help organizations). The sample for the initial survey was collected from June 1, 2001 to May 31, 2002. The survey as a whole ended on May 31, 2004.

To recruit patients for the initial survey, the Medical Sociology Department of Freiburg University collaborated with various types of care providers. The collaboration partners had the following tasks:

- Identify patients with rheumatic diseases who were willing to participate in the study.
- Provide brief patient information about the study and obtain consent.
- Hand out a questionnaire to be returned directly to Freiburg University by mail.

The following procedure was typically used to recruit study participants (Table 13.2): After the partners confirmed their collaboration, the number of patients who may be willing to participate in the study was collaboratively estimated. Most collaboration partners were sent the corresponding number of questionnaires. In a few clinics, research project staff was involved in contacting the patients on site.

The study surveyed a wide spectrum of rheumatism-related diagnosis groups. In this analysis, we only took into account patients whose main diagnosis was chronic polyarthritis (CP) or FM.

Additional inclusion criteria were: (a) age 18+ and (b) consent to participate in the study. Exclusion criteria were: (aa) difficulty in writing and (bb) severe comorbidities or multimorbidity masking the rheumatic illness.

Questionnaires

The study participants were issued questionnaires consisting of individual questions and standardized survey instruments. The questionnaires were largely identical, except for minor differences based on survey time and diagnosis, for instance.

Utilization

The utilization of medical services was recorded at all four time points using the survey instrument V-RHEUMA, which was developed for this study. V-RHEUMA encompasses outpatient and inpatient medical treatment, rehabilitation services, the respective therapy (pharmaceutical, surgical, physical, occupational therapy, psychotherapy, etc.), and supplementary services such as functional training, psychological pain management training, patient training, and self-help groups.

Predictors of PT utilization were examined using the variable "received PT within the last 6 months: yes/no" for the survey times $t_2$and t_4. For direct utilization, only the time point t_2 was taken into account. For calculating predictors of repeat utilization, we analyzed patients who reported having received PT within the previ-

Table 13.2 Recruitment of study participants

Collaborating partners	Number	Questionnaires supplied	Study participants
Rheumatologists	13	199	25
Physicians in private practice	7	55	3
Hospitals	54	1,425	301
Physical therapists	151	1,219	229
Working groups within the League against Rheumatism	49	932	341
Other collaborating partners[a]	7	60	2
Total	283	3,890	901

[a] Pharmacies, social services offices, medical bath practices

ous 6 months for both t_2 and t_4. The comparison group consisted of the patients who reported not having received PT at either one of these time points.

On the basis of the Andersen model (see Chap. 2), the independent variables were categorized as need factors, predisposing factors, or enabling factors.

Need factors

Time of diagnosis The time of diagnosis was categorized as a dichotomous variable, primarily because more differentiated categorization would have resulted in very small sample sizes. We differentiated patients diagnosed before 1990 versus those diagnosed after 1990.

Functional ability Functional ability was surveyed using the Hannover Functional Ability Questionnaire (FFbH-X). The FFbH evaluates the functional ability of patients with rheumatic disorders, that is, the extent to which the patients can manage the activities of daily living within their household, family, occupation, and leisure time (Kohlmann and Raspe 1996). For instance, the FFbH records limitations in mobility, personal hygiene, grasping and moving objects, and dressing and undressing that are caused by rheumatic diseases. The results range from a score of 0 (no functional ability) to 100 (full functional ability). The version FFbH-X comprises the three syndrome-specific versions of the FFbH (polyarticular diseases FFbH-P, back pain FFbH-R, and lower extremity OA FFbH-OA) and allows reconstruction of these specialized versions. The FFbH score was categorized in three levels, with participants achieving up to 50 points being grouped in level 1, those up to 75 in level 2, and those up to 100 points in level 3.

Depression/depressive symptoms Depression was surveyed as a predictor at baseline using the German-language Center for Epidemiological Studies Depression (CES-D) questionnaire (Weissman et al. 1977). As an epidemiological screening instrument, the 20-item scale is a sensitive instrument for measuring depressive symptoms. It is recommended for use in patients with chronic pain since it has few somatic items that may represent a "symptom overlap" with pain questionnaires

(Nagel et al. 2002). An example item is: "During the past week, I've felt depressed or sad." The 4-point scale offers respondents choices from "rarely or none of the time (less than 1 day)" to "most or all of the time (5–7 days)." A cut-off score of 16 is used to identify clinically relevant depressive symptomatology (Parikh et al. 1988, Zich et al. 1990). Using this value, the variable was categorized into clinically relevant versus irrelevant symptomatology.

Predisposing factors

Age Age was recorded using the patient's year of birth. Ages were categorized into 20-year groups, ranging from ages 20–39 to 60+.

Sex Sex was recorded as a dichotomous variable (male/female).

Locus of control To survey general expectations, we used the questionnaire for the assessment of disease and health locus of control [KKG, *Kontrollüberzeugungen zu Krankheit und Gesundheit*] (Lohaus and Schmitt 1989). This questionnaire particularly allows discriminating between internal locus of control (specific events are experienced as a consequence of one's own actions and therefore under one's own control) and external locus of control (specific events are attributed to chance [fatalistic externality] or the influence of other persons [social externality]).

Coping with disease The Freiburg Questionnaire on Coping with Illness [FKV, *Freiburger Fragebogen zur Krankheitsverarbeitung*] assesses a wide range of coping dimensions (Muthny 1989). The test consists of a detailed instrument (FKV 102) with 12 scales and a short form for self-assessment (FKV-LIS) with five scales and 35 items each. This study used the short form because it is particularly suitable for measuring course over time. The five scales describe the following coping mechanisms: depressive coping, active problem-oriented coping, distraction and self-encouragement, religious faith and search for meaning, as well as minimization and wishful thinking.

Enabling factors

Level of education Level of education was categorized in four levels: no degree, lower secondary school degree [*Haupt-/Volksschulabschluss*], mid-level secondary school degree [*Realschulabschluss*], and university entrance qualification *[(Fach-) Abitur*].

Occupational training Occupational training was categorized into five levels: No completed occupational training, completed occupational training, mid-level secondary school degree, academic, and other occupational training.

Income Net household income was recorded in EUR 750 increments, from an income up to EUR 750 to above EUR 1750.

Social support Social support was surveyed on the basis of the "Fragebogen zur soziale Unterstützung-Kurzform 22" questionnaire by Sommer and Fydrich (1991). With its two parts the F-SOZU surveys social support or burden (Part A) as well as the presence of other people who are experienced as socially supportive or burdensome, and hence aspects of the social network (part B). The contents are surveyed with the main scales "emotional support," "practical support," and "social integration," plus the previously neglected component "social burden." With the supplementary scales, additional aspects such as "reciprocity of interaction" and "satisfaction with social support" can be measured.

Analysis

The secondary analysis included the CP or FM respondents' data sets that were available for the times t_1, t_2, and t_4 ($n=426$). Subgroup analyses were conducted separately for each diagnosis. Predictors were examined at the time t_1 for direct utilization (PT at t_2) and repeat utilization (PT at t_2 and t_4).

For the sociodemographic data, descriptive data and distributions were calculated. The predictor analysis was conducted using binary logistic regression. All independent variables were included in the model step by step. The reference category for categorical variables was determined using content considerations. The significance threshold for predictors of utilization was set on p-value of 0.05. The statistical analysis was conducted using the Predictive Analysis Software (PASW) 18 for Windows.

Results

Sample description

A total of 610 participants with CP and FM were recruited for the survey. For this secondary data analysis, the data of 426 respondents were used because their data sets were available for the time points t_1, t_2, and t_4.

Table 13.3 summarizes the most important sociodemographic and disease-related data of the 426 respondents. The average age of the respondents was 52.73 ± 11.44 years. Ninety percent of participants were female. At the time of inclusion, the average time since diagnosis was 6.07 ± 7.42 years. The analysis included more respondents with FM (58 %) than with CP (42 %).

At the time t_2 (6 months after inclusion), 53.6 % of respondents reported having received PT within the past 6 months. Due to missing responses in the questionnaires, the data sets of 170 participants were unavailable for the frequency analysis of repeat PT. Among the remaining 256 participants, 34.4 % reported having

Table 13.3 Sociodemographic, disease-related, and utilization-related variables of the included cases; FFbH: Hannover Functional Ability Questionnaire

Variable		Frequencies *n* ($n=426$)
Age in categories	*20–39*	33
(missing: $n=1$)	*40–59*	217
	60+	175
Sex	*Male/female*	38/388
Main diagnosis:	*Chronic polyarthritis*	179
(missing: $n=0$)	*Fibromyalgia*	247
Year diagnosed, in categories	*1951–1990*	77
(missing: $n=3$)	*1991 or later*	346
FFbH with categories	*Up to 50*	74
(missing: $n=1$)	*51–75 points*	174
	76–100 points	177
PT with the past 6 months (t_2)	*Yes/no*	228/197
(missing: $n=1$)		
PT with the past 6 months (t_2 *and* t_4)	*Yes/no*	88/168
(missing: $n=170$)		

received PT within the past 6 months at times t_2 and t_4 (18 months after inclusion). This was interpreted as repeat utilization (Table 13.3).

Predictors of direct utilization of PT

Total sample

Among the 426 data sets, 366 could be included in the predictor analysis for the total sample. The other data sets were excluded due to missing responses in one or multiple independent variables of the regression analysis. We found no significant differences in selected prognostic variables (age, sex, time since diagnosis, functional ability, quality of life, and depressive symptoms) between analyzed and incomplete data sets.

Two variables were found to significantly influence the utilization of PT in the following 6 months. However, the variance explained by the model was low (Nagelkerke $R^2=0.077$). In the first step, physical functional ability (FFbH) was included in the model. We found that participants with lower scores in the FFbH were more likely to receive PT than patients with higher functional ability (FFbH up to 50 points: odds ratio (OR): 2.25; 95%-confidence interval (CI): 1.20–4.21 ($p<0.01$); FFbH 51–75 points: OR: 2.50; 95%-CI: 1.55–4.02 ($p<0.001$); reference: FFbH 76–100 points). Educational level was the second predictor that was included in the model. Participants with a lower secondary school education exhibited lower utilization than those with university entrance qualification (OR: 0.51; 95%-CI 0.28–0.96 ($p=0.035$)) (Table 13.4). All other variables were not included in the model. Figures 13.1 and 13.2 show the prevalence distributions of PT utilization for the two predictors.

Chronic polyarthritis

Among the 179 participants with CP, we were able to include 150 in the regression analysis. Two of the examined predictors were incrementally included in the model. However, the explained variance was low (Nagelkerke $R^2=0.127$). In the first step, the KKG variable "internal locus of control" was found to be a significant predictor, and in a second step, the FKV subscale "distraction and self-encouragement." High internal locus of control was negatively associated with the utilization of PT (OR=0.91; 95%-CI 0.86–0.97 ($p<0.01$)). Regarding the FKV subscale, higher values in "distraction and self-encouragement" were associated with utilization of PT in the following 6 months (OR: 1.94; 95%-CI 1.12–3.37 ($p<0.05$)).

Fibromyalgia

Among the 247 data sets of participants with FM that were originally included in the analysis, 216 were included in the model. None of the selected variables were identified as significant predictors of PT utilization.

Predictors of repeat utilization of PT

Total sample

Among the 426 included data sets, we were able to analyze 225 for repeat utilization of PT using logistic regression. Again, the remaining data had to be excluded due to missing responses on the variables in the model. The respondents whose data sets could be analyzed had significantly lower scores in the FFbH (67.48 vs. 71.80; $p=0.01$) and in the somatic subscale (25.35 vs. 34.36; $p<0.001$) of the SF-36. Further, a significantly higher percentage of men (10 vs. 28; $p<0.001$) were excluded from the analysis, and included patients had a shorter time since diagnosis (5.44 vs. 6.80; $p=0.01$)

None of the independent variables that were included as predictors in the analysis met the criteria for inclusion in the predictor model.

Chronic polyarthritis

Only 58 of 179 data sets could be included in the model. No significant predictors were identified by the model.

Table 13.4 Significant predictors of direct utilization of PT (t_2); OR = Odds ratio, FFbH = Hannover Functional Ability Questionnaire, KKG = Questionnaire for the assessment of disease and health locus of control, FKV = Freiburg questionnaire on coping with illness

All participants (n=366, missing: n=60)			CP (n=150, missing: n=29)			FM (n=216, missing: n=31)		
Predictor	OR (95% CI)	p-value	Predictor	OR (95% CI)	p-value	Predictor	OR (95% CI)	p-value
FFbH:			*KKG*					
Up to 50 points	2.25 (1.20–4.21)	0.01	Internal locus of control	0.90 (0.85–0.96)	0.002			
51–75 points	2.50 (1.55–4.02)	<0.001						
76–100 points (reference)								
Level of education:			*FKV*					
No degree	1.99 (0.57–6.99)	0.283	Distraction and self-encouragement:	1.94 (1.12–3.37)	0.018			
Lowest secondary school degree	0.51 (0.28–0.96)	0.035						
Mid-level secondary school degree	0.61 (0.31–1.19)	0.148						
University entrance qualification (reference)								

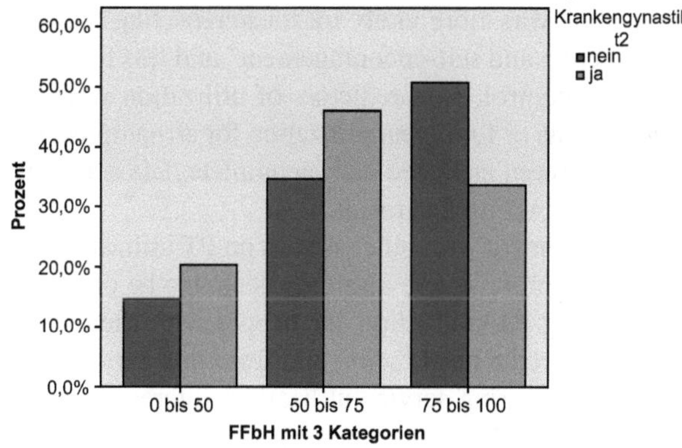

Fig. 13.1 Frequency distribution for functional ability (FFbH) of the total sample

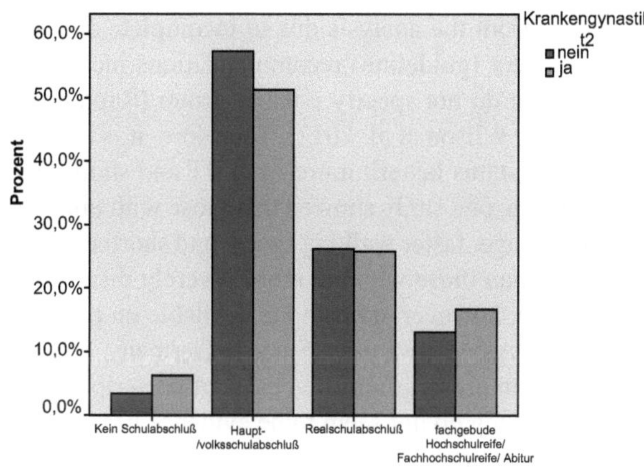

Fig. 13.2 Frequency distribution for level of education in the total sample

Fibromyalgia

Among the 247 data sets of participants with FM that were originally included in the analysis, 216 were included in the model. None of the selected variables were identified as significant predictors of PT utilization.

Discussion

The results of this secondary data analysis show that only direct utilization of PT could be partially predicted by various factors of the model. For the total group, the only significant positive predictor of utilization (which is predominantly based on doctor's prescriptions) was more severe functional disability. Patients with university entrance qualification were almost twice as likely to utilize PT. However, this result barely missed significance level. In the subgroup of RA patients, PT utilization was more likely for those reporting higher scores in the coping strategy "distraction and self-encouragement" and less likely for those with a higher internal locus of control. No predictors of utilization were found for direct utilization by FM patients or for repeat utilization for all samples. However, the significant differences between analyzed and incomplete data sets must be taken into consideration when interpreting this result.

In agreement with other studies on PT utilization in Germany, greater severity of disease or more severe disability seems to be of one of the most significant factors influencing PT utilization for people with rheumatism. Functional disability can be considered a need factor, and from this perspective, it seems to be a reasonable factor for steering service utilization. Interestingly, however, this predictor cannot be confirmed in the subgroups, possibly as a result of insufficient sample size as a limiting factor. It could also be an insignificant predictor of repeat PT utilization because significantly more patients with severe somatic and mental disability were excluded from the analysis due to incomplete data sets, thereby reducing the contrast. Current (guideline) recommendations include a general note that PT should be used but do not specify a target group (Raptopoulou et al. 2008, van den Berg et al. 2012, Wilson et al. 2012). Therefore, it is unclear whether patients with a low functional status benefit more from PT and should receive more therapy. Only for OA patients, one study showed that those with unilateral hip pain, lower pain intensity, lower age, faster walking speed, and shorter duration of symptoms benefit from PT more than those who are more severely disabled (Feldman et al. 2007). To our knowledge, however, no data are available on patients with other diagnoses and or on direct physical disability. Since in Germany, PT utilization is strongly influenced by physician prescriptions, the basis of prescription practices is an important issue. Currently, they do not seem to be evidence based.

Among enabling factors, the predictor "lower secondary school degree" is associated with lower utilization than "university entrance qualification," suggesting that utilization is dependent on social status. It would be interesting to determine the basis of this association. There may be a secondary factor, for instance, patients with lower educational level visiting physicians less frequently and therefore receive fewer prescriptions, or that receiving fewer prescriptions despite equal numbers of physician visits. In Canada, for instance, RA patients of lower socioeconomic status wait longer to consult a physician (Feldman et al. 2007). However, a direct association is conceivable as well. Iversen and colleagues also identified this predictor for RA patients in the USA (Iversen et al. 2011). To our knowledge, no data on this topic are available for Germany. This could indicate that despite SHI, social barriers may limit PT utilization. However, we must note that the results barely missed significance level.

Interestingly, only predisposing factors could be identified as predictors in the subgroup of RA patients. For instance, coping strategies that are largely based on distraction and self-encouragement are associated with greater utilization of PT. It remains unclear whether PT utilization partially results from this strategy or represents part of it. A slightly less pronounced negative predictor in this patient group is a stronger internal locus of control. This may also lead to reduced utilization of support from others, such as physical therapists. Again, it is conceivable that this is influenced by the physician visit.

Although nearly 45 % of FM patients received PT, no predictors could be identified. We can only suspect that this is a sign of noncontrolled utilization. Since nationally and internationally few data are available on utilization and its determinants in FM patients, more research is required in this area.

Repeat utilization could not be predicted by any predictors in any study samples. The small sample size of cases that could be included in the analysis is likely a decisive limiting factor.

In addition to small sample size, limitations include the method of secondary data analysis. For instance, this method makes faulty data or data loss more difficult to trace. In addition, no a priori, theory-based investigation of potential indicators is possible. Another limiting factor is the fact that due to missing or incomplete data, only part of the primarily analyzed data sets was included in the regression analysis on utilization. In the present study, this resulted in a high percentage of incomplete data sets. Some of the variables used to compare complete versus incomplete data sets also differed significantly, although the differences were minor from a clinical perspective. Further, selection bias cannot be ruled out since one-quarter of the respondents were recruited in PT practices, and nearly 100 % utilization prevalence can be assumed for this group. This could have biased results, at least regarding the prevalence of utilization. Nevertheless, this study is important to supplement and expand the existing, very limited data on the PT utilization of rheumatism patients in Germany.

In summary, these data expand and at least partially support existing knowledge. For instance, patients with more severe functional disability more frequently take advantage of PT. This utilization pattern is not supported by evidence-based medicine, however. We also found indications of social influencing variables like educational qualification. In RA patients, in contrast, predisposing factors such as locus of control and coping mechanism influence (indirect) utilization behavior. However, we found no predictors for FM patients and repeat utilization. In the future, a greater effort must be made to increase the available data on determinants and predictors of utilization. In addition, strategies must be developed to optimize utilization.

References

Andersen R. 2008. National health surveys and the behavioral model of health services use. Med Care 46(7):647–653.

Andrianakos AA, Miyakis S, Trontzas P, Kaziolas G, Christoyannis F, Karamitsos D, Karanikolas G, Dantis P. 2005. The burden of the rheumatic diseases in the general adult population of Greece: the ESORDIG study. Rheumatology (Oxford) 44(7):932–938.

Baillet A, Vaillant M, Guinot M, Juvin R, Gaudin P. 2012. Efficacy of resistance exercises in rheumatoid arthritis: meta-analysis of randomized controlled trials. Rheumatology (Oxford) 51(3):519–527.

Baillet A, Zeboulon N, Gossec L, Combescure C, Bodin L, Juvin R, Dougados M, Gaudin P. 2010. Efficacy of cardiorespiratory aerobic exercise in rheumatoid arthritis: meta-analysis of randomized controlled trials. Arthritis Care Res (Hoboken) 62(7):984–992.

Berkanovic E, Hurwicz ML, Batchlor E. 1991. Rheumatoid arthritis and the use of medical services. Arthritis Care Res 4(1):12–21.

Bernatsky S, Joseph L, Pineau CA, Tamblyn R, Feldman DE, Clarke AE. 2007. A population-based assessment of systemic lupus erythematosus incidence and prevalence–results and implications of using administrative data for epidemiological studies. Rheumatology (Oxford) 46(12):1814–1818.

Borgetto B, Stößel U, editors. 2011. Gemeinschaftliche Selbsthilfe und medizinische Versorgung Rheumakranker. LIT-Verlag: Münster.

Borgetto B, Kirchner C, Kolba N, Stößel U. 2008. Selbsthilfe und Ehrenamt in der rheumatologischen Versorgung. Ergebnisse einer empirischen Untersuchung der Struktur und Prozeßqualität der Selbsthilfeaktivitäten und Versorgungsangebote der Rheuma-Liga Baden-Württemberg e.V. LIT-Verlag, Münster.

Brosseau LU, Pelland LU, Casimiro LY, Robinson VI, Tugwell PE, Wells GE. 2002. Electrical stimulation for the treatment of rheumatoid arthritis. Cochrane Database Syst Rev (2):CD003687.

Bundesverwaltungsgericht. 2009. http://www.bverwg.de/enid/0,e7ead8655f76696577092d096465 7461696c093a09636f6e5f6964092d093132343530093a095f7472636964092d093133333232/ Entscheidungen/Entscheidung_8n.html: Zugang: 05.12.2012

Carmona L, Ballina J, Gabriel R, Laffon A. 2001. The burden of musculoskeletal diseases in the general population of Spain: results from a national survey. Ann Rheum Dis 60(11):1040–1045.

Dagfinrud H, Kvien TK, Hagen KB. 2008. Physiotherapy interventions for ankylosing spondylitis. Cochrane Database Syst Rev (1):CD002822.

Dziedzic K, Jordan J, Foster N. 2008. Land- and water-based exercise therapies for musculoskeletal conditions. Best Pract Res Clin Rheumatol 22(3):407–418.

Feldman DE, Bernatsky S, Haggerty J, Leffondre K, Tousignant P, Roy Y, Xiao Y, Zummer M, Abrahamowicz M. 2007. Delay in consultation with specialists for persons with suspected new-onset rheumatoid arthritis: a population-based study. Arthritis Rheum 57(8):1419–1425.

Hsieh JB, Dominick KL. 2003. Use of non-pharmacological therapies among patients with osteoarthritis. Aging Clin Exp Res 15(5):419–425.

IFK. Modellvorhaben/Direct Access. http://www.ifk.de/verband/verband/ifk-positionspapiere/ 562-direct-access-modellvorhaben. Zugang: 05.12.2012

Iversen MD, Chhabriya RK, Shadick N. 2011. Predictors of the use of PT services among patients with rheumatoid arthritis. Phys Ther 91(1):65–76.

Jacobi C, Boshuizen H, Rupp I, Dinant H, van d. 2004. Quality of rheumatoid arthritis care: the patient's perspective. Int J Qual Health Care 16(1):73–81.

Jamtvedt G, Dahm K, Christie A, Moe R, Haavardsholm E, Holm I, Hagen K. 2008. PT interventions for patients with osteoarthritis of the knee: an overview of systematic reviews. Phys Ther 88(1):123–136.

Kahn KL, MacLean CH, Liu H, Rubenstein LZ, Wong AL, Harker JO, Chen W, Fitzpatrick DM, Bulpitt KJ, Traina SB, Mittman BS, Hahn BH, Paulus HE. 2007. The complexity of care for patients with rheumatoid arthritis: metrics for better understanding chronic disease care. Med Care 45(1):55–65.

Kaipiainen-Seppanen O, Aho K. 2000. Incidence of chronic inflammatory joint diseases in Finland in 1995. J Rheumatol 27(1):94–100.

Kelley GA, Kelley KS. 2011. Exercise improves global well-being in adults with fibromyalgia: confirmation of previous meta-analytic results using a recently developed and novel varying coefficient model. Clin Exp Rheumatol 29(6 Suppl 69):S60 2.

Kohlmann T, Raspe H. 1996. [Hannover Functional Questionnaire in ambulatory diagnosis of functional disability caused by backache]: Der Funktionsfragebogen Hannover zur alltagsnahen Diagnostik der Funktionsbeeintrachtigung durch Ruckenschmerzen (FFbH-R). Rehabilitation (Stuttg) 35(1):I–VIII.

Lange A, Vanwanseele B, Fiatarone S. 2008. Strength training for treatment of osteoarthritis of the knee: a systematic review. Arthritis Rheum 59(10):1488–1494.

Li L, Maetzel A, Pencharz J, Maguire L, Bombardier C. 2004. Use of mainstream nonpharmacologic treatment by patients with arthritis. Arthritis Rheum 51(2):203–209.

Lohaus A, Schmitt GM. 1989Fragebogen zur Erhebung von Kontrollüberzeugungen zu Krankheit und Gesundheit (KKG). Handanweisung. Hogrefe, Göttingen.

Mau W, Müller A. 2008. [Rehabilitation and outpatient physiotherapy in rheumatic disease patients. Results of cross-sectional studies of patients with rheumatoid arthritis or ankylosing spondylitis and rheumatologists]: Rehabilitative und ambulante physikalisch-medizinische Versorgung von Rheumakranken. Ergebnisse der Befragungen von Patienten mit rheumatoider Arthritis oder ankylosierender Spondylitis und Rheumatologen. Z Rheumatol 67(7):542–553.

McVeigh J, McGaughey H, Hall M, Kane P. 2008. The effectiveness of hydrotherapy in the management of fibromyalgia syndrome: a systematic review. Rheumatol Int 29(2):119–130.

Muthny F. 1989. Freiburger Fragebogen zur Krankheitsverarbeitung (FKV). Manual. Beltz Test GmbH, Weinheim.

Nagel B, Gerbershagen HU, Lindena G, Pfingsten M. 2002. Entwicklung und empirische Uberprufung des Deutschen Schmerzfragebogens der DGSS. Schmerz 16(4):263–270.

Ottawa Panel Members. 2004. Ottawa Panel evidence-based clinical practice guidelines for therapeutic exercises in the management of rheumatoid arthritis in adults. Phys Ther 84(10):934–972.

Parikh RM, Eden DT, Price TR, Robinson RG. 1988. The sensitivity and specificity of the Center for Epidemiologic Studies Depression Scale in screening for post-stroke depression. Int J Psychiatry Med 18(2):169–181.

Raptopoulou A, Sidiropoulos P, Siakka P, Boki K, Drosos AA, Aslanidis S, Karras D, Pikazis D, Vassilopoulos D, Karassa F, Boumpas DT. 2008. Evidence-based recommendations for the management of ankylosing spondylitis: results of the Hellenic working group of the 3E Initiative in Rheumatology. Clin Exp Rheumatol 26(5):784–792.

Rheumabericht der Bundesregierung 1997. Bundestags-Drucksache 13/8434.

Robinson V, Brosseau L, Casimiro L, Judd M, Shea B, Wells G, Tugwell P. 2002. Thermotherapy for treating rheumatoid arthritis. Cochrane Database Syst Rev (2):CD002826.

Sauer K, Kemper C, Glaeske G. 2011. Fibromyalgia syndrome: prevalence, pharmacological and non-pharmacological interventions in outpatient health care. An analysis of statutory health insurance data. Joint Bone Spine 78(1):80–84.

Scheel K. 2012. Modellvorhaben: Physiotherapie zwischen Autonomie und Fremdkontrolle. Public Health Forum 20(4): 20.e1–20.e3.

Schneider M, Lelgemann M, Abholz HILdfASVD2I3. 2011. Interdisziplinäre Leitlinie-Management der frühen Arthritis. 3rd ed. Springer Verlag, Berlin.

Schneider S, Schmitt G, Richter W. 2006. Prevalence and correlates of inflammatory arthritis in Germany: data from the First National Health Survey. Rheumatol Int 27(1):29–38.

Sommer G, Fydrich T. 1991. Entwicklung und Überprüfung eines Fragebogens zur sozialen Unterstützung. Diagnostica (37):160–178.

Sun J, Gooch K, Svenson L, Bell N, Frank C. 2007. Estimating osteoarthritis incidence from population-based administrative health care databases. Ann Epidemiol 17(1):51–56.

Symmons DPM. 2002. Epidemiology of rheumatoid arthritis: determinants of onset, persistence and outcome. Best Pract Res Clin Rheumatol 16(5):707–722.

Thieme H, Borgetto B. Utilisation of rheumatology care services in Germany: the case of physical therapy and self-help groups. GMS Psychosoc Med 2012: 9.

Thieme H, Borgetto B. 2011. Physiotherapeutische Versorgung von Menschen mit rheumatischen Erkrankungen. In: Borgetto B, Stößel U (Hrsg): Gemeinschaftliche Selbsthilfe und medizinische Versorgung Rheumakranker LIT-Verlag, Münster, Hamburg, Berlin, S. 210–129.

Thieme H, Löffler K, Borgetto B. 2009. Physiotherapeutische und ergotherapeutische Versorgung bei Rheumatoider Arthritis. In: Kemper C, Sauer K, Gläske G (Hrsg): GEK-Heil und Hilfsmittelreport 2009. Asgard-Verlag, St. Augustin, S. 84.96.

Thomas A, Eichenberger G, Kempton C, Pape D, York S, Decker A, Kohia M. 2009. Recommendations for the treatment of knee osteoarthritis, using various therapy techniques, based on categorizations of a literature review. J Geriatr Phys Ther 32(1):33–38.

van den Berg R, Baraliakos X, Braun J, van der Heijde D. 2012. First update of the current evidence for the management of ankylosing spondylitis with non-pharmacological treatment and non-biologic drugs: a systematic literature review for the ASAS/EULAR management recommendations in ankylosing spondylitis. Rheumatology (Oxford).

van den Ende CH, Vliet Vlieland TP, Munneke M, Hazes JM. 2000. Dynamic exercise therapy for rheumatoid arthritis. Cochrane Database Syst Rev (2):CD000322.

Vliet V, Li LC. 2009. Rehabilitation in rheumatoid arthritis and ankylosing spondylitis: differences and similarities. Clin Exp Rheumatol 27(4 Suppl 55):S171–8.

Wagner E, Lackerbauer E, Siegmeth W. 2005. [Direct and indirect costs of rheumatoid arthritis and the socio-emotional effects of this disease–an Austrian study]: Direkte und indirekte Kosten der chronischen Polyarthritis und sozio-emotionale Auswirkungen dieser Krankheit–eine Untersuchung in Osterreich. Wien Med Wochenschr 155(9–10):217–226.

Waltz M. 2000. The disease process and utilization of health services in rheumatoid arthritis: the relative contributions of various markers of disease severity in explaining consumption patterns. Arthritis Care Res 13(2):74–88.

Weissman MM, Sholomskas D, Pottenger M, Prusoff BA, Locke BZ. 1977. Assessing depressive symptoms in five psychiatric populations: a validation study. Am J Epidemiol 106(3):203–214.

Westhovens R, Boonen A, Verbruggen L, Durez P, De C, Malaise M, Mielants H. 2005. Healthcare consumption and direct costs of rheumatoid arthritis in Belgium. Clin Rheumatol 24(6):615–619.

Wilson B, Spencer H, Kortebein P. 2012. Exercise recommendations in patients with newly diagnosed fibromyalgia. PM R 4(4):252–255.

Zich JM, Attkisson CC, Greenfield TK. 1990. Screening for depression in primary care clinics: the CES-D and the BDI. Int J Psychiatry Med 20(3):259–277.

Zink A, Listing J, Ziemer S, Zeidler H. 2001. Practice variation in the treatment of rheumatoid arthritis among German rheumatologists. J Rheumatol 28(10):2201–2208.

Zink A, Thiele K, Huscher D, Listing J, Sieper J, Krause A, Gromnica-Ihle E, von H, Wassenberg S, Genth E, Schneider M. 2006. Healthcare and burden of disease in psoriatic arthritis. A comparison with rheumatoid arthritis and ankylosing spondylitis. J Rheumatol 33(1):86–90.

Zink A, Huscher D, Listing J. 2003. [The National Database of the Regional Collaborative Rheumatic Centers as a tool for clinical epidemiology and quality assessment in rheumatology]: Die Kerndokumentation der Regionalen Kooperativen Rheumazentren als Instrument der klinischen Epidemiologie und der Qualitatssicherung der rheumatologischen Versorgung. Z Arztl Fortbild Qualitatssich 97(6):399–405.

Chapter 14
Participation in Self-Help Activities Among Patients with Rheumatic Diseases

Bernhard Borgetto and Holm Thieme

Introduction

Individual responsibility, self-help, and active cooperation of patients and their relatives are essential for optimizing health care. In the professional health-care system, the limitations of medical and psychosocial care in the treatment of chronic diseases and disabilities often become apparent. Alongside the professional health-care system, self-help associations therefore make an important contribution by helping people with chronic diseases and disabilities as well as their relatives to cope with illness and improve their quality of life. Factors that influence participation and involvement in self-help associations are therefore highly relevant in health services research and in the field of rheumatic diseases,[1] and they are the subject of the secondary analysis of rheumatic disease care data that is presented in this chapter.

Since self-help associations can significantly differ in structure, operation, and offered services, we will first provide a general overview of the definition and concepts of community self-help as well as the principal results of self-help effectiveness research. Using the example of a federal state association [*Landesverband*], we will discuss in detail the German League against Rheumatism [*Deutsche Rheuma-Liga*] as one of the most important and largest rheumatism self-help associations in Germany, and we will present the available results of research on the effectiveness of self-help in rheumatism.

[1] An overview of rheumatic diseases and their epidemiological significance is presented in Chap. 13.

B. Borgetto (✉) · H. Thieme
Faculty of Social Work and Health, HAWK—University of Applied Sciences and Arts, Faculty of Social Work and Health, Hildesheim, Germany
e-mail: borgetto@hawk-hhg.de

H. Thieme
e-mail: agf_thieme@hawk-hhg.de

C. Janssen et al. (eds.), *Health Care Utilization in Germany*,
DOI 10.1007/978-1-4614-9191-0_14,

Definition and Conceptual Foundations

Currently, there are no binding definitions of the terminology associated with the concept of self-help, neither in Germany nor internationally. The definitions presented here from the perspective of self-help research in German-speaking countries (Borgetto 2004) are intended for the scientific systematization of these phenomena; in practice, the usage of the terminology may vary. Self-help associations are voluntary associations of people who strive toward collaborative coping with diseases and/or mental disorders and their sequelae that affect them or their relatives. Generally, self-help groups (SHGs) and self-help organizations (SHOs) are differentiated.

Associations of affected people in groups whose members personally know one another are considered SHGs. Some groups are led by group members. The definition as an SHG significantly depends on whether the leader is personally affected by the disease, regardless of whether this person is a medical/health layperson or expert/professional care provider. SHGs that focus on the concerns and problems of their own members are considered inwardly oriented groups, while SHGs that also counsel and represent the interests of other affected individuals are considered externally oriented groups.

Unlike SHGs, SHOs have national offices representing their interests, typically more members, formalized work and administrative procedures, specific legal forms, and, often, extensive contacts to professional systems. SHOs can arise from mergers of several SHGs or support SHGs and stimulate their foundation. Particularly older SHOs, however, were often established at the suggestion and with the support of health professionals. SHOs provide consultation and information services to people much beyond their own membership.

The principal objectives of SHOs are providing information for consulting affected patients and their relatives, providing services for the regional divisions and SHGs, conducting and promoting research, collaborating within the health-care system, providing therapeutic services, public relations, and representing people with the respective disorder on a national level.

We can further distinguish between people who use and those who actively contribute to self-help activities. While the latter are active in the sense that they use as well as organize the programs and activities of self-help associations, self-help users take advantage of these services without being involved in creating them.

Principal Results of Self-Help Effectiveness Research

The results of existing health services research within the lay system show that particularly SHGs contribute to mutual social support, patient education, and changes in attitude in the affected patients and their social environment (Borgetto 2004). They relieve the patients' primary social networks and support more targeted utilization of professional services. Except for counseling services, the activities and other assistance offered by SHOs have been little researched so far.

The effectiveness of self-help is based on conversations between similarly affected people, particularly when participating in SHGs, during social events in a group, or during counseling (Borgetto 2004). "Self-help communication" is based on the "experienced and suffered expertise" of affected people. Communication serves not only to exchange information but also to strengthen social relationships between affected people that arise through the involvement in self-help associations.

Study results on the operation and activities of SHGs suggest that four dimensions of communication between affected individuals should be distinguished, the intensity and context of which depend on the respective self-help activities: exchanging experiences, conveying information, verbalizing feelings, and holding conversations without specific purpose (see Daum 1984; Borgetto et al. 2008). These dimensions are associated with various mechanisms of action known from stress research and psychotherapy research, for instance, model-based learning, self-discovery, mutual emotional support, broadening of the individual knowledge base, processing of the past, etc. (see Matzat 1999; Borgetto 2004).

Primary effects of self-help are *changes in behavior*, individual *personal development*, and relief or *strengthening of social networks*. Kyrouz, Humphreys, and Loomis (2002) provide an overview of the most important empirical results of international self-help effectiveness research, to which we will further refer below.

Changes in behavior are expected to directly impact health. Empirical studies indicate that this is particularly the case for SHGs for addictions, eating disorders, and diabetes. According to existing studies, more efficient utilization of services within the professional health-care system and increased compliance can be achieved regardless of the respective diagnosis, thereby increasing the effectiveness and efficiency of health care.

Personal development is based on the therapy-esque interactions between affected people. The effects of conversation-based SHGs have been found to be comparable with those of group psychotherapy (Daum 1984). Accordingly, SHGs reduce mental disorders and increase subjective health and quality of life.

Stress research has revealed that successful social relationships generally reduce susceptibility to disease and directly affect health by strengthening the immune system (Borgetto 2010). Many studies, predominantly using a retrospective assessment by group participants, confirm that participation in SHGs relieves and strengthens partnerships for most participants, improves relationships with family members and friends, activates social involvement, and increases the person's social network (Trojan 1986; Braun et al. 1997; Borgetto 2004).

Direct evidence of *salutogenic* and *tertiary preventive* effects of SHGs has also been found, including better coping with and reduction of addictions and other health-impairing behaviors, alleviation of depression and depressive symptoms, improvement of subjective well-being, self-confidence, and quality of life, as well as better coping with diseases and disabilities. Several studies provide indirect evidence of the alleviation of mental disorders through the directly measured, distinctly reduced utilization of inpatient services by participants of SHGs for the mentally ill (Edmunson et al. 1982; Kurtz 1988).

Self-Help in Rheumatic Disorders

People with rheumatic disorders experience their disease as a comprehensive, holistic problem that is continuously present throughout their daily lives. In contrast, medical services—including rheumatology care—are characterized by division of labor and increasing specialization. Simultaneously, the health-care system suffers from growing financing problems that hamper further development of the offered services and even restrict services that are currently available.

In this context, services have been developed for people suffering from a variety of disorders, including rheumatism (see Borgetto 2004); these services pick up on the above deficits and are organized largely in self-help settings by volunteers-affected individuals, dedicated laypeople, and health-care professionals. For rheumatic disorders, the majority of these services are provided by the German League against Rheumatism and its state and member associations.

The German League Against Rheumatism

The German League against Rheumatism is a complex organization that includes a multitude of collective and individual stakeholders. Today's structure of one federal association and several state associations as well as member associations, some of which in turn have their own state associations, did not result from the merger of smaller collective stakeholders such as SHGs on a national level. On the contrary, in 1970, the federal association of the German League against Rheumatism was founded as a nonprofit association, the first association of professionals, patients, and dedicated citizens.

The individual state associations then formed as members of the federal association. Furthermore, three member associations have joined the German League against Rheumatism: the German Bechterew's Disease Association [*Deutsche Vereinigung Morbus Bechterew*], the Lupus Erythematosus Self-Help Association [*Lupus Erythematodes Selbsthilfegemeinschaft*], and Scleroderma Self-Help [*Sklerodermie Selbsthilfe*].

The federal association of the German League against Rheumatism is itself a member of the Federal Association of SHOs [*Bundesarbeitsgemeinschaft Selbsthilfe e.V.*], the Association of Non-affiliated Charities [*Deutscher Paritätischer Wohlfahrtsverband*], and the German Disability Council [*Deutscher Behindertenrat*].

Its operational level consists of the Bonn office with exclusively salaried staff. These staff members are hired without regard to whether they suffer from a rheumatic disorder. In the German League against Rheumatism, the federal association has no authority over the state and member associations; it is one association among many in the League against Rheumatism, albeit with coordinating functions on the federal level.

Baden-Württemberg League Against Rheumatism

Since most of the study participants whose data were used for the secondary data analysis live in Baden-Württemberg, the available range of self-help activities and programs will be presented using the example of the Baden-Württemberg state association of the German League against Rheumatism.

With some 50,000 members, the Baden-Württemberg state association is one of the larger state associations within the German League against Rheumatism (Borgetto et al. 2008). There are some regional coalitions that conduct joint training events, but like other state associations, its true basis are local working groups made up of volunteers. With 80 regional and district-level working groups, we can assume statewide coverage with a network of working groups.

The work of the state office is supported by four full-time social workers who support the volunteers in the working groups using the "help for self-help" principle (Zartmann 1996). Each of the four social workers is responsible for one region (North Baden, South Baden, North Württemberg, and South Württemberg) and specific topic areas (parents of rheumatic children, children and youth, professional support of group leaders, support of most severely affected patients, and seminars). The social workers are in constant contact with the working groups and support them as needed, for instance, in the areas of organization, financing, professional and personal support, conflicts between volunteers, and in case of vacant positions and necessary restructuring.

In 2004, the Baden-Württemberg League against Rheumatism had more than 1,700 volunteers involved in the working groups, and more than 80 % of them are estimated to suffer from rheumatic disorders themselves (Borgetto et al. 2008). Hence, the majority of the work on the ground is performed by rheumatism patients who are members of the Baden-Württemberg League against Rheumatism. The work primarily consists of organizing professional help, lay help, social events, and the discussion groups, which are typically completely independent. In addition to the volunteers, a total of about 500 therapists provide the professional services offered by the Baden-Württemberg League against Rheumatism.

The help offered by the Baden-Württemberg League against Rheumatism includes (help for) self-help, lay help, professional help, information and education, individual counseling, and counseling on social law. Self-help is primarily rooted in the discussion groups and task forces of the local and regional working groups. Some of them are tailored to age-specific and diagnosis-specific target groups, such as discussion groups for parents of children with rheumatic disorders, for young people with rheumatism, or for people who suffer from fibromyalgia (FM), rheumatoid arthritis, lupus erythematosus, or other rheumatic disorders, while other discussion groups are open to all members. Self-help programs also include dance and crafts groups as well as social and information events. Lay help is primarily provided by volunteer staff members of the Baden-Württemberg League against Rheumatism who are themselves affected by rheumatic disorders. It pri-

Table 14.1 Programs and activities of the working groups of the Baden-Württemberg League against Rheumatism in 1997–2000

Programs and activities of the Baden-Württemberg League against rheumatism		Percentage of working groups offering the program in the years: 1997–1999[a]	2000[b]
Direct assistance			
Self-help	Discussion groups	55.9	56.5
	Social events	92.5	91.3
Lay help	Counseling	88.2	81.2
	Support of severely affected individuals	29.4	26.1
Professional help	Warm-water exercise	98.5	98.6
	Nonaquatic exercise	98.5	98.6
	Psychological pain management	29.4	13.0
	Occupational therapy	8.8	5.8
Indirect help			
Public relations		No information available[c]	74.7
Information events		89.6	76.8
Rheumatism meetings (lectures, trips, etc.)		75.9	85.5

[a] A retrospective survey in 2000 asked about 1997–1999. The results are based on the responses from 68 working groups

[b] A prospective survey in 2001 asked about the year 2000. The results are based on the responses of 69 working groups

[c] Questions on public relations were only included in the prospective survey in 2001

marily includes phone counseling, personal counseling, visiting services, neighborhood assistance, etc.

Professional help, which is largely organized by affected patients themselves, is an important part of the work of the Baden-Württemberg League against Rheumatism. Functional training (nonaquatic and warm-water exercise), psychological pain management training, and occupational therapy are conducted in professional-led groups. Furthermore, an extensive seminar and training program is offered. In 2002, the Baden-Württemberg League against Rheumatism centrally offered nine seminars for volunteers and 13 seminars for affected patients. The seminars for patients range from basic seminars on specific diseases for patient education to psychosocial services, seminars on relaxation techniques, and leisure seminars.

Table 14.1 provides an overview of the services and activities of working groups of the Baden-Württemberg League against Rheumatism on the basis of survey results from 2000 and 2001 (Borgetto et al. 2008).

The work of the Baden-Württemberg League against Rheumatism is guided by the so-called guidepost, a written guideline in the form of a loose-leaf collection (see Borgetto et al. 2008). It serves as a central steering instrument for the association's management to guide volunteer work and implement the programs within the working groups. It also offers practical tips and assistance for the organization and the implementation of functional training offered in the form of warm-water and nonaquatic exercises. In addition to information on exercise therapy, a catalog of guidelines applies to the preparation, organization, and conduct of discussion groups and consultation services, and the so-called indirect help, such as public relations activities and social and information events, should be organized following this guide as well.

Effects of Self-Help in Patients with Rheumatic Disorders

A study on the psychosocial and health effects of functional training for rheumatism and discussion groups offered by the Baden-Württemberg League against Rheumatism empirically verified the following findings (Borgetto et al. 2008):

- The self-help programs "functional training" and "discussion groups" are among the three most popular programs offered by the Baden-Württemberg League against Rheumatism.
- FM patients who are self-help users more commonly receive most care from their primary care physicians, in compliance with guidelines, than nonusers.
- In contrast, FM patients who are nonusers more frequently receive pain therapy in compliance with guidelines.
- Chronic polyarthritis (CP) patients who are self-help users receive better rheumatologist care than nonusers.
- CP patients who are self-help users more frequently take substances to protect the gastric lining in conjunction with nonsteroidal anti-inflammatory drugs (NSAIDs).
- FM patients who are self-help users exhibit a slower decrease in functional abilities than nonusers.

The data support the conclusion that under everyday conditions, the activities and programs of the Baden-Württemberg League against Rheumatism positively influence the functional abilities of FM patients, the utilization of specialist rheumatologists by CP patients, and predominant care provision by primary care physicians in FM patients, while they do not promote the utilization of pain therapists by FM patients. Thumboo and Strand (2007) also report that participation in self-help classes improves the health-related quality of life of patients with systemic lupus erythematosus.

Secondary Analysis of Predictors of Participation in Rheumatology Self-Help Activities and Programs

The overview of self-help research in general and specifically in the area of rheumatic disorders shows that self-help activities and programs are available throughout Germany and that their psychosocial, health, and health services-related benefits outweigh their disadvantages. However, the determinants of passive and active participation in self-help activities for patients with rheumatism and their relatives are unknown: A national systematic literature search found no relevant data (Thieme & Borgetto 2012).

In this context, a secondary analysis of the RheumaDat Panel (Borgetto et al. 2008) was conducted to supply data on the predictors of participation in self-help activities.

Methods

The data set used in this analysis is the same as in Chap. 13, and it is only briefly presented here.

The RheumaDat Panel is based on a written survey of a cohort of patients with rheumatism over the time period of 2 years, with standardized questionnaires collected semiannually at four time points (t_1–t_4). The panel surveyed a wide spectrum of rheumatological diagnosis groups. Study participants were assigned to the diagnosis groups on the basis of their self-reported information. Therefore, the survey used the terminology commonly used by the lay public: CP, Bechterew's disease, FM, osteoarthritis, scleroderma, lupus erythematosus, vasculitis, and osteoporosis. This secondary data analysis only included data sets from patients who reported CP or FM as their main diagnosis. Additional inclusion criteria were (a) age 18+ and (b) consent to participate in the study. Exclusion criteria were (aa) difficulty in writing and (bb) severe comorbidities or multimorbidity masking the rheumatic illness.

Questionnaire

The study participants were presented with questionnaires consisting of single questions and standardized survey instruments. Utilization of medical services was recorded at all four time points using the survey instrument V-RHEUMA, which was developed for this study. The investigation of predictors for participation in SHGs was based on the variable "participation in SH activities (functional training and/or discussion group): yes/no" at the time points t_2 and t_4. The time point t_2 was used for the first surveyed participation in the study period (hereafter: direct participation). For calculating predictors of further utilization within the study period, we included the respondents who reported having participated in SHG activities within the previous 6 months for time points t_2 and t_4.

Independent variables were selected on the basis of Andersen's model (Andersen and Davidson 2007). We differentiated between need factors, predisposing factors, and enabling factors. The majority of the independent variables are presented in more detail in Chap. 13.

Need Factors

- Time of diagnosis
- Functional ability (Hannover functional ability questionnaire (FFbH-X))
- Depression/depressive symptoms (CES-D)

Predisposing Factors

- Age
- Sex
- Locus of control (questionnaire on the health locus of control (Lohaus and Schmitt 1989))
- Coping: The Freiburg Questionnaire of Coping with Illness (Freiburger Fragebogen zur Krankheitsverarbeitung, FKV) surveys coping with disease at various levels, such as cognition, emotion, and behavior (Muthny 1989). The brief version of the FKV for self-assessment (FKV-LIS-FE) consists of 35 items and five scales. The five scales are: depressive coping, active problem-focused coping, distraction and self-encouragement, religious faith and search for meaning, as well as minimization and wishful thinking.

Enabling Factors

- Level of education.
- Occupational training.
- Income.
- Social support (F-Sozu) (Sommer and Fydrich 1991).
- Marriage status: The participants were asked whether they were married or not. The variable is therefore dichotomous.

Study Sample

The secondary data analysis included the data sets of CP and FM patients that were available for the times t_1, t_2, and t_4 ($n=426$). Subgroup analyses were conducted separately for patients of the two diagnosis groups. We examined predictors of direct and repeat participation in self-help programs at the time t_1.

Statistical Analysis

For the sociodemographic data, descriptive statistics and frequency distributions were calculated. Group differences were tested for significance using the *t*-test for

Table 14.2 Sociodemographic, disease-related, and care-related variables

Variable		Number of participants *n* (*n*=426)
Age, in categories (missing: *n*=1)	20–39	33
	40–59	217
	60+	175
Sex	Male/female	38/388
Main diagnosis (missing: *n*=3)	Chronic polyarthritis	179
	Fibromyalgia	247
Year diagnosed, in categories (missing: *n*=3)	1951–1989	77
	1990 or later	346
FFbH with categories (missing: *n*=1)	Up to 49 points	74
	50–74 points	174
	75–100 points	177
SHA participation within the preceding 6 months (t2)	Yes/no	257/169
SHA participation within the preceding 6 months (t2 and t4) (missing: *n*=165)	Yes/no	141/120

FFbH Hannover Functional Ability Questionnaire, *SHA* self-help activities

interval-scaled data, the Mann–Whitney U test for ordinal scaled data, and the chi-squared test for dichotomous data. The predictor analysis was conducted using binary logistic regression. All independent variables were incrementally included in the model. The reference category for categorical variables was determined using content considerations. Significant predictors of utilization were determined based on a *p*-value of 0.05. The statistical analysis was conducted using the software PASW 18 for Windows.

Results

Sample Description

A total of 901 participants were recruited for the survey; 610 participants reported the diagnosis CP or FM at the time t_1. Among them, 426 completed the questionnaire at time points t_1, t_2, and t_4 and were therefore, in general, suitable for inclusion in the secondary data analysis. Table 14.2 provides an overview of the most important sociodemographic and disease-related characteristics of this subsample.

Among the analyzed respondents, 60.3 % had participated in self-help activities (functional training and/or discussion group) within the preceding 6 months at time point t_2 (6 months after inclusion). At the time t_4, the information from 165 participants was incomplete for calculating the frequency distribution of continued participation. Among the remaining 261 participants, slightly more than half (54.0 %) reported having participated in self-help activities within the preceding 6 months

Table 14.3 Differences between the total group of generally suitable cases and the subgroup of those excluded from the analysis

Variable	Generally suitable (n=426)	Cases with incomplete data (n=184)	p-value
Age in years (mean ± SD)	55.73 ± 11.44	58.86 ± 12.46	<0.01
Sex (w(%)/m(%))	388/38	160/26	0.06
Duration of illness in years (mean ± SD)	7.02 ± 7.42	9.25 ± 9.85	<0.01
Main diagnosis			
Chronic polyarthritis	179	108	<0.01
Fibromyalgia	248	79	0.001
Somatic functional ability (FFbH) (mean ± SD)	69.51 ± 18.88	65.90 ± 22.25	<0.05
Depressive symptoms (CES-D) (mean ± SD)	19.92 ± 10.81	19.55 ± 10.75	0.69
LQ: Somatic component summary score (SF-36) (mean ± SD)	29.60 ± 23.25	27.93 ± 21.62	0.43
LQ: Mental component summary score (SF-36) (mean ± SD)	55.04 ± 29.67	53.47 ± 31.17	0.57

FFbH Hannover Functional Abilities Questionnaire, *CES-D* Center for Epidemiological Studies Depression Scale, *LQ* quality of life, SF-36 short form-36

at time points t_2 and t_4 (18 months after inclusion). This was classified as "repeat" utilization.

A total of 184 respondents had to be excluded from the analysis because data relevant to the problem asked by the secondary analysis were missing. We analyzed the data of participants who were generally suitable and those who were excluded because of incomplete data sets for differences in important characteristics (Table 14.3).

Predictors of Direct Participation in Self-Help Programs

Total Sample

We were able to include 367 of the 426 data sets into the analysis. The remaining data sets were missing answers in one or more variables of the analysis. No significant differences in selected prognostic variables (age, sex, time since diagnosis, functional ability, quality of life, and depressive moods) were found between analyzed and incomplete data sets.

The identified predictors explained a substantial proportion of variance (Nagelkerne R^2=0.19). Significant predictors were sex, the FKV subscale "active problem-focused coping," the F-Sozu subscales "emotional support" and "satisfaction with emotional support," and participant marriage status. Men were less likely to participate in self-help activities than women were. Participants with a higher score in active problem-focused coping more frequently participated in self-help activities, and so did participants with lower scores in social support and satisfaction with social support. Married participants were more than twice as likely to participate in self-help activities (Table 14.4).

Chronic Polyarthritis

Among 179 respondents with CP, 150 were included in the analysis. However, the predictor model only explained a small proportion of variance (Nagelkerne $R^2=0.10$). The following predictors were included in the model: sex and the "practical support" subscale of F-Sozu. Men were less likely than women were to participate in self-help activities, as were participants with low scores in practical support (Table 14.4).

Fibromyalgia

Among 247 respondents with FM, 217 were included in the analysis. The model explained a substantial proportion of variance (Nagelkerne $R^2=0.21$). Significant predictors in the model were the FKV subscales "distraction and self-encouragement" and "minimization and wishful thinking," marriage status, and somatic functional ability (FFbH). Patients with high scores in coping, "distraction and self-encouragement," and "minimization and wishful thinking" were more likely to participate in self-help activities, and so were married patients. In contrast, patients with higher scores in somatic functional ability were less likely to participate (Table 14.4).

Predictors of Continued Participation in Self-Help Programs

Total Sample

Among 426 data sets, 230 were included in the analysis on repeat participation in self-help services. Respondents whose information could be included in the analysis were significantly older (53.45 vs. 51.88 years; $p<0.001$) and had been more recently diagnosed (5.5 vs. 6.76 years; $p<0.05$). In addition, they had significantly lower scores in the FFbH (67.65 vs. 71.72; $p<0.05$) and in the somatic component summary score (25.79 vs. 34.07; $p<0.001$) of the SF-36. Differences in sex, depressive symptoms, and the mental component summary score of the SF-36 were not significant.

In the total sample, the following predictors explained a substantial proportion of variance (Nagelkerke $R^2=0.18$): age, coping (FKV: active problem-focused coping), social support (F-Sozu: trusted person), and somatic functional ability (FFbH). Patients up to age 39 were less likely and patients aged 40–59 were more likely to participate in SHGs than those of age 60+. Higher scores in active problem-focused

Table 14.4 Significant predictors of the regression analysis of the utilization of self-help services

All participants (n=367, missing: n=59)			CP (n=150, missing: n=29)			FM (n=217, missing: n=30)		
Predictor	OR (95 % CI)	p-value	Predictor	OR (95 % CI)	p-value	Predictor	OR (95 % CI)	p-value
Sex			*Sex*			*FKV*		
Male	0.23 (0.10–0.53)	0.001	Male	0.21 (0.07–0.67)	<0.01	Distraction/ self-encouragement	2.68 (1.5–4.78)	0.001
Reference: female			Reference: female					
						Minimization and wishful thinking	1.49 (1.0–2.21)	0.05
FKV			*F-Sozu*			*Marriage status*		
Active problem-focused coping	1.68 (1.19–2.37)	<0.01	Practical support	0.66 (0.44–0.98)	<0.05	Married	2.41 (1.17–4.95)	<0.05
						Reference: not married		
F-Sozu						*FFbH*		
Emotional support	0.75 (0.57–0.99)	<0.05				51–75 points	0.26 (0.06–1.23)	0.09
Satisfaction with emotional support	0.81 (0.66–0.99)	<0.05				76–100 points	0.13 (0.03–0.59)	<0.01
						Reference: 0–50 points		
Marriage status								
Married	1.94 (1.18–3.18)	<0.01						
Reference: not married								

CP chronic polyarthritis, *FM* fibromyalgia, *FKV* Freiburg Questionnaire on Coping with Illness, *F-Sozu* Social support questionnaire, *FFbH* Hannover Functional Abilities Questionnaire coping were associated with greater participation in self-help activities. In contrast, high scores in social support were associated with a lower likelihood of participation. Patients with high functional ability according to the FFbH were more likely to participate in SHGs than those with low functional ability (Table 14.5).

Chronic Polyarthritis

Among the 179 participants with CP, 59 data sets were included in the analysis. The model explained a high proportion of variance (Nagelkerke $R^2=0.40$). Age, coping (FKV: active problem-focused coping), and marriage status were significant predictors in the model. Participants aged 40–59 were much more likely to participate in self-help activities than those of age 60+, as were participants with a high score in active problem-focused coping. Married patients, in contrast, were less likely to participate.

Fibromyalgia

Among the 247 participants with FM, 171 were included in the analysis. The model explained a substantial proportion of variance (Nagelkerke $R^2=0.19$). Sex and somatic functional ability (FFbH) were significant predictors in the model. Being male as well as a high score in the FFbH were identified as negative predictors.

Discussion

Summary of Results

In summary, the study identified predictors in all areas described by the Andersen model. For direct participation in self-help programs, being female and higher scores in active problem-focused coping were positive predisposing factors, and being married was a positive enabling factor. However, it remains unclear if patients who are unmarried but living with their partners participate in self-help activities more than those living alone do. Higher scores in experienced social support, in contrast, were negatively associated with SHG participation. Positive coping promoted participation, but fewer functional limitations were negatively associated with repeat participation in SHGs in the overall sample. The latter result underscores the influence of need factors in this predictive model.

In addition to the duration of utilization, differences were found between diagnostic groups as well. For instance, in CP patients, males and those with high social support scores (practical support subscale) were less likely to participate in SHGs. In contrast, repeat participation is promoted by younger age. Being married was a

Table 14.5 Significant predictors of repeat utilization of self-help programs

All participants ($n=230$, missing: $n=196$)			CP ($n=59$, missing: $n=120$)			FM ($n=171$, missing: $n=76$)		
Predictor	OR (95 % CI)	*p*-value	Predictor	OR (95 % CI)	*p*-value	Predictor	OR (95 % CI)	*p*-value
FKV			*Age*			*Sex*		
Active problem-focused coping	1.95 (1.26–3.03)	<0.01	Up to age 39	10.30 (2.15–49.5)	<0.01	Male	0.13 (0.01–1.24)	0.08
						Reference: female		
			Age 40–59	4.56 (0.27–7.8)	0.20			
			Reference: 60+					
F-Sozu			*F-Sozu*			*FFbH*		
Trusted person	0.69 (0.51–0.94)	<0.05	Practical support	3.5 (1.18–10.35)	<0.05	51–75 points	0.48 (0.17–1.34)	0.16
						76–100 points	0.22 (0.08–0.65)	<0.01
						Reference: 0–50 points		
FFbH			*Marriage status*					
51–75 points	0.78 (0.35–1.74)	0.54	Married	0.13 (0.03–0.66)	0.01			
			Reference: not married					
76–100 points	0.37 (0.16–0.85)	<0.05						
Reference: 0–50 points								

CP chronic polyarthritis, *FM* fibromyalgia, *FKV* Freiburg Questionnaire on Coping with Illness, *F-Sozu* Social support questionnaire, *FFbH* Hannover Functional Abilities Questionnaire negative predictor. However, this analysis included only 59 patients, which reduces the reliability of the findings.

In patients with FM, high coping scores and lower functional limitations were negative predictors of participation, while being married was positively associated. The only negative predictors of repeat participation in SHGs were higher functional ability and male sex.

Need Factors

The analysis shows that severe functional disability is positively associated with SHG participation, particularly in patients with FM. This seems plausible since patients with physically impairing disorders expect self-help programs to improve their functional abilities, and this effect has been described in the literature (Borgetto et al. 2008). Studies on other disorders, such as stroke patients, also show that greater perceived somatic limitations are positive predictors of SHG participation (Kimmel 2007). Particularly functional training within SHGs is presumably utilized as an additional therapeutic program if the therapeutic services available through the professional health-care system are perceived as insufficient or too limited.

Participation was not influenced by time of diagnosis or severity of depressive symptoms. The latter is surprising, particularly in light of the fact that psychological well-being influences SHG utilization in mourning persons (Levy & Derby 1992), Alzheimer family caregivers (Martichuski et al. 1997), and stroke patients (Kimmel 2007). Although depression is two to four times more common in patients with rheumatoid arthritis than in the healthy population (Margaretten et al. 2011), and up to 90 % of FM patients have symptoms of depression (Graceley et al. 2012), our study found no association with SHG participation. Since SHGs have a positive effect on symptoms of depression and anxiety in patients with rheumatic disorders (Garnefski et al. 2012), strategies are needed to motivate patients with symptoms of depression to participate in SHGs.

Predisposing Factors

Remarkably, age was a predictor only in CP patients, where younger people were far more likely to participate repeatedly. In stroke patients (Kimmel 2007), age was not a significant predictor. It is unclear why this study shows such a high predictive influence particularly for this subgroup; however, the early onset of disease may be a decisive factor. In patients with CP, peak morbidity is around 55 years. Patients who are diagnosed very young (<40 years of age) may perceive a greater need for self-help.

Sex is a much more striking predisposing factor. Men were often far less likely to participate in SHGs, which was not the case in the stroke patients studied by Kimmel (2007). In another study, however, the authors showed that a much higher percentage of women participated in SHGs on coping with mental disorders, particularly SHGs on the psychological coping with physical disorders (Hartmann & Zepf 2005).

In this study, higher coping scores in various dimensions were often associated with a higher likelihood of SHG participation. This can be interpreted as a positive sign since patients with positive coping apparently consider and use self-help programs as part of their coping strategy. Volle et al. (1990) found that among patients with rheumatism, self-help users dealt with disorders more actively and deliberately than nonusers. This is an important starting point for motivating patients to participate in SHGs since coping may be positively influenced and participation in SHGs thereby promoted. Volle et al. (1990) also found that the locus of control significantly differed between SHG participants and nonparticipants: SHG participants had stronger internal locus of control and less pronounced external locus of control. We could not confirm this finding in this study, although it is very plausible and can be related to the stronger coping strategies we found.

Enabling Factors

In this study, perceived social support was often a significant predictor. However, results were sometimes heterogeneous. While higher perceived social support was often negatively associated with SHG participation, this was only true for direct participation in CP patients. Social support actually promoted repeat participation in this group. A similar situation was found for the variable "marriage status." While being married was typically a positive predictor of participation, it negatively predicted repeat participation in CP patients. In stroke patients and those with heart disease, higher perceived social support was a positive predictor of SHG participation as well (Hildingh & Fridlund 2001; Kimmel 2007), but in patients with psychosomatic disorders, SHG participants reported lower perceived social support (Höflich et al. 2007). It is unclear what causes these heterogeneous results. In principle, both phenomena can be logically explained: SHG participation can at least partially compensate for lower perceived social support. On the other hand, patients with greater social support may be encouraged to participate in SHGs by their positive experiences with social relationships. In stroke patients, the level of actually received social support by the closest friend or family member was very closely associated with SHG utilization. This may correspond to our finding that spouses frequently represented a positive promoting factor. Patients' primary social contacts could act as gatekeepers for community self-help programs and also provide very practical help, for instance, transport to the SHG meeting point.

It is unclear to what extent the timing of the survey influences results. In those who have participated in an SHG for an extended period of time, results may be significantly influenced since the positive social effect of SHGs has been described as particularly important. Social status was not found to be a relevant influencing factor for the utilization of self-help programs.

Limitations of the Study

This study is primarily limited by the underlying type of data analysis. Our results stem from a secondary data analysis, which is associated with a series of problems, such as difficulty in checking of erroneous or lost data post hoc. Another major disadvantage of secondary data analyses involves the theory-based a priori selection of indicators. An associated significant limitation of our study is the unclear causal direction of the identified associations. For some of the associations we found, reciprocal relationships are likely. Nevertheless, this research is very important for the exploration of potential predictors of SHG participation. This is particularly true in light of the very limited available data on SHG participation of patients with rheumatic disorders in Germany.

The participant recruitment process is a further limiting factor. The majority of the respondents were recruited through the Baden-Württemberg League against Rheumatism. Since this League is involved in organizing self-help programs, selection bias cannot be ruled out.

In addition, the study is limited by small sample sizes, particularly for the subgroups. For instance, missing or incomplete data meant that only about half of the data sets that were included in the primary analysis could be included in the secondary data analysis on utilization.

Outlook

The available data give rise to various implications for research and practice. Further efforts must be made to collect additional data on predictors of SHG utilization by patients with rheumatic disorders in Germany. In particular, longitudinal studies should be conducted with theory-based a priori specification of predictor variables. These studies can be particularly helpful for identifying a clear causal relationship between the variables and SHG utilization.

In addition, our research has shown that Andersen's model can be used as a heuristic for predictors of SHG utilization. With the aid of this model and the research results, we successfully conducted a theory-guided identification of potential predictor variables.

Our data offer initial implications for promoting SHG participation. For instance, patients should be supported in developing active coping strategies, which, in conjunction with information about self-help associations, can promote participation in SHGs. Further, all stakeholders in the health-care system should increase their efforts to involve more men in SHGs. Barriers to the utilization of male patients must be further studied and focused on in practice. In addition, potential gatekeepers to SHGs must focus on social environment and perceived social support. Since the direction of results is highly heterogeneous in this regard, either high or low perceived social support can be viewed as an access barrier. Stakeholders must be sensitized to this issue, and the social environment of the affected patients must be involved.

In addition, the self-help concept should be further promoted among health professionals, particularly physicians and therapists, in an effort to gain their support in disseminating constructive information about self-help activities and programs.

References

Andersen, R.M., Davidson, P.L. (2007): Improving access to care in America: individual and contextual indicators. In R.M. Andersen, T.H. Rice, G.F. Kominski (Hrsg.), Changing the U.S. health care system: key issues in health services, policy, and management (S. 3–31). 3. Auflage. San Francisco, CA: Jossey-Bass

Borgetto, B. (2004): Selbsthilfe und Gesundheit. Analysen, Forschungsergebnisse und Perspektiven. Buchreihe des Schweizerischen Gesundheitsobservatoriums. Bern, Göttingen, Toronto, Seattle: Hans Huber-Verlag

Borgetto, B. (2010): Soziale Beziehungen und Gesundheit. In: Badura, B., Walter, U., Hehlmann, T. (Hg.): Betriebliche Gesundheitspolitik. Der Weg zur gesunden Organisation. 2., völlig neu überarbeitete Auflage, Berlin: Springer, S. 339–349

Borgetto B, Kirchner C, Kolba N, Stößel U (2008): Selbsthilfe und Ehrenamt in der rheumatologischen Versorgung. Ergebnisse einer empirischen Untersuchung der Struktur- und Prozessqualität der Selbsthilfeaktivitäten und Versorgungsangebote der Rheuma-Liga Baden-Württemberg e.V. LIT-Verlag, Münster

Braun, J., Kettler, U., Becker, I. (1997): Selbsthilfe und Selbsthilfeunterstützung in der Bundesrepublik Deutschland. Schriftenreihe des BMFSFJ, Bd. 136, Stuttgart; Berlin; Köln: Kohlhammer

Daum, K.-W. (1984): Selbsthilfegruppen. Eine empirische Untersuchung von Gesprächs-Selbsthilfegruppen. Rehburg-Loccum: Psychiatrie-Verlag

Edmunson E D, Bedell J R, et al. (1982) Integrating Skill Building and Peer Support in Mental Health Treatment: The Early Intervention and Community Network Development Projects. In: Jeger A M, Slotnick R S (Hrsg) Community Mental Health and Behavioral Ecology. Plenum Press, New York, S 127–139

Garnefski N, Kraaij V, Benoist M, Bout Z, Karels E, Smit A. 2012. Cognitive behavioral self-help intervention reduces depression and anxiety and improves coping self-efficacy in people with rheumatism. Arthritis Care Res (Hoboken). doi: 10.1002/acr.21936

Gracely RH, Ceko M, Bushnell MC. 2012. Fibromyalgia and depression. Pain Res Treat. 2012; 486590. doi: 10.1155/2012/486590. Epub 2011 Nov 19

Hartmann S & Zepf S. 2005. Hilfe zur Selbsthilfe – Ergebnisse von Laienbehandlungen in unterschiedlichen Selbsthilfegruppen. In: DAG SHG (Hrsg.) Selbsthilfegruppenjahrbuch, Gießen, S. 110–120

Hildingh, C. & Fridlund, B. 2001. Patient participation in peer support groups after a cardiac event. *British Journal of Nursing 10*: 1357–63

Höflich A, Matraz J, Meyer F, Knickenberg RJ, Bleichner F, Merkle W, Reimer C, Franke W & Beutel ME. 2007. Inanspruchnahme von Selbsthilfegruppen und Psychotherapie im Anschluss an eine stationäre psychosomatisch–psychotherapeutische Behandlung. Psychother Psych Med 57: 213–20

Kimmel A. 2007. Gemeinschaftliche Selbsthilfe nach einem Schlaganfall. Die Determinanten der Inanspruchnahme. Dissertation, Universität Bielefeld: 213 Seiten

Kurtz L F (1988) Mutual Aid for Affective Disorders: The Manic Depressive and Depressive Association. American Journal of Orthopsychiatry 58, 1: 152–155

Kyrouz E M, Humphreys K, Loomis C (2002) A Review of Research in the Effectiveness of Self-Help Mutual Aid Groups. In: White B J, Madara E J (Hrsg) American Self-Help Clearinghouse Self-Help Group Sourcebook. Saint Clares Health Services, New Jersey, S1–16. Online verfügbar unter (Link zuletzt geprüft am 9.11.2006) http://www.chce.research.med.va.gov/chce/pdfs/Kyrouz%20Humphreys%20Loomis%202002.pdf

Levy L & Derby JF. 1992. Bereavement support groups: who joins; who does not; and why? *American Journal of Community Psychology 20*: 649–62

Lohaus A, Schmitt GM. 1989. Fragebogen zur Erhebung von Kontrollüberzeugungen zu Krankheit und Gesundheit (KKG). Handanweisung. Hogrefe, Göttingen

Margaretten M, Julian L, Katz P, Yelin E. 2011. Depression in patients with rheumatoid arthritis: description, causes and mechanisms. Int J Clin Rheumtol 6(6):617–23

Martichuski DK, Knight BL, Karlin NJ & Bell PA. 1997. Correlates of Alzheimer's Disease caregivers support group attendance. *Activities, Adaptation & Aging 21*: 27–39

Matzat, J. (1999). Selbsthilfe als therapeutisches Prinzip. Therapeutische Wirkungen der Selbsthilfe. In: Günther, P., Rohrmann, E. (Hg.): Soziale Selbsthilfe: Alternative, Ergänzung oder Methode sozialer Arbeit? Heidelberg: Ed.S, S. 105–126

Muthny F. 1989. Freiburger Fragebogen zur Krankheitsverarbeitung (FKV). Manual. Beltz Test GmbH, Weinheim

Sommer G, Fydrich T. 1991. Entwicklung und Überprüfung eines Fragebogens zur sozialen Unterstützung. Diagnostica (37):160–178

Thieme, H., Borgetto, B. (2012): Utilisation of rheumatology care services in Germany: the case of physical therapy and self-help groups. In: GMS Psycho-Social-Medicine, Vol. 9, Doc08, S. 1–7, *DOI: 10.3205/psm000086, URN: urn:nbn:de:0183-psm0000862*

Thumboo J, Strand V. Health-related quality of life in patients with systemic lupus erythematosus: an update. Ann Acad Med Singapore 2007; 36(2):115–22

Trojan, A. (Hrsg.) (1986): Wissen ist Macht. Eigenständig durch Selbsthilfe in Gruppen. Frankfurt/M.: Fischer-alternativ

Volle B, Wiedebusch S, Lohaus A. 1990. Psychological correlates of self-help group membership in patients with rheumatic diseases. Psychother Psychosom Med Psychol 40(6): 230–7

Zartmann, E. (1996). Wohnortnahe Betreuung rheumakranker Menschen. Die Aufgaben hauptamtlicher Sozialfachkräfte. In: 20 Jahre Rheuma-Liga Baden-Württemberg e.V. Bruchsal: Eigenverlag

Part VI
Results: Selected Sectors of Care

Chapter 15
Social Determinants of the Utilization of Psychotherapeutic Care in Germany

Mirjam Körner, Birte A. Maschke and Christian Janssen

Introduction

Mental Illness in German Society

Mental illness (psychological or behavioral disorder) affects an estimated one-fourth of the European population at least once in their lifetime (Sonntag 2007; Wittchen and Jacobi 2005, 2006; Wittchen et al. 2011). A shift from somatic to mental illnesses has recently been observed in Germany as well (Klingberg et al. 2011). This is the result of a variety of societal changes and the associated strains, such as growing poverty, middle-class social uncertainty, new occupational demands, fears about the future, higher stress due to tighter deadlines, faster work pace, greater complexity, disputes over competence, fear of losing jobs, and lack of future prospects, among other things (Klingberg et al. 2011; Wieland 2009). The 1998/1999 German National Health Survey determined a 12-month prevalence of 31% for mental disorders in the general adult population (age 18–65) of Germany (Jacobi et al. 2004a). Mental disorders are more common in women than in men (Harfst and Marstedt 2009) and are more frequently found in people of lower social status (Wittchen and Jacobi 2001). Busch et al. (2011), for instance, report that the probability of experiencing depression is twice as high for people of low social status as it is for people of average or high social status.

More than half of all mental illnesses begin before the 14th year of life (Margraf 2012). They become chronic in 40% of cases, in part due to the considerable latency period between the onset of the mental disorder and the start

M. Körner (✉)
Medical Psychology and Medical Sociology, Medical Faculty,
University of Freiburg, Freiburg, Germany
e-mail: mirjam.koerner@mps.unifreiburg.de

B. A. Maschke · C. Janssen
Department of Applied Social Sciences,
Munich University of Applied Sciences, Munich, Germany
e-mail: christian.janssen@hm.edu

C. Janssen et al. (eds.), *Health Care Utilization in Germany*,
DOI 10.1007/978-1-4614-9191-0_15,

of professionally indicated psychotherapy (more than 5 years, chronification period; Potreck-Rose and Koch 1994; Zielke et al. 2004). Depression, anxiety, and eating disorders are even chronic in 50–80 % of cases (Margraf 2012). Women are more commonly affected than men, and older employed people age 45 and above more commonly than younger workers. Particularly high rates of mental disorders are found in people in social and educational occupations, health occupations, and in the paper production and print industry (The Parliament of the Federal Republic of Germany 2012). Unemployed people more commonly suffer from mental and behavioral disorders than the employed. This is confirmed by international meta-analyses as well as by analyses of health insurance data surveys in Germany (Hollederer 2008).

Mental and behavioral disorders negatively affect workplace productivity, fulfillment of duties, and quality of life and are associated with high direct and indirect costs of illness. In 2010, these disorders were the third most common diagnoses in incapacity to work days, at 13.1 % (Federal Chamber of Psychotherapists 2012). Across health insurance funds, the percentage of incapacity to work cases caused by mental illness has increased by 1 % since 2000, which is a considerable rise as they initially made up only 3–3.5 % of all incapacity to work cases (Federal Chamber of Psychotherapists 2010).

Mental and psychosomatic disorders are the most common causes of early retirement on medical grounds. Nearly one-third (31 %) of early retirement cases are approved as a result of a reduction in earnings for psychological reasons. On average, mentally ill patients leave the labor force 20 years before the legal retirement age or almost 13 years before the actual average retirement age (currently age 60.4; Federation of German Pension Insurance Institutes 2004; Weber et al. 2006). In 2008, 18 % of all lost working years were due to mental and behavioral disorders, which corresponds to a productivity loss of EUR 26 billion and a loss in gross value added of EUR 45 billion—equaling 1.8 % of the gross domestic product (The Parliament of the Federal Republic of Germany 2012). In Germany, the cost of mental and behavioral disorders was EUR 28.6 billion in 2008, representing a rise of EUR 5.2 billion compared to 2002. This is the highest increase when compared with other types of disease. In 2008, the costs of mental illness equaled 11.3 % of total costs, making them some of the most cost-intensive disorders in Germany (The Parliament of the Federal Republic of Germany 2012).

Psychotherapeutic Care in Germany

Psychotherapeutic care is continuously growing in importance in the German health-care system because of the rising percentage of incapacity to work cases (Wieland 2009) and early retirement cases (Weber et al. 2006) that are caused by mental disorders. The German mental health-care system is highly complex. Psychotherapeutic care can be provided on an inpatient basis (e.g., psychiatry department, psychosomatic hospital, rehabilitation facility), semi-inpatient basis (day clinic), or outpatient basis (e.g., psychotherapist in private practice, psychosocial counseling center, basic psychosomatic care provided by primary care physicians).

Since the Psychotherapist Act [*Psychotherapeutengesetz*] has come into effect, outpatient psychotherapeutic care has been provided primarily by medical and psychological psychotherapists in private practice (statutory health insurance (SHI)-accredited physician services). The treatment procedures recognized by social law (the so-called guideline therapies) are psychoanalytic and depth psychology services as well as behavioral therapy. Self-pay patients can also choose treatment by psychological psychotherapists using other therapies (e.g., person-centered psychotherapy, systemic therapy) and by alternative medical practitioners who are licensed in psychotherapy. In addition, outpatient care is offered at psychotherapeutic outpatient clinics, semi-inpatient facilities, and psychotherapeutic and psychosocial counseling facilities. Low-threshold therapies for the mentally ill are also offered in the context of primary care through basic psychosomatic care provided by primary care physicians (Schulz et al. 2008).

Inpatient care in psychiatric and psychosomatic hospitals is characterized by a multimodal treatment strategy. The patient receives care from a team of physicians, psychological psychotherapists, "special therapists" (non-psychologist, nonphysician therapists), nursing staff, occupational therapists, physical therapists, etc. Treatment focuses on verbal interventions in group and individual therapy sessions. Inpatient facilities include hospitals (psychiatry, psychosomatic medicine, and psychotherapy departments or hospitals) and rehabilitation facilities specializing in mental health and psychosomatic medicine. While hospitals primarily treat patients insured through the SHI system (§ 39 SGB V [SGB = Sozialgesetzbuch, Code of Social Law]), rehabilitation facilities chiefly treat patients insured through the statutory pension insurance (§ 15 SGB VI) as well as a smaller percentage of SHI patients (§ 40 SGB V).

Semi-inpatient facilities or day clinics are typically affiliated with hospitals that provide inpatient treatment; only 11 % of them are independent (Schulz et al. 2008). Therapy is provided in the daytime during the workweek, and the patients spend the night at home. The offered treatments vary widely and range from supportive services to intensive, multimodal treatment strategies. Their advantage is that stress situations encountered in everyday life (e.g., relationship conflicts) can be directly discussed in therapy.

The question when inpatient or semi-inpatient treatment is indicated has not yet been definitively answered. Numerous patient variables and the social environment must be taken into consideration. The concept of the German Federal Rehabilitation Council (2003) suggests that this type of treatment is indicated in the case of "extensive psychological and/or somatic comorbidity, severely reduced psychophysical resilience that requires continuous support and structure, very pronounced symptoms that require close monitoring and continuous availability of crisis intervention options, and need for external control of harmful behaviors" (quote according to Schulz et al. 2008).

Utilization of Psychotherapy

The 1998/1999 German National Health Survey (supplementary survey mental disorders) reveals that nationwide, only 36.4 % of need is met on the basis of the per capita existing number of therapists (Wittchen and Jacobi 2001), despite the favorable overall cost-benefit ratio of psychotherapy and the associated significant cost reduction (Margraf 2009). Among the affected patients, 42% received care from their primary care physician, 27% from psychological psychotherapists, 17% from medical psychotherapists, 32% from psychiatrists or neurologists, and 23% at inpatient psychiatric or psychotherapeutic hospitals (multiple answers possible) (Jacobi et al. 2004b). In their international comparison, Jacobi et al. (2004b) highlighted a relatively high percentage of inpatient treatment and treatment by psychological psychotherapists. Patients with mental illnesses remain untreated in 35–50% of cases (Demyttenaere et al. 2004; Alonso et al. 2007).

The cost of psychotherapeutic services is estimated to equal much less than 1% of the overall costs of mental illness (Wittchen and Jacobi 2005). Therefore, it is important to examine how mentally ill people can receive adequate help in a timely manner (Klingberg et al. 2011).

In primary care, only about half of all mental illnesses are detected, and most of them are treated by the primary care physician (Wittchen and Jacobi 2001). The utilization rate of professional psychotherapeutic services is 45% in women, a higher rate than in men (34%) (Jacobi et al. 2004b). In part, this is the result of greater fear of stigmatization in men (Eisenberg et al. 2009). In addition, people with a higher level of education are more likely to be treated (ten Have et al. 2005). Apparently, numerous individual-based barriers (age, gender, education, income, fear of stigmatization, denial of need for help, information deficits, etc.) as well as structural barriers (regional undersupply of services, long waiting times, refusal by therapists, failure to recognize the disorder in primary care, service interface problems, etc.) can complicate the utilization of psychotherapy (Eisenberg et al. 2009; Grohn 2008; Körner 2009; Maercker et al. 2005; Oelsner 2000; Schulz et al. 2008; Zepf et al. 2001). Löcherbach et al. (2000) showed that patients who visit a psychotherapist are in poorer psychosocial health and complain of more health problems than those who do not take advantage of psychotherapy, so a large percentage of them should be considered as requiring treatment and willing to receive it. However, only half of all requests for an initial consultation lead to probationary sessions, and after the probationary sessions, 35% of patients are not accepted into outpatient therapy (Zepf et al. 2003). It is likely that patients of higher social status, who may be better informed and have superior communication skills, can more easily access psychotherapeutic treatment than patients of lower social status, for instance, due to migration background and/or language barriers. People with a migration background are likely to suffer from at least equal or even higher rates of illness than people without a migration background but simultaneously exhibit lower utilization (Bermejo 2010). The available data on the utilization of psychotherapy by people with migration background suggest inappropriate utilization or an undersupply of services (Baschin et al. 2012).

On behalf of the Federal Ministry of Health and the National Association of SHI Physicians, Löcherbach et al. (2000) developed an indicator-supported model for requirements planning that takes into account the levels of *mental disorder, patient, treatment provider, and health-care system*. They determined the current situation in terms of treatment providers and patients for individual German regions.

Key patient-related predictors of the utilization of psychotherapy were gender, age, concepts of illness, level of suffering, existential problems, social stressors, attitude toward psychotherapy, awareness, financial and time resources, and "fit" (Löcherbach et al. 2000). Patients in inpatient psychotherapeutic care were in poorer health than those in outpatient psychotherapy. On the provider side, demand-modulating factors included the primary care physician's awareness as well as referral practice, which in turn depends on the offered services and their transparency. The economic situation, state interventions, waiting times, health services structures, and spatial proximity are indicators related to the health-care system (Löcherbach et al. 2000).

Andersen's model of health services utilization (Andersen 1995; Andersen & Davidson 2007) contains the following three categories: health-care system (politics, resources, and organization), patient or population characteristics (predisposing, enabling, and need), and provider characteristics. However, no model-based systematic analysis of the individual characteristics and contextual characteristics applicable to psychotherapeutic care in Germany has been conducted so far.

The available data on the utilization of psychotherapy in Germany are unsatisfactory (Nübling 2009; Kordy 2008; Schulz et al. 2006, 2008). Outpatient psychotherapy is considered a particularly "great challenge for psychosocial health services research" (Kordy 2008, p. 249). This research is necessary to meet the patients' need for information, create transparency, offer choices between the various alternatives, and develop new models of care (Richter 2009). The development of steering mechanisms and models of care for groups who have not yet found access to outpatient psychotherapy would enormously improve care (Richter 2009).

On the basis of the sociological question to what extent social inequality influences the utilization of psychotherapy, we will focus on the individual predisposing factor "social structure," which according to the Andersen model encompasses education, occupation, and ethnicity, and examine the influence of social status on the utilization of outpatient psychotherapy in Germany.

Methods

For this purpose, we conducted systematic literature searches in the Medline and PsycINFO databases using the following terms: utilization, social inequality, socioeconomic factors, sociodemographic factors. The specific search strategy was structured as follows: "utilization" OR "utilization" OR "access" AND "psychotherapy" AND "social inequalities" OR "social inequality" OR "social disparities" OR "social disparity" OR "socio-economic" OR "socioeconomic" OR *"socio-demographic" OR "socio-demographic."* We limited the search to Germany and the time period from 2002 through 2012.

Additional literature searches were then conducted for 2002 through 2012 in the databases Leibniz Institute for the Social Sciences (GESIS), the virtual technical library medicine (MEDPILOT), and Springer using the terms "social inequality and psychotherapy" ["Soziale Ungleichheit und Psychotherapie"], "health inequality and psychotherapy" ["gesundheitliche Ungleichheit und Psychotherapie"], "education and psychotherapy" ["Bildung und Psychotherapie"], "occupational status and psychotherapy" ["Beruflicher Status und Psychotherapie"], "income and psychotherapy" ["Einkommen und Psychotherapie"]. Finally, we conducted a manual search for scripts, dissertations, research reports, etc., as well as for literature cited in the articles selected for the chapter.

Results

In the Medline database, the above search strategy brought up 17 publications, of which the majority was found to be unsuitable upon closer examination. The 17 search results only included one relevant paper (Gallas et al. 2008). The second search used an identical search strategy in the PsycINFO database and resulted in 12 hits. Again, only one paper (Albani et al. 2010) was found to be relevant to our research question.

No additional relevant publications resulted from the search in the GESIS and MEDPILOT databases. Through the manual search, we found two additional publications on the topic: (1) a dissertation by Bembenneck (2006) on the characteristics of patients that utilize outpatient psychotherapy and (2) a brochure on the 2010 survey of outpatient psychotherapeutic care, published by the German Association of Psychotherapists (Walendzik et al. 2011; Fig. 15.1).

Overall, we analyzed four empirical papers on the utilization of psychotherapy in view of social status (Albani et al. 2010; Gallas et al. 2008; Walendzik et al. 2011, Bembenneck 2006). These studies measured social status in various ways. While Walendzik et al. (2011) surveyed the level of education, extent of occupational activity, and occupational position, Albani et al. (2010) use level of education, occupation, and net household income per capita to measure social status. Gallas et al. (2008) and Bembenneck (2006) recorded the level of schooling and professional training. With the exception of Bembenneck, all studies investigated the guideline therapies (psychoanalytic psychotherapy, depth psychotherapy, and behavioral therapy). The most current survey by Walendzik et al. (2011) included the greatest number of patients, with 29,594 members of statutory or private health insurance funds as well as self-payers. The study by Gallas et al. (2008) focuses on 717 privately insured patients. The study of Albani et al. (2010) analyzed 1,212 patients using a standardized telephone interview; Bembenneck (2006) analyzed 997 applications for psychotherapy. Table 15.1 provides an overview of the variables used for measuring social status, the survey methods, the study populations, the included therapy types, and the insurance type of treated patients.

The 2010 survey of outpatient psychotherapy conducted by the German Association of Psychotherapists used questionnaires to ask psychological psychotherapists about their current patients. The research question was "to what extent indications of undersupply of services, and possibly (partial) oversupply and inappropriate services can be identified" (Walendzik et al. 2011, p. 10). Among other things, they researchers examined the care situation in various sociodemographic groups. The representative population survey by Albani et al. (2010) used a standardized

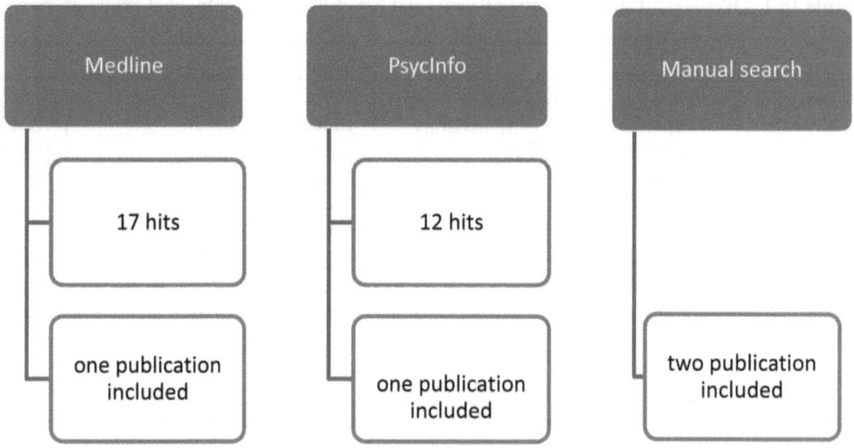

Fig. 15.1 Results of the literature search

telephone interview to survey 1,212 people who were in outpatient psychotherapy at the time or within the previous 6 years. The data from Gallas et al. (2008) were collected using a written survey in the context of the larger study Transparency and Outcome Orientation in Outpatient Psychotherapy (TRANS-OP) ("Optimizing psychotherapy service provision via transparency and outcome orientation: evaluating outpatient psychotherapy"). Bembenneck (2006) used 997 initial applications (time period 1998–2001) for analytical or depth psychotherapy. Comparing only the highest school degrees earned by the patients receiving outpatient psychotherapy, there are no significant differences between patients with a university entrance qualification [*Abitur*] (24.5%) and the lowest secondary school degree [*Hauptschulabschluss*] (19.8%). However, when comparing these results with the distribution of degrees in the overall German population age 15 and above (2007 Microcensus by the Federal Statistical Office), it becomes clear that 40.4% of the working German population hold the lowest secondary school degree, but they represent only about one-fifth of patients in outpatient psychotherapy. In contrast, while 11.5% of the population holds a university entrance qualification, this group makes up a considerable 24.5% of patients (Walendzik et al. 2011). Albani et al. (2008) arrive at a similar result in their study on outpatient psychotherapy in Germany. This study confirms a higher representation of better-educated people among psychotherapy patients. Like the study by the German Association of Psychotherapists, this analysis showed that people with lowest secondary school degrees made up 20% of the group of psychotherapy patients but represent 40% of the overall population. Among the surveyed individuals, almost 17% indicated that they held a university entrance qualification, which is very close to the 25% of the overall population with this qualification. The representation of people with a middle-level secondary school degree [*Mittlere Reife*] is nearly 6% higher in psychotherapy patients than in the overall population. More than half of the surveyed individuals reported a monthly per capita net

Table 15.1 Overview of studies on social status and the utilization of outpatient psychotherapy

Author	Survey method	Study population	Social status indicators	Treatment type	Insurance type
Albani et al. (2010)	Standardized telephone interview	1,212 patients (response rate: 74 %)	Level of education, occupation, household net income per capita	PA, DPP, bT	Statutory, private, self-pay
Bembenneck (2006)	Analysis of applications for psychotherapy using a data collection sheet	997 applications	Completed schooling and occupational position	PA, DPP	Statutory, private, self-pay
Gallas et al. (2008)	Written survey of members of a private health insurance	714 of 939 members	Level of schooling and occupational training	PA, DPP, bT	Private
Walendzik et al. (2011)	Written survey of members of the German Association of Psychotherapists (psychological psychotherapists) about their patients (data analysis of the last 10 patients)	7,508 psychological psychotherapists, response rate of 33 % $N=2{,}497$ therapists, documentation of 29,594 patients	Level of education, extent of occupational activity, occupational position (Winkler Index)	PA, DPP, bT	Statutory, private, self-pay

PA psychoanalysis, *DPP* depth psychology-based psychotherapy, *bT* behavior therapy

income of less than EUR 1,000, slightly more than one-fourth up to EUR 1,499, and almost 13 % up to EUR 1,999. Only 5 % of psychotherapy patients dispose of a per capita net income of more than EUR 2,000 per month. Gallas et al. (2008) collected data of privately insured individuals. In this study, only 6.9 % of participants hold a lower secondary school degree, 17 % a middle-level secondary school degree, and a high 73 % hold a university entrance qualification. However, this study is not representative of the total population of psychotherapy patients since private insurance is only available to people with a certain minimum gross annual income (2012: EUR 50,850). Therefore, it can be safely assumed that few people of low socioeconomic status (SES) are privately insured.

Bembenneck (2006) also revealed socioeconomic differences in applicants for psychotherapy when compared to the general population. Some 20 % of applicants held a lower secondary school degree, while this population made up 47 % of the general population in 2002. The relationship is reversed in people with university entrance qualification: 40 % of the applicants held a university entrance qualification, although this group makes up only 20 % of the general population. This study again showed that the percentages for those with middle-level secondary school degree are nearly equal (25 % versus 27 %). Differences can also be observed in the highest level of occupational training, which was surveyed by Bembenneck (2006). At nearly 67 %, most applicants reported a completed apprenticeship as their highest occupational training, followed by academics at nearly 23 %. These percentages differ only slightly from those in the general population, where 53 % have completed an apprenticeship and 11 % hold a university degree. More distinct differences can be observed in people without any completed occupational training. They make up only 8.7 % of outpatient psychotherapy patients although they make up 28.4 % of the general population. Nearly 2 % of the patient sample reported holding a trade or technical school degree or master craftsman qualification—although they represent 8.3 % of the general population.

A direct comparison of the studies (see Table 15.2) is limited by differences in study design and in operationalization of social status. In all four publications, level of education was surveyed as a key variable of social status and was analyzed as it relates to the utilization of psychotherapy. The studies by Walendzik et al. (2011), Albani et al. (2010), and Bembenneck (2006) all find that some 20 % of patients hold a lower secondary degree. In the study by Gallas et al. (2008), this percentage is only about 7 %, probably because the study surveyed only privately insured individuals. In contrast, 40 % of the general German population holds a lower secondary school degree. The Microcensus shows that an average of 28 % holds a middle-level secondary school degree. This relationship is approximately reflected by the study results by Bembenneck (2006; 25 %), Albani et al. (2010; 35 %), and Walendzik et al. (2011; 32 %). Gallas et al. (2008) diverge from these results, at 17 %, for the reasons discussed above. Albani et al. (2010) found that some 17 % of their study participants held a university entrance qualification. This was the lowest percentage among the included studies. As people with this qualification make up only 11 % of the general population, however, it becomes clear that people with a higher education level take greater advantage of outpatient psychotherapy. The studies by Gallas et al. (2008), Bembenneck (2006), and Walendzik et al. (2011) report a higher percentage of participants with university entrance qualification, resulting in an even greater difference to the Microcensus numbers. In the study of privately insured individuals, the percentage is as high as 70 %, but this value is not representative due to the private insurance status. The results of the four studies demonstrate that the utilization of outpatient psychotherapy is in fact influenced by social status.

Table 15.2 summarizes these results. The selected categories were lowest secondary school degree, middle-level secondary school degree, university entrance qualification, and university degree. The study combined special education and lower-level secondary school as well as technical college entrance qualification [*Fachhochschulreife*] and university entrance qualification [*Abitur*] into one category each, and students and those without degree, who provided no information, or held another degree were excluded from the analysis. Next to the results of the four studies, the last column shows the Microcensus results, that is, data from the

Table 15.2 Overview of the results of the included studies

Highest degree earned	Walendzik et al. (2011)		Albani et al. (2010)		Gallas et al. (2008)		Bembenneck (2006)		2007 Microcensus	
	N=29,594		N=1,212		N=710		N=997		N=70,496,000	
Lowest secondary school degree [*Hauptschulabschluss*]	19.8%	5,802	20.0%	242	6.9%	49	20.3%	201	40.4%	28,477
Middle-level secondary school degree [*Mittlere Reife*]	32.1%	9,320	39%	434	17.0%	121	24.8%	246	27.6%	19,466
University entrance qualification [*Hochschulreife/Abitur*]	24.5%	7,472	16.9%	204	73.0%	518	40.3%	400	11.5%	8,135
University degree	19.1%	5,569	26.8%	325	–	–	–	–	12.4%	8,735

Federal Statistical Office about the level of education of people 15 years and older in Germany, for comparison purposes. This information is from 2007.

Discussion and Conclusion

We found four studies that investigated the influence of social status on the utilization of outpatient psychotherapy in Germany. The results consistently show that mentally ill people with a higher level of education are more commonly in therapy than those with a lower level of education. This is the case despite the fact that people with a lower level of education more commonly suffer from mental and behavioral disorders than people with a higher educational level. The combined analysis of the epidemiological findings and the utilization data indicate severe undertreatment of people with low levels of education (Walendzik et al. 2011). On the individual level, causes conceivably include higher strains (financial concerns, fear of losing job, unemployment, etc.) as well as various barriers to utilization (lack of information, absence of contact persons, fear of stigmatization, etc.). On the structural level, obstacles include health services bottlenecks, particularly for low-threshold services, regional differences (e.g., undersupply of services in former East Germany), and long waiting times for therapists in private practice. These obstacles to the utilization of outpatient psychotherapy have not yet been extensively researched.

Limitations of the included studies result from the study populations (e.g., only privately insured individuals, only psychological psychotherapists, only members of the German Association of Psychotherapists), survey designs, and the exclusion of non-guideline therapies. This limits the representativeness of general health-care practices. The study designs, survey methods, and operationalization of social status also vary widely in the included studies, which limits their comparability. The studies aimed to characterize the patients that utilize outpatient psychotherapy. Albani et al. (2010) surveyed social status as well as the reason for visit, access paths, insurance or other payers, and contact persons for mental illness. The results confirm a great need for improving access to outpatient psychotherapy. Walendzik et al. (2011) supplied comprehensive insights into psychotherapeutic care in Germany. They call for a precise analysis of the barriers to access for lower SES patients. Psychosocial services research could make an important contribution to generating meaningful data on the utilization of psychotherapy in the various health services sectors and, thereby, provide important evidence for needs-appropriate psychotherapeutic care that follows the principles of "quality, humanity, and economic efficiency" (SGB [Sozialgesetzbuch, Code of Social Law] V § 70) by determining the individual and contextual characteristics of utilization nationwide, both representatively and systematically.

The investigation of the outpatient sector only supplies part of the picture and should be expanded to include the inpatient and semi-inpatient sectors to determine whether less-educated people are treated at higher rates in the inpatient sector (e.g., in psychiatric hospitals). In the German health-care system, patients often still receive inpatient treatment far too late rather than undergoing early outpatient treatment (Margraf 2009; Nübling 2009). This practice results in high treatment costs, which could be distinctly reduced by early outpatient treatment, as the effectiveness and efficiency of outpatient therapy have been demonstrated (Margraf 2009). Direct and indirect costs can be reduced by improving access to outpatient therapy, for instance, by reducing barriers, creating incentives for (early) treatment, and developing new models of care and steering mechanisms. Knowledge of access paths and service interfaces can improve the integration of outpatient psychotherapeutic care into primary care and reduce undertreatment and inappropriate treatment. On the basis of the Andersen model of utilization (1995; Andersen & Davidson 2007), supply bottlenecks, coordination problems at service interfaces, and barriers to access could be identified for psychotherapeutic care as well so that further actions can be taken.

References

Albani C., Blaser G., Geyer M., Schmutzer G., Brähler E. (2010) Ambulante Psychotherapie aus Sicht der Patienten Teil 1: Versorgungssituation. *Psychotherapeut*, 55 (6) 503–514.

Alonso, J., Codony, M., Kovess, V., Angermeyer, M.C., Katz, S.J., Haro, J.M. et al. (2007) Population level of unmet need for mental healthcare in Europe. *Br J Psychiatry*, 190, 299–306.

Andersen, R.M. (1995). Revisiting the behavioral model and access to medical care: does it matter?. *Journal of Health and Social Behavior*, 36, 1–10.

Andersen, R.M., Davidson, P.L. (2007). Improving access to care in America: individual and contextual indicators. In R.M. Andersen, T.H. Rice, G.F. Kominski (Hrsg.), Changing the U.S. health care system: key issues in health services, policy, and management (S. 3–31). 3. Auflage. San Francisco, CA: Jossey-Bass.

Baschin, K., Ülsmann, D., Jacobi, F., Fydrich, T. (2012). Inanspruchnahme psychosozialer Versorgungsstrukturen. Theoretisches Modell für Personen mit Migrationshintergrund. *Psychotherapeut*, 2012, 7–14.

Bembenneck, C. (2006). Welche Merkmale kennzeichnen die Inanspruchnahmepatienten ambulanter Psychotherapie? Dissertation, Medizinische Hochschule, Hannover.

Bermejo, I., Mayninger, E., Kriston, L., Härter, M. (2010). Psychische Störungen bei Menschen mit Migrationshintergrund im Vergleich zur deutschen Allgemeinbevölkerung. *Psychiatrische Praxis*, 37, 225–232.

Busch, M., Hapke, U., Mensink, G.B.M. (2011). *Psychische Gesundheit und gesunde Lebensweise*. Hrsg. Robert Koch-Institut Berlin: GBE kompakt 2(7).

Demyttenaere, K., Bruffaerts, R., Posada-Villa, Gasquet, I., Kovess, V., Lepine, J.P. et al. (2004). Prevalence, severity and unmet need for treatment of mental disorders in the World of Health Organization World Mental Health Surveys. *JAMA*, 291 (21), 2581–2590.

Eisenberg, D., Downs, M.F., Golberstein, E., Zivin, K. (2009). Stigma and help seeking for mental health among college students. *Medical Care Research & Review*, 66 (5), 522–541.

Federal Chamber of Psychotherapists (2010). Komplexe Abhängigkeiten machen psychisch krank—BPtK-Studie zu psychischen Belastungen in der modernen Arbeitswelt. http://www.bptk.de/fileadmin/user_upload/Publikationen/BPtK-Studien/belastung_moderne_arbeitswelt/20100323_belastung-moderne-arbeitswelt_bptk-studie.pdf.

Federal Chamber of Psychotherapists (2012). Psychische Störungen sind die dritthäufigste Ursache für Krankschreibung Wirtschaftspsychologie aktuell. Zeitschrift für Personal und Management. http://www.wirtschaftspsychologie-aktuell.de/nachrichten/nachrichten–20120814-psychische-stoerungen-sind-dritthaeufigste-ursache-fuer-krankschreibung.html. Accessed 14 Aug 2012.

Federation of German Pension Insurance Institutes (2004). Rentenzugangsstatistik: Rentenzugänge wegen Erwerbsminderung. Frankfurt/Main: Federation of German Pension Insurance Institutes.

Gallas, C., Kächele, H., Kraft, S., Kordy, H., Puschner, B. (2008) Inanspruchnahme, Verlauf und Ergebnis ambulanter Psychotherapie. Befunde der TRANS-OP-Studie und deren Implikationen für die Richtlinienpsychotherapie. *Psychotherapeut*, 53(6), 414–423.

Grohn, J. (2008). Psychotherapeutische Versorgung in Deutschland—das teure Tabu. *Die BKK Zeitschrift der Betrieblichen Krankenversicherung*, 1, 8–14.

Harfst, T., Marstedt, G. (2009). Psychische Gesundheit in Deutschland: Erkrankungen bleiben oft unentdeckt. *Gesundheitsmonitor, Newsletter der Bertelsmann Stiftung*, 1, 1–7.

Hollederer, A. (2008). Psychische Gesundheit im Fall von Arbeitslosigkeit. *Praktische Arbeitsmedizin*, 12, 29–32.

Jacobi, F., Wittchen, H.U., Hölting, C., Höfler, M, Pfister, H., Müller, N. et al. (2004a). Prevalence, comorbidity and correlates of mental disorders in the general population: results from the German Health Interview and Examination Survey (GHS). *Psychological Medicine*, 34 (5), 597–611.

Jacobi, F., Klose, M., Wittchen, H.-U. (2004b). Psychische Störungen in der deutschen Allgemeinbevölkerung: Inanspruchnahme von Gesundheitsleistungen und Ausfalltage. *Bundesgesundheitsbl-Gesundheitsforsch-Gesundheitsschutz*, 47, 736–744.

Klingberg A. Lahme M., Rabe-Menssen, C., Willms S. (2011). Wie finden Patienten Zugang zu einer ambulanten Psychotherapie? Ergebnisse einer schriftlichen Befragung in psychotherapeutischen Praxen. Psychotherapie aktuell,1, 18–23.

Kordy, H. (2008). Psychosoziale Versorgungsforschung. Eine wissenschaftliche und politische Herausforderung. *Psychotherapeut*, 53, 245–253.

Löcherbach, P., Henrich, T., Kemmer, H., Kinstler, H.-J., Knopp-Vater, M., Rieckmann, N. et al. (2000). *Indikatoren zur Ermittlung des ambulanten psychotherapeutischen Versorgungsbedarfs*. Schriftenreihe des Bundesministeriums für Gesundheit, Band 125. Baden-Baden: Nomos.

Margraf, J. (2009). *Kosten und der Psychotherapie. Eine kritische Literaturanalyse*. Berlin: Springer.

Margraf, J. (2012). Versorgung psychisch kranker Menschen: Impulse aus der Forschung. http://www.ptk-nrw.de/fileadmin/user_upload/pdf/Aktuelle_Informationen/2012/09_2012/Vortrag_Prof_Dr._Juergen_Margraf.pdf. Accessed 15. Jan 2013.

Maercker, A., Enzler, A., Grimm, G., Helfenstein, E., Ehlert, U. (2005). Inanspruchnahme und Psychotherapiemotivation in einer repräsentativen Bevölkerungsstichprobe über 65-Jähriger—Ergebnisse der Zürcher Altersstudie. *Psychotherapie, Psychosomatik, Medizinische Psychologie*, 55 (3–4), 177–182.

Nübling, R. (2009). Verankerung und Veränderung der psychotherapeutischen Versorgung seit dem Psychotherapeutengesetz—aktueller Stand und Ausblick. *Psychotherapeutenjournal*, 3, 239–252.

Oelsner, S. (2000). *Determinanten für die Bereitschaft zur Psychotherapie: Eine empirische Studie*. Dissertation, Universität Trier.

Potreck-Rose, F. & Koch, U. (1994). Chronifizierungsprozesse bei psychosomatischen Patienten. Stuttgart: Schattauer-Verlag.

Richter, R. (2009). Psychotherapie für psychisch kranke Menschen: Gesundheitspolitische Vorstellungen für die kommenden Jahre. *Psychotherapeutenjournal*, 3, 278–281.

Schulz, H., Barghaan, D., Harfst, T., Dirmaier, J., Watzke, B. & Koch, U. (2006). Versorgungsforschung in der psychosozialen Medizin. *Bundesgesundheitsbl—Gesundheitsforsch—Gesundheitsschutz*, 49, 175–187.

Schulz, H., Barghaan, D., Harfst, T., Koch, U. (2008). Gesundheitsberichtserstattung des Bundes, Heft 41. Psychotherapeutische Versorgung. Berlin: Robert Koch-Institut.

Sonntag, U. (2007). Das Grünbuch zur psychischen Gesundheit. *Impulse Newsletter zur Gesundheitsförderung*, 57, 3–4.

ten Have, M., Meertens, V., Scheepers, P., te Grotenhuis, M., Beekman, A., Vollebergh, W. (2005). Demand for mental health care and changes in service use patterns in the Netherlands, 1979 to 1995. *Psychiatric Services*, Vol. 56 (11), 1409–1415.

The Parliament of the Federal Republic of Germany (2012). Zahl psychischer Krankheiten nimmt zu. http://www.bundestag.de/presse/hib/2012_05/2012_247/06.html. Accessed 15. Jan 2013.

Walendzik, A., Rabe-Menssen, C., Lux, G., Wasem, J., Jahn, R. (2011). *Erhebung zur ambulanten psychotherapeutischen Versorgung 2010*. Berlin: Deutsche PsychotherapeutenVereinigung.

Weber, A., Hörmann, G., Köllner, V. (2006). Psychische und Verhaltensstörungen: Die Epidemie des 21. Jahrhunderts? *Dtsch Aerzteblatt*, 103(13), 834–41.

Wieland, R. (2009). Barmer Gesundheitsreport 2009. *Psychische Gesundheit und Psychische Belastungen*. Wuppertal: Barmer Ersatzkasse.

Wittchen, H.U. & Jacobi, F. (2001). Die Versorgungssituation psychischer Störungen in Deutschland: Eine klinisch-epidemiologische Abschätzung anhand des Bundesgesundheitssurveys 1998. *Bundesgesundheitsblatt, Gesundheitsforschung Gesundheitsschutz* 44, 993–1000.

Wittchen, H.-U. & Jacobi, F. (2005). Size and burden of mental disorders in Europe—a critical review and appraisal of 27 studies. *European Neuropsychopharmacology*, 15, 357–376.

Wittchen, H.-U. & Jacobi, F. (2006). Psychische Störungen in Deutschland und der EU—Größenordnung und Belastung. *Verhaltenstherapie & Psychosoziale Praxis*, 38, 189–192.

Wittchen, H.-U., Jacobi, F., Rehm, J., Gustavvson, A., Svensson, M., Jönnson, B., et al. (2011). Size and burden of mental disorders and other disorders of the brain in Europe 2010. *European Neuropsychopharmacology*, 21, 655–679.

Zepf, S., Mengele, U., Marx, A. (2001) *Zur ambulanten psychotherapeutischen Versorgungslage in der Bundesrepublik Deutschland*. Gießen: Psychosozial-Verlag.

Zepf S., Mengele U., Hartmann S. (2003). Zum Stand der ambulanten psychotherapeutischen Versorgung der Erwachsenen in der Bundesrepublik Deutschland—Psychotherapie, Psychosomatik, *Medizinische-Psychologie*, 53, 152–162.

Zielke, M., Borgart, E.-J., Carls, W. et al. (2004). Ergebnisqualität und Gesundheitsökonomie verhaltensmedizinischer Psychosomatik in der Klinik. Lengerich: Pabst.

Chapter 16
Utilization of Prevention Services by Gender, Age, Socioeconomic Status, and Migration Status in Germany: An Overview and a Systematic Review

Christoph Kowalski, Julika Loss, Florian Kölsch and Christian Janssen

Introduction

In the early 1970s, Marmot identified a social gradient in health, meaning that the higher the social position, the better the health of a person (Marmot et al. 1978). This gradient, which he termed a "status syndrome," means that not only is the lowest social class at a disadvantage or that the poorest of the poor are affected, but that this gradient runs through society as a whole (Marmot and Wilkinson 2006;Marmot 2006;Siegrist and Marmot 2006) as well. Similar results were found for many other countries, e.g., the USA (Antonovsky 1967; Hinkle et al. 1968; Kitagawa and Hauser 1973), and the social gradient can now be seen as a typical phenomenon in Western industrialized countries, although it is not limited to them (Mackenbach and Backer 2002; Marmot and

C. Kowalski (✉)
Faculty of Human Sciences and the Faculty of Medicine,
Institute for Medical Sociology,
Health Services Research, and Rehabilitation Science,
University of Cologne, Cologne, Germany
e-mail: christoph.kowalski@uk-koeln.de

J. Loss
Division of Medical Sociology, Institute for Epidemiogy and Social Medicine,
University of Regensburg, Regensburg, Germany
e-mail: julika.loss@klinik.uni-regensburg.de

F. Kölsch
Faculty of Human Sciences and the Faculty of Medicine,
Institute for Medical Sociology, Health Services Research,
and Rehabilitation Science, University of Cologne, Cologne, Germany
e-mail: florian.koelsch@uk-koeln.de

C. Janssen
Department of Applied Social Sciences,
Munich University of Applied Sciences, Munich, Germany
e-mail: christian.janssen@hm.edu

C. Janssen et al. (eds.), *Health Care Utilization in Germany*,
DOI 10.1007/978-1-4614-9191-0_16, © Springer Science+Business Media New York 2014

Wilkinson 2006; Siegrist and Marmot 2006; Berkman and Kawachi 2000). In Germany, for example, the mean difference in life expectancy between members of the highest and the lowest income group is 8.4 years for women and 10.8 years for men (Lampert, Kroll, and Dunkelberg 2007). Those most impacted by social status-based health inequalities are young children and middle-aged adults, while fewer inequalities are observed during adolescence and old age (Kuh and Ben-Shlomo 2004). There are also differences between genders. Men's health seems to be more impacted by individual social status—measured at least in terms of level of education, occupation, and income—than women's health (Arber and Thomas 2001). For women, a relatively high impact was found for contextual social status (regional, neighborhood, as found by Lengerke and Mielck 2010; Breckenkamp, Mielck, and Razum 2007).

Among the many models that provide pathways to analyze the causes of the social gradient, Mielck's model for explaining health inequality (Mielck 2006) is among the most comprehensive. According to this model, less knowledge/formal education, less power, less occupational prestige, and less income lead to increased health burdens at one's place of residence or work, to fewer coping resources, to poorer medical care, and to less healthy behavior. This increases the risk of illness and premature death. Other direct pathways described in the model are those linking social and health inequalities, for instance, illness potentially leading to a social "downgrade" as well as direct relationships between physical and social characteristics.

To determine whether differences in the use of prevention services in Germany can be attributed to health inequalities between different social status groups, this chapter focuses on the associations between the individual factors gender, age, migration status, and socioeconomic status and their associations with health care in terms of the utilization of prevention services. We provide an overview of the health-care system with regard to health promotion and prevention as well as a review of the literature. The following section will provide a brief description of the German health-care system with regard to prevention. This overview will focus on the legal framework for prevention services in Germany. Following the overview, the methods and results of the review will be presented. The review investigates the impact of the individual factors gender, age, migration status, and socioeconomic status (Andersen and Davidson 2001) on the use of prevention services in Germany. In doing so, it contributes to answering the questions as to why there are such strong differences in morbidity and mortality based on individuals' social status characteristics (e. g., education, occupation, and income) and whether tackling inequalities in the utilization of prevention services might help tackle health inequalities. The findings of the reviewed empirical studies on differences in utilization will be synopsized in a table and briefly analyzed in consideration of systematic criteria. The final section will discuss the review's findings as well as the limitations and strengths of the review methods.

Responsibilities and Legal Bases for Disease Prevention and Health Promotion in Germany

In Germany, many private individuals, institutions, and companies engage in health promotion and disease prevention. Preventive services are offered by public, semi-public, and nongovernmental actors. These services can be directly medical in nature (e.g., vaccinations or screening examinations) or involve health education or "settings projects" (e.g., at companies or in municipalities) that facilitate health-promoting behaviors.

Public institutions Public institutions primarily include federal and state ministries or senates for health, nutrition, social affairs, agriculture, consumer protection, etc. The Federal Centre for Health Education (*Bundeszentrale für gesundheitliche Aufklärung* (BZgA)) is a lead government institution in disease prevention. The BZgA is a federal agency under the Federal Ministry of Health. It aims to reduce health risks and encourage health-promoting lifestyles in the German population. Key topics include acquired immunodeficiency syndrome (AIDS) prevention, sex education and family planning, addiction prevention, nutrition, exercise, stress management, and influenza protection. The BZgA is also involved in health equality.

In addition to these national and state institutions, public health offices, schools, and daycares are responsible for prevention and health promotion on a municipal level.

By law, the duties of municipal public health offices include identifying, recording, preventing, and fighting transmissible diseases (legal basis: Infection Protection Act [*Infektionsschutzgesetz*]); providing consultation on issues of environmental health and medicine (legal basis: Law on Public Health and Consumer Protection, [*Gesundheitsdienst- und Verbraucherschutzgesetz* (GDVG)]); and offering medical examinations (legal basis: Education Law [*Erziehungs- und Unterrichtsgesetz*], Civil Servant Act [*Beamtengesetz*], school regulations, etc.). A variety of disease prevention and health promotion programs and activities are conducted in schools (healthy school meals, addiction prevention programs, etc.), but there are no applicable national or state standards. As the highest education authorities, states are responsible for occupational safety, security, and health protection at schools. Occupational safety regulations apply at schools as well. The legal bases of health promotion in daycares are also not standardized in Germany.

In addition, numerous municipal tasks indirectly affect citizens' health, such as urban development projects; residential, leisure area, and traffic planning; municipal sports; youth, family, senior, and educational facilities; and business development programs. Hence, health and health promotion are affected by decisions and planning in many municipal policy fields, and there is no common legal basis for municipal health promotion.

Semipublic Institutions Among the so-called semi-public institutions that are active in disease prevention and health promotion, the statutory health insurances (SHIs) play a particularly important role (see below). Additional semipublic institutions include the federal and state dental and pharmacists associations.

After multiple revisions, § 20 SGB (Code of Social Law [*Sozialgesetzbuch*]), which was originally intended to promote the general entry of SHIs into the realm of health promotion, has been limited to primary prevention (see below) and self-help (§ 20 SGB V Prevention and self-help). In addition, SHIs can conduct activities for workplace health promotion and support self-help groups and organizations in their prevention or rehabilitation activities. Prevention within the meaning of § 20 is therefore not limited to specific disease avoidance but also includes the general improvement of health. Since 2003 (SHI Modernization Act [*GKV-Modernisierungsgesetz*]), health insurances can offer a bonus to members who regularly utilize screening or primary prevention services. This also applies to employers and members who participate in workplace health promotion activities. The bonus can be offered in the form of reduced co-payments, lower contributions, or another reward, as independently determined by each SHI.

According to SGB V, the following prevention services are included in the SHI catalog of services: workplace health promotion, prevention of work-related health hazards, promotion of self-help (§ 20a–c); vaccinations according to the recommendations of the German Standing Committee on Vaccination (Ständige Impfkommission (STIKO)) (§ 20d); diagnosis and prevention of dental diseases in group or individual prevention programs for children and adolescents (§§ 21, 22); medical prevention services (including convalescence treatments) (§ 23); services for the early detection of diseases such as the "Health Check-up," particularly for cardiovascular diseases, renal diseases, and diabetes, which the SHI covers every 2 years for members 35 years-of-age and above, and various cancer screenings (§ 25) (see Table 16.1) as well as services for the early detection of diseases that can negatively affect the physical or mental development of children (U1–U9[1]) (§ 26).

There is no compulsory vaccination in the Federal Republic of Germany. The highest health authorities of the states "publicly recommend" vaccinations on the basis of the STIKO recommendations in accordance with § 20 paragraph 3 of the Protection against Infection Act (IfSG, *Infektionsschutzgesetz*). The federal states assure care in case of vaccination-induced injury from "publically recommended" vaccinations. Table 16.2 shows an overview of the currently recommended routine vaccinations beyond the first year of life. Other vaccinations may be indicated in particular epidemiological situations or in case of risks to children, adolescents, and adults (indicated vaccinations). Indicated vaccinations also include travel vaccinations, which may be required by international health regulations (yellow fever vaccination) or may be recommended for individual protection.

Screening examinations for children in the first 6 years of life include a total of ten examinations in accordance with the information in the examination booklet for children, the expanded newborn screening, and the newborn hearing screening program (Joint Federal Committee). In some federal states, laws that aim to ensure participation in preventive medical checkups by transmitting data from registry offices and pediatricians have now come into effect.

[1] Series of health checks for children starting directly after birth (U1) until age five (U9: 60th–64th month).

Table 16.1 SHI-financed cancer screening examinations (Loss and Eichhorn 2013)

Cancer type	Entitled individuals	Examination interval	Examination method
Cervical cancer	Women from their 20th year of life	Annually	Specific history, cervical examination, pap smear, gynecological palpation, consultation
Breast cancer	Women from their 30th year of life	Annually	Specific history, inspection and palpation of the breast and the regional lymph nodes, instructions for self-examination, consultation
	Women between their 50th and 70th year of life	Every 2 years	Invitation to certified screening center, pamphlet, written history, mammography, second opinion, notification of findings
Prostate cancer	Men from their 45th year of life	Annually	Specific history, inspection and palpation of external genitalia, prostate palpation, palpation of the regional lymph nodes, consultation
Colon cancer	Women/men aged 50–54	Annually	Consultation, rectal palpation, Guajak-based fecal occult blood testing (FOBT)
	Women/men from the 55th year of life	Two examinations, 10 years apart	Consultation, colonoscopy
		or. every 2 years	Guajak-based fecal occult blood testing
Skin cancer	Women/men from their 35th year of life	Every 2 years	Targeted history, standardized visual full-body inspection of skin, consultation

Nongovernmental Institutions Nongovernmental actors that plan and implement prevention activities and services include individual health professionals, such as physicians and pharmacists; private health insurances; welfare associations, consumer advocacy centers; federal or state-wide associations as platforms for various actors within the health-care system, such as the Federal Association for Prevention and Health Promotion [*Bundesvereinigung für Prävention und Gesundheitsförderung*], state associations for health, the German Centre for Addiction Issues [*Deutsche Hauptstelle für Suchtfragen*], or the Platform for Diet and Physical Activity [*Plattform Ernährung und Bewegung (peb)*]; associations for specific diseases, such as the German Cancer Aid *[Deutsche Krebshilfe*], German AIDS Service Organization [*Deutsche AIDS-Hilfe*], the Blue Cross addiction self-help association [*Blaues Kreuz*]; national networks such as the Healthy Cities Network, the German Network of Health Promoting Hospitals or the working group Health Promoting Universities; medical working groups, such as the Association of Dermatological Prevention [*Arbeitsgemein-*

Table 16.2 Vaccination schedule (routine vaccinations) for children 2 years and above, adolescents, and adults (source: Robert Koch-Institut 2012)

<table>
<tr><th rowspan="2">Vaccination</th><th colspan="6">Age in years</th></tr>
<tr><th>2-4</th><th>5-6</th><th>9-11</th><th>12-17</th><th>18+</th><th>60+</th></tr>
<tr><td>Tetanus</td><td>C</td><td>Booster 1</td><td colspan="2">Booster 2</td><td colspan="2" rowspan="3">Booster</td></tr>
<tr><td>Diphtheria</td><td>C</td><td>Booster 1</td><td colspan="2">Booster 2</td></tr>
<tr><td>Pertussis</td><td>C</td><td>Booster 1</td><td colspan="2">Booster 2</td></tr>
<tr><td>Hemophilus influenza B</td><td>C</td><td colspan="5"></td></tr>
<tr><td>Poliomyelitis</td><td colspan="2">C</td><td colspan="2">Booster 1</td><td colspan="2"></td></tr>
<tr><td>Hepatitis B</td><td colspan="4">C</td><td colspan="2"></td></tr>
<tr><td>Meningococcal C</td><td colspan="4">C</td><td colspan="2"></td></tr>
<tr><td>Measles</td><td colspan="4">C</td><td>Standard vaccination*</td><td></td></tr>
<tr><td>Mumps, rubella</td><td colspan="4">C</td><td></td><td></td></tr>
<tr><td>Varicella</td><td colspan="4">C</td><td></td><td></td></tr>
<tr><td>Influenza</td><td colspan="5"></td><td>Standard annual vaccination</td></tr>
<tr><td>Pneumococcal</td><td colspan="5"></td><td>Standard vaccination</td></tr>
<tr><td>Human papillomavirus</td><td colspan="3"></td><td>Standard vaccination (girls)</td><td colspan="2"></td></tr>
</table>

C Catch-up vaccination (primary vaccination for all individuals who have not yet been vaccinated or completion of an incomplete series)
*One-time vaccination, preferably using an Measles, mumps, and rubella (MMR) vaccine, of all persons born after 1970 and ≥18 years of age who have an unclear vaccination status, are unvaccinated, or received only one vaccination in childhood

schaft Dermatologische Prävention]; private foundations that combat a specific disease, such as the Felix Burda Foundation (colon cancer prevention) and the Michael Stich Foundation (for HIV-infected children); self-help organizations and groups; and sports clubs, and information centers.

While the statutes, professional codes of conduct, or mission statements of these institutions often explicitly list prevention tasks, there is no federal or state-level legal basis specifying the responsibility for or implementation of prevention activities.

The legal framework and cost reimbursement by the health insurances strongly affect the utilization of preventative services. In the two following sections, we present the methods and results of the literature review and investigate to what extent utilization behavior is additionally influenced by socioeconomic status, age, migration status, and gender.

Systematic Review

Methods

The search strategy employed here is an extension of the strategy used in two recent papers, published in 2009 and 2012 (Janßen, Grosse Frie, and Ommen 2009; Janßen, Sauter, and Kowalski 2012). In 2009, a systematic literature review was conducted to determine the extent to which social status characteristics are associated with the utilization of services within the entire German health-care system (Janßen, Grosse Frie, and Ommen 2009). Thirty-two studies were identified that were published between 2000 and 2008. According to the results of these studies, the overall level of health care provided to all social status groups in Germany is relatively high, and hardly any differences were found in the curative or rehabilitative care received across status groups. There were, however, marked differences with regard to the groups' use of prevention and health promotion services, suggesting that prevention and health promotion programs aimed at influencing individuals' use of such services, providing them with relevant health and disease information, and impacting the way this information is used must be tailored to less privileged social status groups.

In light of the findings of the 2009 review, the 2012 review only focused on the utilization of prevention and health promotion services using search terms only for the mentioned topics, while the first review and its search terms included the medical system in general. A new literature search was conducted using MedPilot to identify relevant articles published between 1998 and 2010; 23 papers were identified, of which 20 showed a clear association between socioeconomic status and the utilization of prevention and health promotion measures. However, no studies were retrieved that presented results on tertiary prevention services and measures.

The search strategy for this review was extended by including a number of additional (medical subject headings (MeSH)) terms and by including the term "rehabilitation," which includes measures of tertiary prevention. On the other hand, the search was restricted to the PubMed database. The search strategy used on 8 October 2012 was:

> health AND german* AND (socioeconomic factors [MeSH] OR education* OR profession* OR occupational groups [MeSH] OR occupation* OR gender identity [MeSH] OR gender OR sex OR age* OR emigrants and immigrants [MeSH] OR migration*) AND (preventive health services [MeSH] OR preventive medicine [MeSH] OR prevent* OR early diagnosis [MeSH] OR rehabilitation [MeSH] OR rehabilitation* OR disability evaluation [MeSH] OR recovery of function [MeSH]) AND (utilization OR use OR usage) AND (german [Language] OR english [Language]) AND ("2002"[Date—Publication]: "3000"[Date—Publication])

Retrieved papers were considered for the review if they were published in English or German and reported empirical findings (original articles). Papers that otherwise fulfilled the inclusion criteria were not considered if relevant models were used in the analyses but not reported in the tables or results section, e.g., if they were variables for which the authors "controlled" or "adjusted" in the analyses. If multivariate and bivariate results were reported for the same variables, only multivariate results are presented in the table. If no significance test was performed, differences were reported if they appeared to be substantial to the authors. Some studies reported differences according to the health insurance status, which—although correlated with socioeconomic status—was not part of the search strategy and therefore not reported. In some studies, coefficients for some variables of interest were reported for the whole sample but not broken down by country; results of such studies were only reported if separate analyses were undertaken for Germany. Studies were excluded if they generally referred to utilization of health-care services without differentiating for prevention. Studies were excluded if they referred to rehabilitation in general without providing information on concrete tertiary preventive measures. Studies were also excluded if the results only referred to the individuals' utilization behavior with regard to preventive/health promoting measures outside the health-care services. In addition, studies that reported on the utilization of health-related website or health-related information-seeking behavior were excluded. Titles and abstracts of the 438 references retrieved were screened by two independent researchers (FK, CK) to see if they meet these criteria. A total of 71 full articles were assessed for eligibility, of which 23 were excluded, resulting in 48 articles that are presented in Table 16.3.

Results

Table 16.3 presents the results of the systematic review. Only study findings pertaining to socioeconomic status, education, occupation, income, age, gender, and migration are listed. In many of the studies, additional factors were also investigated for associations with the utilization of prevention services, but these are not presented in the table. In the "area of interest" column, we distinguish between primary, secondary, and tertiary prevention, knowing that these categories are not necessarily mutually exclusive. We omit the primordial prevention category that is used by the World Health Organization (WHO) (Bonita, Beaglehole, and Kjellström 2006), which is still rarely used in the German literature.

For secondary prevention, results by and large demonstrate a substantial association between socioeconomic status, gender, and German citizenship/nonmigrant status on the one hand and the utilization of health care on the other. This is especially true for cancer screening programs. For primary and tertiary prevention, however, the findings are less conclusive with regard to socioeconomic status and gender. Vaccination rates, for example, tend to be higher for adults with higher socioeconomic status. However, results show that children of higher socioeconomic status (SES) parents are less vaccinated. Overall, migrants/non-German citizens show the least utilization of primary, secondary, and tertiary prevention services. Age is positively or negatively associated with the utilization of a number of preventive measures, in many cases due to recommendations; for example, people over

Table 16.3 A breakdown of the reviewed studies by area of interest, design/participants, region of study, dependent variable, and findings

Study	Area of interest	Design/Participants	Region(s) of study	Dependent variable(s)	Findings
Albert et al. 2012 (G)	Secondary prevention	Cross-sectional paper-based survey/3,226 participants from a representative sample (50–69-year-old women)	Ten federal states in Germany	Mammography screening participation rate	Bivariate analyses: Higher participation in screening by women with lower education, lower HHI; no significant differences for age, employment status
Bader et al. 2004 (G)	Primary prevention	Documentation of immunization coverage by occupational physicians at occupational health checks for 12,720 workers	Schleswig- Holstein	Immunization coverage for diphtheria, tetanus, poliomyelitis, measles, mumps, rubella, hepatitis A and B	Bivariate analyses without significance tests: "immunization coverage was higher in women, young adults and health-care workers."
Beitz et al. 2004 (G)	Primary prevention (OTC/CAM)	Population-based cross-sectional survey/7,099 individuals aged 18–79.	Germany	OTC use for preventive (self-medication) purposes	Bivariate analysis: More women reported using OTC for preventive purposes
Bergmann et al. 2005	Primary, secondary, and tertiary prevention	Population-based, cross-sectional telephone survey/8,318 individuals	Germany	Influenza vaccination coverage, health checkup utilization, cancer screening, medical rehabilitation	Bivariate analyses: Men and 50–79-year-old individuals go in for health checkups more often, no association with social status. Women and higher social status groups use cancer screening services more often. No gender differences were found in the current uptake of flu vaccinations; an association found between flu vaccinations and social status was no longer present after controlling for overall health status. Medical rehabilitation slightly more often used by women

Table 16.3 (continued)

Study	Area of interest	Design/Participants	Region(s) of study	Dependent variable(s)	Findings
Blank et al. 2009[a] (E)	Primary prevention	Population-based cross-sectional telephone survey with 2,002 respondents aged 14 years or older	Germany	Influenza vaccination coverage rates	Multivariate analyses: lower coverage in older patients, no differences regarding "work in medical field" and income groups
Böhmer et al. 2011 (E)	Primary prevention	Population-based cross-sectional household telephone survey with 21,262 adults	Germany	Tetanus and seasonal influenza vaccine coverage	Multivariate analyses: tetanus vaccination coverage associated with being male, younger age, high/medium socioeconomic status, no/only one-sided migration status; older age associated with influenza vaccination coverage, two-sided migration background, no sign. association with gender and SES
Chenot et al. 2008 (E)	Primary/tertiary prevention	Longitudinal telephone survey among participants of an RCT/1,342 individuals aged 18 and older with low back pain from 116 general practices	two medium-size university cities and surrounding small towns and rural areas	Participation in back schools	Bivariate analysis: No gender differences in participation in back schools
Freund et al. 2010 (G)	Primary/ secondary prevention	Cross-sectional paper-based survey/299 patients from five general practices	Germany (Berlin, Wiesbaden)	Participation in health screening program "Check up 35", vaccine coverage	Bivariate analyses without significance tests: Women indicated incomplete vaccination coverage more often, decreasing coverage from 18 to age 75, >75 years indicate highest coverage; no gender difference for the Check up 35, higher utilization among participants with lower formal education

Table 16.3 (continued)

Study	Area of interest	Design/Participants	Region(s) of study	Dependent variable(s)	Findings
Friedrichs et al. 2009 (G)	Primary prevention	Analyses of data from approx. 5.2 million insured individuals from 74 company health insurance funds	Germany	Participation in prevention bonus programs	Bivariate analyses: Higher level of education and age 30–49 years (female) and 40 and older (male) are positively associated with participation in bonus programs
Geyer & Micheelis 2012 (E)	Secondary prevention	Three population-based cross-sectional surveys (conducted in 1989, 1997, 2005)/500, 655, 921 respondents aged 35–44	Germany	Routine-based/problem-based dentist utilization pattern	Multivariate analyses: For the 2005 survey, male gender, lowest education, and lowest HHI were signficantly associated with problem-based dentist utilization pattern. For the 1989 survey, male gender, lowest HHI were sign. associated with problem-based dentist utilization pattern. No sign. associations for 1997
Gölder et al. 2007 (E)	Secondary prevention	Data from 631 individuals aged 40 and older	Regensburg	Participation in flexible sigmoidoscopy (FS)	Bivariate analysis: Male patients participated in the FS screening more often than female patients
Grande et al. 2002 (G)	Tertiary prevention (Rehabilitation)	Prospective paper-pencil survey/668 acute myocardial infarction patients from 67 clinics	North Rhine-Westphalia	Participation in various cardiac rehabilitative measures	Bivariate analyses: Males participate in cycling, group sports, stress prevention training more frequently. No sign. gender differences for a number of other measures, like smoking cessation courses

Table 16.3 (continued)

Study	Area of interest	Design/Participants	Region(s) of study	Dependent variable(s)	Findings
Hauswaldt et al. 2010 (G)	Primary prevention	Secondary analysis of 1) contract physicians' union of Lower Saxony data with all physicians vaccinating against influenza in the winter seasons of 1995/1996, 2002/2003, and 2005/2006, and 2) from direct access to the electronic practice record system of 79 general practices	Lower Saxony	Influenza vaccine coverage	Patients over 60 more likely to be vaccinated
Huber et al. 2009 (E)	Primary prevention	Analyses of 5,013 enquiries from 4,091 patients	Germany (two thirds of users from Saxony)	Utilization of a drug information service	Univariate analyses: Women and older patients used information service more often
Jung 2011 (G)	Secondary prevention	Data from 1,351 HIV-antibody tests	Bremen/Cologne	Participation in HIV-antibody test	Univariate analysis: People with higher education, younger age overrepresented among the users; no gender differences
Kamtsiuris 2007 (G)	Secondary prevention	Population-based interview and examination survey/17,418 children and adolescents aged 0–17	Germany	Participation in early diagnostic tests for children	Bivariate analyses: Participation increases with higher social status, nonmigration status; no association with gender; no differences between 7-to-10-year-olds and 11-to-13-year-olds

Table 16.3 (continued)

Study	Area of interest	Design/Participants	Region(s) of study	Dependent variable(s)	Findings
Klug et al. 2005 (E)	Secondary prevention	Cross-sectional paper-and-pencil survey/532 women aged 25–75	Bielefeld	Participation in breast and cervical cancer screening	Bivariate analyses: Social class was positively associated with younger age at first pap smear/first breast examination by a medical doctor; negatively associated with ever having had a mammography (among those who ever had a mammography, social class was positively associated with younger age at first mammography)
Koller et al. 2009 (E)	Primary/ Secondary prevention	Analysis of medical checkup prior to school enrollment/9,353 children ~ 6 years	Munich	Participation in health checkups and immunization	Multivariate analyses: Other than German mother tongue, significantly associated with incomplete U1–U9 checkups and with complete immunizations. DVs have no significant associations with gender. High number of low-education households on school district level sign. associated with incomplete U1–U9 checkups and complete immunizations
Maywald et al. 2005 (G)	Primary prevention	Analyses of 3,080 enquiries	Metropolitan region of Dresden	Utilization of a drug information service	Univariate analyses: Women and older patients used information service more often

Table 16.3 (continued)

Study	Area of interest	Design/Participants	Region(s) of study	Dependent variable(s)	Findings
Mielck et al. 2006 (E)	Tertiary prevention	Analyses of data from a myocardial infarction registry and from a population-based survey/378 patients with type 2 diabetes	Augsburg	Participation in Diabetes training courses	Multivariate analysis: Diabetic persons with a low educational level and oldest patient group (70–87 years) participated in diabetes training courses least often, especially in the subsample with a previous myocardial infarction. No association between gender and participation
Morgenroth et al. 2005 (G)	Primary prevention	Analyses of documentation of 15,682 children aged 24–30 months from 196 pediatric practices	KV-district Nordrhein	Vaccination coverage	Multivariate analyses: Other than German household language, associated with complete vaccination for diphtheria and tetanus (DT)/ measles, and rubella (MMR). Mother having Abitur sign. associated with incomplete MMR vaccination, mother having Realschulabschluss (intermediate degree) associated with complete DT vaccination (ref. no formal school leaving certificate)
Müller & Szucs 2007 (E)	Primary prevention	Population-based cross-sectional telephone survey/5,990 individuals aged 14 years or older	Germany	Influenza vaccination coverage	Bivariate analyses: Vaccination coverage rate increases with age (except youngest, oldest age group); females more likely to be vaccinated (not sign. in one of the three cohorts)
Poethko-Müller et al. 2009 (E)	Primary prevention	Population-based interview and examination survey/14,826 children and adolescents aged 2–17	Germany	Measles vaccination coverage	Multivariate analyses: Foreign-born and 2-year-olds more likely to be unvaccinated. No impact of gender, SES

Table 16.3 (continued)

Study	Area of interest	Design/Participants	Region(s) of study	Dependent variable(s)	Findings
Poethko-Müller et al. 2007 (G)	Primary prevention	Population-based interview and examination survey/16,460 children and adolescents aged 0–17	Germany	Tetanus, diphtheria, pertussis, Hib, hepatitis B and polio vaccination as well as first dose of measles, mumps and rubella (MMR) coverage	Bivariate analyses: Vaccination coverage for pertussis, Hib and hepatitis B is higher in younger than in older age groups. No sign. overall gender differences. In higher age groups, lower vaccination coverage in migrants for tetanus, diphtheria, Hib, and polio. Complete vaccination for tetanus, diphtheria, and polio higher for middle compared to low, high SES. MMR vaccination rate lower in high SES group.
Reuss et al. 2010 (E)	Primary prevention	Analyses of billing data of the German Associations of SHI Physicians/61.5 million individuals	14 of 17 regions in Germany	Influenza vaccination coverage	Bivariate analyses: Influenza vaccination coverage increases with age
Richter et al. 2002 (G)	Secondary prevention,	Cross-sectional, population-based survey/1920 individuals aged 18–79	North Rhine-Westphalia	Participation in cancer screening, health checkup, health promotion programs	Bivariate analyses: Women undergo cancer screening exams and use health promotion programs more often. More upper class individuals took part in a health promotion program. Multivariate analyses: Men in the middle and upper classes took part in cancer screening programs more often than men in low social classes. No gender differences or social gradient was found for participation in health check-ups

Table 16.3 (continued)

Study	Area of interest	Design/Participants	Region(s) of study	Dependent variable(s)	Findings
Ringwald et al. 2006 (E)	Primary prevention	Cross-sectional standardized survey/6,812 whole blood donors	Baden-Wuerttemberg/Hesse	Hepatits B vaccination coverage	Multivariate analyses: Younger age was significantly associated with higher hepatitis B vaccination. Beside health-care workers, teaching professions and students showed the highest Hepatitis B vaccination rate. No significant gender differences
Röckl-Wiedmann et al. 2002 (G)	Secondary prevention	Cross-sectional CAPI survey/1938 individuals aged 18–79	Bavaria	Vaccination coverage (tetanus, polio, Hep A, Hep B), participation in screening programs	Multivariate analyses: Level of education, social class, HHI is positively associated with vaccination rates. Higher social class is associated with an increased likelihood of HIV testing, but not with use of mammography
Roggendorf et al. 2011 (G)	Primary prevention	Cross-sectional paper-and-pencil survey/1,670 employees and staff members of a University Hospital	Essen	Influenza vaccination coverage	Bivariate analyses: Vaccination rate increases with age and was highest among medical doctors. Multivariate analysis: vaccination coverage increases with age
Rückinger et al. 2008a (G)	Secondary prevention	Analyses of billing data/2,223,135 women age 20 and older	Bavaria	Participation in screening for cervical cancer	Bivariate, ecological analysis: Participation rates are lower in districts with lower average household income. Bivariate analysis: participation decreases with age

Table 16.3 (continued)

Study	Area of interest	Design/Participants	Region(s) of study	Dependent variable(s)	Findings
Rückinger et al. 2008b (G)	Secondary prevention	Analyses of billing data/2,223,135 women age 20 and older	Bavaria	Participation in screening for cervical cancer	Bivariate analysis: participation decreases with age
Schenk & Knopf 2007 (G)	Secondary prevention	Population-based interview and examination survey/17,641 children and adolescents aged 0–17	Germany	Participation in annual dental checkups, use of pharmaceutical preparations for caries prevention	Bivariate analyses: Higher social status groups and nonmigrants, 3–6-year-olds have annual dental checkups more often. Nonmigrants, 0–2-year-olds use pharmaceutical preparations for caries prevention more often
Schenkel et al. 2008 (E)	Primary prevention	Population-based cross-sectional telephone survey/406 individuals aged 18 and older	Germany	Hepatitis B vaccination coverage	Bivariate analyses: Higher education levels associated with higher vaccination coverage. Multivariate analyses: vaccination coverage decreased with age
Schmitt et al. 2011 (E)	Secondary prevention	Analyses of 12,187 skin screening participants aged 14–34 years	Saxony	Participation in skin cancer screening program	Univariate analyses: Participation in skin cancer screening program more likely in women. Participation increased slightly with age in women
Schultze-Lutter et al. 2008 (E)	Secondary prevention	Analyses of 872 first contacts	Metropolitan area of Cologne	Utilization of center for early detection for mental crisis	German citizens and people with higher education overrepresented among the clients
Schwarz et al. 2005 (E)	Secondary prevention	Population-based cross-sectional survey/2186 women aged 20–79	Western Pomerania	participation in cervical cancer screening	Bivariate analysis: Participation in any cancer screening was less frequent in young (20–29 years) as well as older women (≥70 years)

Table 16.3 (continued)

Study	Area of interest	Design/Participants	Region(s) of study	Dependent variable(s)	Findings
Sieverding et al. 2008 (G)	Secondary prevention	Population-based cross-sectional paper-and-pencil survey/10,659 men aged 45–70	Germany	Participation in prostate cancer early detection (DRE/PSA test)	Multivariate analyses: Use of prostate cancer screening (digital rectal examination and PSA test) is associated with higher age, higher income, and having a college/university degree
Sieverding et al. 2008 (E)	Secondary prevention	Population-based panel survey/15,810 individuals aged 50–70 years without a personal history of cancer	Germany	Fecal occult blood test (FOBT) use	Multivariate analysis: Use of FOBT is associated with age, education level, income, and female gender
Sieverding et al. 2010 (G)	Secondary prevention	Population-based panel survey/15,810 individuals aged 50–70 years without a personal history of cancer	Germany	Colonoscopy use	Bivariate analysis: There are hardly any differences in the percentages of men and women having undergone a colonoscopy. Multivariate analysis: Colonoscopy use is highest in high income group (in women) and higher school degree group (in men)
Simoes et al. 2009 (G)	Secondary prevention	Analyses of perinatal data of 556,948 pregnant women	Baden-Württemberg	Attendance of prenatal checkups	Bivariate analyses: Attendance of prenatal checkups is lower among non-Germans, unskilled and semi-skilled mothers, mothers with low occupational status
Stock & Brenner 2010 (E)	Secondary prevention	Population-based cross-sectional CAPI survey with 1,175 respondents aged 50 years or older	Germany	FOBT/lower gastrointestinal endoscopy use	Age-standardized analyses: FOBT use is higher in women (but not statistically significant). No differences in lower gastrointestinal endoscopy use

Table 16.3 (continued)

Study	Area of interest	Design/Participants	Region(s) of study	Dependent variable(s)	Findings
Stock et al. 2011 (E)	Secondary prevention	Analyses of claims data/170,493 individuals	Hesse	Colonoscopy and fecal occult blood test (FOBT) use	Age-standardized colonoscopy and FOBT participation was higher in women. FOBT rates increased with age
Szucs et al. 2006 (G)	Primary prevention	Population-based cross-sectional telephone survey/5,990 individuals aged 14 years or older	Germany	Influenza vaccination coverage	Bivariate analyses: Respondents > = 60 more likely to be vaccinated than < 60; females more likely to be vaccinated (significant in one of the three cohorts). Health-care workers statistically less likely to be vaccinated in one of three cohorts. Vaccination coverage decreases with higher HHI (survey 2004/2005)
Teich et al. 2011 (E)	Primary prevention	Consecutive sample, cross-sectional survey/203 patients from three institutions suffering from Crohn's disease or ulcerative colitis	Saxony	Vaccination coverage	Univariate analyses: No significant differences in vaccination status for age or educational level
Von dem Knesebeck & Mielck 2009 (G)	Secondary prevention	Cross-sectional CAPI and paper-and-pencil survey/1,921 individuals aged 50 or older	Germany	Participation in mammography in the last 2 years, ever endoscopic examination of colon, eye examination in the last 2 years	Multivariate analyses: Higher education, equivalized income, financial assets are significantly associated with mammography use. Higher education and financial assets are sign. associated with examination of colon, eye examination

Table 16.3 (continued)

Study	Area of interest	Design/Participants	Region(s) of study	Dependent variable(s)	Findings
Wicker et al. 2011 (G)	Primary prevention	Questionnaire survey, serological tests and checkup of the certificates of vaccination in 324 s year medical students	Frankfurt/Main	Measles vaccination coverage	Bivariate analyses: Female (compared to male) and German (compared to foreign) students were sign. more likely to have had two or more measles vaccinations
Zeeb et al. 2004 (G)	Primary/secondary prevention	Cross-sectional survey of accompanying parents at preschool examinations/565 adults	Bielefeld	Utilization of preventive programs	Bivariate analyses: Female Germans utilized preventive programs (cancer screening, cardiovascular, prenatal, general, dental checkup) more frequently than female immigrants. Male Germans only used dental checkups significantly more often than male immigrants

G German, *E* English, *HHI* household income, *SHI* statutory health insurance, *DV* dependent variable, *Abitur* German highschool degree qualifying for university, *SES* socioeconomic status, *PP* primary prevention, *SP* secondary prevention, *W* women, *M* men, *OTC* over-the-counter drug, *DRE* digital rectal exam, *PSA* prostate-specific antigen, *RCT* randomized controlled trial, *Hib* haemophilus influenza type B, *CAPI* computer-assisted personal interview, *Hep* A hepatitis A, *Hep* B hepatitis B, If multi- and bivariate results reported for the same variables, only multivariate results are presented in the table

[a] Analyses for more than one country, only results for Germany are presented in the table

age 60 are a target group for influenza vaccination. Most articles that are included in this review focus on primary or secondary prevention, with few articles investigating the utilization of rehabilitative care or tertiary prevention. None of the identified studies used qualitative methods to explore their research questions.

Discussion

The aim of this study was to examine differences in the utilization of prevention services in Germany with regard to socioeconomic status, age, gender, and migrant status by means of a systematic review of the recent literature. As evidenced by the findings presented in Table 16.3, many of the 48 reviewed studies provided relatively clear evidence of a significant association between higher social status, female gender, as well as a nonmigrant status on the one hand and greater use of preventive services on the other. Evidence of this association was provided for almost the whole of Germany. Our review built on two previous articles (Janßen, Grosse Frie, and Ommen 2009;Janßen, Sauter, and Kowalski 2012) and used a search strategy that was carefully refined after reviewing the results of those two articles. The choice of search terms played a major role in the review process: The search strategy was restricted to articles published in journals listed in the Pubmed database to ensure high quality of the studies and to avoid the identification of too many irrelevant papers. Of course, this strategy might lead to overlooking relevant results from studies published in journals not listed in Pubmed as well as results not published in peer-reviewed journals. When interpreting the review's results, this should be taken into account as well as the fact that significant results tend to be published more often. This may mean that studies finding no differences by social status were not published and therefore not identified during this review. As another form of publication bias, many publishers tend to prefer quantitative methods over qualitative methods. As a result, only quantitative studies were identified in this review.

The search strategy used in this review yielded 48 studies that were considered relevant, compared to 23 in the paper published in 2012. Two studies (Schultze-Lutter et al. 2008;Schultze-Lutter, Ruhrmann, and Klosterkötter 2009) investigated different questions but used the same data set and therefore provided identical descriptive results; they were included as one study in the results table. The higher number of retrieved studies is in part due to the inclusion of studies that investigate the utilization of rehabilitation services. Rehabilitation is considered tertiary prevention and was not included in the first paper. A number of additional search terms were used, resulting in a more elaborate search strategy. However, 13 of the studies that were included in the previous review either were not included in this review because of their focus on individual behavior outside the health services system or were not retrieved by this search strategy—several of them because of the different publication period chosen.

Overall, the review shows that depending on the specific service, there are strong relationships between indicators of socioeconomic status, gender, age, and migration background and the utilization of prevention services. Especially with regard to secondary prevention, utilization increases with higher general socioeconomic status as well as in cases where income and education are investigated as separate indicators. Albert et al. point out that although in their own analyses, nonparticipation in cancer screening was associated with higher social status, a relevant proportion of women in the higher status group use cancer early detection services outside of the established screening programs. This assumption is in accordance with findings from a review by Scheffer et al. (Scheffer, Dauven, and Sieverding 2006), which shows that utilization of cancer early detection services is associated with higher social status.

In some studies, vaccination coverage in children decreases with higher social status, most likely due to parents preferring to not have their children vaccinated rather than a lack of opportunities. Migrant/non-German citizenship status is strongly associated with lower utilization of primary and secondary (and tertiary) prevention. Female gender is associated with higher utilization of secondary, and, to a smaller extent, primary prevention services. The results are less conclusive with regard to age, largely due to different recommendations, for example, with regard to vaccinations. Gender tends to have a greater effect on the use of prevention services than characteristics of vertical social inequality. This is in part due to the greater public awareness of specific preventive measures for women and does not take into consideration the degree to which the offered measures are necessary and under which circumstances they were used. Notably, one study (Geyer and Micheelis 2012) did not regress the utilization/frequency of preventive consultations to SES, age, and the like, but to the ratio of preventive versus problem-based dentist visits. Correlations of lifetime events, e.g., screening and age (like those presented by Siverding et al. 2010), are not listed in the table since it is obvious that older patients have had more time to ever utilize specific measures.

There are still some "blind spots" in the research on this topic, for example, the lack of studies on tertiary prevention. By including search terms related to rehabilitation, we tried to address this shortcoming of the before-mentioned review from 2012 (Janßen, Sauter, and Kowalski 2012), but using this general term does not allow investigating the utilization of specific tertiary prevention measures. Instead, larger sets of services, such as those provided during inpatient rehabilitation, are investigated; as a result, the studies cannot present results on single, clearly preventive measures. The exclusion of papers investigating health-related behavior (such as toothbrushing, sunscreen use, and bicycle helmet use) only led to an exclusion of articles aiming at health promotion measures that are not based on health-care services, such as cancer screening or vaccination. Depending on the outcome measure, it is difficult to distinguish between preventive and problem-oriented care in a number of settings; this is especially true in dental health (Geyer and Micheelis 2012). Although concerted efforts to better reach the socially disadvantaged have been recently undertaken (e.g., by the German Federal Ministry of Education and Research), there is a lack of published intervention studies in this area.

Although the search strategy identified a number of studies reporting associations between rehabilitation participation and the individual factors investigated here, only two of them reported associations with these factors for specific tertiary prevention measures within rehabilitation. Studies not reporting on specific measures are not presented in the table. The interpretation of participation rates in tertiary prevention measures during inpatient rehabilitation is always difficult. As Grande et al. point out, the utilization of specific services cannot be interpreted independently of an individual's needs. This is true for the utilization of all preventive services and especially for tertiary prevention within rehabilitation. Although we generally support the distinction between four dimensions of prevention, the rare use of the category "primordial prevention" in the German literature led to its omission in this review.

All of the determinants of service utilization that were examined in this review (i.e., education, occupation, income, gender, age, and migration status) may be categorized either as predisposing or as enabling (i.e., income) individual factors (Andersen and Davidson 2001;Andersen 2008). Finding causal explanations of the findings is challenging. Both education and migration status might be considered proxies for difficulties in understanding and navigating through the health services system, i.e., of limited health literacy, a concept with high potential of being integrated more strongly in the behavioral model. For a number of measures, variations in utilization by age and gender are explained by health insurance coverage. Some studies, for instance, by Rückinger and colleagues, use data on average income in individual regions rather than individual or household income, not in an effort to include these as contextual factors but because individual-level data are not available (Rückinger et al. 2008). This particular type of ecological analysis makes it difficult to derive causal inferences, particularly since the individual characteristic is not (and cannot be) controlled for. Multilevel approaches are needed, and besides representative surveys, claims data are key to identify individual and contextual factors for certain preventative measures, particularly those covered by health insurance.

Many of the indicators used in the studies are operationalized very heterogenously, which makes cross-study comparisons difficult. This is true for both the utilization of different thresholds/cutpoints, for example, with regard to income, age, or educational groups, as well as for the grouping of occupational groups and the definition of migrant status (citizenship, mother tongue, etc.). The data that were analyzed in the selected studies differed in various respects, for example, with regard to study design, sampling method, or sample size, which must be considered when interpreting the results. Some studies investigated samples of service users, without "controls" (Jung 2011;Schultze-Lutter et al. 2008;Schultze-Lutter, Ruhrmann, and Klosterkötter 2009). Differences between participants and nonparticipants were therefore made by comparisons with the general population. However, no studies were excluded because of a weak study design or small/unrepresentative sample. As mentioned by several authors (for example Schenk & Knopf 2007), self-reports of respondents/patients often overestimate actual utilization. More reliable data, however, are often scarce, not generalizable, or do not allow for correlation with indicators of socioeconomic status. We did not discuss the effectiveness of the different preventive measures presented here. This has been done elsewhere, for example, with regard to general routine health checks in a recent publication (Krogsbøll et al.2012; Boulware et al. 2007).

In the long term, it seems imperative to more strongly fight the causes of health inequality on a prevention level instead of merely focusing on curative and rehabilitative activities. In our view, there are essentially three strategies to tackle differences in utilization of prevention services and the general problem of differences in morbidities and mortalities between population groups. Firstly, we must strengthen target group-specific prevention programs and increase the number of program participants, for instance, through a stronger emphasis on the settings approach. Programs in the school setting, for example, are promising since they reach all members of a school grade, who can also take these activities to the family setting. Target group-specific prevention programs can therefore compensate for health inequalities resulting from differences in social status in an effort to optimize care.

Secondly, we must examine the causes of differences in health services provision and the distribution of disease to build a dual strategy. The results of socio-epidemiological studies that show a significant connection between socioeconomic inequality and health principally suggest the following: The best prevention is reducing socioeconomic inequality while adapting activities to meet the particular needs of those most affected. Specifically, this can mean that schools and companies play a dual role in reducing health inequalities: By acting as short-term, medium-term, and long-term settings for prevention and health promotion programs, reaching people where they already spend time, as well as by combating inequalities in (continued) education, which represent a cause of health inequalities, in the medium and long term.

The third approach focuses on each individual's responsibility to take specific action. It requires stronger appeals to personal responsibility and freedom of choice. No one is forced to smoke, consume harmful amounts of alcohol, lead a sedentary lifestyle, or eat unhealthy foods.

References

Albert, U. S., et al. "Das populationsbezogene Mammografie-Screening-Programm in Deutschland: Inanspruchnahme und erste Erfahrungen von Frauen in 10 Bundesländern." *Das Gesundheitswesen* 74 (2012): 61–70.

Andersen, R. M. and Davidson, P. L. "Improving Access to Care in America: Individual and Contextual Indicators." *Changing the U.S. health care system: key issues in health services, policy, and management*. Ed. R. M. Andersen, T. H. Rice, and E. F. Kominski. San Franisco: Jossey-Bass, 2001. 3–30.

Andersen, R. M. "National health surveys and the behavioral model of health services use." *Medical Care* 46 (2008): 647–53.

Antonovsky, A. "Social Class, Life Expectancy and Overall Mortality." *The Milbank Memorial Fund Quarterly* 45 (1967): 31–73.

Arber, S. and Thomas, H. "From Women's Health to a Gender Analysis of Health." *The Blackwell companion to medical sociology*. Ed. W. C. Cockerham. Oxford: Blackwell, 2001.

Bader, H.-M. and Egler, P. "Initiativen zur Steigerung der Impfbereitschaft in Schleswig-Holstein: Impfschutz bei Erwachsenen in der Arbeitswelt 2003." *Bundesgesundheitsblatt—Gesundheitsforschung—Gesundheitsschutz* 47 (2004): 1204–15.

Beitz, R., et al. "Selbstmedikation mit Over-the-Counter-(OTC-) Präparaten in Deutschland." *Bundesgesundheitsblatt—Gesundheitsforschung—Gesundheitsschutz* 47 (2004): 1043–50.

Bergmann, E., Kalcklösch, M., and Tiemann, F. "Inanspruchnahme des Gesundheitswesens: Erste Ergebnisse des telefonischen Gesundheitssurveys 2003." *Bundesgesundheitsblatt—Gesundheitsforschung—Gesundheitsschutz* 48 (2005): 1365–73.

Berkman and Kawachi, I. *Social Epidemiology*. New York: Oxford University Press, 2000.

Blank, P. R., Schwenkglenks, M., and Szucs, T. D. "Vaccination coverage rates in eleven European countries during two consecutive influenza seasons." *Journal of Infection* 58 (2009): 446–58.

Böhmer, M. M., et al. "Determinants of tetanus and seasonal influenza vaccine uptake in adults living in Germany." *Human Vaccines* 7 (2011): 1317–25.

Bonita, R., Beaglehole, R., and Kjellström, T. *Basic Epidemiology*. 2 ed. Geneva: World Health Organization, 2006.

Boulware, L. E., et al. "Systematic review: the value of the periodic health evaluation." *Annals of Internal Medicine* 146 (2007): 289–300.

Breckenkamp, J., Mielck, A., and Razum, O. "Health inequalities in Germany: do regional-level variables explain differentials in cardiovascular risk?" *BMC Public Health* 7 (2007): 132.

Chenot, J.-F., et al. "Sex differences in presentation, course, and management of low back pain in primary care." *The Clinical Journal of Pain* 24 (2008): 578–84.

Freund, T., et al. "Gesundheitsuntersuchung und Impfstatus: Ergebnisse einer Patientenbefragung in deutschen Hausarztpraxen." *Das Gesundheitswesen* 72 (2010): 804–07.

Friedrichs, M., Friedel, H., and Bödeker, W. "Teilnehmerstruktur und ökonomischer Nutzen präventiver Bonusprogramme in der betrieblichen Krankenversicherung." *Das Gesundheitswesen* 71 (2009): 623–27.

Gemeinsamer Bundesausschuss. *Richtlinien des Bundesausschusses der Ärzte und Krankenkassen uber Die Früherkennung von Krankheiten bei Kindern bis zur Vollendung des 6. Lebensjahres („Kinder-Richtlinien")*. Ed. Gemeinsamer Bundesausschuss. Gemeinsamer Bundesausschuss, 2011.

Geyer, S. and Micheelis, W. "Changes in problem-based and routine-based healthcare attendance: a comparison of three national dental health surveys." *Community Dentistry and Oral Epidemiology* 40 (2012): 459–67.

Gölder, S., et al. "Acceptance of flexible sigmoidoscopy as a screening examination for colorectal cancer in an outpatient clinic." *International Journal of Colorectal Disease* 22 (2007): 387–94.

Grande, G., et al. "Frauen und Männer nach Herzinfarkt: Gibt es in Deutschland geschlechtsspezifische Unterschiede in der Inanspruchnahme rehabilitativer Leistungen?" *Die Rehabilitation* 41 (2002): 320–28.

Hauswaldt, J., Kersting, M., and Hummers-Pradier, E. "Influenza vaccination by lower saxonian general practitioners: a secondary analysis of physicians' data from 1995/1996, 2002/2003 and 2005/2006." *Das Gesundheitswesen* 72 (2010): 332–39.

Hinkle, L. E. Jr., et al. "Occupation, education, and coronary heart disease." *Science* 161 (1968): 238–46.

Huber, M., Kullak-Ublick, G. A., and Kirch, W. "Drug information for patients—an update of long-term results: type of enquiries and patient characteristics." *Pharmacoepidemiology and Drug Safety* 18 (2009): 111–19.

Janßen, C., Grosse Frie, K., and Ommen, O. "Der Einfluss von Sozialer Ungleichheit auf die medizinische und gesundheitsbezogene Versorgung in Deutschland—Effect of Social Inequality on Medical and Health Care in Germany." *Gesundheitliche Ungleichheit: Grundlagen, Probleme, Perspektiven.* Ed. Matthias Richter and Klaus Hurrelmann. Wiesbaden: VS, Verl. für Sozialwiss., 2009. 149–65.

Janßen, C., Sauter, S., and Kowalski, C. "The influence of social determinants on the use of prevention and health promotion services: results of a systematic literature review." *GMS Psycho-Social Medicine* 9 (2012): Doc07.

Jung, F. "Der HIV-Antikörpertest—Antworten der Nutzerinnen und Nutzer." Das Gesundheitswesen 73 (2011): 97–104.

Kamtsiuris, P., et al. "Inanspruchnahme medizinischer Leistungen. Ergebnisse des Kinder- und Jugendgesundheitssurveys (KiGGS)." *Bundesgesundheitsblatt—Gesundheitsforschung—Gesundheitsschutz* 50 (2007): 836–50.

Kitagawa, E. M. and Hauser, P. M. *Differential Mortality in the United States: a Study in Socioeconomic Epidemiology*. Camebridge: Harcard University Press, 1973.

Klug, S. J., Hetzer, M., and Blettner, M. "Screening for breast and cervical cancer in a large German city: participation, motivation and knowledge of risk factors." *European Journal of Public Health* 15 (2005): 70–77.

Koller, D. and Mielck, A. "Regional and social differences concerning overweight, participation in health check-ups and vaccination: Analysis of data from a whole birth cohort of 6-year old children in a prosperous German city." *BMC Public Health* 9 (2009): 43.

Krogsbøll, L. T., et al. *General Health Checks in Adults for Reducing Morbidity and Mortality From Disease:* Cochrane Systematic Review and Meta-analysis. *British Medical Journal* 345 (2012): e7191.

Kuh, D. and Ben-Shlomo, Y. *A Lifetime Course Approach to Chronic Disease Epidemiology* Oxford: Oxford University Press, 2004.

Lampert, T., Kroll, L. E., and Dunkelberg, A. "Soziale Ungleichheit der Lebenserwartung in Deutschland." *Aus Politik und Zeitgeschichte* 42 (2007): 11–18.

Lengerke, T. and Mielck, A. "Unzufriedenheit mit dem eigenen Körpergewicht nach Einkommensarmut: Eine Mehrebenenanalyse in der Region Augsburg." *Psychologie und Medizin—Traumpaar oder Vernunftehe?* Ed. Hendrik Berth. Lengerich: Papst, 2010. 69–80.

Loss, J. and Eichhorn, C. "Prävention und Gesundheitsförderung." *Das Gesundheitswesen in Deutschland. Struktur, Leistungen, Weiterentwicklung*. Ed. Eckard Nagel. Köln: Deutscher Ärzteverlag, 2013. 213–27.

Mackenbach, J. P. and Backer, M. J. *Reducing Inequalities in Health: a European Perspective*. London: Routledge, 2002.

Marmot, M. G., et al. "Employment grade and coronary heart disease in British civil servants." *Journal of Epidemiology and Community Health* 32 (1978): 244–49.

Marmot, M. "Health in an unequal world." *The Lancet* 368 (2006): 2081–94.

Marmot, M. and Wilkinson, R. G. *Social Determinants of Health*. Ed. Michael Marmot and Richard G. Wilkinson. 2 ed. Oxford: Oxford Univ. Press, 2006.

Maywald, U., et al. "Arzneimittelberatung für Patienten—Bedarfsanalyse, Evaluation und Einfluss auf die Compliance." *Deutsche Medizinische Wochenschrift* 130 (2005): 1485–90.

Mielck, A., Reitmeir, P., and Rathmann, W. "Knowledge about diabetes and participation in diabetes training courses: The need for improving health care for diabetes patients with low SES." *Experimental and Clinical Endocrinology & Diabetes* 114 (2006): 240–48.

Mielck, A. *Soziale Ungleichheit und Gesundheit*. Bern: Huber, 2000.

Morgenroth, H., et al. "Die Durchimpfung von 24–30 Monate alten Kindern in pädiatrischen Praxen im Zeitraum von November 1999 bis Mai 2001– Der Einfluss soziodemografischer Faktoren." *Das Gesundheitswesen* 67 (2005): 788–94.

Müller, D. and Szucs, T. D. "Influenza vaccination coverage rates in 5 European countries: a population-based cross-sectional analysis of the seasons 02/03, 03/04 and 04/05." *Infection* 35 (2007): 308–19.

Poethko-Müller, C., Kuhnert, R., and Schlaud, M. "Durchimpfung und Determinanten des Impfstatus in Deutschland Ergebnisse des Kinder- und Jugendgesundheitssurveys (KiGGS)." *Bundesgesundheitsblatt—Gesundheitsforschung—Gesundheitsschutz* 50 (2007): 851–62.

Poethko-Müller, C., et al. "Vaccination coverage against measles in German-born and foreign-born children and identi?cation of unvaccinated subgroups in Germany." *Vaccine* 27 (2009): 2563–69.

Reuss, A. M., et al. "Influenza vaccination coverage in the 2004/05, 2005/06, and 2006/07 seasons." *Deutsches Ärzteblatt International* 107 (2010): 845–50.

Richter, M., Brand, H., and Rössler, G. "Sozioökonomische Unterschiede in der Inanspruchnahme von Früherkennungsuntersuchungen und Maßnahmen der Gesundheitsförderung in NRW." *Das Gesundheitswesen* 64 (2002): 417–23.

Ringwald, J., et al. "Hepatitis B vaccination status among healthy adults in Germany." *Health Policy* 79 (2006): 306–12.

Robert-Koch-Institut. "Empfehlungen der Ständigen Impfkommission (STIKO) am Robert Koch-Institut/Stand: Juli 2012." *Epidemiologisches Bulletin* 2012 (2012): 283–310.

Röckl-Wiedmann, I., et al. "Schichtspezifische Inanspruchnahme medizinischer Leistungen und Vorsorgeverhalten in Bayern: Ergebnisse einer repräsentativen Bevölkerungsbefragung." *International Journal of Public Health* 47 (2002): 307–17.

Roggendorf, H., et al. "Die Influenza-Impfrate bei Mitarbeitern eines Universitätsklinikums Status Quo und geeignete Verbesserungsstrategien." *Deutsche Medizinische Wochenschrift* 136 (2011): 1299–304.

Rückinger, S., et al. "Participation in cervical cancer screening by age and region—a cohort study with a 3 1/2 year follow-up on 2 223 135 women in Bavaria." *Das Gesundheitswesen* 70 (2008a): e17-e21.

Rückinger, S., et al. "Die Krebsfrüherkennungsuntersuchung für Frauen wird in Regionen mit niedrigem Haushaltseinkommen seltener in Anspruch genommen—Analyse von Daten der Kassenärztlichen Vereinigung Bayerns." *Das Gesundheitswesen* 70 (2008b): 393–97.

Scheffer, S., Dauven, S., and Sieverding, M. "Sociodemograhic differences in the participation in, early detection of cancer examinations‘ in Germany: a review." *Das Gesundheitswesen* 68 (2006): 139–46.

Schenk, L. and Knopf, H. "Mundgesundheitsverhalten von Kindern und Jugendlichen in Deutschland: Erste Ergebnisse aus dem Kinder- und Jugendgesundheitssurvey (KiGGS)." *Bundesgesundheitsblatt—Gesundheitsforschung—Gesundheitsschutz* 50 (2007): 653–58.

Schenkel, K., et al. "Viral hepatitis in Germany: poor vaccination coverage and little knowledge about transmission in target groups." *BMC Public Health* 8 (2008): 132.

Schmitt, J., et al. "Effectiveness of skin cancer screening for individuals age 14 to 34 years." *Journal of the German Society of Dermatology* 9 (2011): 608–16.

Schultze-Lutter, F., et al. "Das Kölner Früh-Erkennungs- & Therapie-Zentrum für psychische Krisen (FETZ): Evaluation der Inanspruchnahme." *Medizinische Klinik* 103. (2008): 81–89.

Schultze-Lutter, F., Ruhrmann, S., and Klosterkötter, J. "Early detection of psychosis e establishing a service for persons at risk." *European Psychiatry* 24 (2009): 1–10.

Schwarz, S., et al. "Gynaecological health care utilization and use of sex hormones-the study of Health in Pomerania." *Human Reproduction* 20 (2005): 2916–22.

Siegrist, J. and Marmot, M. "Introduction." *Social inequalities in health: new evidence and policy implications*. Ed. J. Siegrist and M. Marmot. Oxford: Oxford University Press, 2006. 1–25.

Sieverding, M., Matterne, U., and Ciccarello, L. "Gender differences in FOBT use: evidence from a large German survey." *Zeitschrift für Gastroenterologie* 46 (2008): S47-S51.

Sieverding, M., et al. "Colonoscopy use in a country with a long-standing colorectal cancer screening programme: evidence from a large German survey." *Zeitschrift für Gastroenterologie* 48 (2010): 1351–57.

Sieverding, M., et al. "Prostatakarzinomfrüherkennung in Deutschland: Untersuchung einer repräsentativen Bevölkerungsstichprobe." *Der Urologe* 47(2008): 1233-8.

Simoes, E., Kunz, S. K., and Schmahl, F. W. "Inanspruchnahmegradienten in der Schwangerenvorsorge fordern zur Weiterentwicklung des Präventionskonzepts auf." *Das Gesundheitswesen* 71 (2009): 385–90.

Stock, C. and Brenner, H. "Utilization of lower gastrointestinal endoscopy and fecal occult blood test in 11 European countries: evidence from the Survey of Health, Aging and Retirement in Europe (SHARE)." *Endoscopy* 42 (2010): 546–56.

Stock, C., et al. "Colonoscopy and fecal occult blood test use in Germany: results from a large insurance-based cohort." *Endoscopy* 43 (2011): 771–79.

Szucs, T. D., Wahle, K., and Müller, D. “Grippeimpfung in Deutschland: Eine bevölkerungsbezogene Querschnittsanalyse der drei Influenzasaisons von 2002 bis 2005.” *Medizinische Klinik* 101 (2006): 537–45.

Teich, N., et al. “Vaccination coverage in immunosuppressed patients.” *Deutsches Ärzteblatt International* 108 (2011): 105–11.

von dem Knesebeck, O. and Mielck, A. “Soziale Ungleichheit und gesundheitliche Versorgung im höheren Lebensalter.” *Zeitschrift für Gerontologie und Geriatrie* 42 (2009): 39–46.

Wicker, S., et al. “Masern im Jahr 2010: Wissensstand und Impfstatus von Medizinstudenten.” *Bundesgesundheitsblatt—Gesundheitsforschung—Gesundheitsschutz* 54 (2011): 238–42.

Zeeb, H., et al. “Gesundheitliche Lage und Gesundheitsversorgung von erwachsenen Migranten—ein Survey bei der Schuleingangsuntersuchung.” *Das Gesundheitswesen* 66 (2004): 76–84.

Chapter 17
Utilization Dynamics of an Integrated Care System in Germany: Morbidity, Age, and Sex Distribution of *Gesundes Kinzigtal Integrated Care's* Membership in 2006–2008

Achim Siegel, Ingrid Köster, Ingrid Schubert and Ulrich Stößel

Background: Population-Based Integrated Care in Germany

One feature of Germany's health service system is its organizational fragmentation: primary and secondary outpatient care, inpatient (hospital) care, and public health services are organized largely independently from each other and are financed according to different reimbursement principles and by strictly separate budgets (Schlette et al. 2009, Hildebrandt et al. 2010).

This fragmentation is considered a source of ineffectiveness and inefficiency, particularly in those health services which constitute an "interface" between different sectors of care. A prominent example is the often insufficient follow-up care after patients have been discharged from a hospital: Very often, patients' medication regimens differ before, during, and after hospitalization. This is not only a constant object of dispute between hospitals and primary care providers but also confuses—and sometimes even harms—the concerned patients (Hildebrandt et al. 2009, 2010). Commonly, it takes two or more weeks for German primary care physicians to "receive a full report from a hospital once their patient has been dis-

A. Siegel (✉)
Division of General Practice, University Medical Center Freiburg, Freiburg, Germany
e-mail: achim.siegel@uniklinik-freiburg.de

A. Siegel · U. Stößel
Division of Medical Psychology and Medical Sociology,
University of Freiburg, Freiburg, Germany
e-mail: ulrich.stoessel@mps.uni-freiburg.de

I. Köster · I. Schubert
PMV research group at the Department of Child and Adolescent Psychiatry,
University of Cologne, Cologne, Germany
e-mail: ingrid.koester@uk-koeln.de

I. Schubert
e-mail: ingrid.schubert@uk-koeln.de

C. Janssen et al. (eds.), *Health Care Utilization in Germany*,
DOI 10.1007/978-1-4614-9191-0_17, © Springer Science+Business Media New York 2014

charged" (Schlette et al. 2009). Insufficient communication between providers is a problem not only at sector interfaces, but also within sectors, for instance, leading providers to perform redundant services (e.g., repeat X-rays). Poor communication between providers is also regarded a main reason for (non-coordinated) polypharmacy, which is risky for the concerned patients as well as unnecessarily costly (Hamilton et al. 2011).

Starting in 2000 and—more intensively—2004, German health care legislation has attempted to solve these problems by creating incentives for health insurers and care providers to introduce more integration: From 2004 to 2008, for instance, the so-called Statutory Health Modernization Act ("GKV-Modernisierungsgesetz") incentivized Germany's statutory health insurers to spend 1 % of their total expenditures on integrated care programs (Schlette et al. 2009, Hildebrandt et al. 2010). From July 2009, statutory health insurers were even obliged to offer 'family-doctor centered-care' (in German: 'Hausarzt-zentrierte Versorgung' or simply 'HzV') options to their insurants because 'family-doctor-centered care' was thought to create a higher degree of patient-centered integration than usual care (Schlette et al. 2009, Sachverständigenrat 2009).

From 2004 through 2008, more than 6000 integrated care projects were launched in Germany (Bundesgeschäftsstelle Qualitätssicherung 2009). The bulk of these projects, however, target only one or a few indications—such as knee or hip surgery—and encompass only one or two sectors of care, such as inpatient care and post-surgery outpatient care. The so-called population-based integrated care systems are more ambitious: 'Population-based integration' means that health care is organized for a defined resident population by one management center across all (or nearly all) indications, encompassing all sectors of health care. To date, only a few population-based integrated care systems operate in Germany.

These population-based integrated care models were inspired by managed care models in the USA and in Switzerland (Preuß et al. 2002, Berchtold and Hess 2006, Jakobs and Schulze 2006, Amelung 2007). As a rule, those 'classic' managed care models relied on a fairly simple form of capitation which led to relative cost savings but also had some problematic effects: First, health insurers and/or health care providers preferably enrolled the so-called good risks, i.e., comparatively healthy people, at least as long as there was no effective morbidity-based risk structure compensation between health insurers. Thus, the comparative cost savings realized by managed care models were in part due to risk selection (Reich et al. 2012, Beck et al. 2011). Second, capitation incentivized a tendency toward under-use of some necessary health services (such as diagnostic procedures, drug prescriptions, etc.). These two side effects—risk selection and at least a trend toward under-utilization of health care resources—are considered characteristic drawbacks of classic managed care models.

One of the few population-based integrated care systems in Germany is located in the Kinzigtal region in Baden-Württemberg (the southwestern-most federal state of Germany) and is called Gesundes Kinzigtal Integrated Care (in German: 'Integrierte Versorgung Gesundes Kinzigtal'). While following some basic ideas of managed care, the founders of Gesundes Kinzigtal Integrated Care (hereafter called 'GKIC') deliberately attempted to avoid the two above-mentioned tendencies of classic managed care models through a series of contractual and economic regulations. GKIC was founded in late 2005 and has been operating since the beginning of 2006. The system is run by a regional health management company (Gesundes Kinzigtal GmbH) in cooperation with the physicians' network in the region (Medizinisches Qualitätsnetz—Ärzteinitiative Kinzigtal e.V.— MQNK), a German health care management company (OptiMedis AG), and two statutory health insurers (Allgemeine Ortskrankenkasse—AOK— and Landwirtschaftliche Krankenkasse—LKK—Baden-Württemberg).

In this chapter, we analyze whether GKIC succeeded in enrolling first and foremost patients with above-average morbidity, i.e., in avoiding the traditional selection of 'good risks'. Before explaining GKIC's economic and contractual regulations designed to avoid such risk selection (Sect. 3), we will outline the main characteristics of the GKIC system (Sect. 2). In Sect. 4, we will analyze in detail whether GKIC has reached its aim to avoid the above-mentioned risk selection. In this analysis, we rely on insurants' claims data (Schubert et al. 2008, Swart & Ihle 2005, cf. also Swart in this issue), supplied by the involved health insurers. In Sect. 5, we discuss our findings and paraphrase them in terms of Andersen's behavioral model of health services use, one of the seminal models of health care utilization (Andersen 1995, Andersen 1998).

Characteristics and Aims of GKIC

The total population in the western and central Kinzigtal region—the service area of GKIC—amounts to about 69,000 inhabitants. Slightly less than half of them (31,000) are insured by either AOK Baden-Württemberg (about 29,300 insurants) or LKK Baden-Württemberg (about 1,700 insurants). Both are statutory health insurers: AOK is open to anyone, whereas LKK is open only to farmers and their dependents. All 31,000 AOK and LKK insurants are entitled to enroll as members of GKIC. The enrollment is both voluntary and free for these 31,000 insurants, meaning that GKIC membership does not cost any additional membership fee. As of February 5, 2013, there were 9,047 GKIC members. GKIC members are entitled and invited to use special health programs and services which are, with a few exceptions, reserved for enrolled insurants. These programs are listed in Table 17.1. As a rule, participation in these programs is free. Those AOK and LKK insurants who do not wish to enroll receive at least usual care according to statutory health care regulations.

As of February 5, 2013, there were 92 health care providers ('Leistungspartner') working with GKIC on the basis of a formal cooperation contract. The contract specifies principles and details of the cooperation, special reimbursement regulations, patients' rights etc. Among these 92 partner providers, there are

Table 17.1 Specific care management and preventive programs offered by GKIC or in cooperation with either AOK specialists or third parties, as of February 5, 2013

Subject and name of program	Year of implementation	No. of participants in the program
Prevention/treatment of congestive heart failure ('Starkes Herz')	2006	84
Smoking cessation ('Rauchfreies Kinzigtal')	2007	199
Lifestyle intervention for patients with metabolic syndrome ('Gesundes Gewicht')	2007	180
Early intervention by psychiatrists or psychotherapists in case of acute personal crises ('Psychotherapie akut')	2007	320
Diet counseling[a]	2007	71
Sponsored membership vouchers in sports clubs[a]	2008	281
Social case management (by social workers according to general practitioner's recommendation)[a]	2008	210
Prevention of osteoporosis and osteoporotic fractures ('Starke Muskeln—Feste Knochen')	2008	770
Ophthalmological checkup for children (amblyopia, U10 & U11)	2008	755
Aqua fitness[a]	2008	529
Patient university (lectures on health issues)[a]	2009	2,713
Medical care for the elderly in nursing homes ('Ärzte plus Pflege')	2009	119
Prevention of falls for the elderly[a]	2009	144
Special intervention for patients with depression ('Besser gestimmt')	2010	23
Back pain prevention program ('Starker Rückhalt—Mein gesunder Rücken')	2011	42
Prevention of secondary diseases for patients with hypertension ('Im Gleichgewicht—Mein Blutdruck im Griff')	2011	22
Early intervention for patients with rheumatism ('Beweglich bleiben—Rheuma frühzeitig behandeln')	2011	6

[a] Third parties

- 26 family doctors (thereof one with the additional title 'psychotherapist'),
- 24 practice-based specialists (thereof one with the additional title 'psychotherapist'),
- 7 pediatricians,
- 5 psychotherapists,
- 8 physiotherapists,
- 6 hospitals,
- 11 nursing homes,
- 4 outpatient nursing services, and
- 1 outpatient social-therapeutic service.

Furthermore, 16 pharmacies, 30 sports clubs, and 6 fitness centers continuously cooperate with GKIC, but not on the basis of formal provider contracts.

The aim of GKIC is to make the regional health services system more efficient without reducing the quality of health services, neither in absolute terms nor in comparison with the surrounding usual care system.

To realize this aim, the GKIC management pursues two strategies: On the one hand, GKIC attempts to advance and foster the cooperation of the different health care providers across professions and sectors of care so as to overcome—or at least alleviate—the fragmentation of health services and the resulting inefficiencies. This is done by common treatment guidelines, by enabling a cross-linking of providers' means of communication and information, and the like (Hildebrandt et al. 2010). This strategy is thought to be effective and efficient even in the short and medium term (Hildebrandt et al. 2010, Siegel et al. 2012). On the other hand, GKIC focuses on prevention: through carefully targeted preventive programs, GKIC attempts to prevent—or at least delay—the onset of chronic diseases and their associated secondary diseases. This strategy is thought to be effective and efficient in the medium and long term. Both strategies are to bring about improved population health as well as relative cost savings, i.e., a smaller increase of risk-adjusted health care costs in the intervention region than in regions where usual care dominates (Hildebrandt et al. 2010, Siegel et al. 2012). This strategy is based on the assumption that carefully targeted preventive programs may reduce total health care costs for a given population (*ceteris paribus*) at least in the medium and long term. GKIC strives to realize its aim without any risk selection (Hermann et al. 2006, Hildebrandt et al. 2010).

Three years after starting to operate, GKIC seems to be well on the way to achieving its financial objective: During the years 2006 through 2008, GKIC realized a successively growing contribution margin for the insurants of AOK and LKK in the intervention region—a growing contribution margin over time means that standardized health care costs of the Kinzigtal insurants increase at a smaller rate than those of the average German insurant (Hildebrandt 2010, Siegel et al. 2012).

GKIC's Attempt to Avoid Risk Selection: the Concept

GKIC's operative activities are based on provision contracts, which were concluded in 2006 by the two statutory health insurers AOK and LKK Baden-Württemberg on the one hand and the management company 'Gesundes Kinzigtal GmbH' on the other. The management company acts as an 'integrated care management company' according to §§ 140 a–d of the German Social Code Book V (Fünftes Buch Sozialgesetzbuch—SGB V) which is the statutory basis of organizing integrated care in Germany. The provision contract runs until December 31, 2014, and may be renewed thereafter.

When designing the details of the provision contracts, the contracting parties wanted to block any incentives that could stimulate a selection of 'good risks' by GKIC and its partner providers or a strategy of postponing necessary medical services or even withhold necessary services from patients (Hermann et al. 2006). The following regulations are to serve this aim:

1. Enrollment into the GKIC's integrated care system and becoming a member of GKIC is completely voluntary for the insurants. If an insurant chooses not to enroll, she or he will continue to be served according to statutory health care regulations (usual care). If an enrolled insurant wants to opt out of GKIC, she or he may quit at the end of each quarter and without giving reasons.
2. Insurants' enrollment into GKIC is not incentivized through direct financial means (such as a reduced insurance premium). Nonetheless, enrolled insurants are invited to participate in special health programs (cf. Table 17.1) largely free of charge.
3. Enrolled insurants' free choice of physician and/or hospital is not restricted.

These three regulations ensure that health care providers and the management company can convince insurants to enroll simply by using the argument that GKIC provides a higher 'health utility' or 'health benefit' than usual care. Moreover, in a system characterized by those three regulations, it would make no sense to achieve relative cost savings by withholding or postponing necessary health services, i.e., by under-utilization: In that case, insurants would opt out of GKIC or claim such services later (the contract period is at least 9 years). The 'exit option' may be exercised in two different ways: First, the insurant may cancel only GKIC membership without changing the current primary care physician (who might have convinced him or her to enroll). Second, the insurant might wish to cancel GKIC membership *and* switch to a primary care physician who is in no way associated with GKIC. This latter option is actually available as about 45 % of all registered physicians in the region are not associated with GKIC. In other words: in a competitive environment, in which GKIC has to prove itself, those three regulations will probably foil any hypothetical attempt of GKIC to achieve relative cost savings by under-use of health services.

The probably most effective regulation with which a selection of 'good risks' is to be prevented is the following:

4. The financial result of GKIC is calculated using the contribution margins of *all* AOK resp. LKK insurants residing in the Kinzigtal region *regardless of whether they are enrolled or not*. This means that the costs of *all potential enrollees* are the decisive variable, rather than the costs of a subgroup of enrollees which might be more or less arbitrarily selected by GKIC.

This means that it makes no economic sense for GKIC and its partner providers to preferably enroll only a subgroup consisting of those insurants who are 'good risks' in the traditional sense of the term. Instead, the fourth stipulation incentivizes a different enrollment policy: By first and foremost enrolling those insurants with above-average health care costs or a high morbidity risk (and presumably fast-growing health care costs in the future), the potential for relative cost savings and thus a growing total contribution margin is obviously the greatest. In contrast, if the traditional 'good risks' were preferably enrolled, the contribution margin's growth potential would be comparatively small because if actual health care costs are low (and the morbidity risk is low, too), potential cost savings in the future will be low, too. This means that the comparatively healthy insurants—that is, those who are traditionally regarded as 'good risks'—do *not* constitute GKIC's primary target group. On the contrary, if GKIC and its partnering providers act rationally, they will first and foremost convince insurants with exceptionally high health care costs and/or an above-average morbidity risk to enroll so that these insurants can be treated more effectively and more efficiently by exploiting GKIC's extended preventive and treatment potential.

Structural Characteristics of GKIC's Membership: an 'Inverted Risk Selection' in Action

If GKIC's factual enrollment process works in accordance with this theoretical concept, we should be able to find, e.g., higher morbidity among enrolled insurants than in non-enrolled ones—at least during the first years of GKIC's existence. The following analysis is based on insurants' claims data gathered in 2006 through 2008, i.e., the first 3 years of GKIC's existence. As the absolute number of enrolled LKK insurants is very low during that time period—only 120 LKK insurants had enrolled by December 31, 2007—we refer hereafter to AOK insurants only.

Insurant Characteristics Among Enrolled vs. Non-Enrolled Insurants

The distribution of AOK insurants according to year and insurant group is found in Table 17.2. The dimension 'year' contains each of the first 3 years of GKIC's existence, with December 31 as the effective date of a given year. The dimension 'insurant group' consists of the three categories 'continually insured throughout a given year', 'deceased during the year', and 'change to or from another health insurer during the year'. Table 17.2 and all following analyses refer to a cohort of AOK insurants who resided in the Kinzigtal region as of July 2006. This means AOK insurants who were born later than July 2006 or who moved into the region after July 2006 are not considered here.

Table 17.2 shows a continually growing number of enrolled insurants ('IC'), with 3997 insurants being enrolled on December 31, 2008. On that date, 24,056 AOK insurants residing in the Kinzigtal region were not (yet) enrolled. Furthermore, the second half of Table 17.2 shows that the number and proportion of those insurants who joined or quit AOK during the year is lower among the enrolled (2.2 % in 2008) than among the non-enrolled insurants (3.9 % in 2008).

Table 17.3 contains the distribution of enrolled vs. non-enrolled insurants according to sex and age group as of December 31, 2008. To simplify the description,

Table 17.2 Distribution of AOK insurants residing in the Kinzigtal region according to year and insurant subgroup in 2006–2008 (enrollment status as of December 31 of a given year)

	AOK insurants according to year and insurant group (count)											
	Continually insured throughout year			Deceased during the year			Change to/from other health insurer during the year			Total		
Year	IC[a]	NIC[b]	Total	IC[a]	NIC[b]	Total	IC[a]	NIC[b]	Total	IC[a]	NIC[b]	Total
2006	934	27,306	28,240	0	391	391	12	1,146	1,158	946	28,843	29,789
2007	1,970	25,519	27,489	24	352	376	40	1,381	1,421	2,034	27,252	29,286
2008	3,884	22,823	26,707	25	306	331	88	927	1,015	3,997	24,056	28,053
	Proportion of AOK insurants (in %) according to year and insurant group											
2006	98.7	94.7	94.8	0.0	1.4	1.3	1.3	4.0	3.9	100.0	100.0	100.0
2007	96.9	93.6	93.9	1.2	1.3	1.3	2.0	5.1	4.9	100.0	100.0	100.0
2008	97.2	94.9	95.2	0.6	1.3	1.2	2.2	3.9	3.6	100.0	100.0	100.0

[a] IC—enrolled insurants (members of GKIC)
[b] NIC—non-enrolled insurants (nonmembers of GKIC)

Table 17.3 Distribution of enrolled vs. non-enrolled AOK insurants according to sex and age group as of December 31, 2008 (only insurants who were continually insured by AOK throughout 2008)

	IC/enrolled		NIC/non-enrolled		Total	
	Count	%	Count	%	Count	%
Women	2,174	56.0	11,798	51.7	13,972	52.3
Men	1,710	44.0	11,025	48.3	12,735	47.7
< 18 years	346	8.9	4,050	17.7	4,396	16.5
18–29 years	278	7.2	3,141	13.8	3,419	12.8
30–39 years	258	6.6	2,523	11.1	2,781	10.4
40–49 years	579	14.9	3,713	16.3	4,292	16.1
50–59 years	564	14.5	2,925	12.8	3,489	13.1
60–69 years	631	16.2	2,336	10.2	2,967	11.1
70–79 years	813	20.9	2,583	11.3	3,396	12.7
80–89 years	389	10.0	1,367	6.0	1,756	6.6
> 89 years	26	0.7	185	0.8	211	0.8
Total	3,884	100.0	22,823	100.0	26,707	100.0

Table 17.3 contains only those insurants who were continually insured by AOK throughout the year 2008.

It can be seen from Table 17.3 that women are overrepresented among the enrolled insurants: Among all (continually insured) insurants residing in the Kinzigtal region, women make up 52.3 %, whereas their proportion among the enrolled insurants is 56 %. Furthermore, the older age groups of continually insured AOK insurants—i.e., insurants who are 50 years or older—are clearly overrepresented among GKIC members (enrolled insurants): 62 % of the enrolled insurants are 50 years or older, whereas among all (continually insured) AOK insurants, only 44 % are 50 years or older. The mean age among the enrolled insurants (continually insured throughout 2008 by AOK) is 54.5 years, in contrast to 45.4 years among all AOK insurants in 2008 (continually insured 2008 by AOK).

These differences are a first hint that insurants with above-average morbidity might have been enrolled into GKIC as a primary target group. To confirm this suspicion, one needs to analyze morbidity data.

Morbidity Characteristics Among Enrolled vs. Non-Enrolled Insurants

Table 17.4 contains the multi-morbidity prevalence among enrolled vs. non-enrolled insurants residing in the Kinzigtal region. An insurant with 'multi-morbidity' has been defined as follows: An insurant is 'multi-morbid' if her or his claims data contain at least three International Classification of Diseases (ICD)-10 codes from different ICD-10 subgroups according to the DIMDI classification scheme (cf. Deutsches Institut für Medizinische Dokumentation und Information—DIMDI 2013), documented in at least three quarters of the year in question. Thus, an insur-

Table 17.4 Proportion of insurants with multi-morbidity according to year and enrollment status (enrollment status as of December 31 of a given year)

	Number and proportion of insurants with multi-morbidity				
	IC/enrolled insurants		NIC/non-enrolled insurants		Total
Year	Count	Proportion in %	Count	Proportion in %	Proportion in %
2006	543	58.1	6,326	23.2	24.4
2007	1,146	58.1	6,157	24.1	26.5
2008	2,027	52.2	5,672	24.9	28.8

ant is classified as multi-morbid in a given year if her or his claims data contain, e.g., (1) one code from the subgroup 'affective disorders' (ICD-10: F30-F39), (2) another code from the subgroup 'hypertension' (I10-I15), and still another code from the subgroup 'ischemic heart diseases' (I20-I25), with each code documented in at least three quarters of the year in question. As the number of quarters (3 out of 4) is crucial for the prevalence calculation, only those insurants were considered who were continually insured by AOK throughout a given year—all other insurants were excluded from the analysis.

Table 17.4 shows that in each year, multi-morbidity is more than twice as prevalent among the enrolled as among non-enrolled insurants: In 2006, the first year of GKIC's operation, the multi-morbidity prevalence among the enrolled was 2.5 times higher, and in 2008, it was still 2.1 times higher. The differences between enrolled and non-enrolled insurants are statistically significant for all 3 years ($p<0.001$).

A similar pattern of results is found when considering another variable quantifying the morbidity of a population: the Charlson comorbidity index (Charlson et al. 1987, Quan et al. 2005). The Charlson index contains 19 comorbidity categories, ranging from myocardial infarction and congestive heart failure to metastatic solid tumor and acquired immunodeficiency syndrome (AIDS). Each category has a specific weight (with, e.g., '1' for a myocardial infarction and '6' for AIDS). The sum of all 19 weighted categories for a given person makes up her or his overall Charlson comorbidity score. The overall score reflects the person's cumulative increased likelihood of 1-year mortality: The higher the score, the more severe is the person's burden of comorbidity.

Table 17.5 presents the mean total Charlson score of enrolled vs. non-enrolled insurants. Like Table 17.4, 17.5 includes only those insurants who were continually insured by AOK throughout a given year.

Table 17.5 shows that the morbidity in 2006—as measured by the mean Charlson index score—is about 2.4 times higher for the enrolled than for the non-enrolled insurants. The differences between enrolled and non-enrolled insurants are statistically significant for all 3 years ($p<0.001$). This ratio decreased a bit by 2008, but as of December 31, 2008, it was still twice as high as among non-enrolled insurants.

As the enrolled insurants are considerably older than the non-enrolled, the higher morbidity is not surprising at all. To check if GKIC has realized an 'inverted risk selection' in the sense explained above, the morbidity figures for the two subpopulations have to be adjusted for age and sex.

Table 17.5 Mean value of the Charlson comorbidity index according to year and enrollment status (enrollment status as of December 31 of a given year)

	Charlson comorbidity index (mean)		
Year	IC/enrolled insurants	NIC/non-enrolled insurants	Total
2006	1.16	0.48	0.51
2007	1.12	0.50	0.54
2008	1.04	0.51	0.59

Age- and Sex-Standardized Morbidity Among Enrolled vs. Non-Enrolled Insurants

Tables 17.6 and 17.7 present results analogous to those in Tables 17.4 and 17.5, but standardized with respect to age and sex. In both cases, the reference group for this standardization is the age and sex distribution of all (continually insured) AOK insurants residing in the Kinzigtal region in a given year.

Tables 17.6 and 17.7 show that the age- and sex-standardized morbidity is considerably higher for enrolled insurants than for the non-enrolled ones. These differences are statistically significant for each given year ($p<0.001$). Thus, the standardized prevalence of multi-morbidity in 2008 amounts to 39.6 % among the enrolled compared with 26.6 % among the non-enrolled insurants (ratio: 1.49). Both prevalence figures rose somewhat over the years: in 2006, e.g., the corresponding figures amounted to 37.8 % (enrolled) versus 23.7 % (non-enrolled), resulting in a prevalence ratio of 1.59. These results are rather similar to those using the Charlson comorbidity index: for 2006, the mean score was 0.72 for the enrolled and 0.50 for the non-enrolled (ratio: 1.44). For 2008, the mean score was slightly higher in both groups: 0.77 for the enrolled and 0.55 for the non-enrolled insurants (ratio: 1.40).

Conclusion and Outlook

Having considered morbidity figures that have been standardized by age and sex, we may conclude that average morbidity is considerably higher among the enrolled AOK insurants, i.e., among the members of GKIC, than among the non-enrolled AOK insurants living in the Kinzigtal region. The ratio indicating the 'surplus morbidity' among the enrolled ranges between 1.4 and 1.6, depending on which indicator and which year we use: When we consider multi-morbidity prevalence as of December 31, 2006, we get a ratio of 1.59 (prevalence among the enrolled 37.9 vs. 23.7 % among the non-enrolled). The Charlson comorbidity index score as of December 31, 2008 shows a morbidity ratio of 1.40 (0.77 among the enrolled vs. 0.55 among the non-enrolled). Whatever indicator we use: GKIC has obviously enrolled first and foremost insurants with above-average morbidity to treat them with the full potential of integrated care and special preventive programs.

Table 17.6 Proportion of insurants with multi-morbidity according to year and enrollment status (enrollment status as of December 31 of a given year), standardized for age and sex (reference group: all insurants residing in the Kinzigtal region in a given year)

	Proportion with multi-morbidity in %		
Year	IC/enrolled	NIC/non-enrolled	Total
2006	37.8	23.7	24.4
2007	38.3	25.3	26.5
2008	39.6	26.6	28.8

Table 17.7 Mean value of the Charlson comorbidity index according to year and enrollment status (enrollment status as of December 31 of a given year), standardized for age and sex (reference group: all insurants residing in the Kinzigtal region in a given year)

	Charlson comorbidity index (mean)		
Year	IC/enrolled	NIC/non-enrolled	Total
2006	0.72	0.50	0.51
2007	0.72	0.52	0.54
2008	0.77	0.55	0.59

These results confirm that GKIC's recruitment policy has indeed worked in accordance with the plan of the GKIC founders: GKIC has avoided the selection of the traditional 'good risks'. The results mean that there is even a kind of 'inverted risk selection' in the sense that those insurants with above-average morbidity have been preferably enrolled.

Thus, GKIC has demonstrated that managed care systems do not necessarily produce the kind of risk selection known from the history of managed care systems in the USA and Switzerland. By carefully designing the rules of provision contracts, risk selection may not only be avoided but even reversed in a managed care system: The founders of GKIC have obviously created a managed care system in which insurants with above-average morbidity are the preferred target group.

These results are even more noteworthy if we consider that a morbidity-oriented risk compensation scheme among Germany's statutory health insurers—which in part compensates those health insurers whose insurants' morbidity is above the average—was not introduced in Germany until 2009 (Göpffarth et al. 2009, Göpffarth et al. 2010, Göpffarth 2010, Drösler et al. 2011).

Nonetheless, one important limitation of our analysis must be mentioned: The foregoing arguments and conclusions are based on the assumption that the health conditions of enrolled and non-enrolled insurants are coded in the same way, i.e., that the fact of enrollment does not lead to a specific kind of 'disease-coding' by the concerning physicians. A critic may argue that enrolled insurants might receive more attention by their physicians, which could lead in effect to a more 'ambitious' disease coding in enrolled insurants compared with non-enrolled insurants. If this was the case, higher documented morbidity among enrolled insurants, derived from ICD-10 codes, would not necessarily reflect an objectively higher morbidity but rather—to an unknown degree—physicians' higher attention vis-à-vis the enrolled insurants. On the basis of our present data, we admittedly cannot completely rule out this possibility. On the other hand, however, it seems rather implausible that the above-mentioned 'surplus morbidity' among the enrolled insurants can be attributed largely (or even solely) to such a coding effect, given the sheer size of that surplus morbidity. Hence, we stand by our conclusions.

Finally, what do these results mean from the perspective of Andersen's behavioral model of health services use (Andersen 1995, Andersen 2008)? As is widely known, Andersen conceived three categories of factors to predict the use of health care services: predisposing factors, enabling factors, and need factors, with the latter category containing factors that reflect either 'subjective' or 'evaluated' need (Andersen 2008). Our finding that GKIC has indeed enrolled first and foremost insurants with above-average morbidity may be paraphrased in Andersen's terms as follows: Among AOK insurants residing in the Kinzigtal region, there is a positive correlation between evaluated need, i.e., morbidity, and use of the GKIC system. Evaluated need is, then, a positive predictor of the use of GKIC: The higher the need for more intensive, i.e., integrated, care, the higher is the insurants' likelihood to enroll in GKIC. If GKIC were just another cream-skimming model, we would have found a negative correlation between evaluated need (morbidity) and enrollment status. Thus, insurants' evaluated need, i.e., their morbidity, seems to be a substantive factor that predicts their use of GKIC, independently of some predisposing factors such as age or gender (as the association between insurants' enrollment status and their morbidity still remained significant after adjusting for the influence of age and sex). At the moment, however, we cannot compare the relative importance of need factors with the relative importance of relevant predisposing and enabling factors simply because we currently have no valid data on enabling factors such as patients' knowledge or educational level. This is certainly an interesting question, but it can only be answered when additional (primary) data have become available.

A potentially even more interesting question regarding utilization dynamics within the GKIC system is whether GKIC has successfully avoided the under-use of health services, both in absolute figures and in comparison with usual care. As mentioned above, the tendency toward an under-use of health services is another potential drawback of managed care systems. In this chapter, we did not focus on this question in detail but point to some interim analyses that have been published elsewhere (Köster et al. 2011, Siegel & Stössel 2011, Siegel & Stössel 2012, Siegel et al. 2012). These interim analyses show that the GKIC system is *not* subject to a trend toward a comparative under-use of necessary health services. Detailed results of the latter study will be published after its completion.

References

Amelung VE (2007): Managed Care. Neue Wege im Gesundheitsmanagement. Wiesbaden: GWV

Andersen RM (1995): Revisiting the Behavioral Model and Access to Medical Care: Does it Matter? Journal of Health and Social Behavior 36: 1–10.

Andersen RM (2008): National Health Surveys and the Behavioral Model of Health Services Use. Medical Care 46 (7): 647–653.

Beck K, Kunze U, Buholzer M, Trottmann M (2011): Steigern Schweizer Ärztenetzwerke die Effizienz im Gesundheitswesen? Eine Analyse auf mittlere Frist. CSS Institut für empirische Gesundheitsökonomie. Available online: http://www.css-institut.ch/de/home/wissenschaftliche_publikationen/managed_care_und_capitation.html, last access: February 25, 2013.

Berchtold P, Hess K (2006): Evidenz für Managed Care. Europäische Literaturanalyse unter besonderer Berücksichtigung der Schweiz: Wirkung von Versorgungssteuerung auf Qualität und Kosteneffektivität. Neuchatel: Schweizerisches Gesundheitsobservatorium.

Bundesgeschäftsstelle Qualitätssicherung (2009): Entwicklung der integrierten Versorgung in der Bundesrepublik Deutschland 2004–2008. Available online: http://bqs-register140d.de/, last access: February 28, 2013.

Charlson ME, Pompei P, Ales KL, MacKenzie CR (1987): A new method of classifying prognostic comorbidity in longitudinal studies. Development and validation. J Chron Dis 40 (5): 373–383.

DIMDI (Deutsches Institut für Medizinische Dokumentation und Information) (2013): Internationale statistische Klassifikation der Krankheiten und verwandter Gesundheitsprobleme. 10. Revision, German Modification, Version 2013. Available online: http://www.dimdi.de/static/de/klassi/icd-10-gm/kodesuche/onlinefassungen/htmlgm2013/index.htm, last access: February 28, 2013.

Drösler S, Hasford J, Kurth BM, Schaefer M, Wasem J & Wille E (2011): Evaluationsbericht zum Jahresausgleich 2009 im Risikostrukturausgleich. Endfassung vom 22.06.2011. Available online: http://www.mm.wiwi.uni-due.de/fileadmin/fileupload/BWL-MEDMAN/Aktuelle_Meldungen/Gutachten_mit_Anlagen.pdf, last access: Februrary 25, 2013.

Göpffarth D (2010): Auswirkungen des Morbi-RSA auf Kassenhandeln. Public Health Forum 18 (66): 12–13.

Göpffarth D, Greß St, Jacobs K, Wasem J (eds.) (2009): Jahrbuch Risikostrukturausgleich 2008–Morbi-RSA, St. Augustin: Asgard.

Göpffarth D, Greß St, Jacobs K, Wasem J (eds.) (2010): Jahrbuch Risikostrukturausgleich 2009/10—Von der Selektion zur Manipulation? Heidelberg: medhochzwei.

Hamilton H, Gallagher P, Ryan C, Byrne S, O'Mahony D (2011): Potentially inappropriate medications defined by STOPP criteria and the risk of adverse drug events in older hospitalized patients. Arch Intern Med 171 (11): 1013–1019.

Hermann C, Hildebrandt H, Richter-Reichhelm M, Schwartz FW, Witzenrath W (2006): Das Modell "Gesundes Kinzigtal". Managementgesellschaft organisiert Integrierte Versorgung einer definierten Population auf Basis eines Einsparcontractings. Gesundheits- und Sozialpolitik (5–6): 11–29.

Hildebrandt H, Richter-Reichhelm M, Trojan A, Glaeske G, Hesselmann H (2009): Die Hohe Kunst der Anreize: Neue Vergütungsstrukturen im deutschen Gesundheitswesen und der Bedarf für Systemlösungen. Sozialer Fortschritt 58 (7): 154–160.

Hildebrandt H, Hermann C, Knittel R, Richter-Reichhelm M, Siegel A, Witzenrath W (2010): Gesundes Kinzigtal Integrated Care: Improving population health by a shared health gain approach and a shared savings contract. International Journal of Integrated Care (10): 1–15. Available Online: http://www.ijic.org/index.php/ijic/article/view/539/1051, last access February 25, 2013.

Jakobs K, Schulze S (2006): Managed Care und integrierte Versorgung in den USA—Erfahrungen und Lehren für die Diskussion in Deutschland. In: Klauber J, Robra BP, Schellschmidt H (eds.): Krankenhaus-Report 2005. Schwerpunkt: Wege zur Integration. Stuttgart: Schattauer: 81–97.

Zwischenbericht 2004–2008 für Gesundes Kinzigtal GmbH, hier: AOK-Daten. Evaluationsmodul der Integrierten Versorgung „Gesundes Kinzigtal“: "Identifizierung und Abbau von Über-, Unter- und Fehlversorgung“, hier: Zwischenbericht mit Status-Quo-Daten des Jahres 2004 sowie Analyse der Jahre 2005–2008. Köln: unpublished manuscript.

Quan H, Sundararajan V, Halfon P, Fong A, Burnand B, Luthi JC, Saunders LD, Beck CA, Feasby TE, Ghali WA (2005): Coding algorithms for defining comorbidities in ICD-9-CM and ICD-10 Administrative data. Med Care 43 (11): 1130–1139.

Reich O, Rapold R, Flatscher-Thöni M (2012): An empirical investigation of the efficiency effects of integrated care models in Switzerland. International Journal of Integrated Care 12: 1–12. Available online: http://www.ijic.org/index.php/ijic/article/view/685/1506, last access: February 25, 2013.

Sachverständigenrat zur Begutachtung der Entwicklung im Gesundheitswesen (2009): Koordination und Integration. Gesundheitsversorgung in einer Gesellschaft des längeren Lebens. Bundestagsdrucksache 16/13770. Berlin 2009; Available online: http://dip21.bundestag.de/dip21/btd/16/137/1613770.pdf, last access: February 25, 2013.

Schlette S, Lisac M, Blum, K. Integrated Primary Care in Germany: the road ahead. International Journal of Integrated Care 2009; 9: 1–11. Available online: http://www.ijic.org/cgi-bin/pw.cgi/articles/000424/article_print.html, last access: February 25, 2013.

Schubert I, Köster I, Küpper-Nybelen J, Ihle P. Versorgungsforschung mit GKV-Routinedaten. Nutzungsmöglichkeiten versichertenbezogener Krankenkassendaten für Fragestellungen der Versorgungsforschung. Gesundheitsblatt—Gesundheitsforschung—Gesundheitsschutz 2008; 51 (10): 1095–1105.

Siegel A, Stössel U (2011): Kurzbericht zur Evaluation der Integrierten Versorgung Gesundes Kinzigtal 2010. Available online: http://www.ekiv.org/pdf/EKIV-Evaluationsbericht_2010_Kurzfassung_fin_2011–02-24.pdf, last access: February 25, 2013.

Siegel A, Stössel U (2012): Kurzbericht zur Evaluation der Integrierten Versorgung Gesundes Kinzigtal 2011. Available online: http://www.ekiv.org/pdf/EKIV-Evaluationsbericht_2011_Kurzfassung_FINAL_2012–06-30.pdf, last access: February 25, 2013.

Siegel A, Köster I, Schubert I, Stössel U (2012): Integrierte Versorgung Gesundes Kinzigtal: Ein Modell für regionale Prävention und Schnittstellenoptimierung. In: Kirch W, Hoffmann T, Pfaff H (eds.): Prävention und Versorgung. Stuttgart and New York: Thieme: 148–164.

Swart E & Ihle P (Hrsg.). (2005) Routinedaten im Gesundheitswesen. Handbuch Sekundäranalyse: Grundlagen, Methoden und Perspektiven. Bern: Huber.

Preuß KJ, Räbiger J, Sommer JH (eds.) (2002): Managed Care. Evaluation und Performance-Measurement integrierter Versorgungsmodelle. Stand der Entwicklung in der EU, der Schweiz und den USA. Stuttgart: Schattauer.

Part VII
Extroduction

Chapter 18
Health Care Utilization: A Concluding Note on Research Prospects

Thomas von Lengerke, Christoph Kowalski, Enno Swart and Christian Janssen

This volume set out to provide a coherent, albeit selective, account of the social determinants of health care utilization in Germany. To this end, theoretical, methodological, and empirical perspectives have been presented. Within each of these perspectives, different issues were taken up. Finally, the behavioral model (BM) [1] has been used as the recurrent model of health care utilization throughout the volume. On this basis, a variety of findings and conclusions have been presented. However, some of them raised more questions than they answered. For instance, while in Chap. 7 *Babitsch* et al. have stated that there is ample evidence of differences in utilization between women and men, including in Germany, empirical explanations for these differences are largely lacking. This may be due to scarce research on the interconnectedness of sex/gender and psychosocial variables, such as health beliefs and socioeconomic status (SES). Even more indicative of a research void, in Chap. 9 *Ciupitu-Plath* et al. found no utilization studies in adult migrant populations in Germany at all. For SES, clear results are available: Higher status groups prefer specialists, while those with lower status tend to visit primary care

T. von Lengerke (✉)
Center of Public Health and Health Care, Medical Psychology Unit,
Hannover Medical School, Hannover, Germany
e-mail: lengerke.thomas@mh-hannover.de

C. Kowalski
Faculty of Human Sciences and the Faculty of Medicine,
Institute for Medical Sociology, Health Services Research, and Rehabilitation Science,
University of Cologne, Cologne, Germany
e-mail: christoph.kowalski@uk-koeln.de

E. Swart
Institute of Social Medicine and Health Economics, Medical Faculty,
Otto von Guericke University of Magdeburg, Magdeburg, Germany
e-mail: enno.swart@med.ovgu.de

C. Janssen
Department of Applied Social Sciences,
Munich University of Applied Sciences, Munich, Germany
e-mail: christian.janssen@hm.edu

C. Janssen et al. (eds.), *Health Care Utilization in Germany*,
DOI 10.1007/978-1-4614-9191-0_18, © Springer Science+Business Media New York 2014

physicians, but the strongest inequalities exist in prevention, to the disadvantage of lower status groups, as *Klein* et al. have reported in Chap. 8. Taking a more specific look at this developing "fourth pillar of health care" *Kowalski* et al. found inequalities to be largely due to differences in the utilization of early detection programs, i.e., secondary prevention (Chap. 16). Other services are interesting in the SES context as well. For instance, according to *Körner* et al. (Chap. 15), use of psychotherapeutic care (while being under-researched) is higher in groups with higher levels of education even though they are less affected by mental disorders. According to *Lüdecke* et al. (Chap. 10), services for caregivers—a field of increasing significance due to the demographic transition—are also utilized more often by educated caregivers of elderly dependents, which agrees with the findings of *Donath* et al. regarding caregivers of dementia patients (Chap. 11). At the same time, some differences emerge: e.g., highly educated caregivers tended to use services even in case of low perceived burden of care in the former analysis, but this was not the case for all services in the latter. Another form of differentiation has been pursued by *von Lengerke* et al. in Chap. 12. By deliberately restricting their analysis of general practitioner (GP) utilization by obese adults to a small number of variables and a predefined interaction term, they found excess GP use in men with severe obesity only, but in women already at the pre-obese stage. Among other things, this raises the question whether sex/gender may (also) represent an enabling factor. A similar relationship is suggested by *Thieme* and *Borgetto* in their analyses of physical therapy and utilization of self-help activities among patients with rheumatic diseases (Chaps. 13 and 14), in which they discuss education (a predisposing factor in the BM) as an enabling factor. In terms of key findings, need factors played a major utilization-triggering role in both fields of services. Also, factors from both the predisposing and enabling clusters were important, e.g., active problem-oriented coping and being married (with social support, however, negatively impacting utilization). Finally, *Siegel* et al. highlight the option of an integrated care system as a viable contextual factor that can reduce risk selection and bring care to the groups most in need (Chap. 17).

As for these empirical results, not all theoretical and methodological questions could be answered in the present volume, and new questions even emerged in our discussions within the NWIn research network (*Netzwerk Inanspruchnahme*). To begin with, however, *Bormann* and *Swart* (Chap. 3) have provided an up-to-date outline of the German statutory health insurance system for English-language audiences, describing its expenses, remuneration principles, outpatient, inpatient, as well as nursing sectors as contextual enabling factors that strongly modulate the health services utilization of roughly 85% of the German population (i.e., those with statutory insurance). Also, those interested in the possibilities and challenges of operationalizing health care utilization in Germany are provided with abundant information on secondary data by *Swart* (Chap. 5) and on primary data by *Swart* and *Griehl* (Chap. 4). In this context, they provide a challenging but at the same time most promising perspective of linking both types of data, which is possible despite a series of legal, technical, and organizational difficulties. Another multi-method research option is raised by *Babitsch* et al. (Chap. 6), who discuss mixing qualita-

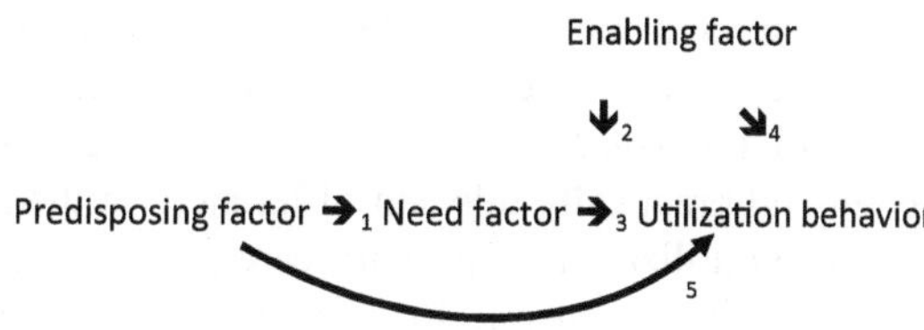

Fig. 18.1 Simple case of applying the mediator vs. moderator distinction on BM explanations of utilization (need factor = mediator; enabling factor = moderator)

tive and quantitative analyses, the latter being an infrequently used and possibly underused approach in German health care utilization research.

But how can researchers link these data while at the same time accounting for the interconnectedness of different variables in a theoretical and empirically consistent manner? In this regard, two main strands of analytical tools look promising for research, as suggested by *von Lengerke* et al. in Chap. 1. On the one hand, the mediator vs. moderator distinction from social psychology [2, 3] might disentangle some conceptual ambiguities, especially of predisposing and enabling factors. As a reminder, Andersen [4] had originally defined predisposing factors as predictors of families' propensity to use services "which exist prior to the onset of specific episodes of illness" (p. 25) even though they "are not directly responsible for health service use" (ibid.), and enabling factors as conditions which "permit a family to act upon a value or satisfy a need regarding health service use" (p. 27). These definitions have remained essentially unchanged in the latest version of the BM [1]. Applying the mediator vs. moderator distinction, where a mediator is a variable intervening between predictor or a causal variable and an outcome, and a moderator is a variable that alters the strength of the causal relationship, this would mean that processes depicted by the BM, in which need is the "most immediate cause of health service use" ([1], p. 28), should always be modeled as follows given a four-variable situation (Fig. 18.1).

The relationships depicted by arrows 1, 2, and 3 represent equitable access, if they are the only ones found. If direct associations emerge between predisposing and/or enabling factors and utilization as shown by arrows 4 and 5, access is inequitable. In any case, the actual analysis would involve both a test of mediation (in terms of "Are effects of predisposing factor on utilization mediated by need factors?" [2, 3, 5]) and moderation ("Are effects of need factors on utilization moderated by enabling factors?" [2, 3, 6]). For didactic reasons, one can consider a simplistic example: assuming that the prevalence of breast cancer is higher in women than in men, women should use more cancer care services because they experience symptoms of illness or worry about their condition (i.e., perceived need) or seek help in terms of professional evaluations (e.g., in early detection programs; evaluated need), and not because they are women (and despite the low subjective health in male breast cancer patients [7]). At the same time, the probability of utilization should be higher if, e.g., the density of the relevant services in one's own residential area is high, one's partner supports the decision to use the services (social support), or one's spending power is high (provided co-payments are involved). Each of these hypotheses would require statistically testing interactions defined by at least one need factor and one enabling factor. Finally, predisposing factors should not moderate associations between need factors and utilization behavior (a counterexample is reported by *von Lengerke* et al. in Chap. 12, where women and men showed different and practically relevant differences in the association between body weight status and utilization of primary care physicians), and enabling factors should not be indirectly responsible for use (which is contradicted, e.g., by the finding that poverty is an important predictor of adverse health outcomes [8]). Tying these arguments together, the problem is that in reality, research oftentimes is not conducted this way (and surely not flawlessly in the primary data analyses in the present volume), probably due to the "traditional" and sometimes practically ubiquitous use of cross-sectional nonhierarchical regression modeling in social epidemiology and medical sociology. Here, methods such as stepwise regression (as used by *Thieme* and *Borgetto* in Chaps. 13 and 14) and hierarchical regression analysis, models for different degrees of disease severity (e.g., *Donath* et al., Chap. 11), path analysis and structural equation modeling, tests of predefined interaction terms (as in *von Lengerke* et al., Chap. 12) or tree-based models (e.g., *Lüdecke* et al., Chap. 10), and ultimately examinations of moderated mediation, mediated moderation, and conditional process analysis as outlined in contemporary methodological texts will be essential [3].

Finally, the picture tends to become even more complicated in light of the most appropriate and consistent description of predisposing, enabling, and need factors on both the contextual and individual levels of the BM, starting with its fifth revision [9]. Multilevel modeling approaches that account for both mediation and moderation effects as described above are required for the theoretical and empirical analysis of health services utilization (and, frankly, have probably been neglected to some extent in the empirical parts of the present volume). As *von Lengerke* et al. have argued in the introductory theoretical chapter of this volume (Chap. 2), integrating biopsychosocial perspectives as described by Engel [10] and the taxonomy of individual and collective properties developed by Lazarsfeld and Menzel [11] may further promote this endeavor (including links to the natural sciences [12]). In addition, there is precedent work by the originators of the BM, especially regarding the assessment of environmental and provider-related variables [13] and low-income populations in general [14, 15] and concerning dental care in particular [16, 17]. Taking social ecological reasoning into account, which depicts environmental factors as enablers [18], contextual variables may be most likely to function as moderators when the criterion to be predicted or explained is individual utilization behavior. If the BM eventually develops into a model that intends to explain prevalences and incidences of utilization behavior as well, as *von Lengerke* et al. have argued to be both possible and useful in terms of health services epidemiology and policy (Chap. 2), the issue of which aggregate biopsychosocial variables predispose and enable, or mediate or moderate, utilization behavior on the level of groups will probably arise anew. Also, it will be exciting to see whether ecological associations will have practical added value in their own right (as argued by some authors, e.g., [19]). In sum, we hope that these prospects in particular, and the volume in your hands in general, will make a contribution in terms of the closing words of David

Mechanic in his 1979 paper on the correlates of physician utilization over 30 years ago: "Examining the role of cultural and social-psychological processes with the constraining influences of economic and organizational factors will result in better theory and, it is to be hoped, more adequate prediction" ([20], p. 395). Not least with its adoption of present-day health-related issues, such as genetic susceptibility and quality of life, the sixth revision of the BM [1] will, in our opinion, be both a guiding and thought-provoking theory for the current generation of health services researchers (like ourselves) as well as future generations—and hence will be of extraordinary importance in this field.

References

1. Andersen RM, Davidson PL, Baumeister SE. Improving access to care in America. In: Kominski GF, editor. Changing the U.S. health care system: key issues in health services, policy, and management. 4th edition. San Francisco, CA: Jossey-Bass; 2013. p. 33–69.
2. Baron RM, Kenny DA. The moderator-mediator variable distinction in social psychological research: conceptual, strategic and statistical considerations. J Pers Soc Psychol. 1986;51:1173–82.
3. Hayes AF. Introduction to mediation, moderation and conditional process analysis: A regression-based approach. New York, NY; Guilford; 2013
4. Andersen RM. Families' use of health services: a behavioral model of predisposing, enabling, and need components [Dissertation]. http://docs.lib.purdue.edu/dissertations/AAI6902884 (1968). Accessed 5 June, 2013.
5. Kenny DA. Mediation. 2013. http://davidakenny.net/cm/mediate.htm. Accessed 5 June, 2013.
6. Kenny DA. Moderation. 2013. http://davidakenny.net/cm/moderation.htm. Accessed 5 June, 2013.
7. Kowalski C, Steffen P, Ernstmann N, Wuerstlein R, Harbeck N, Pfaff H. Health-related quality of life in male breast cancer patients. Breast Cancer Res Treat. 2012;133:753–7.
8. Raphael D. Poverty in childhood and adverse health outcomes in adulthood. Maturitas. 2011;69:22–6.
9. Andersen RM, Davidson PL. Improving access to care in America: individual and contextual indicators. In: Andersen RM, Rice TH, Kominski GF, editors. Changing the U.S. health care system: key issues in health services, policy, and management. 3rd edition. San Francisco, CA: Jossey-Bass; 2007. p. 3–31.
10. Engel GL. The need for a new medical model: a challenge for biomedicine. Science. 1977;196:129–36.
11. Lazarsfeld PF, Menzel H. On the relation between individual and collective properties. In Etzioni A, Lehman EW, editors. A sociological reader on complex organizations (3rd ed.). New York: Holt, Rinehart and Winston: 1980. p. 508–21.
12. Glass TA, McAtee MJ. Behavioral science at the crossroads in public health: extending horizons, envisioning the future. Soc Sci Med. 2006;62:1650–71.
13. Phillips KA, Morrison KR, Andersen R, Aday LA. Understanding the context of healthcare utilization: assessing environmental and provider-related variables in the Behavioral Model of Utilization. Health Serv Res. 1998;33;571–96.
14. Brown ER, Davidson PL, Yu H, Wyn R, Andersen RM, Becerra L, Razack N. Effects of community factors on access to ambulatory care for lower-income adults in large urban communities. Inquiry. 2004;41:39–56.
15. Davidson PL, Andersen RM, Wyn R, Brown ER. A framework for evaluating safety-net and other community-level factors on access for low-income populations. Inquiry. 2004;41:21–38.

16. Baumeister SE, Davidson PL, Carreon DC, Nakazono TT, Gutierrez JJ, Andersen RM. What influences dental students to serve special care patients? Spec Care Dentist. 2007;27:15–22.
17. Davidson PL, Carreon DC, Baumeister SE, Nakazono TT, Gutierrez JJ, Afifi AA, Andersen RM. Influence of contextual environment and community-based dental education on practice plans of graduating seniors. J Dent Educ. 2007;71:403–18.
18. Stokols D. Establishing and maintaining healthy environments: Toward a social ecology of health promotion. Am Psycholog. 1992;47:6–22.
19. Lubinski D, Humphreys LG. Seeing the forest from the trees: When predicting the behavior or status of groups, correlate means. Psycholog Public Policy Law. 1996;2:363–76.
20. Mechanic D. Correlates of physician utilization: why do major multivariate studies of physician utilization find trivial psychosocial and organizational effects? J Health Soc Behav. 1979;20:387–96.

FSC
www.fsc.org

MIX
Papier aus verantwortungsvollen Quellen
Paper from responsible sources
FSC® C105338

If you have any concerns about our products,
you can contact us on
ProductSafety@springernature.com

In case Publisher is established outside the EU,
the EU authorized representative is:
Springer Nature Customer Service Center GmbH
Europaplatz 3, 69115 Heidelberg, Germany

Printed by Libri Plureos GmbH
in Hamburg, Germany